Europe':

MW00779121

 **French**
With Ease Series

by Anthony Bulger
with the editorial assistance of Jean-Loup Chérel

Illustrated by J.-L. Goussé

B.P. 25
94431 Chennevières-sur-Marne Cedex
FRANCE

ASSIMIL®
The intuitive method

Languages available

Optional recordings on audio and mp3 CDs are available for all courses.

Beginner - Intermediate

Arabic - Brazilian portuguese*** - Chinese With Ease volume 1 - Chinese With Ease volume 2 - Writing Chinese With Ease - Dutch With Ease - French* - German** - Hebrew - Hungarian With Ease - Italian - Japanese With Ease volume 1 - Japanese With Ease volume 2 - Writing Japanese With Ease - Russian** - Spanish** - Yiddish

For Kids

Sing Your Way To French

Advanced

Using French

Phrasebooks

Chinese*
French
German*
Italian
Japanese*
Russian
Spanish

* available soon

* e-course (downloadable) available on www.assimil.com
** e-course available soon
*** available soon

Contents

Preface

French is a "living" language in more ways than one. Not only is it spoken by some 200 million people in over 40 countries; it is also widely used in diplomacy, science, the arts, fashion and a host of other areas. Also, because of its grammatical precision, French is used as an official language by several major organisations, including the Organization for Economic Co-operation and Development (OECD) and the International Labour organization (ILO). Furthermore, France plays an active role in defending and promoting its language and culture, with initiatives such as **La Francophonie**, the community of French-speaking countries and governments.

But France does not have a monopoly on French! The Belgians and Swiss make a vital contribution (indeed, one of the classic works of reference, *Le Mot Juste*, is written by a Belgian) while the Canadians are arguably the most ardent defenders of **la langue française**. Immigration, too, has played a part, with ethnic groups in France and other francophone countries adding to the language's lexical treasure trove and literature. Last but not least, the Internet, although dominated by English, is like an electronic Tower of Babel, helping to spread French to the four corners of the globe.

When this book was first written, we could not have foreseen in detail the impact that all these factors would have on the French language. To keep it up to date, we have revised it at regular intervals, adding new material and, as far as possible, adapting the content in order to reflect changes in usage, vocabulary and society as a whole. This is an ongoing process.

When selecting language elements for new material, we always try to choose between the ephemeral – words and expressions that spring up overnight and disappear just as quickly – and the perennial. Naturally our choice is subjective but it is based on usage in the media (in the broadest sense of the term).

One thing will never change, however: the Assimil method, which relies on your natural powers of learning, a relaxed (and often humorous) approach and short periods of daily study.

We hope you enjoy our *French (With Ease Series)*.

Introduction

This method is not complete. It still requires one vital element: your intuitive gift of learning.

We will help you to learn French in much the same way as you learned English: by listening, repeating and drawing conclusions. And finally, by speaking.

There is no miracle nor mystery. We have divided the course into two parts, or 'waves'. The first wave requires little effort: it is passive. You listen, repeat and try to understand. The second wave will draw on the knowledge you have acquired, prompting you to form new sentences and to express your ideas.

True, we have cheated slightly by choosing a grammatical progression that introduces the particularities of French little by little, instead of all mixed together as would be the case if you 'picked up' the language with native speakers. (Remember, that was how you learned English.) But even so, we have tried not to impair your natural gift by explaining everything immediately. Instead, we'll use a word or phrase once or twice before giving you a detailed explanation. In this way, you organise your knowledge after the fact rather than trying to learn through sets of rules. Don't worry! Just relax and learn.

And if you approach the course in a relaxed fashion, if you accept rather than analyse (the problem of most adult learners), if you appreciate the pleasure of understanding, then you will assimilate the language naturally and in a relatively short space of time. Don't worry! Just relax and soak up the language.

How to use this French course

Which "French"?

Our apologies to the purists. We have deliberately ignored the more literary aspects of French. Right from the start, the conversations are written 'with the ear' and are as natural as any language method can make them. They rely on everyday speech, colloquialisms and vocabulary that the visitor to France or a French-speaking country will hear all the time. After about four months of regular study, you should be able to understand normal conversations and to express yourself in everyday situations, both formal and informal.

Also, we have not attempted to cover all the grammar. We have concentrated on those elements that will allow us to achieve our aim as efficiently as possible. There are two good reasons for this. Firstly, what often deters English speakers from learning a Romance language is the seeming over-emphasis on grammatical exactitude to the detriment of expression – an emphasis not shared by the type of French speaker you will encounter in this volume. We believe, as the great writer Rivarol said, that 'grammar is the art of lifting the difficulties out of a language; the lever must not be heavier than the burden.'

The second reason, as we have explained, is one of expediency. This book will provide you with the tools to continue your exploration of the language at your own pace.

How?

Our key rule is: do a little every day. Only through constant contact can you make the most of your natural powers of learning. Try and set aside some time every day – even if it's only ten minutes – and make sure that you treat the course as pleasure, not work.

During the first wave (lesson 1-50), you simply listen to the lessons, look at the translation and notes and repeat the text aloud. From lesson 50 onwards – the second wave – you move into the active phase. For each new lesson, you go back to a corresponding first-wave lesson (starting from lesson 1) and translate from English into French.

During both phases, the exercises will help you to consolidate your knowledge.

Complex points of grammar are examined in a series of chapters called Révision, which you'll come across once a week (i.e. every seventh lesson). In this way, when you reach the Révision at the end of each week, you really will be revising what you have already learned.

One last rule: don't try to do too much at once. Admittedly, we have made things as simple as possible. But we believe – as Albert Einstein said – that 'things should be as simple as possible, but no simpler'.

Pronunciation

Obviously, the only way to acquire a perfect accent is to listen to the recordings. However, to make things easier on the page, we have reproduced French pronunciation using, not the International Phonetic Alphabet, but the nearest equivalent English phoneme. This system is highly practical, but, unfortunately, not perfect, so please remember the following points:

1) Vowel sounds in French are constant (except in regional accents) and are half-way between a short vowel and a long vowel in English. For example *[i]* in French is neither the *[i]* of *ship* nor the long *[i:]* of *sheep* but somewhere in between.

2) Nasal vowels **-en -in -on** and **-un** occur at the end of a syllable. They do not exist in standard English (Americans and Liverpudlians often produce them naturally – or you can always hold your nose!). We have reproduced them by placing an 'h' before the consonant to soften it, but this is not the authentic pronunciation. Let your breath out through your nose rather than through your lips, and you'll find that, in fact, the consonant is not pronounced.

3) Word endings. Many grammatical nuances in French are discernible only in print, not in the spoken language. For example,

the final **s** is not pronounced (with certain exceptions, chiefly foreign words); and the endings of the pronouns (**il/ils**) and the verbs (**regarde/regardent**) are pronounced in the same way in the third person singular and plural. Don't worry. These details will seem less ominous after two weeks' practice.

4) Stress. Possibly the biggest problem for an English-speaking learner. We tend to stress one syllable of a word much more strongly than the rest (e.g. *comfortable*), sometimes to the extent that a shade of meaning is lost: for example, you can't tell whether the word *firemen* is singular or plural.

In French, syllables are pronounced fully and in an even tone (but pay special attention to verb endings). If there is a tendency to stress, it is less marked than English; the emphasis falls regularly on the last syllable of a word.

Enough for now. Remember that no one speaks a language without making mistakes – especially a beginner, but it's those mistakes that help us to learn.

Vous êtes prêt ? Allons-y !
(Ready? Let's go!)

*The liaison is the name given to the sound produced by carrying over
the last consonant of one word to the first vowel of the next, rather like
"an apple". So, for example, we pronounce* **nous allons** *as [noozallon].*

1

Première leçon

À Paris

1 – Pardon, madame [1]. Où est le métro [2] Saint-
   Michel ?
2 – Le métro Saint-Michel ? Attendez une minute...
3   Nous sommes au boulevard Saint-Michel. La
   fontaine est là-bas.
4 – Oui, d'accord. Mais où est le métro, s'il vous
   plaît [3] ?
5 – Mais bien sûr ! Voilà la Seine, et voici [4] le pont.
6 – C'est joli ; mais s'il vous plaît...
7 – Ce n'est pas_à gauche, alors c'est_à [5] droite.

Pronunciation
a paree **1** *pardohn madam. oo ay le metro sah meeshel*
2 *... attenday oon minyoot* **3** *noo somm oh boolevar sah meeshel.*
la fonten ay la-ba **4** *wee daccor. may oo ay le metro seel voo play*
5 *may biehn syoor ! vvala la senn ay vwassi le pohn* **6** *say zholi ...*
7 *se nay paza gohsh alor seta drwat*

Notes

1   French is quite a formal language in many ways, and the use of **monsieur** and **madame** when addressing strangers of almost any age is the
   general rule.

   * Notice that in this lesson there are several words which are similar
   in spelling and meaning to English words. Pay close attention to their
   pronunciation!

1 •   **un** *[eun]*

Liaisons are not indicated in standard written French, so we point it out in our text with the symbol ‿.

1

First Lesson

In *(At)* Paris

1 – Excuse me *(Pardon)* madam. Where is the metro [station] St. Michel?

2 – The metro [station] St. Michel? Wait a minute...

3 We are at [the] boulevard St. Michel. The fountain is over there.

4 – Yes, O.K. But where is the metro [station] please?

5 – But of course! There [is] the Seine and here [is] the bridge.

6 – It's pretty; but please...

7 – It's not *(at)* [on the] left, so it's *(at)* [on the] right.

---

2 **le métro** (short for **métropolitain**) is the Parisian underground railway system. The word is also used to mean *the metro station*. **Le métro République**, *The République station*.

3 **s'il vous plaît** (literally "if it pleases you") is the usual way of saying *please*. Don't ask why, just memorise it! (On formal invitations in both English and French, we use the abbreviation "RSVP" which stands for **Répondez, s'il vous plaît**, *Please reply*.)

4 **voici** is equivalent to *here is/are* and **voilà** to *there is/are*. In line 8 we see an idiomatic use of **Voilà**, *There we are... I've found it!*

5 Prepositions are less numerous in French than in English, and they often serve several functions. "**À**" in the title translates as *in*. In sentence 7, it translates as *on*. Just memorise each individual use. It will soon become a reflex.
Note: **c'est**, *it is*; **ce n'est pas**, *it is not*.

8   Voilà. Le métro est_à droite !
9 – Mais vous_êtes sûre ?
10 – Non. Je suis touriste aussi !   □

8 … le metro eta drwat 9 may voozet syoor 10 noh. zhe swee tooreest osee

***

▶ Exercice 1 – Traduisez
Exercice 1 – Translate
❶ Je suis à Paris ; nous sommes à Paris. ❷ Vous êtes sûr ?
❸ Attendez une minute, s'il vous plaît. ❹ Voilà la fontaine et voici le métro. ❺ Mais bien sûr !

Exercice 2 – Complétez
Exercice 2 – Fill in the blanks with the correct word(s).
Each dot represents a letter; it can also be an apostrophe or a dash.

❶ You're in Paris
   Vous .... à Paris.

❷ We're at the Boulevard St Michel
   Nous ...... au Boulevard Saint-Michel.

❸ Yes, OK, but where's the metro station please?
   Oui, ... mais où est le métro, s'il vous ..... ?

❹ The fountain's on the left.
   La fontaine est . gauche.

❺ It's not on the left.
   Ce . ' est .... gauche.

8 There we are. The metro [station] is *(at)* [on the] right!

9 – But are you sure?

10 – No. I'm [a] tourist, too!

***

Answers to Exercice 1

❶ I am in Paris; we are in Paris. ❷ You are sure? ❸ Wait a minute please. ❹ There is the fountain and here is the metro. ❺ But of course!

Answers to Exercice 2

❶ – êtes – ❷ – sommes – ❸ – d'accord – plaît ❹ – à – ❺ – n' – pas à –

Please remember that for the time being, all you are required to is to understand the French text and to repeat each paragraph immediately after you have heard it. Don't worry about little differences in construction or a word that isn't explained immediately. We want you to use your natural gift of assimilation before learning rules.

2

Deuxième leçon

Au magasin

1 – S'il vous plaît, madame, est-ce qu'il ¹ est cher, ce chapeau ?

2 – Non, il n'est pas cher. Le prix est très raisonnable.

3 – Bon. Et... Où sont les gants ?

4 – Les gants sont là-bas. Vous voyez ² ?

5 – Ah, merci... Mais, est-ce qu'ils ³ ‿sont en laine ?

6 – Non, ils ne sont pas‿en laine, ils sont‿en acrylique.

7 – Bon. Euh... est-ce qu'il est cinq heures ?

🗨 Pronunciation

1 ... eskeel ay shair se shapoh 2 ... pri ay tray rayzonahbl 3 bohn ... oo sohn lay gohn 4 ... voo vwayay 5 ... merssee may eskeel sontohn len 6 ... ohn akrileek 7 ... bohn. eu ... sank eur

◻ Notes

1 This is one way of asking questions, and perhaps the simplest and most common. **Est-ce que** *[eskë]* (literally: "Is it that?") is placed before the phrase you wish to make interrogative... and **voilà**, you have your question. The final **e** of **que** is "elided" (i.e. removed) before a vowel, giving us **Est-ce qu'il est cinq heures ?** or **Est-ce qu'elle est jeune ?**, *Is she young?* We will see other ways of asking questions later on.

2

Second Lesson

In *(At)* **the shop**

1 – *(If you)* please madam, is it dear, this hat?
2 – No, it's not dear. It is very reasonably priced *(the price is very reasonable)*.
3 – Good. And... where are the gloves?
4 – The gloves are over there; [do] you see?
5 – Ah, thank you... But, are they in [made of] wool?
6 – No they are not in wool, they are in [made of] acrylic.
7 – Good. Um... is it 5 o'clock *(hours)*?

2 Another simple way of asking questions, which is the same as in English. The affirmative statement **vous voyez**, *you see*, is pronounced with a rising intonation, just like *You see?* Listen carefully to the recording. Both this and **est-ce que** are conversational, rather informal ways of asking questions. They may not be very "elegant", but they are used in everyday speech.

3 Notice that we cannot hear the plural **s**. The sound is exactly the same as in the first sentence.

8 – Comment ? Ah, je comprends, vous_attendez
votre mari !

9 – Oui, c'est ça [4]... et... il pleut dehors, alors...

10 – Non, madame... Il n'est [5] pas cinq heures !   ☐

*8 kommohn ? ... zhe komprohn, vooz attohnday vot maree **9** ... eel
pleu deor alor*

***

Exercice 1 – Traduisez

❶ Est-ce que vous êtes sûr ? **❷** Est-ce qu'il est cher, ce
chapeau ? **❸** Est-ce que vous voyez la fontaine ? **❹** Il n'est
pas cinq heures. **❺** Est-ce que le prix est raisonnable ?

***

Exercice 2 – Complétez
Exercice 2 – Fill in the blanks

❶ Is it five o'clock?
Est-ce qu'. . .... cinq heures ?

❷ You are waiting for your husband!
Vous attendez ..... mari !

❸ Are they [made] of wool?
Est-ce qu'. . . .. en laine ?

8 – **What?** *(How?)* **Ah, I see, you're waiting [for] your husband!**

9 – **Yes, that's right** *(it is that)*... **and... it** *(rains)* **[is raining] outside, so...**

10 – **No, madam, it's not 5 o'clock** *(hours)***!**

Notes

4 A very useful idiom, literally "it is that". It expresses agreement, and can be translated as *That's it* or *Yes, you're right* or *That's right*.

5 **Ils ne sont pas**, *They are not*; **Il n'est pas**, *It is not*. Once again (note 1) we elide the **e** of **ne** before a word beginning with a vowel to make pronunciation easier.

***

Answers to Exercice 1

❶ Are you sure? ❷ Is this hat expensive? ❸ Can you see the fountain?
❹ It's not five o'clock. ❺ Is it reasonably priced?

***

❹ You're waiting for Mr Legrand? – Yes, that's right.
   Vous attendez monsieur Legrand ? – Oui, c' .. .. ..

❺ The St Michel metro station is over there.
   Le métro Saint-Michel est là- .. .. .

Answers to Exercice 2

❶ – il est – ❷ – votre – ❸ – ils sont – ❹ – est ça ❺ – bas

3

Troisième leçon

Au café

1 – Messieurs ¹, vous désirez ² ?
2 – Deux cafés, s'il vous plaît, et deux croissants chauds ³.
3 – Ah... vous‿êtes anglais ?
  – Oui, je suis de *London*, pardon, Londres. ⁴
4 – Mais vous parlez bien le français.
  – Merci, vous‿êtes gentil.
5 – Nous, les Français ⁵, nous sommes tous gentils !

Pronunciation

1 messyeu voo deziray 2 deu kaffay ... krwassohn show 3 ... voozet onglay ... zhe swee ... pardohn londr 4 may voo parlay ... voozet zhentee 5 ... noo somm tooss ...

Notes

1 messieurs is the plural of monsieur; mesdames is the plural of ma-dame. In both cases, the plural s is silent.

2 See Deuxième leçon: désirer is a formal way of saying *to want* and is used by salespeople, waiters, etc.

3 First notice the silent plural s. Adjectives usually come after the noun in French and "agree" in number, which means that if the nouns they qualify are plural, the adjectives must take a (silent) s also. E.g. **un livre rouge**, *a red book* → **deux livres rouges**, *two red books*.

croissant: These delicious pastries, traditionally eaten for breakfast in France, are in fact a symbol of victory! Croissant literally means "crescent" as in a crescent moon. In 1689, the Ottoman Turks were marauding through Europe. They stopped and laid siege to Vienna. The city resisted and finally managed to beat off the invaders. To

3

Third Lesson

In *(At)* the café

1 – Sirs *(Gentlemen)* **what do you want?** *(desire?)*
2 – Two coffees, please, and two hot *croissants*.
3 – Ah, you are English?
 – Yes, I'm from London, excuse me *(pardon)*, *Londres*.
4 – But you speak French well *(well the French)*.
 – Thank you, you are kind.
5 – We *(the)* French [people] we are all kind!

commemorate the event, a baker made a pastry in the shape of a crescent moon… the symbol of the Turks. Today, in a more peaceful environment, you can choose your **croissant "ordinaire"**, *plain*, or **au beurre**, *with* (more!) *butter*.

4 A handful of British cities are "gallicised". In addition to London, there is **Douvres**, *Dover*, **Edimbourg**, *Edinburgh* and **Cantorbéry**. In the USA, we have **La Nouvelle-Orléans**, *New Orleans*. In all cases, the cities in question have played a part in French history.

5 We do not put an initial capital on adjectives of nationality, or on the noun when it refers to the language. So, **Vous parlez bien le français** or **C'est un café anglais**. However, when the noun means "a French person", we use a capital. **Nous, les Français, nous sommes gentils.**

(Le garçon, à une autre table.)

6 – Pardon messieurs, voici les cafés et les tartines beurrées [6].

7 – Et alors ? Où sont les croissants ?

8 – Excusez-moi, messieurs...
– Et dépêchez-vous ! [7]
(À notre table)

9 – Alors, vous_êtes sûr qu'ils sont toujours gentils, les Français ?   □

6 ... *lay tarteen beuray* ... *le garssohn oon ohtr tahbl* ...
8 ... *daypeshay-voo* ... *not tahbl* **9** ... *toozhoor* ...

Notes

6 Nouns in French have a "gender"; they are either masculine or feminine. A masculine noun is preceded by the indefinite article **un** or the definite article **le**, feminine nouns are preceded by the indefinite article **une** or the definite article **la**. The plural definite article is **les** for masculine and feminine. If the noun begins with a vowel, **la** and **le** become **l'**: **un arbre → l'arbre**; **une école → l'école**.

***

Exercice 1 – Traduisez

❶ Vous parlez bien le français. ❷ Deux cafés, s'il vous plaît.
❸ Voici les cafés et les croissants. ❹ Ah, vous êtes Anglais ?
– Oui, c'est ça. ❺ Est-ce que vous êtes toujours gentil ?

***

Exercice 2 – Complétez

❶ We French [people] are all very nice!
Nous, les Français, nous ...... tous .... !

❷ Where are the croissants?
Où .... les croissants ?

❸ Here are your tartines, gentlemen.
Voici les tartines ...., messieurs.

(The waiter at another table)

6 – Excuse me gentlemen *(Pardon, sirs)* here are the coffees and the buttered slices [of bread].

7 – So what *(And so)*? Where are the *croissants*?

8 – Excuse me, gentlemen...
  – And hurry up *(you)*!
  (At our table)

9 – So, are you sure they are always kind, the French?

Adjectives must agree not only with the number of the noun they qualify (see 1), but also with its gender. For example **le beurre**, *butter*, can be made into an adjective, **beurré**, *buttered*. In sentence 6, the noun **tartines** is in the feminine plural, so the adjective is written **beurrées** (the pronunciation does not change).

As you've probably realised by now, it's vital to learn each noun with its gender.

7 This is the imperative form of our first class of verbs (there are three classes, each marked by the ending of the infinitive). The infinitive of this class ends in **-er** (**excuser**, **dépêcher**, **parler**). The "you" form of the verb ends in **-ez**: **vous parlez**. Like in English, we can use this form to give an order or a command: *Hurry!*, *Wait!*, but in French we must also add the pronoun: **Dépêchez-vous !**, **Excusez-moi !**

***

Answers to Exercice 1
❶ You speak French very well. ❷ Two coffees, please. ❸ Here are the coffees and the croissants. ❹ Are you English? – Yes, that's right. ❺ Are you always nice?

***

❹ You speak very good French. – Thank you, that's very nice of you.
  Vous ...... bien le français. – Merci, vous .... gentil.

❺ I'm from London.
  Je ... . Londres.

Answers to Exercice 2
❶ – sommes – gentils ❷ – sont – ❸ – beurrées – ❹ – parlez – êtes –
❺ – suis de –

You may have noticed that the translation we give in the Answers to Exercise 1 is sometimes slightly different from the one in the text. We're trying to build up your ability to match one

4

Quatrième leçon

Au café (suite)

1 – Commandons : [1]
2   deux tartines beurrées, s'il vous plaît, et deux cafés noirs !
3   Trois bières [2] allemandes et un verre de vin blanc.

Au tabac [3]

4 – Trois paquets de cigarettes brunes [4], s'il vous plaît, et un cigare hollandais !
5 – C'est tout ?

Pronunciation
1 kommohndohn 3 trwa beeair almohnd ay eun vair de van blohn … oh taba … 4 trwa pakay … broon … seegah ollohnday 5 say too

Notes
1 We saw yesterday that **Excusez** was the imperative form (lesson 3, note 7). There is another type of imperative, which in English has the form "Let's…" (*Let's go*, etc.). In French we form this by using the first person plural of the verb without the pronoun, so: **nous commandons**, *we order*; **Commandons !**, *Let's order!*

2 la bière, *beer*, is a feminine noun, so our adjective must take an **e** to "agree". So **un livre allemand**, *a German book*; **une bière allemande**, *a German beer*. Remember our rule on initial capitals? (Lesson 3, note 5.)

13 • **treize** *[trez]*

expression with several possible equivalents in English. Don't worry. You'll soon get the hang of it.

4

Fourth Lesson

In *(At)* the café (continued)

1 – Let's order:
2 Two buttered slices [of bread], please, and two black coffees!
3 Three German beers and a glass of white wine.

In *(At)* the tobacco [shop]

4 – Three packets of brown [tobacco] cigarettes please, and a Dutch cigar!
5 – Is that *(It is)* all?

---

3 **un tabac** is a café which also has a cigarette counter. The sale of tobacco in France is a state monopoly and cigarettes can usually only be sold in specially licensed places. A **tabac** also sells stamps, metro tickets and lottery tickets. Not every café is a **tabac**. You can recognize a **tabac** from afar by its red diamond-shaped sign, called **une carotte**. There is no relationship to the vegetable – when tobacco is harvested it is tied into spindle-shaped bundles called **carottes** (in English, we call them *carrots*, too!).

4 **une cigarette** is feminine. **Brun**, *brown*, refers to the dark tobacco popular in France (as opposed to Virginia tobacco, which the French call **blond**). In order to agree with the feminine plural form **les cigarettes**, the word **brun** must add an **e** and an **s**. So **un cigare brun** but **une cigarette brune** and **deux cigarettes brunes**. <u>Remember</u> that the final **s** is not pronounced.

6 – Non ; est-ce que vous_avez un briquet rouge ?
7 – Non monsieur. Je suis désolé [5].

Dans la rue

8 – Pardon monsieur. Est-ce que vous avez du feu [6], s'il vous plaît ?
9 – Non, je ne fume pas.
10 – Alors, moi non plus [7] !   □

6 … eun breekay roozh **8** … eske voozavay dyoo feu … **10** … mwa nohn plyoo

Notes

5 **désolé** reminds us of *desolate*: **Je suis désolé** is a common way of saying *I'm sorry* in a polite conversation. The feminine form (i.e. when a woman is speaking) is **désolée**. In practice, the expression is shortened to **Désolé(e)**.

6 **Est-ce que vous avez…**, *Do you have…* (We could also say – Deuxième leçon, note 2 – **Vous avez… ?** with a rising intonation). This is an idiomatic way of asking for a light. It literally translates as *Do you have some fire?* However, as smoking is becoming increasingly frowned upon, you may not be able to use this expression in a few year's time!

***

Exercice 1 – Traduisez

❶ Un paquet de cigarettes brunes, s'il vous plaît. ❷ Est-ce que vous avez du feu ? ❸ Désolé, je ne fume pas. ❹ Deux tartines beurrées et deux cafés noirs. ❺ Est-ce que vous avez un briquet rouge ?

6 – No. Do you have a red lighter?
7 – No sir. Very sorry.

In the street

8 – Excuse me *(Pardon)* sir. Do you have a light *(some fire)* please?
9 – No; I don't smoke.
10 – So, neither can I *(me not more)*!

7 **Alors** is one of these wonderful words that can be used almost anywhere. Its literal translation is *then*, but it is used like *Well* as in *Well, I agree,* etc. It can variously be translated as *Right!*, *Well then...*, *In that case...*, and much more. Watch out for it!

***

Answers to Exercice 1
❶ A packet of brown tobacco cigarettes, please. ❷ Do you have a light? ❸ Sorry, I don't smoke. ❹ Two buttered slices of bread and two black coffees. ❺ Do you have a red lighter?

Exercice 2 – Complétez
Look at the following nouns and write down their genders:
❶ une voiture
❷ un homme
❸ une table
❹ une route
❺ un arbre

Now put the correct definite article (le or la) in front of these nouns:
❻ ..... tartine
❼ ..... café
❽ ..... chapeau
❾ ..... métro
❿ ..... magasin
⓫ ..... arbre

5

Cinquième leçon

▶ ## Une conversation téléphonique...

1 – Bonjour. Est-ce que monsieur Legrand est là, s'il vous plaît ?
2 – Non, il est_absent pour le moment.
3 – Ah bon [1]. Est-ce qu'il est là cet_après-midi [2] ?

Pronunciation
oon konversasseohn … 1 … messye legrohn … 2 … eelet absohn poor le momohn

Notes
1 Literally "oh good", **Ah bon** is used when responding to a piece of information. It is best translated as *I see* or *Really?* **Il est Allemand. – Ah bon ?** *He's German. – Really?*

17 • **dix-sept** *[deess-set]*

Now, look at the following adjective in the masculine singular form: vert *(green),* rond *(round),* haut *(high),* court *(short),* intelligent. *Write the following* pairs *in French:*

⑫ Two green cars ....
⑬ A round table ....
⑭ A short road ....
⑮ Two high trees ....
⑯ Two intelligent men ....

Answers to Exercice 2
❶ feminine ❷ masculine ❸ feminine ❹ feminine ❺ masculine

❻ la ❼ le ❽ le ❾ le ❿ le ⓫ l'

⑫ Deux voitures vertes ⑬ Une table ronde ⑭ Une route courte
⑮Deux arbres hauts ⑯ Deux hommes intelligents

⑤

Fifth Lesson

A telephone *(telephonic)* conversation...

1 – Good morning. Is monsieur Legrand there please?
2 – No, he is out *(absent)* for the moment.
3 – Oh really *(good)*? Is he in *(there)* this afternoon?

2 Lines 3 and 4: As in English, the French present tense can be used to express future time (e.g.: *I'm flying to London tomorrow*). Here, the person replies to the question in the present with a statement in the present – but both refer to the afternoon. (We will see later how to use the 24-hour clock.)

4 – Oui. Il arrive à trois heures.
5 – Merci beaucoup, mademoiselle.
– De rien, monsieur. [3]

... des idées toutes faites...

6 Les Français aiment les histoires romantiques,
7 mais les Anglais préfèrent les histoires drôles.

... et des dictons...

8 Les bons comptes font les bons amis [4].
9 Une hirondelle ne fait pas le printemps [5].

4 ... eel arreev a trwazeur 5 merssee bowkoo madmwazel. de ree-ehn ... day zeeday toot fet ... 6 ... emm lay-zeestwar romohntic 7 ... layzonglay prefayr ... deektohn ... 8 ... bohn cohnt fohn lay bohnzamee 9 oon eerondel ne fay pa le prahntohn

Notes

3 **De rien** is the polite answer to **Merci beaucoup** and is equivalent to our *You're welcome*.

4 This commonly used expression basically means "Let's not owe each other money if we want to remain friends". Note how French always uses an article before a noun. The English equivalent for this saying (now obsolescent) is "Short reckonings make for long friendships" – not "the short reckonings, etc." This takes a little getting used to, but you'll quickly acquire the habit. Look at the examples in the lesson carefully.

4 – Yes. He arrives at 3 o'clock *(hours)*.
5 – Thank you [very] much, miss.
 – You're welcome *(For nothing)* sir.

... set ideas...

6 The French like *(the)* romantic stories,
7 but the English prefer funny ones *(the funny stories)*.

... and some sayings...

8 *(The)* good accounts make for long friendships *(The good accounts make good friends)*.
9 One swallow does not make a summer *(the spring)*.

5 Here is our first irregular verb **faire**, which means *to do* or *to make*. It is used extensively, so we want you to start remembering it now. Note the following forms: **il** (or **elle**) **fait**, *s(he) does* or *makes*, **ils** (or **elles**) **font**, *they do* or *they make*. Also, note the difference between the English and French expressions: in English, a swallow does not make a *summer*; in French, it's the *spring*. Colder climes, perhaps?

Exercice 1 – Traduisez

❶ Les Anglais aiment les histoires drôles. ❷ Est-ce que monsieur Legrand est là, s'il vous plaît ? ❸ Merci beaucoup, mademoiselle. – De rien, monsieur. ❹ Est-ce qu'il arrive à trois heures ? ❺ Les Français préfèrent les histoires romantiques.

Exercice 2 – Complétez

❶ Short reckonings make for long friendships.
. . . bons comptes . . . . amis.

❷ One swallow does not make a summer.
Une hirondelle ne . . . . pas . . printemps.

❸ French cigarettes are *(made with)* brown tobacco.
. . . cigarettes françaises . . . . brunes.

❹ You're not English, Mr Legrand? – No, I'm French.
Vous n'. . . . . anglais, monsieur Legrand ? – Non, je . . . . français.

***

*Don't try to analyse constructions like **est-ce que** or expressions like **eh bien**. Just let them sink in. You will soon be able to use them naturally. Practise repeating them aloud!*

Answers to Exercice 1

❶ The English like funny stories. ❷ Is monsieur Legrand there please?
❸ Thank you very much, miss. – You're welcome sir. ❹ Is he arriving
at 3 o'clock? ❺ The French prefer romantic stories.

Answers to Exercice 2

❶ Les – font les bons – ❷ – fait – le – ❸ Les – sont – ❹ – êtes pas
– suis –

6

Sixième leçon

Les achats

1 – Bonjour, monsieur Lefèvre. Comment ça va [1] ?

2 – Bien, merci, et vous ?

– Ça va, merci.

3 Est-ce que vous_avez du [2] beurre ?

– Oui, bien sûr.

4 – Alors, une plaquette de beurre. Est-ce que vous_avez du fromage italien ?

5 – Du parmesan ? Non, je n'ai pas de [3] fromage italien.

– Dommage ! [4]

6 Eh bien, donnez-moi du fromage ordinaire.

🗩 Pronunciation

layzasha **1** *bohnzhoor … kohmohn sa va* **3** *… beur … bee-ehn syoor* **4** *… plaket … fromahzh eetaleeahn* **5** *… pahmayzohn … dohmahzh*

Notes

1 **Comment ça va ?** is a familiar, but widely used expression. It literally means: "How it goes?" and is the equivalent to an expression like: *How's life?* or *How's things?* The "ritual" answer is **Bien merci, et vous ?** Very often, however, such an exchange (known as a "phatic communication") is shortened to **Ça va** ↗ (with a rising intonation) with the answer **Ça va** ↘ (with a falling intonation).

2 To say *some* or *any* in statements or questions, we replace the article (**le** or **la**) by the words **du** (masculine) and **de la** (feminine). For the plural, we use **des** for both genders. So, **Vous avez des pâtes ?**, *Do you have*

6

Sixth Lesson

(The) **purchases**

1 – Good morning *(Good day)*, monsieur Lefèvre. How's
   things *(How it goes)*?
2 – Well, thanks, and you?
   – Fine *(It goes)*, thanks.
3   Do you have any butter?
   – Yes, of course.
4 – Well *(So)*, a pat of butter. Do you have any Italian
   cheese?
5 – Any parmesan? No, I don't have any Italian cheese.
   – Pity!
6   *(And)* well, give me some ordinary cheese.

noodles (pasta)?; **Je veux de la bière,** *I want some beer*; **Est-ce que**
vous avez du vin ?, *Do you have any wine?*

3   (See also note 2). **Du, de la, des** becomes simply **de** in the negative:
   Vous n'avez pas de fromage ?; Vous n'avez pas de cigarettes ? etc.
   Simple, isn't it?

4   **Dommage** or **Quel dommage** means *What a pity* or *What a shame.*

7 – Mais, monsieur Lefèvre, nous n'avons pas de fromage ordinaire en France.

8 Nous_avons un fromage pour chaque jour de l'année [5] !

9 – Alors, donnez-moi le fromage d'aujourd'hui ! □

7 ... ohn frohnss 8 noozavohn ... shak zhoor de lannay 9 ... dohzhoordwee

***

Exercice 1 – Traduisez
❶ Je n'ai pas de café aujourd'hui. ❷ Bonjour monsieur, comment ça va ? ❸ Bien, merci, et vous ? ❹ Donnez-moi du fromage et de la bière. ❺ Est-ce que vous avez des cigarettes anglaises ?

***

Exercice 2 – Complétez
❶ We don't have any ordinary cheese in France.
Nous n'..... pas .. fromage ordinaire en France.

❷ Do you want beer? – Yes, of course.
Est-ce que vous voulez .. la bière ? – Oui, bien ... !

❸ Give me some butter, some cheese and some pasta, please.
Donnez- moi .. beurre, .. fromage et ... pâtes, s'il vous plaît.

***

We have seen many things in this first week. Of course, we don't expect you to remember everything: all the important elements will be repeated and examined in detail in later lessons. Just relax, listen to the French text and look at the English translation. We'll do the rest!

7 – But, monsieur Lefèvre, we don't have any ordinary cheese in France.

8 We have a cheese for each day of the year!

9 – So, give me today's cheese *(the cheese of today)*!

Note

5 General de Gaulle, France's charismatic post-war leader and first president of the 5th Republic, famously complained that it was impossible to govern a country with more than 300 cheeses. He may have underestimated the real number!

***

Answers to Exercice 1

❶ I don't have any coffee today. ❷ Good morning sir. How are you?
❸ Well, thank you, and you? ❹ Give me some cheese and some beer.
❺ Do you have English cigarettes?

***

❹ I don't have any English cigarettes. – Well, give me a cigar.
Je n'ai pas .. cigarettes .... – Eh .... donnez-moi
.. cigare.

❺ Do you have any Italian cheeses?
Est- .. .... vous avez ... fromages .... ?

Answers to Exercice 2

❶ – avons – de – ❷ – de – sûr ❸ – du – du – des – ❹ – de – anglaises
– bien – un – ❺ – ce que – des – italiens

7

Septième leçon

Révision – Revision

At the end of each set of six lessons, you will find a revision lesson that reviews the most important points covered in the previous week.

1 Gender

This is perhaps the major difficulty facing an English speaker: we have to accept the fact that nouns are either masculine or feminine. Each time you learn a new word, learn its gender at the same time. Remember the following words:
le métro; **le pont**; **le chapeau**; **le croissant**; **le briquet**; **le fromage**; **la bière**; **la cigarette**; **la voiture**; **la tartine**; **la fontaine**.

un, **le** for masculine; **une**, **la** for feminine; **les**, plural for both genders.

2 Adjectives

Adjectives usually follow the noun they describe. If the noun is plural, the adjective takes a plural form, and if the noun is feminine, we put the feminine form, usually by adding an **e** or by doubling the final consonant and adding **e**.
un briquet rouge; **deux bières blondes**; **une tartine beurrée**.

Remember: the final **s** is never pronounced.

3 Verbs

We have seen the present tense of several verbs in the first class, whose infinitive ends in **-er**:

parler, *to speak*:	**vous parlez**, *you speak*;
	je parle, *I speak*

7

Seventh Lesson

fumer, *to smoke*:	**vous fumez**, *you smoke*;
	je fume, *I smoke*
arriver, *to arrive*:	**vous arrivez**, *you arrive*;
	j'arrive, *I arrive*.

(We elide the **e** of **je** before another vowel so as not to say **je arrive**, but **j'arrive**. We saw this with **il n'est pas** in lesson 2.)

We also saw three very common irregular verbs; do you remember?
Je suis de Londres, *I am from London*
Il est gentil, *He is kind*
Nous sommes touristes, *We are tourists*
Vous êtes français, *You are French*
Ils sont anglais, *They are English*.
The infinitive of this verb is **être**, *to be*.

We also saw:
Vous avez un briquet, *You have a lighter*
J'ai du fromage, *I have some cheese*.
The infinitive is **avoir**, *to have*

and:
Il fait un exercice, *He does an exercise*
Ils font de bons amis, *They make good friends*.
The infinitive is **faire**, *to make* or *to do*.

One thing that is simpler in French than in English is the present tense: there is only one form, which translates both the simple and progressive forms in English. So **vous parlez anglais** can mean *you speak English* or *you are speaking English*.

***

Enough for now. During the next six lessons, we'll see some of these points put into practice. Remember: don't try to do too much!

8

Huitième leçon

Une visite

1 – Bonjour mademoiselle, est-ce que votre père est_à la maison ?

2 – Non, monsieur ; il est_au [1] bureau.

3 Vous voulez parler à ma mère ?

4 – Non, ne la dérangez pas.

5 À quelle heure est-ce qu'il rentre normalement ?

6 – Oh, pas avant [2] huit_heures.

7 Vous voulez l'adresse de son bureau ?

8 – Oui, s'il vous plaît.

– Attendez, je la cherche [3]

9 Voilà. Sept rue Marbeuf, dans le huitième [4].

10 – Merci beaucoup, mademoiselle. Au revoir.

11 – De rien, monsieur. Au revoir.   □

Pronunciation

1 … madsmwazel … vot pair etala mayzohn **2** *… oh byooroh* **3** *… voolay parlay … mair* **4** *… dayrohnzhay …* **5** *… keleur …* **6** *… pa(z)avohn weeteur* **8** *… shairsh* **9** *… set roo mahbeuf … weetiem* **10** *… orevwar*

Notes

1 We have seen that there are fewer prepositions in French than in English. Thus à la can mean, depending on the preceding verb, *to the*, *at the* or *in the*. We say **à la** if the noun is feminine: **à la maison**, *at home* and **au** if the noun is masculine: **au bureau**, *at the office*.

2 Je ne fume pas, *I don't smoke*. Pas by itself means *not*: **pas aujourd'hui** *– not today*; **pas après deux heures**, *not after 2.00*.

29 • **vingt-neuf** *[vant-neuf]*

8

Eighth Lesson

A visit

1 – Good morning *(Good day)* miss. Is your father at home *(at the house)*?
2 – No, sir; he is at the office.
3 [Do] you want to speak to my mother?
4 – No, don't disturb her.
5 At what time *(hour)* [does] he come back normally?
6 – Oh, not before 8 o'clock *(hours)*.
7 [Do] you want the address of his office?
8 – Yes, *(if you)* please.
– Wait, I [am] looking for it.
9 There [it is]. 7 rue Marbeuf, in the 8th [district].
10 – Thank you very much, miss. Goodbye.
11 – You're welcome, sir. Goodbye.

3 Remember the *present tense*, **temps présent** in French translates both forms of our present tense: **je cherche** – *I look* and *I'm looking*.

4 Major cities (Paris, Lyons, Marseilles) are divided into *districts* called **arrondissements**. Paris has 20 **arrondissements** numbered from *the first*, **le premier**, to *the twentieth*, **le vingtième**. It is usual not to say the word **arrondissement** after the figure. **Elle habite dans le septième**, *She lives in the seventh* (district).

▶ Exercice 1 – Traduisez

① Est-ce que votre mère est à la maison ? **②** Ne la dérangez pas, s'il vous plaît. **③** Voilà l'adresse : il habite dans le sixième. **④** Merci beaucoup, monsieur. – De rien, mademoiselle. **⑤** À quelle heure est-ce qu'il rentre ? **⑥** Pas avant huit heures.

***

Exercice 2 – Complétez

① My mother is in the house and my father is at the office.
Ma mère est . . . . et mon père est . . . .

② You want the address? Wait, I'm looking for it.
Vous . . . . . . l'. . . . . . . ? Attendez, je . . . .

③ At what time does he come back?
. . . . est-ce qu'il . . . . . . ?

***

*Remember to read the numbers **at the beginning of each lesson and at the top of each page.***

9

Neuvième leçon

▶ ## Très simple !

1 Ce monsieur s'appelle Henri Laforge et cette ¹ dame est sa femme.

Note
1 *this* or *that* is **ce** for a masculine noun and **cette** for a feminine noun. **Ce garçon**, *this boy*; **cette femme**, *this woman*. (However if a masculine noun begins with a vowel, or a mute **h**, we write **cet**: **cet_ami**, *this friend*; **cet_homme**, *this man*.) You see, it really is important to learn the genders!

Answers to Exercice 1

❶ Is your mother at home? ❷ Don't disturb her please. ❸ There is the address: he lives in the sixth district. ❹ Thank you very much, sir. – Don't mention it, miss. ❺ At what time does he come home? ❻ Not before 8.00.

***

❹ I'm going to the café, then to the shop and after I'm going back.
Je vais . . . ., puis . . . . et après je . . . .

❺ You want to speak to my mother? – No, don't disturb her.
Vous voulez . . . . . . à . . mère ? – Non, ne . . dérangez pas.

Answers to Exercice 2

❶ – à la maison – au bureau ❷ – voulez – adresse – la cherche ❸ À quelle heure – rentre ❹ – au café – au magasin – rentre ❺ – parler – ma – la –

9

Ninth Lesson

Very simple!

1   This gentleman is called *(calls himself)* Henri Laforge and this lady is his wife.

Pronunciation
1 ... sa famm ...

2 Ils sont_à la mairie pour demander une nouvelle carte d'identité [2] pour leur fils, Jean.

3 – Cet_enfant, il a quel âge [3] ?

– Il a huit_ans, monsieur.

4 – Et il s'appelle Laforge ? Est-ce que c'est votre enfant ?

– Oui monsieur.

5 – Bien. Et il habite chez [4] vous ?

– Mais évidemment ! Il a huit_ans !

6 – D'accord. Je fais mon travail, c'est tout.

7 Est-ce que vous_avez le formulaire B-52 ?

8 – Oui monsieur, nous l'avons.

– Et l'imprimé A-65 ?

9 – Ça aussi, nous l'avons.

– Ah bon ? Mais est-ce que vous_avez son_extrait de naissance ?

10 – Bien sûr. Nous_avons même [5] une photo.

11 – Très bien. Alors je vous fais la carte. Voilà. Vous réglez [6] à la caisse.

12 – Zut [7] ! J'ai oublié mon portefeuille ! □

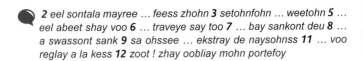

2 eel sontala mayree … feess zhohn 3 setohnfohn … weetohn 5 … eel abeet shay voo 6 … traveye say too 7 … bay sankont deu 8 … a swassont sank 9 sa ohssee … ekstray de naysohnss 11 … voo reglay a la kess 12 zoot ! zhay oobliay mohn portefoy

◻ Notes

2 All French citizens are required to carry an *identity card*, **la carte nationale d'identité**. They are required to produce the cards for official purposes (voting, etc.) and, sometimes, when they pay by cheque.

3 In French, you <u>have</u> your age, whereas in English you <u>are</u> your age: **elle a dix ans**, *she is 10 years old*; **quel âge a cet enfant ?**, *how old is this child?* We always add **ans**, *years*, after the age: **vingt ans**, *20 years old*.

2 They are at the Town Hall to ask [for] a new identity card for their son Jean.

3 – This child, how old is he *(he has what age)*?

– He is *(has)* eight years [old], sir.

4 – And he is called *(calls himself)* Laforge? Is it [he] your child?

– Yes, sir.

5 – Fine. And he lives with you?

– *(But)* obviously! He is *(has)* eight *(years)*!

6 – OK. I'm doing my job, that's all.

7 Do you have *(the)* form B-52?

8 – Yes, sir, we have it.

– And the printed [form] A-65?

9 – That also, we have it.

– Oh really? But do you have his birth certificate *(extract)*?

10 – Of course. We have even a photo.

11 – Very well. So I'll do *(am doing)* [for] you the card. Here it is. *(You)* pay at the cash-desk.

12 – Damn! I've forgotten my wallet!

4 **chez** *[shay]* means basically "home of": **chez moi**, *my place*, *my home* (it comes from the Latin word for *house*, **casa**; and as we know, some English families call their houses **Chez Nous** !). But **chez** can also mean *the shop of*; **chez le boulanger**: *at the baker's*. We'll see some more "abstract" uses of **chez** later on in the book.

5 **même** has several meanings: here it means *even*. Followed by **que** it means *the same as*. For the time being, simply remember this usage. Other forms will crop up later.

6 **régler** is a formal way of saying *to pay* (similar to our *settle up*). **Une caisse** is *a cash-desk*, *checkout* or *other place of payment*.

7 **Zut !** a mild expletive to express annoyance. It is not offensive.

▶ Exercice 1 – Traduisez

❶ Quel âge a cet enfant ? – Il a neuf ans. **❷** Ce monsieur s'appelle Henri et cette dame s'appelle Marie. **❸** J'habite chez un ami. **❹** Est-ce que je règle à la caisse ? **❺** Zut ! J'ai oublié une photo !

Exercice 2 – Complétez

❶ This gentleman, this lady and this child are German.
.. monsieur, ... dame et ... enfant sont Allemands.

❷ Here is Henri and his wife. How's things?
..... Henri et .. femme. Comment .... ?

❸ How old is this woman? – She is fifty years old.
.... dame ? – Elle . cinquante .... .

❹ I'm only doing my job.
.. .., c'est tout.

❺ He lives with us.
Il .... nous.

10
_____

Dixième leçon

Bonsoir, monsieur Duclos

1 Monsieur Duclos rentre chez lui à sept‿heures
tous ¹ les soirs.

🗣 Pronunciation
1 ... rontr shay looee ... too lay swar

Answers to Exercice 1
❶ How old is this child? – He is nine. ❷ This gentleman is called Henri and this lady is called Marie. ❸ I live at a friend's. ❹ Do I pay at the cash-desk? ❺ Damn! I've forgotten a photo!

TRÈS SIMPLE.

Answers to Exercice 2
❶ Ce – cette – cet – ❷ Voici – sa – ça va ❸ Quel âge a cette – a – ans ❹ Je fais mon travail – ❺ – habite chez –

10

Tenth Lesson

Good evening, monsieur Duclos

1   Monsieur Duclos goes back [to] his place at 7.00 every (all the) evening(s).

📖 Note

1   **tout**, *all*, *every*, is an adjective so it must "agree" in number and gender with its noun. **Tous les soirs**, *every evening* (**un soir**; masculine); **toutes les femmes**, *all the women* (**une femme**; feminine); however, **tout le monde** – (lit. "all the world") means *everybody*.

2 D'habitude, il achète quelque chose [2] à manger au supermarché et il monte à son appartement.

3 D'abord, il met le répondeur téléphonique parce qu' [3] il n'aime pas_être dérangé.

4 Puis il dîne, met les_assiettes dans le lave-vaisselle et allume [4] la télévision.

5 Il regarde les_informations [5] et quelquefois un film.

6 D'habitude, il se couche avant minuit [6].

7 Il aime cette vie tranquille et paisible.

8 Mais ce soir, malgré les quatre-vingts chaînes disponibles sur le câble,

9 il ne trouve pas d'émission intéressante.

10 – Eh bien, je vais écouter de la musique et passer une soirée calme [7]. ☐

2 dabeetyood … kelkeshowz a mohnzay … **3** dabor eel may le raypondeuyr taylayfonik parskeel nemm pa etr dayronzhay **4** … eel deen may lay zassiet dohn le lav vayssel … **5** … kelkefwa eun feelm **6** dabeetyood … avon meenwee **7** … set vee tronkeel ay payzeebl **8** … malgray lay katre-vann shen … kabl **9** … daymisyohn antayressont **10** … passay oon swahray kalm

---

: Notes

2 **quelque**, *some, a few*. It takes an **s** in the plural. **Quelques hommes**. **Quelqu'un**, *somebody*; **quelque chose**, *something*; **quelque part**, *somewhere*.

3 **parce que**, *because*; **pourquoi ?**, *why?*

4 Literally "to light the television"! **Allumer le gaz**, *to light the gas*; **allumer la radio**, *to turn on the radio*. *On the radio, television*, **à la radio**, **à la télévision**.

2 Usually, he buys something to eat at the supermarket and he goes up *(mounts)* to his apartment.

3 First of all, he turns on the answering machine because he doesn't like to be disturbed.

4 Then he dines, puts the plates in the dishwasher and turns on *(lights)* the television.

5 He watches the news and sometimes a film.

6 He usually goes to bed before midnight.

7 He likes this quiet and peaceful life.

8 But this evening, despite the 80 channels available on the cable,

9 he does not find an interesting programme.

10 – Well, I'm going to listen to music and spend [pass] a quiet evening.

IL AIME CETTE VIE TRANQUILLE ET PAISIBLE.

5 In the plural, **les informations** means "the news", not just "the information". In modern usage, however, we tend to shorten it to **les infos**. (There is a 24-hour rolling news station on public radio called **France Info** and at least one TV channel with "information" or "info" as part of their name.)

6 **une habitude**, *a habit*. **D'habitude**, *habitually*, i.e. *usually*. Remember that the initial **h** is always silent in French.

7 **calme**, *calm*. **Un homme calme, une soirée calme**. Some adjectives end in **e** in the masculine form, so they *do not change* in the feminine. Another common example is **jeune**, *young*.

Exercice 1 – Traduisez

❶ Il allume la télévision et regarde les informations. ❷ Elle achète quelque chose à manger au magasin tous les soirs. ❸ D'habitude, il rentre chez lui à sept heures. ❹ Il n'y a pas de film à la télévision ce soir. ❺ Je n'aime pas être dérangé.

***

Exercice 2 – Complétez

❶ He has dinner *(dines)* and watches the television.

Il …. et ……. la télévision.

❷ This evening there is no film on the television.

Ce soir ……… de film … télévision.

❸ So he decides to listen to music and spend a quiet evening.

Alors il décide ………… ……… et de …… une

……… …….

11

Onzième leçon

Un peu de révision

1 – À quelle heure est le film ce soir ?
– À huit_heures et demie.

 Pronunciation
… *rayveezeeohn*

Answers to Exercice 2
❶ He turns on the television and watches the news. ❷ She buys something to eat at the shop every evening. ❸ Usually, he comes home at 7.00. ❹ There is no film on the television this evening. ❺ I don't like to be disturbed.

***

❹ First of all, he buys something to eat,
....., il achète .... manger,

❺ and then he goes up to his apartment.
et .... il .... appartement.

Answers to Exercice 2
❶ – dîne – regarde – ❷ – il n'y a pas – à la – ❸ – d'écouter de la musique – passer – soirée calme ❹ D'abord – quelque chose à – ❺ – puis – monte à son –

***

There may seem to be a lot of details, but we don't want you to try and remember everything. We always repeat important points several times in different situations so that you become familiar with them automatically. *So just relax and enjoy yourself!*

11

Eleventh Lesson

A little revision

1 – [At] what time is the film this evening?
 – At half past eight *(eight hours and a half)*.

2 – Et qu'est-ce que c'est [1] ?
  – C'est_un film espagnol.
3 – Et c'est bien ?
  – Je ne sais pas, je ne connais pas le metteur en scène. [2]
4 – Bon. Alors, qu'est-ce qu'il y a à la radio ?
5 – Rien d'intéressant.
  – Alors, je vais lire un roman !

***

6 Un jour, dans un bus à Lyon [3],
7 un jeune homme est assis [4] en face d'une vieille dame ;
8 il mâche du chewing-gum.
9 Elle le regarde pendant [5] cinq minutes et dit :
10 – C'est_inutile d'articuler comme ça, jeune homme,
11 je suis complètement sourde !   □

*2 ... keskesay ? seteun feelm ... 3 ay say ... konnay ... 4 ...
keskeelya ... radeeoh 5 ... antairessohn ... rohmohn 6 ... leeohn
7 ... assee on fas ... veeay ... 8 ... massh ... shooing-gueum 10 set
inooteel dartikyoolay ... 11 ... soord*

Notes

1 These strange-looking expressions (see also line 4) are in fact both easy to pronounce and extremely useful: **Qu'est-ce que c'est ?**, *What's this, what's that?* **Qu'est-ce qu'il y a...?**, *What is there...?* **Qu'est-ce qu'il y a à manger ?**, *What is there to eat?* By itself, **qu'est-ce qu'il y a ?** means *what's the matter?*

2 There are two ways of saying *to know* in French. We say **je sais** when we are referring to a fact or some other abstract *thing*; and **je connais** for a person or a place. **Je connais sa mère**, *I know his/her mother*. **Je connais cette ville**, *I know this town*. **Il sait beaucoup de choses**, *He knows many things*.

2 – And what is it?
  – It's a Spanish film.
3 – And is it *(it is)* good?
  – I don't know, I don't know the director *(putter on stage)*.
4 – OK. So, what is there on the radio?
5 – Nothing *(of)* interesting.
  – Then, I'm going to read a novel!

***

6 One day, in a bus in Lyons,
7 a young man is sitting opposite an old lady;
8 he is chewing gum.
9 She looks at him for five minutes and says:
10 – It's useless to articulate like that, young man,
11 I'm completely deaf!

3 **Lyon** and **Marseille** often take an *s* in English. *Lyons*, France's third largest city and most important cultural centre outside Paris, started life as a Roman settlement (*Lugdunum*) in 43 BC. It was the site of the first Christian church in France and wielded enormous influence. In the 17th century, it was the silk capital of Europe. Today, in addition to being a major industrial and commercial centre, it is renowned for its cuisine.

4 The past participle is also an adjective, so it must "agree": **il est assis**, *he is sitting*; **elle est assise**, *she is sitting*.

5 **pendant**, *for* or *during*. **Pendant le dîner**, *during dinner*; **pendant vingt minutes**, *for 20 minutes*.

▶ Exercice 1 – Traduisez

❶ Qu'est-ce que c'est ? – C'est un livre allemand. ❷ Je ne connais pas sa mère, mais je connais son père. ❸ Qu'est-ce qu'il y a à la télévision ? – Rien d'intéressant. ❹ Il regarde la télévision pendant trois heures tous les jours. ❺ Pardon monsieur, ... – C'est inutile de parler, je suis sourd.

***

Exercice 2 – Complétez

❶ What's on the table? – It's a book.
   Qu'........... a sur .. table ? – ..... un livre.

❷ I'm going to listen to the radio this evening.
   Je .... la radio .. soir.

❸ What's that? – It's my identity card.
   Qu'.......... .....? – ..... ma carte d'identité.

12

Douzième leçon

▶ ## Un tour dans Paris

1 – Bonjour mesdames, bonjour mesdemoiselles, bonjour messieurs [1] ! Je suis votre guide.

💬 Pronunciation
1 ... maydam maydemwazel ... votr geed

Answers to Exercice 1

❶ What is it? – It's a German book. **❷** I don't know his/her mother but I know his/her father. **❸** What is on the television? – Nothing interesting. **❹** He watches television for three hours every day. **❺** Excuse me, sir, … – It's useless speaking, I am deaf.

***

❹ She watches the young man for five minutes.
Elle ……. le …………………… cinq minutes.

❺ What's the matter? – Nothing, nothing!
Qu'………………. a ? – …., … !

Answers to Exercice 2

❶ – est-ce qu'il y – la – C'est – **❷** – vais écouter – ce – **❸** – est-ce que c'est – C'est – **❹** – regarde – jeune homme pendant – **❺** – est-ce qu'il y – Rien, rien

12

Twelfth Lesson

A tour of *(in)* Paris

1 – Good morning ladies, good morning young ladies, good morning gentlemen! I'm your guide.

Note

1 The word for *sir* or *gentleman* is **monsieur** (lit. "my sire"). Likewise *lady* is **madame**, so if we are using the plural, the possessive adjective must agree: **messieurs, mesdames**.

2 Alors, commençons ici par la place du Panthéon : à ma droite, vous voyez le Panthéon même [2],

3 et à ma gauche, l'église Saint-_Étienne du Mont.

4 – Pardon monsieur, dit_un touriste, mais où... ?
  – Tout_à l'heure [3], répond le guide.

5 D'abord une église, le Panthéon...

6 – S'il vous plaît, monsieur, dit le même touriste, mais où sont... ?

7 – Mais laissez-moi terminer, je vous_en prie [4], répond le guide.

8 – Mais monsieur, c'est très_important !

9 – Eh bien, qu'est-ce que vous voulez savoir [5] ?

10 – Où sont les toilettes ?

▢

🗣 *2 ... plass du pontayohn ... drwat ... 3 ... gohsh ... 4 ... tootaleur raypohn ... 5 dabor ... 7 ... lessay-mwa terminay ... 8 ... trayzamportahn 9 ... keske ... savwar 10 ... twalett*

⬛ Notes

2 Here is another meaning of **même**: **moi-même**, *myself*; **elle-même**, *herself*; **lui-même**, *himself*; **vous-même**, *yourself*. If we attach it to a proper noun: **Londres même**, we mean *London*, as opposed to its suburbs. **Le Panthéon même**, *the Panthéon*, as opposed to *the Place du Panthéon*.

Named after the Roman temple dedicated to all the Gods, the Panthéon in Paris was built in a mixture of Greek and Gothic styles between 1764 and 1812. It is the resting place of France's most famous men and – since Marie Curie was inhumed there in 1996 – its women.

2 So let's begin here by the Place du Panthéon: on *(to)* my right, you see the Panthéon itself,

3 and on *(to)* my left, the church Saint-Étienne du Mont.

4 – Excuse me, sir, says a tourist, but where...?
 – Later, replies the guide.

5 Originally *(first)* a church, the Panthéon...

6 – Please, sir, says the same tourist, but where are...?

7 – But let me finish, if you please *(I pray you)*!, answers the guide.

8 – But sir, it's very important!

9 – Oh well, what do you want to know?

10 – Where are the toilets?

3 A tricky expression: it can mean both *earlier* and *later*. However, the context should make the meaning clear.

4 An emphatic way of saying *please*; **je vous en prie** can also be used to reply to someone who thanks you, or who apologises to you: **Oh, excusez-moi, monsieur. – Je vous en prie**, *Oh, I'm sorry, sir. – Don't mention it.*

5 We have seen **je sais**, *I know* (something). **Savoir** is the infinitive. This irregular verb goes: **je sais, il (ou elle) sait, nous savons, vous savez, ils (ou elles) savent.** (The last syllable of the third person plural is always silent.) **Savoir** is the origin of the English slang word *savvy* meaning *knowledge.*

▶ Exercice 1 – Traduisez

❶ Monsieur Legros habite Paris même. ❷ Oh, excusez-moi, monsieur ! – Je vous en prie. ❸ Je vais vous le dire tout à l'heure. ❹ Qu'est-ce que vous voulez savoir ? ❺ Pardon, monsieur, où est l'église Saint-Étienne du Mont ?

Exercice 2 – Complétez
*Put in the correct indefinite article (*un *or* une*)*

1. ..... heure
2. ..... église
3. ..... guide
4. ..... bureau
5. ..... maison
6. ..... adresse
7. ..... cinéma
8. ..... radio
9. ..... carte
10. ..... photo
11. ..... téléphone
12. ..... vie
13. ..... film
14. ..... bus
15. ..... télévision

*Now put the correct definite article (*le*, *la *ou* l'). If the noun begins with a vowel, put the gender in brackets afterwards:*

16. ..... conversation
17. ..... appartement
18. ..... beurre
19. ..... portefeuille
20. ..... mairie
21. ..... supermarché
22. ..... fils
23. ..... café
24. ..... travail
25. ..... dame
26. ..... enfant
27. ..... roman
28. ..... fromage
29. ..... rue
30. ..... tartine

Answers to Exercice 1

❶ Monsieur Legros lives in Paris itself. ❷ Oh, excuse me, sir! – Don't mention it. ❸ I will tell you later. ❹ What do you want to know? ❺ Excuse me, sir, where is the church Saint-Étienne du Mont?

Answers to Exercice 2

1. une heure 2. une église 3. un guide 4. un bureau 5. une maison 6. une adresse 7. un cinéma 8. une radio 9. une carte 10. une photo 11. un téléphone 12. une vie 13. un film 14. un bus 15. une télévision

16. la conversation 17. l'appartement *(m.)* 18. le beurre 19. le portefeuille 20. la mairie 21. le supermarché 22. le fils 23. le café 24. le travail 25. la dame 26. l'enfant *(m.)* 27. le roman 28. le fromage 29. la rue 30. la tartine

It's a little difficult to get used to the idea of different genders, but you can see how important it is. Always memorise the gender of a noun when you come across it for the first time (and don't forget to revise them from time to time!).

13

Treizième leçon

La belle musique

1 – Est-ce que vous_aimez cette chanteuse [1] ?

2 – Bof [2], elle a une assez belle voix...

3 mais je trouve que ses chansons sont_idiotes [3] ;

4 les paroles sont bêtes et la musique est triste.

5 De toute façon [4], j'aime seulement la musique classique.

6 – Vous n'aimez pas du tout [5] la musique moderne ?

7 – Si, mais seulement quand les chansons sont_intelligentes et belles.

8 – Qui aimez-vous [6] par exemple ?

– J'aime bien Coco et les Clowns. [7]

Pronunciation

1 ... shonteuz 2 ... assay bel vwa 3 ... shohnsohn ... ideeot 5 de toot fassohn ... seulmohn ... 7 ... sontantelizhohnt ... 8 ... lay kloon

Notes

1 Masculine nouns that end in **-eur** (see line 10) are "feminised" by adding **-euse** to the root word. For example **un vendeur**, *a salesman*, **une vendeuse**, *a saleswoman*. Here, the root is **chant** (**chanter** = *to sing*); **un chanteur** → *une chanteuse*.

2 **Bof !** is a whole vocabulary in itself: it is a French institution and expresses a basic lack of enthusiasm: **Vous aimez ce vin ? – Bof !**, *Do you like this wine? – Well, I suppose it's alright but...* So expressive is it that teenagers are sometimes referred to (by their elders) as **la génération "bof"** (*the "who cares?" generation...*).

13

Thirteenth Lesson

Beautiful music

1 – Do you like this singer?
2 – Oh, she has a pretty enough voice...
3   but I find that her songs are idiotic;
4   the words are stupid and the music is sad.
5   Anyway *(In any fashion)*, I like only *(the)* classical music.
6 – You don't like at all modern music?
7 – Yes [I do], but only when the songs are intelligent and beautiful.
8 – Whom [do] you like, for example?
   – I like *(well)* Coco and the Clowns.

3 Remember the plural **s** is silent! However we do pronounce the **t**, because there is a vowel after the final consonant: **un idiot** *[idioh]*; **une chanson idiote** *[idiot]*.

4 **façon** means *a fashion, a way of doing something*. **Ne le faites pas de cette façon**, *Don't do it that way*. **De toute façon** – *in any case, anyway*. *Fashion* meaning *style* is **la mode** *[mod]*. Note that the **d** is pronounced because there is a vowel after the final consonant.

5 Notice the construction of the sentence: **du tout** must follow **pas** directly: **Vous l'aimez ? – Pas du tout !**, *Do you like him? – Not at all!*

6 We said that forming questions with **est-ce que** was very common but not elegant. Here is the other interrogative form – and very simple it is. We simply invert the verb and the pronoun; **vous aimez... aimez-vous ?** This works for all forms and tenses. A famous novel, written by Françoise Sagan in 1959, is titled **Aimez-vous Brahms ?** An easy way to remember this construction!

7 Notice the pronunciation *[kloon]*.

9   Une affiche sur la vitrine [8] d'un magasin :
10   "Nous recherchons un vendeur : jeune
       ou vieux ; plein temps ou temps partiel ;
       expérimenté ou débutant".
11   Et en dessous, ajouté au crayon : "Mort ou vif".□

*9 … afeezh … vitreen … 10 … vohndeur … vyeu plahn tohn …
tohn parsee-el eksperimontay oo debyootohn 11 … on desoo … oh
krayohn "mor oo vif"*

Note

8 *window*, une fenêtre; une vitrine, *a shop-window*; faire du lèche-
vitrine (lit. "shop-window licking"), *to go window-shopping*.

***

Exercice 1 – Traduisez
❶ Dites-moi, Jean, vous aimez ce chanteur ? – Bof ! ❷ Et
vous, Pierre ? – Moi ? Pas du tout ! ❸ J'aime bien la musique
classique, mais j'aime aussi la musique moderne. ❹ De
toute façon, ses chansons sont bêtes. ❺ Elle n'aime pas du
tout le vin.

***

Exercice 2 – Complétez
❶ Do you like this shop? – Not at all!
      . . . . ce magasin ? – . . . . !

❷ Anyway, he only likes good wine.
      . . . ., il aime . . . . le bon vin.

❸ Her songs are sad and the music is beautiful.
      . . . chansons sont . . . . et la musique est . . . .

9 A sign on the window of a shop:

10 "We [are] looking [for] a salesman: young or old; full time or part time; experienced or beginner".

11 And, underneath, added in pencil: "Dead or alive".

LA BELLE MUSIQUE

Answers to Exercice 1

❶ Tell me, Jean, do you like this singer? – Not much! ❷ And you, Pierre? – Me? Not at all! ❸ I like classical music a lot, but I also like modern music. ❹ In any case, his/her songs are stupid. ❺ She doesn't like wine at all.

***

❹ She has quite a pretty voice.

Elle . une .... voix.

❺ He doesn't like modern music at all.

Il n'aime .... musique moderne.

Answers to Exercice 2

❶ Aimez-vous – Pas du tout ❷ De toute façon – seulement – ❸ Ses – tristes – belle ❹ – a – assez jolie – ❺ – pas du tout la –

14

Quartorzième leçon

Révision – Revision

1 Possessive adjectives

Look at these examples:

my father, **mon père**   *my mother*, **ma mère**
my brother, **mon frère**   *my sister*, **ma sœur**

The possession word (adjective) thus changes if the singular noun is masculine or feminine. For the plural, the word is **mes** irrespective of the gender: **mes parents**, **mes enfants**.

For *your*, *our* and *their*, we have one singular form and one plural form, irrespective of gender: **votre carte**, *your card*; **votre père**; **vos parents**; **notre radio**; **notre appartement**; **nos‿amis**; **leur adresse**; **leur maison**; **leurs photos**. (This plural **s** is silent unless the noun begins with a vowel: **leurs‿amis**.)

his and *her* (*its*) is slightly different from English. We say *his* if the <u>possessor</u> is masculine and *her* if she is feminine. In French however, the words for *his/her/its* are <u>adjectives</u> and must therefore <u>agree with the noun they qualify</u>.

So **son bureau** can mean: *his* or *her office*; we use **son** because **bureau** is masculine. In the same way **sa photo** can be *his* or *her photo*. The plural is **ses**: **ses romans** – *his* or *her novels*.

There is one exception to these rules of agreement: if the noun qualified begins with a vowel, we use the masculine adjective to make pronunciation easier. e.g. ***sa amie** would be difficult to pronounce (rather like *a apple*); so we say **son‿amie** and **mon‿amie** and allow the context to show whether the friend is male or female!

14

Fourteenth Lesson

2 Verbs ending in -er

In the last week, we have seen many different verbs, the infinitives of which end in **-er**. This is the largest category of French verbs, with literally thousands of "members". Let's look at an example: **aimer**; *to like, love*: **j'aime, il/elle aime, nous aimons, vous aimez, ils/elles aiment** (the final **-ent** is silent).

This is the pattern for all these verbs. Do you remember these? **rentrer**; **acheter**; **monter**; **décrocher**; **déranger**; **manger**; **allumer**; **regarder**; **laver**; **se coucher**; **penser**; **écouter**. Go back to lesson 10 and review them.

The past participle – which corresponds to the English *I have loved* – is simply: **aimé, dérangé**, pronounced the same as the infinitive. **Il n'aime pas être dérangé**, *He doesn't like to be disturbed*. Choose four of the above verbs and write out the forms with: **je, il/elle, nous, vous** and **ils/elles**. (Remember: the final **-ent** is silent.)

3 It is, C'est

We have seen two ways of saying *it is*: **c'est** and **il est**. Now let's explain the difference.
We use **c'est** to explain what a thing (or who a person) is.
Qu'est-ce que c'est ? – C'est une photo de famille.
What is it? – It's a family photo.
Regarde, c'est mon frère, *Look, that's my brother.*

or to say:
It's me – *C'est moi*
It's you – *C'est vous*
or if the noun is qualified by an adjective:
c'est un bon ami, *He's a good friend.*
The plural is **ce sont**. **Ce sont mes bons amis**, *They are my good friends*.

Il est is used to refer to a noun just mentioned:
Où est mon portefeuille ? – Il est sur la table.
(if the noun is feminine, we say **elle est**, – *Where is my wallet? – It's on the table.*)
Où est l'église ? – Elle est en face du Panthéon.
Where is the church? – It's opposite the Panthéon.

15

Quinzième leçon

▶

Petites_annonces

1   Recherche jeune fille pour garder mes_enfants le soir.
2   Téléphoner [1] le matin au 04 56 52 39 01 [2]

3   Je vends un canapé et deux fauteuils en cuir. Prix à débattre.

4   À louer. Petit studio. Calme et clair. Salle d'eau [3]
5   Écrire à Mme Delaye, 3 boulevard Malesherbes, Paris huitième.

🗨 Pronunciation
1 … zheun fee … mayzohnfohn … 2 … oh zehrow kat sinkont seess sinkont deu tront neuf zehrow eun 3 … vohn … fotoy ohn kweer … pree … 4 a looay. petee … sal doh 5 … malzerb …

📓 Notes
1   The infinitive is often used on public notices, signs, etc. as an imperative: **Ne rien jeter à terre**, *Don't throw anything on the floor.* (Of course, we could say **Ne jetez rien**…)

or if we are talking about the weather:
il pleut, *it's raining*. **il fait beau**, *it's fine*.
or telling the time:
il est huit heures et demie, *it's half past eight.*

***

So much for the rules. In time you will "feel" the correct usage,
so don't try to do too much at once.
Remember: learn each noun with its gender!

15

Fifteeth Lesson

Classified (small) advertisements

1 Looking [for] young girl (for) to look after (keep) my children [in] the evening.
2 Telephone [in] the morning (to) 04 56 52 39 01.

3 I am selling a sofa and two (in) leather armchairs. Price to [be] discussed.

4 To rent. Small studio. Quiet (Calm) and light (clear). Bathroom.
5 Write to Mrs Delaye, 3 boulevard Malesherbes, Paris 8th [district].

2 In France, phone numbers are grouped in sets of two figures and pro-nounced as real numbers (i.e. not "five six" but "fifty-six"). This takes some getting used to, so let's start today!

3 **une salle de bains**, *a bathroom*; **une salle d'eau** (lit. "waterroom") – *a small bathroom*, generally with a shower and washbasin.

6 – Bonjour, madame. Je vous‿appelle au sujet de votre annonce pour garder les‿enfants.

7 – Très bien. Comment vous‿appelez-vous [4] ?

8 – Je m'appelle Martine Lenoir, madame.

9 – Et quel âge avez-vous, Martine ?

10 – J'ai quatorze ans, madame.

11 – Oh, mais vous‿êtes beaucoup trop jeune !

12 Je suis désolée [5]. Au revoir.   □

🗣 **6** … *oh soozhay de votranonss* **10** … *katorzohn* … **11** … *voozet bowkoo troh* … **12** … *dayzolay* …

🗂 Notes

4 je m'appelle; il/elle s'appelle; nous nous appelons; vous vous appelez; ils/elles s'appellent. This is called a "reflexive" verb: the subject and the object are the same. You will have noticed the change in spelling, from double ll to single l – **appelle/appelons**. We'll explain why at a later stage.

5 **Excusez-moi**, *Excuse me; I'm sorry*. **Pardon**, *Pardon*. Remember? We saw **désolé** in lesson 4, note 5.

***

▶ Exercice 1 – Traduisez

❶ Je n'ai pas d'argent pour acheter des meubles. ❷ Il y a un petit studio à louer dans le huitième. ❸ Bonjour ! Je m'appelle Pierre Lefèvre. ❹ Mais vous êtes beaucoup trop jeune ! ❺ Comment vous appelez-vous ?

6 – Good morning, madam. I [am] calling you about the *(your)* advertisement to look after *(the)* children.

7 – Very well. What is your name *(How do you call yourself)*?

8 – My name is *(I call myself)* Martine Lenoir, madam.

9 – And how old are you, Martine *(what age have you)*?

10 – I am *(have)* 14 years [old], madam.

11 – Oh, but you are much too young!

12 I am very sorry. Goodbye.

***

Answers to Exercice 1

❶ I haven't any money to buy furniture. ❷ There is a little studio to rent in the 8th district. ❸ Hello! My name's Pierre Lefèvre. ❹ But you are much too young! ❺ What is your name?

Exercice 2 – Complétez

❶ What is your name?
.... appelez- .... ?

❷ How old are you, miss?
.... âge ...., mademoiselle ?

❸ I'm terribly sorry; my father isn't in.
Je suis ...... ; mon père n'... pas ....•

16

Seizième leçon

Des_achats... !

1 – Bonjour, madame. Je cherche un piège à rats [1].
Vous_en [2] avez ?

2 – Bien sûr, monsieur. Attendez une minute, je
vais vous_en chercher un.

3 – Dépêchez-vous, madame. J'ai un avion à
prendre.

4 – Un avion ? Oh, monsieur, je suis désolée,

5 je n'ai pas_un modèle assez grand [3] !

Pronunciation
*1 ... pee-ezh a ra voozonavay 2 ... zhe vayvoozon ... eun 3 ... eun
aviohn ...*

Notes

1 une bouteille de vin, *a bottle of wine*; une bouteille à vin, *a wine
bottle*. The second construction explains the <u>purpose</u> of the object; une
brosse à dents, *a toothbrush*; un verre à champagne, *a champagne
glass*.

❹ I am calling you about your advertisement.
Je vous .... votre annonce.

❺ I'm looking for a young girl to look after my children.
Je cherche une ..... fille .... mes enfants.

16

Sixteenth Lesson

Purchases...!

1 – Good morning, madam. I am looking for a rat trap.
[Do] you have one?
2 – Of course, sir. Wait a minute, I'm going to look for
one *(for you)*.
3 – Hurry *(yourself)*, madam. I have a plane to catch *(take)*.
4 – A plane? Oh sir, I'm very sorry.
5 I don't have a model big enough!

Note the pronunciation of *rat*, un rat *[ra]*. *A female rat*, une rate *[rat]* because of the final vowel (see lesson 13, note 4). (**La rate** also means *the spleen*.)

2 en: This little word means *of it* or *of them*. **Vous avez des enfants ? – J'en ai deux**, – *Do you have any children? – I have two*. Its use is idiomatic and we will see some more examples later.

3 Notice the word order: **je n'ai pas un sac assez grand**, *I don't have a bag big enough*.

6 Un douanier arrête un voyageur à la sortie de la douane [4] :

7 – Bonjour monsieur. Ouvrez votre sac, s'il vous plaît.

8 Le voyageur ouvre son sac... qui est plein de diamants.

9 – Ces diamants sont pour mes lapins, dit le voyageur.

10 – Pour vos lapins, vous dites ? s'exclame le douanier.

11 – Parfaitement. Et s'ils ne veulent [5] pas de diamants, ils n'auront [6] rien à manger ! ☐

🗣 **6** ... dooaniay ... vwoyazheur ... dooann **8** ... plan de deeamohn **9** say ... lapan ... **10** ... seksklam ... **11** parfetmohn ... seel ne veul ... norohn ...

Notes

4 la douane, *customs, the customs area*; un douanier, *a customs officer*; un policier, *a police officer*. *A custom in the sense of a tradition*: une coutume.

5 je veux; il/elle veut; nous voulons; vous voulez; ils/elles veulent. The infinitive of this verb is **vouloir**, *to want*. Il veut partir, *He wants to leave*.

***

▶ Exercice 1 – Traduisez

❶ Nous cherchons notre sac. **❷** Il va en apporter un, je pense. **❸** Si vous ne voulez pas de café, nous avons du thé *[tay]*. **❹** Je n'ai pas un modèle assez grand. **❺** Ces diamants sont pour mes lapins.

6 A customs officer stops a traveller at the exit of the customs [hall]:

7 – Good morning sir. Open your bag, please

8 The traveller opens his bag... which is full of diamonds.

9 – These diamonds are for my rabbits, says the traveller.

10 – For your rabbits, you say? exclaims the customs officer.

11 – Exactly *(Perfectly)*. And if they don't want diamonds, they will have nothing to eat!

DES ACHATS...

6 This is our first encounter with the future tense. We will see it in greater detail later on.

***

Answers to Exercice 1

❶ We are looking for our bag. ❷ He is going to bring one, I think. ❸ If you don't want coffee, we have tea. ❹ I don't have a model big enough. ❺ These diamonds are for my rabbits.

Exercice 2 – Complétez

❶ Do you have a cigarette, please? – I have two.
Vous .... une cigarette, ... vous plaît ?

– J'.... deux.

❷ Wait a minute; I'll just go and bring one.
.... une minute ; je ...... apporter une.

❸ Where is my toothbrush?
.. est .. brosse ...... ?

17

Dix-septième leçon

Au téléphone

(This is one side of a telephone conversation. The other side is in the next lesson.)

1 – Allô ? ¹... Oui, c'est moi. Qui est à l'appareil ?
2 ... Ah, bonjour Sophie... Bien, et vous ? ... Oh, quel dommage ² !
3 J'espère que ce n'est pas grave ? ... Heureusement.
4 Jacques ? ... Oh, il va assez ³ bien, mais il a beaucoup de travail en ce moment.

Pronunciation
konvairsasseeohn 1 ... kee etalaparay 2 ... kel domahzh 3 ... grahv ... eureusmohn 4 ... onsemomohn

Notes
1 **Allô ?** is only used on the telephone; it is not a greeting. To greet someone, we say **bonjour** or **bonsoir** if it is the evening. (**bonne nuit** means *good night*). **Qui est à l'appareil ?** is telephone vocabulary for

❹ He opens his bag to find a lighter.

Il ouvre ... sac .... chercher un briquet.

❺ These books are for my children.

... livres sont ... ... enfants.

❶ – avez – s'il – en ai – **❷** Attendez – vais en – **❸** Où – ma – à dents
❹ – son – pour – **❺** Ces – pour mes –

17

Seventeenth Lesson

On the telephone

1 – Hello? Yes, it's me. Who's speaking *(on the apparatus)*?

2 ... Ah, hello Sophie... well, and you? Oh, what [a] pity!

3 I hope that it's not serious? ... Fortunately.

4 Jacques? ... Oh, he's quite well, but he has a lot of work at the *(in this)* moment.

Who's speaking? Note, too, that French says **au téléphone** for *on the telephone*.

2 Quel livre voulez-vous ?, *Which book do you want?*
Quelle heure est-il ?, *What time is it?*
Quels livres aimez-vous ?, *Which books do you like?*
Quelles cartes voulez-vous acheter ?, *Which cards do you want to buy?*
All these forms are pronounced the same.
quel; quelle; quels; quelles, *which?* or *what?*
In exclamations, it means *What a...!* **Quelle ville !**, *What a town!*
Quel nom !, *What a name!* **Quel dommage !**, *What a pity!*

3 **assez** has two principal meanings. Before an adjective or adverb, it means *quite*: il est‿assez grand, *He is quite big*; Elle chante assez bien, *She sings quite well*. Before a noun, it means *enough*: je n'ai pas‿assez de temps, *I don't have enough time*.

5   ... Des vacances ? Ne me [4] faites pas rire ! Nous n'avons pas_assez d'argent. Et vous ?

6   ... Comme tout le monde... Avec plaisir. Quand ? Samedi prochain ?

7   Attendez, je vais voir. Ne quittez pas.

8   Non, samedi, ma mère vient dîner à la maison.

9   Dimanche ? Je pense que nous sommes libres [5]. Oui, dimanche, c'est parfait.

10 À huit heures. D'accord. Soignez-vous ! ... Merci, au revoir.   □

6 ... toolemond ... plezeer. kon ? samdi proshan 7 ... keetay ... 8 ... vee-en ... 9 ... leebr. ... parfay 10 ... weeteur swanyayvoo

Notes

4 With an affirmative imperative, *me* is **moi**. It comes after the verb and is joined to it by a hyphen: **Parlez-moi !**, *Speak to me!* **Répondez-moi**, *Answer me. He* becomes **lui**: **Dites-lui**, *Tell him.*
With a negative imperative, *me* is **me** and comes before the verb: **Ne me regardez pas comme ça**, *Don't look at me like that.*

5 **Ces livres sont gratuits**, *These books are free* (i.e. they cost nothing). **Il n'est pas libre ce soir**, *He is not free this evening* (i.e. he is busy). **Du temps libre**, *free time.*
If a shop announces **libre-service**, it is our *self-service store.*

***

Exercice 1 – Traduisez

❶ Il a beaucoup de travail en ce moment. ❷ Samedi, ma mère vient à la maison. ❸ Je pense que je suis libre dimanche. ❹ Ne quittez pas, je vais voir. ❺ Comme tout le monde, nous n'avons pas assez d'argent.

5 ... Holidays? Don't make me *(to)* laugh! We don't have enough money. And you?

6 ... Like everybody... With pleasure. When? Next Saturday?

7 Wait, I'll have a look *(I'm going to look)*. Don't go away *(leave)*.

8 No; [on] Saturday, my mother [is] coming to dinner *(dine at home)*.

9 Sunday? I think that we are free. Yes, Sunday *(it)* is perfect.

10 At 8.00. Fine. Look after yourself! ... Thank you. Goodbye.

Answers to Exercice 1

❶ He has a lot of work at the moment. ❷ On Saturday, my mother is coming to the house. ❸ I think that I am free on Sunday. ❹ Don't hang up, I'll go and see. ❺ Like everybody, we haven't enough money.

Exercice 2 – Complétez

❶ You are not free? What a pity!
Vous n'.... pas .....? .... !

❷ Don't make me laugh!
Ne .. faites pas .... !

❸ My husband is quite well but he has a lot of work.
Mon mari .... bien mais il a .... travail.

18

Dix-huitième leçon

Au téléphone (suite)

1 – Allô, Anne-Marie ? ... C'est Sophie.
Comment_allez-vous ?

2 Moi, j'ai la grippe... Non, ce n'est pas trop grave.

3 Et comment va Jacques ? ... Vous prenez des
vacances bientôt [1] ?

4 Non, malheureusement, ça coûte trop cher.

5 Dites-moi, est-ce que vous voulez venir dîner un
soir ?

6 Disons samedi prochain... Tant pis [2]. Eh bien,
dimanche ? ... Ça vous va [3] ?

Pronunciation

*1 ... komontalayvoo 2 ... greep ...3 ... byantoh 4 ... malereuzmohn
... koot ... 5 deetmwa ... 6 ... tohnpee ...*

Notes

1 tôt, *early*; Venez tôt, *Come early.* tard, *late*; Il se couche tard, *He goes to
bed late.* to be early, être en avance. to be late, être en retard. bientôt,
soon; À bientôt !, *See you soon!*

❹ I hope that it's not serious.
   J'...... que .. n'... pas ......

❺ Are you free next Saturday?
   ... ... libre .... ?

Answers to Exercice 2
❶ – êtes – libre – Quel dommage ❷ – me – rire ❸ – va assez –
beaucoup de – ❹ – espère – ce – est – grave ❺ Êtes-vous – samedi
prochain

18

Eighteenth Lesson

On the telephone (continued)

1 – Hello, Anne-Marie? ... It's Sophie. How are you?
2   Me, I have the flu'... Not, it's not too serious.
3   And how is *(goes)* Jacques? [Are] you taking holidays
    soon?
4   No, unfortunately. It costs too much *(expensive)*.
5   Tell me, do you want to come to dinner *(to dine)* one
    evening?
6   Let's say next Saturday... Bad luck. Well, Sunday?
    Does that suit you? *(that goes you?)*

2   An idiom meaning *hard luck, there is nothing we can do*. **Ils ne viennent
    pas. Tant pis**, *They are not coming. Shame.* (Note that the final **s** of **pis**
    is silent...)

3   We've seen several ways in which the verb **aller** is used idiomatically.
    Comment va Jacques ?, *How is Jacques?*; **Vous_allez bien ?**, *Are you
    well?*; **Ça vous va ?**, *Does that suit you?*; **Ce chapeau vous va bien**, *This
    hat looks good on you, suits you nicely*; **Ça me va**, *That's fine by me*.

7 Parfait. Venez vers huit_heures. Pas trop tôt.

8 ...Oui, oui. Je prends beaucoup de médicaments, beaucoup trop [4] !

9 Allez, dites bonjour à Jacques pour moi.

10 Je vous_embrasse [5]. Au revoir. À dimanche. □

7 ... vair ... troh toh **10** *zhevoozombrass ...*

Notes

4 In French, we make no difference between *much* and *many*: **beaucoup d'argent**, *much money*; **beaucoup de voitures**, *many cars*. Before **beaucoup**, we often use an expression you have seen: **il y a**, *there is / there are*; **beaucoup de**, *a lot of*; **beaucoup** – *a lot*; **vous fumez beaucoup**, *you smoke a lot!* **beaucoup trop**, *far too much / many*.

5 It is a custom in France for friends to kiss each other on both cheeks as a greeting (men usually shake hands), so it is not unusual to finish a letter or a phone call to a friend with **Je vous embrasse**, *I kiss you*. **Un baiser**, *a kiss* (the title of the famous sculpture by Rodin) is modified

***

Exercice 1 – Traduisez

❶ Il fume beaucoup trop ! ❷ Est-ce que vous voulez dîner ? ❸ Venez à huit heures et demie. Ça vous va ? ❹ Dites bonjour à votre mari pour moi. ❺ Ça coûte trop cher !

7   Perfect. **Come around** *(towards)* **8.00. Not too early.**

8   **...Yes, yes. I [am] taking a lot of medicines, far too many!**

9   **OK.** *(Go)***, say hello to Jacques for me.**

10   **Lots of kisses** *(I kiss you)***. Goodbye. Until** *(to)* **Sunday.**

to **une bise** or **un bisou** *[beezoo]* in familiar language. So, if the two people in this conversation were close friends, they could have finished the conversation with **Bisous.**

***

Answers to Exercice 1

❶ He smokes far too much! ❷ Do you want to have dinner? ❸ Come at 8.30. Does that suit you? ❹ Say hello to your husband for me. ❺ It costs too much!

Exercice 2 – Complétez

❶ I'm taking a lot of medicines; far too many!

Je prends .... médicaments ; beaucoup .... !

❷ He always arrives late.

Il ...... toujours ....

❸ Don't come too early. Does that suit you?

Ne ..... pas .... tôt. Ça ...... ?

❹ There are a lot of children in this school.

.... beaucoup .. enfants dans cette école.

19

Dix-neuvième leçon

Deux conversations au restaurant

1 – Qu'est-ce que vous mangez ? Ça sent bon !

2 – C'est‿une daube ¹ de bœuf. Vous‿en ² voulez ?

3 – Non merci. Je n'ai pas faim. J'ai déjà mangé.

4 – Alors, prenez un verre de vin.

5 – Non merci ; je n'ai pas soif non plus. Mais je
vais prendre un café.

Pronunciation

*1 ... sa sohn bohn **2** ... dowb de beuf ... **3** ... fan ... dayzha
mohnzhay **5** ... swaf nohn plyoo ...*

Notes

1 **une daube** is a rich stew, made with wine, meat and vegetables. Note
that because of the Norman French influence, the English language
has one word for the animal and another for its meat (e.g. *a cow*, *beef*).
French does not make that distinction: **un bœuf**, *an ox*; **du bœuf**, *beef*;

❺ How are you, and how is your husband?
  Comment ……. …… et comment .. votre …. ?

Answers to Exercice 2
❶ – beaucoup de – trop ❷ – arrive – en retard ❸ – venez – trop – vous
va ❹ Il y a – d' – ❺ – allez-vous – va – mari

*Don't try to learn all these new expressions at once. We will see
them again in later lessons.*

19

Nineteenth Lesson

Two conversations at the restaurant

1 – What are you eating? It smells good!
2 – It's a beef stew. [Do] you want some?
3 – No, thank you. I'm not hungry *(I have not hunger)*. I
  have already eaten.
4 – Well, have *(take)* a glass of wine.
5 – No, thank you. I'm *(have)* not thirsty either. But I will
  (going to) have *(take)* a coffee.

un agneau, *a lamb*; de l'agneau, *lamb* (meat); un veau *[voh]*, *a calf*; du
veau, *veal*. But in case you thought it was too easy, un cochon, *a pig*;
du porc, *pork*!

2 Je veux du beurre, *I want some butter*; J'ai du beurre, vous en voulez ?, *I have some butter; do you want some?* en avoids the repetition,
  in the second part of the sentence, of du beurre. Note that du, de la
  and des can never stand by themselves.

6 – Bien. Garçon ! Deux cafés et l'addition, s'il vous
plaît !

7 – Je ne vais pas prendre de vacances cette année.

8 Ça coûte beaucoup trop cher. Et vous ?

9 – Moi [3] je vais en [4] Grèce en septembre [5] pour
deux semaines.

10 – En Grèce ? Vous_avez de la chance ! Je suis
jaloux.

☐

6 ... *ladeeseeohn* ... **9** *gress* ... *septombr* ... **10** ... *shonss* ...
zhaloo

Notes

3 This declarative use of the pronoun is colloquial and adds emphasis to
the statement. If someone has given their opinion and you wish to give
yours, you can start the sentence with **moi**, *as for me*. **Moi, je pense
qu'il a raison**, *Well, I think he's right*.
We can use the same construction with other pronouns, as we'll see
later.

4 **Vous le trouvez en Grèce**, *You find it in Greece*. **Elle va en Grèce**, *She
is going to Greece*. However, if the country has a plural name (the

***

▶ Exercice 1 – Traduisez

❶ Je n'ai pas faim. J'ai déjà mangé. ❷ Prenez un verre
de vin ! – Non merci. ❸ Vous avez soif ? – Oh oui, très.
❹ Qu'est-ce que vous mangez ? Ça sent très bon. ❺ Garçon !
Un café et l'addition, s'il vous plaît !

6 – Good. Waiter! Two coffees and the bill, please!

7 – I'm not going to take holidays this year.

8   It costs too much *(expensive)*. And you?

9 – Me, I'm going to *(in)* Greece in September for two weeks.

10 – To *(in)* Greece? You're lucky *(you have luck)*! I'm jealous.

Netherlands, the United States, etc.) we use the plural form **aux** after **aller**. Ils vont aux **États-Unis**, *They go/are going to the United States.*

5   Here are the names of the months: janvier *[zhonveeay]*; février *[fevreeay]*; mars *[marss]*; avril *[avreel]*; mai *[may]*; juin *[zhwan]*; juil-let *[zhweeyay]*; août *[oot]*; septembre *[septombr]*; octobre *[oktobr]*; novembre *[novombr]*; décembre *[dessombr]*.

***

Answers to Exercice 1

❶ I am not hungry. I have already eaten. ❷ Have a glass of wine! – No thank you. ❸ Are you thirsty? – Oh yes, very. ❹ What are you eating? It smells very good. ❺ Waiter! A coffee and the bill please!

Exercice 2 – Complétez

❶ I have some wine. Do you want some?

J'ai .. vin. Vous .... ?

❷ As for me, I'm going to Italy and to the United States this year.

..., je vais .. Italie et .. États-Unis cette ....

❸ You're thirsty? Well, have a glass of water.

Vous .... ? Alors, ... un verre .. eau.

20

Vingtième leçon

Encore ¹ un peu de révision

1 Aujourd'hui, nous_allons revoir ²
   quelques_expressions utiles :

2 – Venez vers huit_heures, d'accord ?
   – Parfait.

                    ***

3 Elle est malade et elle prend beaucoup de
   médicaments.

🗣 Pronunciation
onkor … reveezeeon 1 … revwar … kelkezekspresseeohn …

📇 : Notes

1 Remember how we shout **Encore!** at a concert, to ask the band to play
   another number? Well, the word comes from French. **Encore du vin ?**,
   Some more wine? **Vous_en voulez encore ?**, *You want some more of
   it?* **Encore un peu, s'il vous plaît,** *A little bit more, please.*
   (Funnily enough, the French would never shout **Encore !** at a concert;
   the equivalent is **Bis !**, which means *twice.*)

④ What are you eating? Beef?
.... vous ......? .. bœuf ?

⑤ They aren't going to take holidays in August.
Ils ne .... pas .... vacances ....

20

Twentieth Lesson

A little more *(Again a little)* revision

1 Today we are going to see again some useful expressions:

2 – Come around *(towards)* 8.00, O.K. ?
   – Perfect.

*** *

3 She is ill and she [is] taking a lot of medicines.

COMMENT S'APPELLE
SA FEMME ?

2 English tends to modify its verbs by using "postpositions" (look <u>at</u>, look <u>after</u>, look <u>for</u>, etc.); In contrast, French adds a prefix to the verb: **voir**, *to see*; **revoir**, *to see again*; **brancher**, *to plug in*; **débrancher**, *to unplug*.

4 – Je cherche un grand sac en cuir. Vous_en_avez
un ?

***

5   Il n'a pas faim et il n'a pas soif : il a déjà mangé.

***

6 – Qui est à l'appareil ? Ah, Sophie.
Comment_allez-vous ?

***

7 – Ma femme ³ a beaucoup de travail en ce
moment.

8 – Des vacances ? Ne me faites pas rire !

***

9 – Vous voulez un verre de vin ?
   – Avec plaisir.

***

10 – Comment vous_appelez-vous ?
   – Je m'appelle Sophie Delaye.

***

11 – Je suis désolé, je suis pris ⁴ samedi soir.
   – Eh bien tant pis !

***

12 – Cette nouvelle robe vous va très bien.   ☐

4 ... kweer 6 ... laparay

4 – I'm looking for a big leather bag. [Do] you have *(one)* ?

***

5 He is *(has)* not hungry and he is *(has)* not thirsty; he has already eaten.

***

6 – Who is on the phone? Oh, Sophie. How are you?

***

7 – My wife has a lot of work at the *(in this)* moment.
8 – Holidays? Don't make me laugh!

***

9 – [Do] you want a glass of wine?
 – With pleasure.

***

10 – What is your name?
 – My name is Sophie Delaye.

***

11 – I'm very sorry, I'm taken [on] Saturday evening.
 – Oh well, hard luck!

***

12 – That new dress suits you very well.

Notes

3 une femme, *a woman*; BUT ma femme, *my wife*. We have a similar confusion with une fille, *a girl*; sa fille, *his/her daughter*. The context should make the meaning clear: un homme, un mari, *a man*, *a husband*; un garçon, un fils, *a boy*, *a son*.

4 This is the <u>past participle</u> of the verb prendre, *to take*.

▶ Exercice 1 – Traduisez

❶ J'ai du café. Est-ce que vous en voulez ? **❷** Encore un petit peu, s'il vous plaît. **❸** Ce nouveau chapeau et cette nouvelle robe sont très jolis. **❹** Mon mari est pris ce soir. – Quel dommage ! **❺** Comment s'appelle sa femme ? **❻** Je veux revoir cet exercice, s'il vous plaît.

Exercice 2 – Complétez
Put the correct indefinite article (un, une).

❶ ... fauteuil
❷ ... salle de bains
❸ ... douanier
❹ ... sac
❺ ... femme
❻ ... voyageur
❼ ... monde

❽ ... grippe
❾ ... verre
❿ ... addition
⓫ ... brosse à dents
⓬ ... livre
⓭ ... agneau

21

Vingt et unième leçon

Révision – Revision

1 Verbs

Vendre, *to sell*; **prendre**, *to take*; **attendre**, *to wait for*. These verbs – which we have already used – are part of a second "class" or category whose infinitives end in **-re**.
Here is how they look:
je vends, ils/elle vend, nous vendons, vous vendez, ils/elles vendent.
Remember that the final **s** and the **-ent** are silent; but there is a difference in pronunciation between the "(s)he" and the "they" forms. **Il vend** *[eel vohn]*; **ils vendent** *[eel vohnd]*. Remember our rule about the final vowel?

Answers to Exercice 1

❶ I have some coffee. Do you want some? ❷ A little more, please.
❸ This new hat and this new dress are very pretty. ❹ My husband is
busy this evening. – What a pity! ❺ What's his wife called? ❻ I want to
see this exercise again please.

Answers to Exercice 2

❶ un fauteuil ❷ une salle de bains ❸ un douanier ❹ un sac ❺ une
femme ❻ un voyageur ❼ un monde ❽ une grippe ❾ un verre ❿ une
addition ⓫ une brosse à dents ⓬ un livre ⓭ un agneau

21

Twenty-First Lesson

If the verb begins with a vowel, of course, we "liaise" (join up) the
s of **ils, elles**.
elle attend *[el attohn]*; **elles_attendent** *[elzattohnd]*.

The past participle of these verbs usually ends in **-u**: **vendu,
attendu.**
Let's remind ourselves of three irregular verbs:
savoir, *to know*; **je sais, il/elle sait, nous savons, vous savez, ils/
elles savent.**
prendre, *to take*; **je prends, il/elle prend, nous prenons, vous prenez, il/elle prennent.** (past participle: **pris**).
aller, *to go*: **je vais, il/elle va, nous allons, vous allez, ils/elles vont.**

2 Days of the week

The days of the week are: **lundi, mardi, mercredi, jeudi, vendredi,
samedi, dimanche.**

Notice that, unless they are used at the beginning of a sentence, they are not spelled with an initial capital letter.
We do not need a preposition to express *on*...:
Il vient jeudi, *He's coming on Thursday*;
Téléphonez-moi mardi, *Phone me on Tuesday*.

If we want to say: *he works Saturdays* (meaning every Saturday), we put the definite article before the noun, thus:
Il travaille le samedi (no final **s**) because proprer nouns in French are never pluralised.
À samedi !, *Until Saturday!* (See you on Saturday);
Bon week-end !, *Have a nice weekend!* (Officially, *the weekend* is **la fin de la semaine**, but English has gained the upper hand here!)

3 A few expressions constructed with *avoir*

avoir faim: Certain expressions which in English use *to be* are constructed with **avoir**, *to have* in French. Thus:
Avez-vous faim ?, *Are you hungry?*
Elle n'a pas soif, *She is not thirsty*.

22

Vingt-deuxième leçon

Les passe-temps nationaux

1 Les Français sont passionnés par les jeux [1] d'argent.

Pronunciation
*lay pastohn nassionoh **1** … pass-i-onay … zheu …*

Note
1 The plurals of most nouns and adjectives are formed by adding a silent **s** to the end of the word. However, those ending in **-eu** and **-eau** take a

Vous avez de la chance, *You are lucky*.
Quel âge a votre enfant ?, *How old is your child?*

Here are some new ones:
Elle a peur la nuit, *She's frightened at night*.
Vous avez raison, *You are right*.
Il a tort *[tor]*, *He's wrong*.
Excusez-moi, j'ai sommeil *[sommey]*, *Excuse me, I'm sleepy*.

4 Numbers

un (1), **deux** (2), **trois** (3), **quatre** (4), **cinq** (5), **six** *[seess]* (6), **sept** *[set]* (7), **huit** (8), **neuf** (9), **dix** *[deess]* (10), **onze** (11), **douze** (12), **treize** (13), **quatorze** (14), **quinze** (15), **seize** *[sez]* (16), **dix-sept** *[deesset]* (17), **dix-huit** *[deezweet]* (18), **dix-neuf** (19), **vingt** *[van]* (20).

Continued next week. Look back at the past 20 lessons and practise saying the numbers aloud.

22

Twenty-Second Lesson

The national pastimes

1 The French are fascinated by gambling *(games of money)*.

(silent) x. un jeu – des jeux; un étau (*a vice*) – des étaux; un château – des châteaux.
Similarly, nouns and adjectives ending in -al change to -aux *[oh]*. un cheval – des chevaux; un journal – des journaux; national – nationaux. There are a couple more exceptional plurals, but we needn't worry about them for the time being.

2 Chaque semaine, des millions d'hommes et de femmes jouent ²

3 à l'un ³ des principaux jeux ⁴ : le loto, les jeux instantanés et le P.M.U.

4 Les deux premiers sont des jeux de hasard :

5 il faut soit ⁵ choisir des numéros dans un certain ordre,

6 soit gratter des cases sur un ticket qu'on‿achète dans‿un bureau de tabac.

7 En revanche, les courses demandent un peu plus de connaissances :

8 on doit sélectionner les chevaux en fonction de leur performance dans d'autres courses.

9 Il y a aussi des jeux de casino, mais‿ils sont très strictement réglementés.

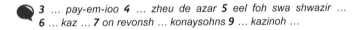

3 ... pay-em-ioo **4** *... zheu de azar* **5** *eel foh swa shwazir ...*
6 *... kaz ...* **7** *on revonsh ... konaysohns* **9** *... kazinoh ...*

Notes

2 **jouer**, *to play*. For games and sports, we use the preposition **au** (or **à la** in the feminine). **Il joue au football**, *He plays soccer*. But for an instrument, the preposition is **du** (or **de la**). **Elle joue de la guitare**, *She plays the guitar*.

3 We add the **l'** before **un** as an aid to pronunciation (try saying **à un**!). It does not affect the meaning in any way.

4 Basically, gambling is not permitted by the French civil or penal codes. But the law makes certain exceptions, and the state takes a percentage of the winnings! The **loto** and scratch-card games are organised by state-controlled bodies. The P.M.U. (**Pari Mutuel Urbain**), which started at the end of the 19th century, is a totalisator betting system for horse

2 Each week, millions of men and women play

3 *(at)* one of the main games: the Loto, scratchcard *(instant)* games and the horse races (P.M.U.).

4 The first two are games of chance:

5 you must *(it is necessary to)* either choose numbers in a certain order

6 or scratch boxes on a card *(ticket)* that you *(one)* buy*(s)* in a tobacconist's.

7 In contrast, the races require a little more knowledge:

8 you *(one)* must select the horses according to their performance in other races.

9 There are also casino games, but they are very strictly regulated.

races (note that the term "pari-mutuel" can also be used in English). **Un pari**, *a bet.*

5 **soit... soit** *[swa]* is the most common way of saying *either... or.* As in English, the words are placed before the alternatives: **Il faut soit gratter la case, soit choisir des numéros**, *You must either scratch the box or choose a number.* **Il y a soit de la bière soit du vin**, *There's either beer or wine.*

10   Dans tous les cas, les joueurs ont tous [6] la
même idée en tête : faire fortune.

11   Mais du fait qu'ils sont très nombreux, il y a
peu de gros [7] gagnants...

12   C'est ça, les jeux de hasard : un jour vous
perdez, et le lendemain...

13   vous perdez encore !   □

🗨 *10 ... zhou-err ... **11** ... nombreu ... gro ...*

Notes

6   Beware! If **tous** comes before a plural noun, it means all and is pronounced *[too]*. **Tous les journaux**, *All the newspapers*; BUT if it comes
after a verb, it means *all of you/them*, *everyone*, and is pronounced
[toos]. **Venez tous à huit heures**, *All of you come at 8 o'clock*. The secret
is to notice the position of **tous**.

***

▶ Exercice 1 – Traduisez

❶ Elle joue à l'un des jeux les plus difficiles : les échecs.
❷ En revanche, les dames* demandent moins d'habileté.
❸ Venez soit tôt le matin, soit tard le soir. ❹ Dans tous les
cas, vous risquez de perdre. ❺ C'est ça la vie !

* **une dame** = *a lady*, **les dames** = *ladies*, BUT **les dames** is also the game of
draughts / checkers.

***

Exercice 2 – Complétez

❶ What are the principal national games?
Quels sont les .... ?

❷ They all hope to win the jackpot.
Ils espèrent .... le ....

❸ He plays football every day.
Il .... football .... les jours.

10 In every case, the players have the same idea in mind *(head)*: to make [their] fortune[s].

11 But [because] of the fact that they are very numerous, there are few big winners...

12 That's what games of chance are all about *(It is that, games of chance)*: one day you lose, and the next day...

13 you lose again!

---

7 gros *[groh]* and the feminine **grosse** *[grohss]* basically mean *fat*. But the adjective is used very extensively to refer to anything *big, important, heavy, significant*, etc. For example **un gros mensonge**, *a huge lie*; **une grosse somme d'argent**, *a big sum of money*; **un gros buveur**, *a heavy drinker*. Get the idea? Here, **un gros gagnant** is someone who wins... big time! Finally, note the expression: **Il a gagné le gros lot !** *[groh loh]*, *He's won the jackpot!*

***

Answers to Exercice 1

❶ She plays one of the most difficult games: chess. ❷ In contrast, draughts requires less skill. ❸ Come either early in the morning or late in the evening. ❹ In any case, you risk losing. ❺ That's life!

***

❹ They've both the same idea [in their heads].
   Ils ont . . . . la . . . .

❺ You find the racing results in all the newspapers.
   Vous trouvez les . . . . dans . . . .
   . . . .

Answers to Exercice 2

❶ – principaux jeux nationaux ❷ – tous gagner – gros lot ❸ – joue au – tous ❹ – tous les deux – même idée en tête ❺ – résultats des courses – tous les journaux

23 ——————————————————————

Vingt-troisième leçon

▶

Le loto

1 – Qu'est-ce que vous faites, Jean ?
2 – Je fais mon loto. C'est_un jeu très_intéressant.
3 Regardez : vous prenez cette carte et vous choisissez une série de numéros.
4 Par exemple, ici, j'ai le cinq, le sept, le onze, le vingt-deux, le quarante-trois et le quarante-huit.
5 Ensuite, vous mettez une croix sur ces numéros
6 et vous donnez la carte au patron du tabac.
7 – Et alors ?
  – Ben [1] vous_attendez les résultats.
8 Si vous_avez choisi les bons [2] numéros, vous gagnez.
9 – Et vous_avez gagné ?
  – Non, pas_encore.
10 – Bon, moi je vais jouer : je choisis le deux ;
11 ensuite, le treize, le quatorze, le vingt, le trente et le trente-deux. □

🔊 Pronunciation
7 bahn … 8 … shwazee … ganyay 9 … ganyay 11 … trez katorz … vahn …

📑 Notes
1 ben *[bahn]* is not really a noun, but a sound. Its meaning is something like *Well…*, *You know…*

It is not particularly elegant, but very common and useful. (It's a contraction of "**Eh bien**".)

23

Twenty-Third Lesson

The loto

1 – What are you doing, Jean?
2 – I'm doing the *(my)* Loto. It's a very interesting game.
3 Look, you take this card and you choose a series of numbers.
4 For example, here I have *(the)* 5, *(the)* 7, *(the)* 11, *(the)* 22, *(the)* 43 and *(the)* 48.
5 Next you put a cross on these numbers
6 and you give the card to *(the boss of)* the tobacconist's.
7 – And then?
– Then you wait for the results.
8 And if you have *(chosen)* the right *(good)* numbers, you win.
9 – And have you won?
– No, not yet.
10 – Right *(good)*: *(me)* I'm going to play: I choose *(the)* 2,
11 next *(the)* 13, *(the)* 14, *(the)* 20, *(the)* 30 and *(the)* 32.

2 un bon vin, *a good wine.* Cette soupe est très bonne, *This soup is very good.* BUT: Est-ce que vous_avez le bon numéro ?, *Do you have the right number?*
Voilà la bonne réponse, *There's the right answer.*
Wrong is faux (feminine: fausse); un faux numéro, *a wrong (phone) number.* *Bad* is mauvais (mauvaise). Un mauvais_élève, *a bad pupil.*

► Exercice 1 – Traduisez

❶ Qu'est-ce que vous faites là ? ❷ Vous choisissez la bonne réponse. ❸ C'est un jeu qui est très intéressant. ❹ Il va jouer du piano ce soir. ❺ Qu'est-ce que je fais ? Ben j'attends.

Exercice 2 – Complétez

❶ Play the 13, the 14 and the 20.
..... le ......, le .... et le .....

❷ If you choose the right figures, you win.
Si vous avez ...... les ...., vous gagnez.

❸ And you have won? – Not yet.
Et vous ....? – Pas ......

❹ You put a cross and you give the card to the boss.
Vous ...... une ..... et vous ...... la carte .. patron.

❺ What do you choose? – I choose the 16.
.... vous ....? – Je .... le seize.

24

Vingt-quatrième leçon

► ### Le passe-temps numéro un

1   Il y a un_autre jeu que nous_avons oublié :
2   c'est le jeu de boules, ou la "pétanque",

🗨 Prononciation
passtohn ... 2 ... bool ... paytonk

Answers to Exercice 1

❶ What are you doing there? ❷ You choose the right answer. ❸ It's a game which is very interesting. ❹ He is going to play the piano this evening. ❺ What am I doing? Well, I'm waiting.

IL VA JOUER DU PIANO CE SOIR.

Answers to Exercice 2

❶ Jouez – treize – quatorze – vingt ❷ – choisi – bons chiffres – ❸ – avez gagné – encore ❹ – mettez – croix – donnez – au – ❺ Qu'est-ce que – choisissez – choisis –

24

Twenty-Fourth Lesson

The number one pastime

1   There is another game which we have forgotten.
2   It is the game of bowls, or *(the)* "pétanque",

3 un jeu qui vient du sud [1] de la France.
4 Partout où il y a un peu d'espace [2],
5 vous voyez des joueurs de boules
6 qui jouent dans les parcs ou sur la place du marché.
7 C'est un jeu qui demande beaucoup d'habileté,
8 beaucoup de concentration... et un peu de passion.
9 Mais il y a un autre passe-temps en France.
10 Les gens le pratiquent, ils en parlent, ils le vivent à chaque [3] moment.
11 C'est la passion nationale numéro un : bien manger [4]. □

3 … vyehn … syood … 4 partoo … ayspass 6 … park … marshay 7 … demohnd … abiltay 8 … konsontrassiohn … passeeohn 10 … parl … veev … shak …

: Notes

1 le nord *[nor]*, *north*, l'ouest *[west]*, *west*, l'est *[lest]*, *east*, le sud, *south*. The South of France is often called **le Midi** (literally: midday). This is similar to Italy, where the south is called *il mezzogiorno*. Beware if you travel to Brussels by train: **Bruxelles-Midi** in French is *Brussel-Zuid* (*south*)! The South of France has a reputation for being more easy-going and expansive than the north. It also has a very particular accent.

2 un peu de, *a little*... un peu de lait, *a little milk*. **Vous voulez du sucre ? – Un peu, s'il vous plaît**, *Do you want some sugar? – A little, please*. **Peu de** (without **un**): *little, few*. **Peu de temps**, *not much time* (or *shortly*).

3   a game which comes from the South of France.

4   Everywhere where there is a little space

5   you see players of bowls

6   who play in *(the)* parks or on the market-place.

7   It is a game which requires *(asks for)* a lot of skill,

8   a lot of concentration... and a little passion.

9   But there is another pastime in France.

10 *(The)* people do it, they talk about it, they live it at every moment.

11 It is the number one national passion: eating *(to eat)* well.

Nous avons peu de temps, *We've not got much time.* Le train part dans peu de temps, *The train is leaving shortly.* Il y a peu de gens qui l'aiment, *Few people like it/him/her. Much – many – a lot of,* beaucoup de.

3   chaque, *each, every.* Chaque jour, elle fait la même chose, *Every day, she does the same thing.*

4   The infinitive, e.g. **manger**, is also used where English would use a gerundive, *eating.* **Défense de fumer,** *No smoking.* Il aime faire la cuisine, *He likes cooking.*

▶ Exercice 1 – Traduisez

❶ C'est un jeu qui vient du sud de la France. ❷ Vous voyez des joueurs partout. ❸ J'aime beaucoup de sucre et un peu de lait dans mon café. ❹ C'est un jeu que j'aime beaucoup. ❺ Il y a peu de gens qui le font.

***

Exercice 2 – Complétez

❶ It's a game which demands a little concentration.
   C'est un jeu … demande un … … concentration.

❷ *(There's)* a book which I like a lot.
   Voilà un livre … j'aime … … … ….

❸ One sees bowls-players everywhere.
   .. voit des … … de boules … … ….

25

Vingt-cinquième leçon

▶ ## Deux histoires drôles

1 Après une audition, un producteur dit_à une
       chanteuse :

2 – Mademoiselle, votre chanson est comme l'épée
       de Charlemagne [1].

3 Toute fière, la fille dit "Ah bon ? Comment ça ?"

4 – Eh bien, elle est longue, plate et mortelle [2] !

🗩 Pronunciation
*deuzeestwar drowl **1** … ohdeesseeon … **2** … epay … sharlemanye*
***3** tootfyair … fee … **4** … long plat …*

Answers to Exercice 1

❶ It's a game which comes from the South of France. ❷ You see players everywhere. ❸ I like a lot of sugar and a little milk in my coffee. ❹ It's a game which I like a lot. ❺ Few people do it.

***

❹ He goes to the cinema every Tuesday.

. . . . il va . . cinéma.

❺ He loves eating and playing bowls.

Il aime beaucoup . . . . . . et . . . . . aux boules.

Answers to Exercice 2

❶ – qui – peu de – ❷ – que – beaucoup ❸ On – joueurs – partout
❹ Chaque mardi – au – ❺ – manger – jouer –

25

Twenty-Fifth Lesson

Two funny stories

1 After an audition, a producer says to a singer:
2 – Miss, your song is like Charlemagne's sword.
3 Proudly *(all proud)*, the girl says "Oh really? How [is] that?"
4 – Well, it's long, flat and deadly!

Notes

1 l'ami de Pierre, *Peter's friend*; la voiture de ma femme, *my wife's car*; la photo de la maison, *the photo of the house*.

2 The masculine forms of these adjectives are **long** *[lohn]*, **plat** *[plah]* and **mortel**.

5 Deux_alpinistes sont bloqués dans_une tempête de neige.

6 Après douze_heures, ils voient ³ arriver un Saint-Bernard

7 avec un tonneau de cognac autour du cou ⁴.

8 – Regardez ça ⁵, dit_un des_hommes,

9 voilà le meilleur_ami de l'homme !

10 – Oui, dit l'autre, et regardez le beau chien qui le porte !

11 "Tout_est bien qui finit bien !" ☐

5 … blockay … tompet … nezh 6 … vwa … san bernar 7 … tonnow … 9 … meyeur … 10 … shee-ehn … 11 … finee

Notes

3 voir, *to see.* je vois, il/elle voit, nous voyons, vous voyez, ils/elles voient *[vwah].* Past participle: **vu.**

4 In English, we "personalise" parts of the body (my hand, her foot, etc.). Not in French: **Il a un couteau à la main** – *He has a knife in his hand.*

Autour de, *around.* **J'ai une écharpe autour du cou,** *I have a scarf around my neck.*

***

Exercice 1 – Traduisez

❶ Ce livre est long et il n'est pas très intéressant. ❷ Écoutez ça ! C'est Georges qui arrive. ❸ Elle a un chapeau sur la tête et une écharpe autour du cou. ❹ Vous voyez ceci ? C'est le stylo de Michel. ❺ Voilà le meilleur ami de l'homme.

5 Two climbers *(alpinists)* are blocked in a snowstorm.
6 After 12 hours, they see a Saint-Bernard arriving
7 with a barrel of brandy around its *(the)* neck.
8 – Look [at] that, says one of the men,
9 There is man's best friend!
10 – Yes, says the other, and look at the cute *(handsome)* dog carrying it!
11 "All's well that ends well" *(All is well which finishes well)*.

VOILÀ LE MEILLEUR AMI DE L'HOMME.

5 We use **ceci/cela** when we are pointing something out. We call them "demonstrative pronouns". *This book*: **ce livre**. *Look at this*: **Regardez ceci**. *Listen to that*: **Écoutez cela**.

Ceci and **cela** have only one form each. They are not used to speak of people, nor before nouns. **cela** is usually always shortened to **ça** in conversation. You know the expression: **Comment ça va ?**, *How are you?* In line 3, we see another idiomatic usage **Comment cela (ça) ?** This is like our *How come?*

***

Answers to Exercice 1
❶ This book is long and it is not very interesting. ❷ Listen to that! It's Georges who is arriving. ❸ She has a hat on her head and a scarf around her neck. ❹ You see this? It's Michel's pen. ❺ There is man's best friend.

Exercice 2 – Complétez

❶ The plain is long and flat.
La plaine est ...... et ......

❷ He has an umbrella in his hand.
Il a un parapluie ....

❸ All's well that ends well.
" .... est bien .... bien".

26

Vingt-sixième leçon

Que fait ¹ M. Duclos le matin ?

1 Nous_avons parlé de ce que fait M.Duclos le
soir.

2 Regardons-le maintenant le matin, quand le
radio-réveil sonne.

3 D'abord, il se lève ²... très lentement.

Pronunciation
2 ... mantenohn ... matahn ... revay ... 3 ... lontemohn

Notes

1 Qu'est-ce que vous faites ?, *What are you doing?*
We told you earlier that there were several ways of asking a question,
and that **(qu')est-ce que** was commonly used and a bit "familiar". So far,
we have seen another – and more "elegant" – way of saying: **Qu'est-ce
que vous faites ?**, namely the inversion **Que faites-vous ?**
Qu'est-ce que fait monsieur Duclos ? thus becomes **Que fait monsieur Duclos ?**
Qu'est-ce que vous mangez ? Que mangez-vous ?, *What are you
eating?*

❹ She's my wife's best friend.
    Elle est la meilleur amie ... ...**.**

Answers to Exercice 2
❶ – longue – plate ❷ – à la main ❸ Tout – qui finit – ❹ – de ma femme

---

26

Twenty-sixth Lesson

What does Mr Duclos [do] [in] the morning?

1 We have spoken of what *(that which)* Mr Duclos does [in]-the evening.
2 [Let's] look [at] him now [in] the morning, when the radio alarm clock rings.
3 Firstly, he gets *(himself)* up... very slowly.

The two forms have exactly the same meaning. The difference is simply one of register.

2 We have already seen a couple of "reflexive" verbs. We noted that the reflexive pronoun comes before the verb in French. Let's revise: **se lever**, *to get up*; **je me lève**, **il/elle se lève**, **nous nous levons**, **vous vous levez**, **ils/elles se lèvent** *[lev]*.
Notice in this text that, unlike English, the following verbs must take the reflexive form in French: **se lever**, *to get up*; **s'habiller**, *to get dressed*; **se raser**, *to shave*, etc. Memorise the sequence of events in the lesson: get up, wash, shower, shave and dress. It will help you remember when to use a reflexive verb.

4   Il va à la salle de bains et se lave ³ le visage...
5   à l'eau froide, pour se réveiller ⁴.
6   Ensuite, il se douche, se rase et se brosse les dents.
7   De retour dans sa chambre, il commence à s'habiller.
8   Les jours de travail, il met une chemise blanche ⁵, une cravate bleue
9   et un costume gris foncé ⁶.
10 Il met des chaussettes et des chaussures noires,
11 et un imperméable s'il pleut.
12 Enfin, il prend sa serviette et descend dans la rue. □

4 ... lav ... veezazh 5 ... low frwad ... revayay 7 ... sabiyay 8 ... may ... kravat ... 9 ... gree fonssay 10 ... may ... nwar 11 ... ampermayabl seel pleu 12 ... prohn ... daysohn ...

Notes

3   In lesson 25, we saw how to say: *she has a hat on her head*: **elle a un chapeau sur la tête.** Here, we see another example of how the parts of the body are not "personalised" with the possessive adjective (my, her, etc.). **Elle se lave le visage** – *She washes her face.* **Je me brosse les dents,** *I am brushing my teeth.*
French supposes that, if we have already mentioned the subject of the sentence, it is superfluous to specify on whose head the hat appears.

4 He goes to the bathroom and washes *(himself the)* his face...

5 *(at the)* in cold water, to wake *(himself)* up.

6 Next, he showers *(himself)*, shaves *(himself)* and brushes *(himself)* his teeth.

7 Back *(Of return)* in his room, he begins to dress *(himself)*.

8 [On] work-days, he puts [on] a white shirt, a blue tie

9 and a dark grey suit.

10 He puts [on] socks and black shoes,

11 and a raincoat if it is raining.

12 Finally, he takes his briefcase and goes down in [to] the street.

4 à l'eau chaude, *in hot water*. Écrire à l'encre de Chine, *to write in Indian* (lit. "Chinese") *ink*; poulet à la crème, *chicken in cream sauce*; danser à la russe, *to dance in the Russian manner*. Note that there are in English many examples of this "in the manner of" form in cooking terms such as "chicken à la king" or "apple pie à la mode".

5 The masculine form is blanc *[blahn]*.

6 Light (not heavy) is *léger*, but for a colour, we say clair; similarly, *dark* (of a room etc.) is sombre but for a colour, we say foncé (feminine forms: légère *[layzhair]*; claire; sombre; foncée).

▶ Exercice 1 – Traduisez

❶ Que faites-vous ? – Je me rase. ❷ Regardons ce que fait M. Duclos le soir. ❸ Elle se lave et se brosse les dents... très lentement. ❹ Que mangez-vous ? – Un poulet à la crème. ❺ De retour dans sa chambre, il s'habille.

***

Exercice 2 – Complétez

❶ What are you doing this evening? – I'm going to dinner at Georges'.

Que .... ce ....? – Je vais dîner .... Georges.

❷ Let's look at him: he is washing and shaving.

Regardons- ..: il .. .. et .. ..

❸ He takes his briefcase and goes down into the street.

Il prend .. serviette et .... la rue.

27

Vingt-septième leçon

▶ ## Les commerçants

1 Il y a beaucoup de supermarchés en France – mais‿aussi beaucoup de petits commerçants.

2 Quand vous voulez du pain, vous‿allez chez le boulanger [1].

💬 Pronunciation

*lay komersohn **1** ... soopair-marshay ... kommersahn **2** ... pan ... boolonzhay*

Answers to Exercice 1

❶ What are you doing? – I am shaving. ❷ Let's look at what Mr Duclos does in the evening. ❸ She washes, and brushes her teeth... very slowly. ❹ What are you eating? – A chicken in cream sauce. ❺ Back in his room, he dresses.

***

❹ He puts on a white shirt, a blue tie and black shoes.
Il ... une ...., une cravate ..... et des
.... noires.

❺ She always washes in cold water.
Elle ...... toujours ...... froide.

Answers to Exercice 2

❶ – faites-vous – soir – chez – ❷ – le – se lave – se rase ❸ – sa – descend dans – ❹ – met – chemise blanche – bleue – chaussures – ❺ – se lave – à l'eau –

27

Twenty-Seventh Lesson

(The) **shopkeepers**

1 There are many supermarkets in France – but also many small shopkeepers.
2 When you want bread, you go to the baker's.

⌉ Note

1 In English, we can say: *I go to the baker's* or *to the bakery*. The same distinction exists in French (see line 10). For the first, we say **chez le boulanger** and for the second **à la boulangerie**. We recommend using **chez** because it familiarises you with this extremely common idiom.

3   Là, vous trouvez non seulement des baguettes ²,
4   mais_aussi des croissants, des tartes et des
      gâteaux ³.
5   Si vous_avez besoin ⁴ de viande, vous_allez
      chez le boucher.
6   Vous pouvez ⁵ y ⁶ acheter toutes sortes de
      viandes et de volailles.
7   Et si vous_avez envie de bon jambon, de pâté
      ou de saucisson,
8   vous_allez chez le charcutier ⁷.
9   Le lait, le beurre, la crème et les_œufs ⁸,
10   on les trouve à la crèmerie.
11   Chez l'épicier, il y a des fruits_et légumes – et
      beaucoup d'autres choses.
12   Et quand vous_avez mangé tout ce que
      vous_avez acheté...
13   vous_allez à la pharmacie – pour acheter de
      l'Alka-Seltzer !   □

🗨 Pronunciation

*3 … baget 4 … gatoh 5 … bezwan … veeond … booshay 6 …
voleye 7 … onvee … shombohn … sossissohn 8 … sharkooteeay
9 … lay … krem … layzeu 11 … leppeesseeay … frweezay laygyoom … 12 … monzhay tooske … ashtay 13 … farmassee …*

Notes

2   A **baguette** is a long, thin, crusty loaf baked fresh every day. Other types
      of bread include **un pain** (a thicker baguette) and **un pain de cam-
      pagne**, *country bread* and **un pain complet**, *whole-grain bread*. Note
      that the word for *loaf*, **une miche**, is never used when ordering in a
      baker's.

3   **un gâteau** – **des gâteaux**; **un bateau**, *a boat*, **des bateaux**.

3 There, you find not only *baguettes*,

4 but also *croissants*, tarts and cakes.

5 If you *(have)* need *(of)* meat, you go to the butcher's.

6 You can buy there all sorts of meats and poultry.

7 And if you *(have)* want *(of)* good ham, *(of)* pâté or *(of)* sausage,

8 you go to the *charcutier's*.

9 Milk, butter, cream and eggs

10 are found *(one finds them)* at the creamery.

11 At the grocer's there are fruit*(s)*, vegetables – and much more *(many other things)*.

12 And when you have eaten everything *(all)* that you have bought...

13 you go to the chemist's – to buy *(of)* Alka-Seltzer!

4 Here's another idiom with **avoir: avoir besoin de**, *to need*; **elle a besoin de vacances**, *she needs a holiday*. **J'ai besoin d'une allumette**, *I need a match*; **un besoin**, *a need*.

5 Here's another very common irregular verb: **pouvoir**, *to be able – can*; **je peux, il/elle peut, nous pouvons, vous pouvez, ils/elles peuvent** *[perv]*.

6 We have already seen how **en** is used to avoid repeating a noun: **Vous avez des baguettes ? – J'en ai deux**. In the same way, **y** is used to avoid repeating a place-name or location: **Vous connaissez Paris ? – J'y habite**, *Do you know Paris? – I live here/there*. We'll see **y** in more detail later.

7 A typical French institution! The word **charcutier** comes from **la chair cuite**, *cooked meat*, and a **charcutier** is a butcher specialised in prepared meats ("deli" meats) and dishes. The nearest we can come in English would be a "delicatessen". The shop is called **la charcuterie**. In slang, **un charcutier** is a clumsy surgeon or dentist!

8 **un œuf** *[euf]*, **des œufs** *[eu]*. A similar pronunciation change is found with **un bœuf** *[beuf]*, **des bœufs** *[beu]*, *ox*, *oxen*.

▶ Exercice 1 – Traduisez

❶ Je veux du lait, du beurre et des œufs, s'il vous plaît.
❷ Allez chez le boulanger et achetez deux baguettes.
❸ Que faites-vous quand vous avez mangé ? – Je me couche ! ❹ Vous y trouvez toutes sortes de viandes et de volailles. ❺ Il ne peut pas trouver de jambon.

Exercice 2 – Complétez

❶ This is all you have eaten, my child?
C'est .... vous avez mangé, mon enfant ?

❷ She needs a holiday.
Elle .... de ....

❸ It's warm (weather). I feel like an ice-cream.
Il fait chaud. J'.......... une glace.

❹ They cannot come before eight o'clock.
Ils .... venir avant .... heures.

❺ At the "charcutier" one finds ham and pâté.
.... le charcutier .. trouve du ...... et du pâté.

28

Vingt-huitième leçon

Révision – Revision

1 *L'alphabet* [alfabey] *français*

A [ah]	B [bay]	C [say]	D [day]
E [euh]	F [eff]	G [zhay]	H [ash]
I [ee]	J [zhee]	K [ka]	L [el]
M [em]	N [en]	O [oh]	P [pay]
Q [kiou]	R [air]	S [ess]	T [tay]

Answers to Exercice 1

❶ I want some milk, some butter and some eggs, please. ❷ Go to the baker's and buy two baguettes. ❸ What do you do when you have eaten? – I go to bed! ❹ You find there all sorts of meat and poultry. ❺ He can't find any ham.

Answers to Exercice 2

❶ – tout ce que – ❷ – a besoin – vacances ❸ – ai envie d' – ❹ – ne peuvent pas – huit – ❺ Chez – on – jambon –

28

Twenty-Eighth Lesson

U [oo] *	**V** [vay]	**W** [doublevay]	**X** [eeks]
Y [eegrek]	**Z** [zed]		

* There is no real equivalent to this sound in English: try making an O shape with your lips and then pronouncing [dew] or [you]. It will take some getting used to, but it's important to be able to make the difference between our [oo] sound and the French **u**.

2 One, *On*

On is used extensively, often when in English we could use the passive voice. Note too, that although **on** is similar to the English pronoun *one*, it is much less formal.
On dit qu'en France..., *It is said that in France...*
On chante souvent cette chanson, *This song is often sung.*
On le trouve chez l'épicier, *It can be found at the grocer's.*
Or when the person who is the subject is unknown.
On vous demande au téléphone: *Someone is asking for you on the phone ("You're wanted on the phone").*
And in modern spoken French, **on** is used instead of **nous** (even though this usage is considered "incorrect").
On‿arrive à huit‿heures, *We're arriving at eight.*
You will get the feel of it after a few more examples.

3 Verbs ending in *-ir*

Here is the last group of French verbs: those which end in **-ir**. **choisir**, *to choose*; **je choisis, il/elle choisit, nous choisissons, vous choisissez, ils/elles choisissent** *[shwazeess]*.

finir, *to finish*; **je finis, il/elle finit, nous finissons, vous finissez, ils/elles finissent** *[feeneess]*.
Conjugate these verbs:
dormir (*to sleep*); **sentir** (*to feel/to smell*); **servir** (*to serve*); **définir** (*to define*).

4 Numbers (continued)

20: **vingt**; 21: **vingt et un**; 22: **vingt-deux**, etc.
30: **trente**; 40: **quarante** *[karont]*; 50: **cinquante** *[sankont]*; 60: **soixante** *[swassont]*.
A different system applies for 70, 80 and 90.
70: **soixante-dix** (60 + 10), so we continue to add to the 10 – 71: **soixante et onze**; 72: **soixante-douze**; 73: **soixante-treize**, etc.
80: **quatre-vingts** (4 x 20); so we continue to add to the 20: 81: **quatre-vingt-un**; 82: **quatre-vingt-deux**, etc.
90: **quatre-vingt-dix** (4 x 20 + 10); 91: **quatre-vingt-onze**; 92: **quatre-vingt-douze**; 93: **quatre-vingt-treize**, etc.

This may seem complicated, but it is in fact the same system as that used in old English "four-score" for 80, "four-score and ten", for 90. Evidently the Swiss, Belgian and Canadians thought it too complex because they have their own words: *septante* (70), *octante* (80) and *nonante* (90). However don't use them in France; they would produce a raised eyebrow or a sly smile...

Don't worry about the spelling for the time being and remember that reacting to numbers automatically takes a lot of practice. One excellent way of developing good reflexes is to flip through the pages of this book and read the numbers aloud. The faster you flip, the quicker these reflexes will become.

5 Who... / Which..., *Qui... / Que...*

who... which (that)... In English, the use of this relative pronoun depends on whether the preceding noun is <u>animate</u> (*who*) or <u>inanimate</u> (*which* or *that*). In French, the use of the relative depends on whether the noun is the **subject** or the **object** of the sentence; whether it is animate or not is irrelevant.

<u>Subject</u>: **qui**   <u>Object</u>: **que**

The bread which is on my plate. The bread = subject: **qui**.
Le pain qui est dans mon assiette.
*The bread **which** I am eating. The bread* = object: **que**.
Le pain que je mange.
The man ("whom") I know, **L'homme que je connais**.
The man who is speaking, **L'homme qui parle**.

Any difficulty we might have comes from the English tendency to leave out the object relative pronoun (the man [...] I know, etc.). French is so much clearer!
<u>Never</u> omit the relative pronoun in French.

ce que – ce qui: *what (that)* depending again on whether *what* is subject or object of the verb following:
Vous mangez ce que vous achetez, *You eat what you buy*.
Dites-moi ce qui vous intéresse, *Tell me what interests you*.

Don't worry about these points of grammar: they are simply guide-lines to help you understand. Consider them as explanations, not instructions.

6 To want, *Vouloir*

je veux *[veuh]*, **il/elle veut**, **nous voulons**, **vous voulez**, **ils/elles veulent** *[verl]*.

29

Vingt-neuvième leçon

Questions ridicules

1 – Prenez un kilo de plomb et un kilo de plumes : lequel [1] est le plus lourd ?
2 – Ben, un kilo de plomb, bien sûr.
3   Le plomb est plus lourd que les plumes !
4 – Mais non ! Un kilo, c'est_un kilo. Ils_ont le même poids [2].

***

5 – Qu'est-ce que vous pensez de mon nouveau petit_ami ? [3]

🗣 Pronunciation
1 … plohn … plyoom lekel … loor 4 … pwa 5 … noovow peteetamee

📓 Notes
[1] **Lequel de ces livres voulez-vous ?**, *Which [one] of these books do you want?* **Laquelle de ces montres préférez-vous ?**, *Which of these watches do you prefer?*

lequel, **laquelle** (plural **lesquels**, **lesquelles**) is used to discover a person's choice or preference.

avoir envie de; j'ai envie de, etc. expresses the feeling that one wants something for one's pleasure; it conveys the English idiom *I feel like....*
Je veux une réponse !, *I want an answer!*
J'ai envie d'une glace, *I feel like an ice-cream.*
J'ai envie d'un bain, *I'd like a bath*, etc.
When offering something, French always uses **vouloir**: **Voulez-vous du café ?**, etc.

29

Twenty-Ninth Lesson

Ridiculous questions

1 – Take a kilo of lead and a kilo of feathers: Which is the heavier *(the most heavy)*?
2 – Um, a kilo of lead, of course.
3 *(The)* lead is heavier *(more heavy)* than *(the)* feathers!
4 – *(But)* no! A kilo is a kilo. They have the same weight.

***

5 – What do you think of my new boyfriend *(little friend)*?

2 poids, *weight*, is a singular noun despite the final **s**. Like in English (series, means, etc.), French has a few such singular nouns. There is no plural form.

3 You are probably beginning to "feel" the position of the adjective in French by now. Usually, we place it after the noun. However here are some which we place before: **grand**, *big* – or *tall* for a person; **petit**, *small* or *little*; **long**, *long* – **haut** *[oh]*, *high* (or *tall* for a building, tree, etc.) – **joli**, *pretty* – **beau**, *beautiful, handsome* – **jeune**, *young* – **vieux** *[vieuh]*, *old* – **bon**, *good, kind* – **mauvais**, *bad*.
You will soon be able to position the adjective automatically.

6 – Il est sans doute plus_intelligent que le dernier
7 et il est plus beau [4] et plus gentil aussi.
8 Mais... il a un petit défaut : il bégaie [5].
9 – Oui, d'accord, mais seulement quand_il parle !

***

10 – Dis-moi, ma chérie [6], j'ai trois pommes.
11 Laquelle veux-tu ?
– La plus grosse ! □

6 ... derneeay 7 ... boh ... zhontee ... 8 ... dayfoh ... begay
11 lakel ...

Notes

4 **beau** in the feminine is **belle**. Since we put this adjective before the noun, there is a third form which is used if a masculine noun begins with a vowel: **un bel appartement**. There is no difference in pronunciation between **bel** and **belle**.

5 **bégayer**, *to stammer*, behaves like **payer**, *to pay*. **je paie, il/elle paie, nous payons, vous payez, ils/elles paient** *[pay]*.

***

Exercice 1 – Traduisez

❶ Laquelle de ces deux pommes veux-tu ? ❷ Vous payez à la caisse, monsieur. ❸ Elle est plus belle que ma sœur. ❹ Nous avons une très belle voiture américaine. ❺ Qu'est-ce qu'ils pensent du nouveau film ?

6 – He's without doubt more intelligent than the last
  [one]
7   and he is more handsome and kinder too.
8   But... he has a small failing: he stammers.
9 – Yes, OK, but only when he talks!

***

10 – Tell me, my darling, I have three apples.
11   Which [one] do you want?
     – The biggest *(more big)*!

6 A term of affection meaning *darling*. Note that French uses such endearments less indiscriminately than British English; a shopkeeper is unlikely to call you **ma chérie**!

***

Answers to Exercice 1
❶ Which of these two apples do you want? ❷ You pay at the cash desk, sir. ❸ She is more beautiful than my sister. ❹ We have a very beautiful American car. ❺ What do they think of the new film?

Exercice 2 – Complétez

❶ Which is the heavier of these two?

...... est le .... de ces deux(-là) ?

❷ This exercise is longer than the last [one].

Cet exercice est .... que le ....

❸ They have a beautiful apartment and a large house.

Ils ont un ... appartement et une ....

30

Trentième leçon

▶

Chez M. Duclos

1 L'appartement de M. Duclos est composé de deux pièces [1],

2 d'une cuisine et d'une salle de bains.

3 Il se trouve dans_un vieil immeuble [2] dans la banlieue parisienne.

4 Il y a six_étages... et une concierge [3] !

5 M. Duclos vous_ouvre la porte et vous_arrivez dans l'entrée.

🔊 Pronunciation
*1 ... pee-ess 2 ... kweezeen ... 3 ... vyayimmeubl ... bonlyeu ...
4 ... seezaytahzh ... konsee-airzh 5 ... ontray*

🔲 Notes

1 **une pièce** means *a room* in general; **une chambre** is *a bedroom*. **une salle** is used to mean a large room in a public building, or in compound nouns like **salle de bains** or **salle à manger**, *dining room*. **Il habite un deux-pièces** is a familiar way of saying *he lives in a two-roomed apartment.*

❹ They have the same weight. – Of course not!
Ils ont le ....– .... non !

❺ What do they think of his new girlfriend?
Qu'est-ce qu'.......... de .... petite amie ?

Answers to Exercice 2
❶ Lequel – plus lourd – ❷ – plus long – dernier ❸ – bel – grande maison ❹ – même poids – Mais – ❺ – ils pensent – sa nouvelle –

30

Thirtieth Lesson

[At] Mr Duclos'

1   The apartment of Mr Duclos is composed of two rooms,
2   *(of)* a kitchen and *(of)* a bathroom.
3   It is located *(finds itself)* in an old building in the suburbs of Paris.
4   There are six floors... and a *concierge*!
5   Mr Duclos opens the door [for] you and you arrive in the entrance [hall].

---

2   **vieux** in the feminine is **vieille**, and before a masculine noun beginning with a vowel, **vieil**. **Mon vieil ami** – *my old (male) friend* (see lesson 29, note 4); **un immeuble** is *a block of flats*.

3   **une** (or **un**) **concierge** is a French institution, which, for better or worse, seems to be disappearing. Originally, she or he was the holder of the keys, who would light residents to their doors with a *candle*, **cierge**. Up until the early 1970s, most apartment buildings had a concierge who would clean the common areas, distribute the mail and screen visitors. Owing to economic pressures, they have been replaced by electronic locks, interphones and mailboxes. Those that remain have succumbed to the trend for euphemism and are officially called **gardiens**. But **la concierge** remains rooted in popular culture.

6   À droite, il y a la cuisine et, à côté, la salle de bains.

7   Plus loin, on voit la pièce principale, le salon,

8   qui est meublé [4] avec beaucoup de goût [5].

9   Il y a deux beaux fauteuils et un canapé confortable [6].

10   Au milieu de la pièce, il y a une table basse [7].

11   Les fenêtres du salon donnent sur une petite cour.   □

🗣 **6** ... akotay ... **7** ... lwan ... vwa ... salohn **8** ... meublay ... goo **9** ... fohtoy ... kanapay ... **11** ... koor

Notes

4 un meuble, *a piece of furniture*; des meubles, *furniture*; un appartement non meublé, *an unfurnished flat*.

5 goûter, *to taste*. Goûtez cette soupe !, *Taste this soup!* un goût, *a taste*. La soupe a un goût étrange – *The soup has a strange taste*. Un goût also means *a taste* in the sense of preference. In cafés, you will see the word **déguster**: Dégustez nos vins. This more formal word indicates physical tasting and appreciation. Une dégustation de vins, *a wine-tasting*.

***

▶ Exercice 1 – Traduisez

❶ Ils habitent un vieil immeuble dans la banlieue parisienne. ❷ Goûtez ce gâteau ! Il est délicieux. ❸ Il y a un salon, une chambre et une salle à manger. ❹ Je vais acheter un meuble pour ma cuisine. ❺ La fenêtre donne sur la rue.

6 To *(At)* [the] right there is the kitchen and, next to it
(to side), the bathroom.

7 Further, one sees the main room, the living room

8 which is furnished with much taste.

9 There are two handsome armchairs and a
comfortable couch.

10 In the middle of the room, there is a low table.

11 The windows of the living-room give on [to] a small
courtyard.

LA FENÊTRE DONNE
SUR LA RUE.

6 confortable (notice the spelling) is never applied to a person as it is in
English. *Are you sitting comfortably?* In French: **Êtes-vous bien assis ?**
I am comfortable here: **Je suis bien ici.**

7 basse in the masculine is bas *[ba]*.

***

Answers to Exercice 1
❶ They live in an old building in the Paris suburbs. ❷ Taste this cake!
It's delicious. ❸ There is a living-room, a bedroom and a dining-room.
❹ I'm going to buy a piece of furniture for my kitchen. ❺ The window
looks onto the street.

Exercice 2 – Complétez
Fill in the correct prepositions.

❶ Behind the door
.... la porte

❷ In the middle of the room
.... de la pièce

❸ On the table
... la table

❹ Next to the kitchen
..... de la cuisine

❺ Further
....

31

Trente et unième leçon

Chez M. Duclos (suite)

1 Dans sa chambre, M. Duclos a un grand lit,
2 une armoire où il range – parfois – ses vêtements [1]
3 et une table de nuit ; un radio-réveil est posé dessus [2].
4 Sur les murs, il y a des photographies

Pronunciation
1 ... lee 2 ... armwar ... parfwa ... vetmoh 3 ... nwee ... dessyoo 4 ... fohtografee

Notes
[1] We saw, in the last lesson, that **un meuble** is *a piece of furniture*. Note how easily French can "singularise" words that in English are collec-

❻ In the bedroom
.... la chambre

❼ On the right
. . . .

❽ On the left
. . . .

Answers to Exercice 2
❶ Derrière – **❷** Au milieu – **❸** Sur – **❹** À côté – **❺** Plus loin **❻** Dans –
❼ À droite **❽** À gauche

31

Thirty-First Lesson

[At] Mr Duclos' (continued)

1   In his bedroom, Mr Duclos has a large bed,
2   a wardrobe where he – sometimes – puts away his
       clothes
3   and a night table; a radio alarm clock stands *(is
       placed)* on it.
4   On the walls, there are photographs

tive nouns: **les vêtements**, *clothes*; **un vêtement**, *a piece of clothing*;
les_informations, *the news*; **une information**, *a news item, a piece of
information*.

2 **sur la table**, *on the table*; **sous la chaise**, *under the chair*. When **sur** is
not followed directly by a noun, we say **dessus**. Do not confuse this
preposition with the adjective **sûr**, which means *sure* or *safe*. (We have
seen **bien sûr**.)

5   de paysages de France.
6   Monsieur Duclos est citadin, mais il rêve de
     vivre à la campagne ³.
7   Néanmoins, il a des voisins sympathiques ⁴.
8   L'appartement au-dessus appartient à un pilote
     de ligne
9   qui voyage beaucoup et qui n'est jamais chez
     lui,
10   et en dessous vit un vieil homme sourd.
11   C'est pourquoi M. Duclos n'a jamais de
     problèmes de bruit !   □

5 ... *payeezazh* ... *6* ... *seetadan* ... *kompanye* *7* *nayonmwan* ...
vwazan sampateek *8* ... *ohdessyoo aparteean* ... *peelot de leen*
9 ... *vwayazh* ... *zhamay* *10* ... *vee eun vyayom soor* *11* ... *brwee*

Notes

3   la ville, *the town* or *city*; en ville, *in town*; la campagne, *the coun-*
    try(side); un paysage, *a landscape*. The geographical country is un pays
    [payee] (although the French also use this word to describe a region).

***

Exercice 1 – Traduisez
❶ Ses voisins sont très sympathiques. ❷ En France, il y
a des paysages magnifiques. ❸ Elles rêvent de vivre à la
campagne. ❹ N'avez-vous jamais de problèmes de bruit ?
❺ Où est-ce que vous rangez vos vêtements ?

5 of French landscapes *(of France)*.

6 Mr Duclos is [a] city dweller but he dreams of living *(to live)* in the country.

7 Nevertheless, he has nice neighbours.

8 The flat above belongs to an airline pilot

9 who travels a lot and is never at home;

10 and underneath lives an old deaf man.

11 That is why Mr Duclos never has problems of noise!

4 A very important and common word which translates as *nice*, *kind*, *pleasant*, etc. (but not "sympathetic"!). In familiar speech, people contract it to **sympa**.

***

Answers to Exercice 1

❶ His/Her neighbours are very nice. ❷ In France, there are magnificent landscapes. ❸ They dream of living in the country. ❹ Don't you (n) ever have problems of noise? ❺ Where do you put away your clothes?

Exercice 2 – Complétez

❶ All around the room
. . . . de la chambre

❷ The flat above
L'appartement . . . .

❸ The floor below
L'étage . . . .

❹ A table with a book *(placed)* on it
. . . table avec . . livre posé . . . . . .

❺ She is never at home.
Elle . . est . . . . . . chez . . . .

Trente-deuxième leçon

Le métro

1 La meilleure façon de visiter Paris, c'est_à
pied [1],

2 mais si vous voulez aller d'un endroit à un
autre rapidement [2],

3 faites comme [3] les Parisiens : prenez le métro.

4 Le système est très_efficace et en plus il n'est
pas cher.

Pronunciation
*1 … mayeur fassohn … setappeay 2 … ondrwa … 4 … trayzefeekass
… onplyooss …*

Notes
1 en voiture, *by car*; en bus, *by bus*; en avion, *by plane*; à pied, *on foot.*

6 In the bathroom

.... la salle de bains

7 On the right

. . . .

8 On the left

. . . .

Answers to Exercice 2

1 Tout autour – **2** – au-dessus **3** – au-dessous **4** Une – un – dessus
5 – n' – jamais – elle **6** Dans – **7** À droite **8** À gauche

---

32

Thirty-Second Lesson

The metro *(underground)*

1 The best way *(fashion)* to visit Paris *(it)* is on foot,
2 but if you want to go from one place to another quickly,
3 do like the Parisians [do]: take the metro.
4 The system is very efficient and what's more *(in more)*, it is not expensive.

---

2 By now you know how to form adverbs: we add **-ment** to the feminine form of the adjective. **Lent**, *slow*, **lente** (f.), **lentement**, *slowly*. **Heureux**, *happy*, **heureuse** (f.), **heureusement**: *happily*, *fortunately*. There are a few irregular forms, but don't worry about them for the time being.

3 **comme**, *like*, *as*. **Faites comme moi**, *Do as I do*. **Il parle français comme un Français**, *He speaks French like a Frenchman*. **Elle est belle comme une fleur**, *She's gorgeous* (lit. "She is as beautiful as a flower").

5 Le prix de votre ticket ne dépend ⁴ pas de la longueur du trajet :

6 il coûte le même prix pour deux stations ⁵ que pour dix.

7 Les trains circulent ⁶ tous les jours, de cinq heures et demie

8 jusqu'à une heure du matin.

9 Pour aller en grande banlieue, vous pouvez emprunter le RER ⁷.

10 Pour aller de Vincennes au Quartier latin, prenez la ligne numéro un.

11 Vous changez à Châtelet et vous descendez à Saint-Michel. ☐

5 ... pree ... teekay ... daypohn ... 7 ... too lay zhoor ... 8 ... zhooska ... 9 ... grohn bohn-lyeu ... emprantay ... air-eu-air 10 ... vansen ... karteeay latan ...

Notes

4 dépendre, *to depend*, behaves like vendre, *to sell*. je dépends, il/elle dépend, nous dépendons, vous dépendez, ils/elles dépendent *[dehpond]*. Notice the postposition: de. Il dépend de ses parents, *He depends on his parents*.

5 une station de métro, *a metro station*, but une gare, *a train station*. La Gare du Nord, *Paris North Railway Station*. When asking for a metro station, we usually ask for just the name (see lesson 1). The metro and buses are run by the RATP (Régie autonome des transports parisiens).

6 Here, and in line 9, we see two examples of "formal" uses of common words. Circuler (lit. "to circulate") simply means *to run, to operate*; and

5 The price of your ticket does not depend on *(of)* the length of the journey:

6 It costs the same price for two stations as for ten.

7 The trains run every day, from 5.30

8 to 1.00 in *(of)* the morning.

9 To travel to [go in] the outer suburbs, you can take *(borrow)* the RER.

10 To go from Vincennes to the Latin Quarter, take *(the)* line number one.

11 You change at Châtelet and you get off *(descend)* at Saint-Michel.

emprunter (lit. "to borrow") just means *to take*. This type of usage is common in notices, official pronouncements, etc. but rare in everyday speech.

7 **le Réseau express régional**, commonly known as **le RER** *[air-eu-air]* is an efficient and extensive network of regional trains linking the Parisian suburbs and criss-crossing the capital. It was inaugurated in 1970.

▶ Exercice 1 – Traduisez

❶ Ils veulent y aller à pied. ❷ Les Parisiens prennent le métro tous les jours. ❸ Ce train circule tous les jours sauf dimanches et fêtes. ❹ Nous changeons notre voiture la semaine prochaine. ❺ Le métro est ouvert jusqu'à une heure du matin.

***

Exercice 2 – Complétez

❶ He speaks French like I do.
Il parle .. français ....

❷ These ones cost the same price as those ones.
Ceux-ci coûtent le .... prix ... ceux-là.

❸ It is efficient and, what's more, it is not expensive.
Il est .... et, ..., il ..est ... cher.

❹ She speaks slowly, clearly and distinctly.*
Elle parle ...., ... et ....

33

Trente-troisième leçon

▶ ## Quelques questions

1 Que font les Parisiens quand‿ils veulent voyager rapidement ?

2 Pourquoi le métro est-‿il bon marché ¹ ?

◻ Note

1 **bon marché** literally means a "good market", i.e. not expensive, so, as an adjective, **bon marché** means *cheap* (the opposite is **cher**, *expensive*, *dear*).

Answers to Exercice 1

❶ They want to go there on foot. ❷ The Parisians take the metro every day. ❸ This train runs daily except Sunday(s) and public holidays. ❹ We are changing our car next week. ❺ The metro is open until one o'clock in the morning.

***

❻ He takes the train here, he changes at Châtelet and he gets off at Vincennes.

Il ..... le train ici, il ...... à Châtelet et il .... à Vincennes.

*clear, **clair**; *distinct,* **distinct.**

Answers to Exercice 2

❶ – le – comme moi ❷ – même – que – ❸ – efficace – en plus – n' – pas – ❹ – lentement, clairement – distinctement ❺ – prend – change – descend –

33

Thirty-Third Lesson

A few questions

1 What do the Parisians [do] when they want to travel quickly?
2 Why is the metro cheap?

bon is an irregular adjective (like *good* in English). Its comparative is **meilleur** and its superlative **le meilleur**, so *cheaper* is **meilleur marché**. **Ce magasin est meilleur marché que l'autre,** *This shop is cheaper than the other;* **bon marché** has no feminine or plural forms.

3 Combien de billets y a-_t-_il dans un carnet ?*
4 Comment va-t-on de Vincennes au Quartier latin ?
5 Quel est le nom de la station où on change de ligne ?

* réponse phrase 10

Au guichet

6 *Un touriste demande* [2] *un ticket.*
7 – Un aller-retour [3] pour le musée d'Orsay, s'il vous plaît.
8 – Mais monsieur, il n'y a pas de billets aller-retour,
9 et d'ailleurs [4] le ticket coûte toujours le même prix ;
10 alors prenez plutôt [5] un carnet [6] de dix tickets.
11 – D'accord. Ça fait combien [7] ? □

🗣 Pronunciation
3 … eeyateel … 4 … vaton … 7 … allay retoor … 9 … die-eur … 10 … karnay … dee …

📋 Notes

2 demander means only *to ask for* (*to demand* is exiger *[egzeezhay]*). Notice the lack of postposition: **Demandez le programme !**, *Ask for the programme!*

3 un ticket is used for a bus or metro ticket only, otherwise we use billet *[beeyay]*; un billet aller-retour, *a return (ticket)*, literally "to go, to return". *A one-way (ticket)* is un (billet) aller simple *[sampl]*.

4 ailleurs *[eye-eur]* means *elsewhere, somewhere else*. Je n'en ai pas ; essayez ailleurs, *I don't have any; try somewhere else*. D'ailleurs means *furthermore* or *moreover*, and is often used to start a sentence.

3 How many tickets are there in a carnet?*

4 How [does] one go from Vincennes to the Latin Quarter?

5 What is the name of the station where one changes *(of)* line?

* *answer sentence 10*

At the ticket office

6 *A tourist [is] asking [for] a ticket.*

7 – A return to *(for)* the Orsay Museum, please.

8 – But sir, there are no return tickets,

9 and moreover the ticket costs always the same price,

10 so take rather a "carnet" of 10 tickets.

11 – OK. How much is that?

---

5 plutôt, *rather*. **Il fait plutôt chaud,** *It's rather hot*. But after an imperative verb it means *instead* or *why don't you...?* **Allez plutôt chez Fournier ; c'est meilleur,** *Why don't you go to Fournier's? It's better*. **Essayez plutôt ceci,** *Try this instead*.

6 **un carnet,** *a small book*, is most commonly used in compound nouns: **un carnet d'adresses,** *an address book*; **un carnet de chèques,** *a cheque book* (also **un chéquier**); **un carnet de commandes,** *an order book*. For the métro and buses, you can buy **un carnet** of 10 tickets, which works out much cheaper than buying them individually (London Underground introduced the same system – and the same word – in the mid 1990s). *To buy one*, you simply say: **Un carnet, s'il vous plaît**.

7 **Ça fait combien ?** or **Ça me fait combien ?** are very common idiomatic ways of saying **Combien ça coûte ?**
You use them to ask for a bill, or when the cashier has totalled your purchases, etc.

▶ Exercice 1 – Traduisez

❶ Que faites-vous le samedi ? – Je travaille. ❷ Ces billets coûtent très cher ! ❸ Comment allez-vous de Paris à Lyon ? En train ? ❹ Téléphonez chez Jean et demandez Michel. Il vous attend. ❺ Combien de places y a-t-il dans votre voiture ?

***

Exercice 2 – Complétez

❶ Ask John instead. He's better at *(in)* French.
.... à John. Il est .... en français.

❷ Why is the metro cheaper here?
Pourquoi le métro .... ici ?

❸ How does one get to the Latin Quarter?
Comment .... Quartier latin ?

❹ How many letters are there in this word?
.... de lettres ...-il dans ce mot ?

❺ I don't have any: try somewhere else.
Je n'.... pas : essayez ....

34

Trente-quatrième leçon

▶ ## Au musée

1 Un vieux colonel visite un musée avec un guide.
2 Il s'arrête ¹ devant un tableau et déclare :

🗣 Pronunciation
oh myoozay **1** ... *kolonel* ...

📥 Note

1 **arrêter**, *to stop something* – or *somebody*. **Elle arrête sa voiture**, *She stops her car*. With the reflexive form, we can shift from transitive to

Answers to Exercice 1
❶ What do you do on Saturday? – I work. ❷ These tickets cost a lot!
❸ How do you go from Paris to Lyons? By train? ❹ Telephone Jean's
and ask for Michel. He's waiting for you. ❺ How many seats are there
in your car?

***

Answers to Exercice 2
❶ Demandez plutôt – meilleur – ❷ – est-il meilleur marché – ❸ – va-t-
on au – ❹ Combien – y a-t – ❺ – en ai – ailleurs

34

Thirty-Fourth Lesson

At the [Art] Museum

1 An old colonel is visiting a museum with a guide.
2 He stops *(himself)* in front of a picture and declares:

intransitive: **s'arrêter**, *to stop* (oneself): **le bus s'arrête devant le centre
commercial**, *the bus stops in front of the shopping centre* (**un arrêt de
bus**, *a bus stop*).

3 – Celui-ci [2], c'est_un Monet. Je le reconnais [3].
4 Timidement, le guide dit :
 – Vous vous trompez [4], mon colonel [5],
5 celui-ci est_un Seurat, celui-là est_un Monet.
6 – Oui, bien sûr, dit le connaisseur, un peu gêné [6].
7 Il s'arrête devant une statue ; tout de suite [7], il dit :
8 – Très bien ; cette statue est_un Degas !
9 – Pas du tout, mon colonel ; c'est_un Rodin.
10 – D'accord, mais regardez-moi [8] ça : c'est certainement un Picasso.
11 – Eh bien non, mon colonel ; c'est_un miroir ! □

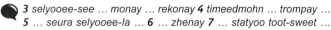

*3 selyooee-see … monay … rekonay 4 timeedmohn … trompay …
5 … seura selyooee-la … 6 … zhenay 7 … statyoo toot-sweet …
8 … deuga 9 … rohdan 10 … sertenmohn … 11 … meerwah*

: Notes

: **2** **celui-ci, celui-là** (lines 3 and 5) – *this one here, that one there*. You must imagine someone pointing to one object, then to the other: we call these "demonstrative" pronouns.

    The feminine forms are **celle-ci** and **celle-là**. We will look at the plural and other uses in later lessons. The construction of the sentence in line 3 is an alternative to that in line 5. The first is more idiomatic.

: **3** **reconnaître**, *to recognize.* **je reconnais, il/elle reconnaît, nous reconnaissons, vous reconnaissez, ils/elles reconnaissent.** *[rekoness]*; past participle: **reconnu.**

: **4** **se tromper**, *to make a mistake, to confuse.* **Il se trompe de sortie à chaque fois,** *He takes the wrong exit every time.* **Si je ne me trompe pas,** *If I'm not mistaken.* Here, the guide tells the colonel that he is confusing two painters (*you are wrong* – **vous_avez tort**).

: **5** In the French army, one always puts "**mon**" before the rank mentioned, except for **sergent** and **caporal; mon capitaine, mon lieutenant,** etc.

3 – This [one] here *(it)* is a Monet. I recognize it.

4 Timidly, the guide says:
  – You're making a mistake, *(my)* colonel,

5 This [one] here is a Seurat; that [one] there is a Monet.

6 – Yes, of course, says the connaisseur, a little embarrassed.

7 He stops *(himself)* in front of a statue; at once, he says:

8 – Very well; this statue is a Degas!

9 – Not at all *(my)* colonel; It's a Rodin.

10 – OK, but look *(me)* [at] that: it's certainly a Picasso.

11 – Well, no, *(my)* colonel; it's a mirror!

un soldat, *a soldier*; l'armée (f.), *the army*. Compulsory military service was abolished in 1996 in France.

6 gêner is a word with many meanings, here we see it as *"to be embarrassed, put out"*. We find it in expressions like: **Est-ce que ça vous gêne si je fume ?**, *Does it bother you if I smoke?* or **Est-ce que le bruit vous gêne ?**, *Does the noise bother you?* We will point out other uses as they come up.

7 Notice the pronunciation: *[toot-sweet]*. This simply means *"straight away"*, *"at once"*. Immediately, **immédiatement**.

8 An emphatic, idiomatic way of attracting someone's attention. You could say **Regardez ça !** Adding **moi** makes the imperative more forceful. It is commonly found with this verb and with **écouter**, *to listen*. **Écoutez-moi cette chanson !**, *Would you listen to this song!*

▶ Exercice 1 – Traduisez

❶ Je commence à huit heures et je m'arrête à quatre heures et quart. ❷ Michel ! Venez ici tout de suite ! ❸ Regardez-moi ça ! C'est un Picasso. – Pas du tout ! ❹ Celui-ci, c'est mon frère et celui-là, c'est mon meilleur ami. ❺ Est-ce que ça vous gêne si je fume ?

Exercice 2 – Complétez

❶ You've got the wrong floor; he lives on the sixth.
Vous . . . . étage ; il habite au . . . .

❷ This one here is a painting and that one there is a statue.
. . . . c'est un . . . . et . . . . . . c'est une statue.

❸ The bus stops in front of his *(her)* door.
Le bus . . . . sa porte.

35

Trente-cinquième leçon

Révision – Revision

1 Comparative and superlative

Whereas English has two ways of comparing adjectives – either by adding the suffixes *-er* and *-est* or by preceding the adjective with "*more*" and "*most*" – French has only one way: adding **plus** and **le plus** before the adjectives.
grand, *big*, *tall*; **plus grand**, *bigger*; **le plus grand**, *the biggest*.
intéressant, *interesting*; **plus intéressant**; **le plus intéressant** – **Ce livre est plus intéressant que l'autre**, *This book is more interesting than the other one*.
Il est plus fort que moi, *He is stronger than me*, **mais je suis plus intelligent que lui**, *but I am more intelligent than him*.

Answers to Exercice 1

❶ I begin at 8.00 and I stop at 4.15. **❷** Michel! Come here at once!
❸ Would you look at that! It's a Picasso. – Not at all! **❹** This one here
is my brother and that one there is my best friend. **❺** Does it bother
you if I smoke?

❹ I hope the smoke doesn't bother you.
   J'espère ... la fumée ne ... ...

❺ Do you recognize this one here?
   Est-ce que vous ... . ?

Answers to Exercice 2

❶ – vous trompez d' – sixième **❷** Celui-ci – tableau – celle-là – **❸** –
s'arrête devant – **❹** – que – vous gêne pas **❺** – reconnaissez celui-ci

35

Thirty-Fifth Lesson

Notice that, in English, when we are comparing only two things, we
must use the comparative: *Which is the bigger of these two?* etc.
French does not make this distinction: **Lequel est le plus lourd des
deux ?**, *Which is the heaviest of the two?* Another simplification!

Elle est aussi intelligente que **sa sœur**, *She is as intelligent as her
sister*.
Less expensive; the least expensive: **moins cher**; **le moins cher**
[mwahn share].
We will look at any irregular forms as and when they occur.

2 Indirect object pronouns

lui is also an "indirect object pronoun"; the others are **me** – **vous** – **nous** and **leur**. Let's see how they are used:
Elle me donne un coup de main, *She's giving me a hand* (lit. "a blow of hand").
Il leur explique la phrase, *He explains the sentence to them.*
Vous lui parlez trop vite, *You are speaking to him/her too quickly.*

In both cases, the pronoun in English is followed by *to*. We call this an "indirect object". We place the French pronoun <u>before</u> the verb except when the verb is an affirmative imperative:
Donnez-moi une réponse !, *Give me an answer!*

Pronoun order is quite a complex subject in French, so we'll tackle it gradually, getting your intuition to work for you. By the end of the course, however, you will have seen all the examples needed to assimilate the rule.

3 Forming questions

We mentioned at the beginning of this course that the question-form **est-ce que**, **qu'est-ce que**, although extremely frequent, was considered a bit "inelegant". We still recommend that you use it when you begin to formulate questions yourself, but we have taken this opportunity to show you how **est-ce que** is replaced in more formal language.

3.1 The inversion of verb and subject pronoun
Est-ce qu'ils sont Anglais ? – Sont-ils Anglais ?
Est-ce que vous avez l'heure ? – Avez-vous l'heure ?

3.2 The inversion of *il y a*
If we tried to pronounce **y a- -il**, it would be rather difficult (try it! *[ee-a-eel]*) so we add the letter **t** before the last word for euphony: **y a-t-il**. The **t** has no meaning.
Est-ce qu'il y a un bus ce soir ? → **Y a-t-il un bus ce soir ?**
Combien de tickets est-ce qu'il y a ? → **Combien de tickets y a-t-il ?**

We find this "euphonic t" each time that a final and an initial vowel would otherwise have to be pronounced together:

Est-ce qu'elle va en Égypte ? → **Va-t-elle en Égypte ?**

This type of language is considered rather stuffy when used in everyday conversation, but is quite normal – even obligatory when written. Because of such formal constructions, there is a wider gap between the written and spoken languages in French than in English. Our course tries to marry the two where possible, but we place greater emphasis on usage and the spoken language.

4 *Vous* and *tu*

Like most languages (including old English), French has two ways of saying *you*. We are learning the polite, formal way – **vous** – which is how you address strangers in everyday situations.

The other, familiar form, is **tu** (like our "thou"); the French themselves sometimes have difficulty knowing when exactly to use it (especially between different generations). Suffice it to say that **tu** is almost always used for family, friends and young children. Most young people use it systematically when talking to each other, even if they have only just met. And in certain professions, notably show business, the **tu** form is *de rigueur*. (Some US and UK companies with French subsidiaries encourage the use of **tu** to create the sense of familiarity that English gets by using first names. This does not always work...)

We do not wish, at this stage, to burden you with another verbal form – especially as its use is often a question of "feeling" a situation. We will, however, (a) include it henceforth when we give a verb conjugation, (b) use it in situations where the **vous** form would be artificial.

In this way, you can start to assimilate it naturally.

36

Trente-sixième leçon

Les secrétaires

1 Une femme téléphone au bureau de son mari :

2 – Je voudrais [1] parler à M. Martin.
 – Il est_absent.

3 Est-ce que je peux prendre un message ?

4 – S'il vous plaît. Je pars en voyage [2], alors dites-lui

5 que j'ai repassé ses chemises, j'ai fait le lit,

6 j'ai envoyé les_enfants chez sa mère

7 et j'ai laissé un repas [3] dans le frigo [4].

8 – Très bien madame. Je vais lui dire. Qui est_à l'appareil ?

Pronunciation
2 … voodray … martan … etabsohn **3** … peu … mesahzh **4** … par … **7** … lessay … freegoh

Notes
1 This is our first encounter with the conditional form: **je veux**, *I want*; **je voudrais**, *I would like*. **Voulez-vous...?**, *Do you want...?* **Voudriez-vous...?**, *Would you like...?* As in English, it is very often used in polite conversation.

2 **un voyage**, *a trip*; **un trajet**, *a journey*; **voyager**, *to travel*; **un agent de voyage**, *a travel agent*; **partir en voyage**, *to go on a trip*; **en voyage d'affaires**, *on a business trip*.

Thirty-Sixth Lesson

(The) **secretaries**

1 A woman telephones *(to)* her husband's office.
2 – I would like to speak to Mr Martin.
   – He is not here *(absent)*.
3 Can I take a message?
4 – [Yes], please. I [am] leaving on a trip, so tell him
5 that I have ironed his shirts, I have made the bed,
6 I have sent the children to his mother's
7 and I have left a meal in the fridge.
8 – Very well madam. I will *(am going to)* tell him. Who is
   speaking?

3 **un repas**, *a meal*. The principal meals are: **le petit-déjeuner**, *breakfast*;
le déjeuner, *lunch*, and **le dîner**, *dinner*. Another loan word is becoming
increasingly common: **le brunch**. (For those interested in etymology,
there is a similarity betwen *breakfast* and **déjeuner**: the verb **jeûner**
means *to fast*, so **dé-jeuner** means *to un-fast*, or *break one's fast*.
Déjeuner, *to have lunch*; **dîner**, *to have dinner*.

4 This is a familiar word for **le réfrigérateur** (like *"fridge"* for *"refrigera-
tor"* in English). A similar formation can be found with **le congélateur**
(*freezer*) and **le congélo**.

9 Une femme rencontre par hasard la secrétaire de son mari.

10 – Je suis très_heureuse de vous connaître, mademoiselle,

11 mon mari m'a dit si peu ⁵ de choses sur vous. □

9 ... parazar ...

***

Exercice 1 – Traduisez

❶ Voudriez-vous parler à M. Bensaid ? – S'il vous plaît. ❷ Il y a tellement de bruit chez lui ! ❸ Nous avons si peu de temps ! ❹ Est-ce que vous aimez voyager ? – Oui, beaucoup. ❺ Je voudrais prendre le petit-déjeuner à huit heures.

***

Exercice 2 – Complétez

❶ There are so many people and so little room!
Il y a .... gens et .... place !

❷ Are you leaving on a trip tomorrow?
Est-ce que vous .... demain ?

❸ We phoned the bank yesterday,
Nous .... à la banque hier *[ee-air]*,

❹ and they sent us a cheque-book.
et ils .... un carnet de chèques.

9   A woman meets by chance the secretary of her husband.

10 – I am very happy to meet *(know)* you, miss,

11   my husband has told me so little *(few things)* about *(on)* you.

] Note

5 *much, many,* **beaucoup**; *little, few,* **peu**. *There is little hope,* **Il y a peu d'espoir**. *There are few people here,* **Il y a peu de gens ici**. *So little, so few,* **si peu de**; *so much, so many,* **tellement**. Note once again that the French make no distinction here between countable and uncountable nouns.

***

Answers to Exercice 1

❶ Would you like to speak to Mr Bensaid? – Yes please. ❷ There is so much noise at his place! ❸ We have so little time! ❹ Do you like travelling? – Yes, very much. ❺ I would like to have breakfast at 8.00.

***

❺ Michel said: "I am very happy to meet you sir".
   **Michel . dit : "Je suis très ……. de …………… ,
   Monsieur".**

Answers to Exercice 2

❶ – tellement de – si peu de – ❷ – partez en voyage – ❸ – avons téléphoné – ❹ – nous ont envoyé – ❺ – a – heureux – vous connaître –

Do you find that you are beginning to understand things without needing detailed explanations? We hope so!

37

Trente-septième leçon

Une soirée [1] au théâtre

1 – Jean et Marie-Claude vont‿au théâtre pour voir une pièce [2]

2 qui s'appelle *L'amour, toujours l'amour*.

3 Ils‿arrivent au théâtre à huit‿heures et quart,

4 un quart d'heure avant le lever [3] du rideau.

5 Ils trouvent leurs places et s'installent.

6 La pièce commence ; deux comédiens [4] entrent en scène :

Pronunciation

… *swaray oh tayatr* **4** … *levay … reedoh* **6** … *komedeean entr …* *sen*

Notes

1 le soir, *the evening*, i.e. from 6 p.m. to 10 p.m. (*Le Soir* is one of the leading French-language newspapers in Belgium.) la nuit, *the night*; le matin, *the morning*. Il se lève tôt le matin, *He gets up early in the morning.*

la soirée, *the evening*, plus the activities involved: the sense is wider than the word soir. Nous avons passé une excellente soirée, *We had a wonderful evening.*

dans la matinée, *in the morning*. Téléphonez-moi en fin de matinée, *Telephone me towards the end of the morning.*

2 We have already seen une pièce meaning *a room*. Here is another meaning: Une pièce de théâtre, *a play*. (Note also une pièce de monnaie, *a coin*; see lesson 39, line 1.)

Thirty-Seventh Lesson

An evening at the theatre

1 – Jean and Marie-Claude go to the theatre *(for)* to see a play
2 which is called "Love, always love".
3 They arrive at the theatre at 8.15 *(8 hours and [a] quarter)*,
4 a quarter of an hour before curtain-up *(the lifting of the curtain)*.
5 They find their seats *(places)* and settle down *(install themselves)*.
6 The play begins; two actors come *(enter)* on *(in)* stage.

3 lever, *to lift, to rise*. **Se lever**, *to get up*. **Le lever du soleil**, *the sunrise*.

4 When we have to refer to a group containing both masculine and feminine nouns, the masculine form takes precedence. Here, for example, we have **un comédien** and **une comédienne** but we say **deux comédiens** (the word means *an actor*; *a comedian* is **un comique** or **un humoriste**). The same for the agreement of adjectives: **le mari et la femme sont très gentils**.

7 – Je t'aime, Gisèle. Tu m'entends ? Je t'aime [5].

8 – Ah bon ? Mais moi je ne t'aime pas. J'aime Pierre.

9 – Pourquoi ?

– Parce qu'il me donne des bijoux [6],

10 et toi, tu ne me donnes jamais rien.

11 À ce moment, Jean commence à ronfler très fort. Il dort [7].

12 Un vieux proverbe dit : "Dieu aide les fous, les ivrognes et les amoureux."

□

9 … parskeel … beezhoo **11** … ronflay … dor **12** … eev-ronye …

Notes

5 What better example of how to use the **tu** form of the verb than to declare your love for someone? (See lesson 35, section 4.) A simple basic rule is never to use **tu** unless you know the person reasonably well...

***

Exercice 1 – Traduisez

❶ Frère Jacques, frère Jacques, dormez-vous ? ❷ À quelle heure vous levez-vous le matin ? ❸ Il leur montre les places ❹ et ils s'installent. ❺ Ils ne me donnent jamais rien. ❻ Montrez-lui le billet.

7 – I love you, Gisèle. You hear me? I love you.

8 – Oh really? But *(me)* I don't love you. I love Pierre.

9 – Why?
   – Because he gives me jewels,

10 and you, you never give me anything *(nothing)*.

11 At this moment Jean begins to snore very loudly *(strong)*. He [is] sleeping.

12 An old proverb runs *(says)*: "God helps *(the)* madmen, *(the)* drunkards and *(the)* lovers."

6 Another irregular plural. The singular is **bijou**. There are seven nouns like this – two more common ones are **genou**, *a knee* (**les genoux**) and **chou**, *cabbage*, (**les choux**). All are masculine.

7 **dormir**, *to sleep*. je dors, tu dors, il/elle dort, nous dormons, vous dormez, ils/elles dorment. S'endormir, *to fall asleep*.

***

Answers to Exercice 1

❶ Brother Jacques, brother Jacques, are you sleeping? ❷ What time do you get up in the morning? ❸ He shows them the seats ❹ and they settle down. ❺ They never give me anything. ❻ Show him/her the ticket.

Exercice 2 – Complétez
❶ He never gives her (*or* him) anything.
   Il ne . . . . rien.

❷ I gave them our address.
   Je . . . . ai donné notre adresse.

❸ He always falls asleep in the theatre.
   Il s'. . . . . au théâtre.

38

Trente-huitième leçon

▶

Le septième art [1]

1　La France possède une longue tradition
　　cinématographique, et le "septième art" est bel
　　et bien [2] vivant aujourd'hui.

2　Beaucoup de gens, surtout les citadins, vont
　　deux – et parfois trois fois par semaine – au
　　cinéma,

3　et les metteurs en scène [3] et comédiens
　　français sont très‿appréciés par le public.

💬 Pronunciation
1 … settiem … 3 … metteu ohn senn … komaydienh …

🔲 Notes
1 A common device in French is to substitute a word referring to an
attribute for the thing that is actually meant (technically, this is
known as "metonymy"). Here, instead of saying *the cinema*, we use

4 His (her) son and his (her) daughter are tall and good-looking.
... fils et .. fille sont ...... et ....

5 She answers him: "I don't love you".
Elle ... répond : "Je ne ...... pas".

38

Thirty-Eighth Lesson

The seventh art

1 France has a long filmic tradition, and the "7th art" is well and truly alive today.
2 Many people, particularly city dwellers, go two – and sometimes three times a week – to the cinema,
3 and French directors and actors are greatly (*very*) appreciated by the public.

a very common substitute: *the seventh art*. This use of metonymy is particularly widespread in the press (see also line 5).

2 **bel et bien** (lit. "beautiful and well") is used for emphasis, rather like our expression *well and truly*. **Elle est bel et bien morte**, *She's well and truly dead*. Note the lack of agreement.

3 A good example of how nouns are derived from verbs. From the verb **mettre**, *to put*, we get **un metteur en scène** (lit. "a putter in stage"), *a film director*; and **la mise en scène** (lit. "the putting in stage"), *the direction*. (Remember that **un comédien** means *an actor*, see lesson 37, note 4.)

4   Le choix de films est_énorme – comédies,
        aventures, policiers, dessins animés, films
        noirs [4] – et des nouveautés sortent chaque
        semaine.

5   Naturellement, il y a aussi beaucoup de films
        étrangers dans nos "salles obscures" [5],

6   qu'on peut voir en version originale ou en
        version française (c'est-à-dire doublés). [6]

7   Deux rendez-vous annuels s'imposent pour
        les cinéphiles : [7] le festival de Cannes avec sa
        Palme d'Or,

8   et la remise des Césars [8] ; ces prix
        récompensent le meilleur du cinéma de l'année
        (meilleur film, meilleur scénario, etc.).

*4 … dessahn animay … 7 … simpohz … 8 … sayzarh … pree ray-
kompohns …*

Notes

4   Two important words for film lovers: **un dessin animé** (lit. "an animated
        drawing") is *a cartoon film*. (*A cartoon in the press*, etc. **un dessin
        humoristique**.) The concept of **le film noir** has no real translation.
        It basically refers to crime or gangster thrillers which are long on
        atmosphere. Many English-speaking film lovers call this… **film noir**.

5   Another example of metonymy (see note 1): **les salles obscures** (lit.
        "the dark rooms") is used – always in the plural – to mean *cinemas*.

6   Before going to see a foreign film in a French cinema, you should
        check the listings to find out whether it is being shown in **VO** (**version
        originale**, i.e. *the original soundtrack with French subtitles*) or in **VF**
        (**version française**, i.e. *dubbed into French*). Most big cities in France
        offer a choice of VO or VF for box-office hits.

4   The choice of films is enormous – comedy, adventure, crime, cartoons, gangster – and new ones *(novelties)* come out each week.

5   Naturally, there are also many foreign films in our "dark rooms"

6   which can be seen in [the] original version or in [the] French version (that is to say dubbed).

7   Two annual get-togethers are a must for film buffs: the Cannes Festival with its Golden Palm

8   and the presentation of the Césars; the *(those)* prizes reward the best of the year's cinema (best film, best screenplay, etc.).

ELLE VA TROIS FOIS PAR SEMAINE À LA PISCINE.

7   The classical origins of French are evident in many everyday words. Here, for example, we have the suffix **-phile** (from the Greek philos, or *friend*). With its Anglo-Saxon roots, English would translate this as *lover*: for example **un bibliophile**, *a book-lover*; **un cinéphile**, *a film-lover* or *movie-buff*. The opposite is **-phobe** (from phobos, or *fear*). **Un xénophobe**: *someone who hates foreigners*. It is important to note that such constructions are not considered to be particularly formal or elitist. You will find them in everyday usage.

8   **les Césars** are France's answer to *the Oscars*. The awards, founded in 1976 to encourage the French film industry, take the form of statuettes awarded for best film, best director, etc. They are named for the sculptor who designed them.

9 – Et maintenant, le moment que nous‿attendons tous : le César du meilleur metteur en scène. Cette année le prix est‿attribué à... Michel Bonnaud !

10 Essayant [9] de rester décontracté, l'heureux gagnant répond :

11 – Merci, je suis très‿ému, mais‿aussi très surpris car je n'ai pas tourné un seul film depuis dix‿ans.

12 – C'est justement pour ça que le jury vous donne cette récompense. □

10 ... eu-reu ganyohn ... **11** ... ay-mioo ... **12** ... zho-ree ...

***

Exercice 1 – Traduisez

❶ Le cinéma est bel et bien vivant en France. ❷ Elle va trois fois par semaine à la piscine. ❸ J'ai beaucoup aimé le scénario, mais pas la mise en scène. ❹ Est-ce que le film passe en VO ou en VF ? ❺ David est un vrai francophile.

***

Exercice 2 – Complétez

❶ And now, the moment we've all been waiting for.
Et maintenant le moment . . . .

❷ She's very moved and also very surprised.
Elle est très . . . . et . . . . . très . . . .

❸ He hasn't made a film for fifteen years.
Il . . . . un film . . . . . . quinze ans.

9 – And now the moment we've all been waiting for: the César of the best director. This year the prize goes to... Michel Bonnaud!

10 Trying to remain relaxed, the happy winner replies:

11 – Thank you. I'm deeply *(very)* moved, but also very surprised because I haven't made *(turned)* a single film for ten years.

12 – That's exactly why the jury is giving you this award *(reward)*.

Note

9 This is the present participle of the verb **essayer**, *to try*. Most present participles of all three verb categories end in -ant: aller → allant; vendre → vendant; finir → finissant. For an example of how the present participle is used as an adjective, look at the word **vivant** in line 1 *(living, alive)*.

***

Answers to Exercice 1

❶ The cinema is well and truly alive in France. ❷ She goes three times a week to the swimming pool. ❸ I really liked the screenplay but not the direction. ❹ Is the film in the original version or dubbed into French? ❺ David is a real Francophile *(i.e; he really loves France and all things French)*.

***

❹ Trying to remain calm, he opened the letter.

.... **calme, il a ouvert la lettre.**

❺ This prize rewards the best screenplay.

. . .. **le meilleur** ....**.**

Answers to Exercice 2

❶ – que nous attendons tous ❷ – émue – aussi – surprise ❸ – n'a pas tourné – depuis – ❹ Essayant de rester – ❺ Ce prix récompense – scénario

39 ─────────────────────────────

Trente-neuvième leçon

Un argument convaincant

1 – Vous n'avez pas une petite pièce pour moi, monsieur ?

2 – Bien sûr que non [1] !

3 – Oh monsieur, je n'ai rien, je n'ai pas d'argent,

4   je n'ai pas de maison et je n'ai plus d'amis.

5   Je n'ai plus qu'une [2] seule chose au monde.
   – Quoi ? [3]

6 – Ce petit revolver ; alors, vous n'avez toujours pas une petite pièce ?

À la fortune du pot

7 – Je vous_ai invité [4] à dîner, mon cher ami, mais regardez :

8   je n'ai plus rien dans mon garde-manger ;

Pronunciation

*… kohnvankohn **5** … plyookyoon … shohz … **6** … revolvair …*
__8__ … gard-monzhay

Notes

1 Bien sûr !, *Of course!* Bien sûr que non !, *Of course not!* The **que** is emphatic. We can also say: Bien sûr que oui.

2 J'ai seulement cinq minutes, *I have only five minutes*, or Je n'ai que cinq minutes. The two sentences mean the same. Ils n'ont qu'un enfant,

39

Thirty-Ninth Lesson

A convincing argument

1 – You don't have any change *(a small coin)* for me, sir
[do you]?

2 – Of course *(that)* not!

3 – Oh sir, I have *(not)* nothing; I haven't any money,

4 I haven't a house and I have no more *(of)* friends.

5 I have only *(no more than)* one thing in *(at)* the world.
 – What?

6 – This little revolver; so, you still haven't any change?

(A the) **Pot-luck**

7 – I have invited you to dine, my dear friend, but look:

8 I have nothing more *(no more nothing)* in my larder:

They have only one child. Je n'ai plus que..., *I have only... left.* Je n'ai plus que trois jours avant de rentrer, *I have only three days left before I return.*

3 Like saying "*What?*" in English, this could be considered impolite or abrupt. More politely we would say **Qu'est-ce que c'est ?** If you want the person to repeat what he or she has said, you would use **Pardon ?** *[pah-dohn]*, with a rising intonation.

4 J'ai invité Jean; je l'ai invité. So, our word order is subject-object-auxiliary-verb. **Elle nous a dit...**, *She told us...* (S+O+A+V). **Ils leur ont donné...**, *They gave them...* (S+O+A+V).

9 plus [5] de sucre, plus de pain, plus de riz, plus de biscuits,

10 plus de conserves... tenez [6]... si, il y a quelque chose :

11 une énorme toile d'araignée ! Bon_appétit [7] ! □

9 ... ree ... biskwee 11 ... twal daraynyay ! ... apaytee

Notes

5 Il n'y a plus *[pliou]* de sucre means *there is no more sugar*. **Donnez-moi plus** *[plious]* **de sucre**: means *Give me more sugar*. In order to avoid a possible confusion, the French themselves often use **davantage**: **Davantage de sucre, s'il vous plaît**, *More sugar, please*.

6 tenir, *to hold*; je tiens, tu tiens, il/elle tient, nous tenons, vous tenez, ils/elles tiennent *[tyenn]*; j'ai tenu, *I (have) held*. **Tenez !**, *Hold on! Wait a minute!*

***

Exercice 1 – Traduisez

❶ Est-ce que vous avez deux enfants, ma chère amie ? ❷ Bien sûr que non ! Je n'ai qu'un enfant ! ❸ Il nous a invités à déjeuner vendredi prochain. ❹ Je n'ai plus d'argent ! Qu'est-ce que je vais faire ? ❺ Il n'a plus qu'une chose au monde. – Qu'est-ce que c'est ?

9   no] more *(of)* sugar, [no] more *(of)* bread, [no] more
       (of) rice, [no] more *(of)* biscuits,

10 [no] more *(of)* tinned food... wait a minute *(hold)* ...!
       yes, there is something:

11 an enormous spider's web! Bon appétit!

7 In most European countries, it is usual to wish your table companions
       a *"good appetite"*. Strangely enough, the British have no equivalent...
       (Note that the American usage *"Enjoy your meal!"* would be roughly
       the same.)

***

Answers to Exercice 1

❶ Do you have two children, my dear friend *(f.)*? ❷ Of course not!
I have only one child! ❸ He has invited us to lunch next Friday. ❹ I
have no more money! What am I going to do? ❺ He has only one
thing left in the world. – What is it?

Exercice 2 – Complétez

❶ I have no more sugar, no more bread, no more anything!

Je ..ai ...... sucre, ... pain, ... !

❷ Hurry up! They only have ten minutes!

Dépêchez-vous ! Ils .... dix minutes !

❸ I have only three days left before returning.

Je .... trois jours avant de rentrer.

40

Quarantième leçon

La rue Mouffetard

1 Le dimanche matin, Mᵐᵉ *(madame)* Ferrandi va au marché de la rue Mouffetard.

2 C'est un très vieux marché en bas d'une [1] petite rue étroite.

3 Il y a toujours beaucoup de monde [2] et c'est très vivant.

4 On y trouve des gens qui jouent de l'accordéon ou de la guitare,

Pronunciation

... mouftar 2 ... on ba ... aytrwat 3 ... veevohn 4 ... geetar

Notes

1 bas (f. basse), *low*. **En bas de**, *at the bottom of*. **En haut de**, *at the top of*. **Au milieu de**, *in the middle of*. **Autour de**, *around* (these forms are invariable).

❹ They told us to come early.
Ils ……… … de venir tôt.

❺ I have nothing left to give you.
Je ………… à …. donner.

Don't forget to read the text aloud: it is important to get the rhythm of the language, and to "feel" the liaisons.

40

Fortieth Lesson

The rue Mouffetard

1   On *(The)* Sunday morning, Mrs Ferrandi goes to the rue Mouffetard market.
2   It is a very old market at the bottom of a small, narrow street.
3   There are always lots of people *(world)* and it is very lively.
4   One finds *(there)* people who play *(of)* the accordeon or *(of)* the guitar

---

2   We have seen a couple of idiomatic uses of **le monde** (*the world*): **tout le monde**, *everybody*; **il y a beaucoup de monde**, (≠ **très peu de monde**): *a lot of people*, *crowded*.

Dans le monde, *Throughout the world*. **Une seule chose au monde**, *One single thing in the world*. (*Le Monde* is also the title of France's leading daily newspaper.)

5 et d'autres ³ qui distribuent des tracts
politiques et des journaux...

6 et il y a même des gens qui achètent des fruits
et des légumes !

7 Tous ces gens se parlent ⁴ en même temps.

8 Mᵐᵉ Ferrandi s'arrête devant l'éventaire d'un
marchand de primeurs.

9 – Quelle est la différence entre ces deux sortes
de haricots ?

10 – Ceux-ci ⁵ sont cultivés en France et ceux-là
sont_importés.

11 – Je vais prendre les moins chers. Avez-vous aussi
des carottes ?

12 – Oui, bien sûr. Celles-ci sont très bonnes. Je
vous_en mets un kilo ⁶ ?

🗣 *5 ... distreebyoo ... trakt ... 6 ... laygyoom 8 ... ayvontair ... marshohn ... preemeur 9 ... de arrekoh 10 se-see ... se-la amportay 11 ... mwah ... 12 ... voozonmay ...*

Notes

3 autre, *other*, is usually followed by a noun (**un autre journal**, *un autre endroit*). If we want to say *others* by itself (e.g. *Some like tea, others prefer coffee*), we must say **d'autres** (**Certains aiment le thé, d'autres préfèrent le café**). We will see more differences between the two forms later.

4 Il se parle, *He talks to himself*, but ils se parlent, *they talk to one another*; il se connaît, *he knows himself* (i.e. his own faults and virtues); ils se connaissent, *they know each other*.

5 and others who distribute political tracts and newspapers...

6 and there are even people who buy fruit and vegetables!

7 All these people talk [to] each other at the same time.

8 Mrs Ferrandi stops in front of the stand of a greengrocer.

9 – What is the difference between these two sorts of beans?

10 – These here are grown (*cultivated*) in France and those there are imported.

11 – I will (*am going to*) take the least expensive. Have you as well any carrots?

12 – Yes, of course. These are very good. I will put (*you*) one kilo (*of them*)?

5 We have seen **celui-ci** and **celui-là** (f. **celle**), our demonstrative pronouns (lesson 34 note 2); this is the plural.

6 This is the type of idiomatic language you are likely to hear in shops and markets. Instead of the formal: **Je voudrais un kilo de**..., we hear **Mettez-moi un kilo de** ...
The stallholder does not say: **En voulez-vous un kilo, madame ?** but **Je vous en mets un kilo ?**

▶ Exercice 1 – Traduisez

❶ Tout le monde est content de ce livre. **❷** On y trouve des gens qui jouent de la guitare. **❸** Que faites-vous le dimanche matin ? **❹** Quelle est la différence entre ces deux sortes de riz ? **❺** Tout le monde se parle en même temps !

***

Exercice 2 – Complétez

❶ There are always a lot of people there.

Il y a .... de ..... là-bas.

❷ Some *(people)* like tea, others prefer coffee.

Certains aiment le thé, ... préfèrent le café.

❸ We speak to each other every day.

.... tous les jours.

41

Quarante et unième leçon

Réservons une table

1 – Bonsoir. Je suis bien [1] au restaurant "Les Savoyards" ?
– Oui monsieur.

🗨 Pronunciation
1 ... zhe swee ... restorohn lay savwayar

▢ Note

[1] In this lesson we see two polite uses of the adverb **bien**, *well*. For the time being, just make a mental note of them: they are forms you are likely to hear in polite conversation. **Vous êtes bien M. Duclos ?**, *You are Mr Duclos, aren't you?* **Est-ce bien "Les savoyards" ?**, *This is "Les Savoyards", isn't it?* **Voulez-vous bien me suivre ?**, *Would you kindly follow me?* **Vous voulez bien me dire...**, *Kindly tell me...*

Answers to Exercice 1

❶ Everybody is happy with this book. ❷ You find there people who play the guitar. ❸ What do you do on Sunday morning? ❹ What is the difference between these two sorts of rice? ❺ Everybody speaks to each other at the same time!

***

❹ What is the difference between these two types of carrots?
  – These ones are imported.
  .... la différence entre ces deux sortes de carottes ? – ......-.. sont importées.

❺ And these ones are French. You want a kilo?
  Et ......-.. sont .... Je .... en .... un kilo ?

Answers to Exercice 2

❶ – toujours beaucoup – monde – ❷ – d'autres – ❸ Nous nous parlons – ❹ Quelle est – Celles-ci – ❺ – celles-là – françaises – vous – mets –

41

Forty-First Lesson

Let's book a table

1 – Good evening. Is this *(Am I well at)* the restaurant "Les Savoyards"?
  – Yes sir.

VOUS ÊTES SÛR QUE VOUS N'AVEZ RIEN ?

2 – Je voudrais réserver une table pour quatre
personnes pour ce soir.

3 – Quatre couverts ² ? Vers ³ quelle heure ?

4 – Vers huit_heures, si c'est possible.

5 – Désolé, monsieur, mais nous sommes complet ⁴
jusqu'à dix_heures.

6 – Ça fait un peu tard ⁵. Vous_êtes sûr que vous
n'avez rien ?

7 – Rien, à part une toute petite table

8 qui est près de la cuisine et...

9 – Ça ne fait rien ⁶. Je la prends. Je m'appelle
Desroches.

10 – Voulez-vous bien l'épeler, s'il vous plaît ?

11 – D.E.S.R.O.C.H.E.S.

– Merci monsieur. À tout_à l'heure.

12 "L'appétit vient_en mangeant, la soif s'en va ⁷
en buvant." – *Rabelais.*

*2 ... voodray ... kat person ... 3 kat koovair? vair ... 5 ... komplay
... 7 ... a par ... 9 ... prohn 10 ... laypeulay ... 11 day-eu-ess-air-oh-
say-ash-eu-ess ... atootaleur 12 ... monzhon ... byoovohn*

Notes

2 un couvert is literally the place-setting in a restaurant, but restaurant
staff often talk of **couverts** instead of *people*. On a fait cinquante couverts à midi, *We served fifty people at lunchtime.*
Le couvert includes le couteau, *the knife*; la fourchette, *the fork*; la
cuillère *[kwee-air]*, *the spoon*; le verre, *the glass*; le sel, *the salt*; le
poivre, *the pepper* and la serviette, *the napkin*. (We saw that the latter
also means *brief-case*.)

3 Il vient vers moi, *He is coming towards me*. Vers huit heures, *Around
8.00.*

4 plein *[plahn]*, *full*. The feminine form is pleine *[plen]*. The opposite,
empty, is vide *[veed]* in the masculine and feminine.

2 – I would like to reserve a table for four persons for this evening.
3 – Four people (*places*)? Around what time?
4 – Around 8.00 if it is possible.
5 – [Very] sorry, sir, but we are full [up] until 10.00 p.m.
6 – That's a bit late. You're sure you have (*not*) nothing ?
7 – Nothing, apart [from] a really small table
8 which is near the kitchen and...
9 – That doesn't matter. I [will] take it. I'm called Desroches.
10 – Would you kindly spell it, please?
11 – D.E.S.R.O.C.H.E.S.
  – Thank you, sir. Until later on.
12 "(*The*) appetite comes with (*in*) eating, (*the*) thirst goes away with (*in*) drinking." – *Rabelais*

Remplir (conjugated like **finir**), *to fill* but for theatres, hotels and restaurants we use **complet**. If you see a **Complet** sign on the door of a hotel, etc., it means *full up*, or *no vacancy*.
If you have eaten well, you often say in English: "*I'm full*". Never translate this literally into French, because it would mean either that you are drunk or expecting a baby! A polite way of refusing an offer of more food is to say: **Non merci, j'ai très bien mangé**, *No thank you, I've eaten very well*. However, if you <u>do</u> come out with a howler, don't worry! You will very rarely offend anyone – and you'll certainly remember not to make the same mistake again!

5 An idiomatic way of saying: **C'est un peu tard**, *It's a bit late*.

6 Another useful idiom, literally "it makes nothing", which means *it's not important*, *it doesn't matter*. **Ça ne fait rien** is invariable. (The expression was adopted into upper-class English in the 1930s as "sanfarryan"!)

7 **aller**, *to go*. **S'en aller**, *to go away*. je m'en vais, tu t'en vas, il/elle s'en va, nous nous en allons (on s'en va), vous vous en allez, ils/elles s'en vont. **Allez-vous en !** – *Go away!* **On s'en va dans trois minutes**, *We're leaving in three minutes*.

▶ Exercice 1 – Traduisez

❶ Je m'en vais en vacances la semaine prochaine. ❷ Elles ne peuvent pas venir. – Ça ne fait rien. ❸ J'arrive vers neuf heures. ❹ Vous êtes bien français ? – Non, désolé ! ❺ Tous les hôtels sont complets jusqu'à demain.

***

Exercice 2 – Complétez

❶ She's leaving around eight o'clock.
Elle ……… …… huit heures.

❷ Are you sure that you have nothing?
…… -vous sûr que vous ……… …… ?

❸ Apart [from] a really small table, we are full [up].
…… une toute petite table, nous sommes ……… .

42

Quarante deuxième leçon

Révision – Revision

1 The past tense

This tense expresses two different English concepts, the simple past and the present perfect. In other words, French makes no difference between "I bought" and "I have bought", thus making life much simpler for us!

You have already come across the past tense before. It is formed with the present tense of **avoir** (which becomes an "auxiliary") and the past participle of the verb we wish to use.

The past participles are formed thus:

verbs like **acheter**	with é → **acheté**
verbs like **finir**	with i → **fini**
verbs like **vendre**	with u → **vendu**

Answers to Exercice 1

❶ I'm going away on holiday next week. ❷ They can't come.
– Never mind. ❸ I'm arriving around 9.00. ❹ You are French, aren't
you? – No, terribly sorry! ❺ All the hotels are full until tomorrow.

***

❹ Will you kindly spell your name, sir?
Voulez-vous . . . . nom, monsieur ?

❺ I would like to reserve a table for this evening.
Je . . . . réserver une table pour . . . .

Answers to Exercice 2

❶ – s'en va vers – ❷ Êtes – n'avez rien ❸ À part – complet ❹ – bien
épeler votre – ❺ – voudrais – ce soir

42

Forty-Second Lesson

Elle a vendu sa voiture, *She sold* (or *has sold*) *her car.*
Nous avons fini de manger, *We (have) finished eating.*
Ils ont acheté un lecteur de DVD, *They (have) bought a DVD
player.*

The negative form is simple: we use **ne** before the auxiliary and
pas after it:
Nous n'avons pas fini ; ils n'ont pas acheté ; elle n'a pas vendu.
Est-ce qu'elle a acheté cette nouvelle imprimante ?, *Did she buy*
(or *has she bought*) *that new printer?*
Certain verbs have irregular participles: some you will pick up
naturally, others you can look up in the Grammatical appendix at
the end of the book. Here are two common ones to start with: **j'ai
eu**, *I (have) had*; **il a dit**, *he (has) said.*

NOTE: French also has a "historic" past tense which has exactly the same use as the past tense we have just seen, but it is basically a literary form and is not found in conversation or modern writing.

2 What time is it?, *Quelle heure est-il ?*

To tell the time, we must first announce the nearest hour.
So, for example, *3.00 p.m*:

Il est trois heures...

Then, the number of minutes past, i.e. 5:
Il est trois heures cinq... Simple!
(No conjunction between the hour and the minute.)

The nearest hour is 4:

Il est quatre heures...

Now, we announce the number of minutes to go: 20.
Il est quatre heures moins **vingt** (lit. "minus 20"):

For the quarter and three-quarter, we say:

Il est deux heures et quart
(note the **et**) or **un quart** *[kah]*.

Il est onze heures moins le quart.

For the half, we say:

Il est neuf heures et demie.

(However, *a half-hour* is written **une demi-heure**, without an **e**; **demi** never agrees with its noun before a hyphen.)
For public announcements (trains, cinema-times, television programmes, etc.), the 24-hour clock is used. We will see this later.

3 Negative sentences

An important point of grammar is that French negatives are always composed of <u>two</u> parts: the **ne** and another particle.
Je ne fume pas, *I don't smoke*;
Je ne fume jamais, *I never smoke*;
Elle n'a rien à manger, *She has nothing to eat*;
Il ne travaille plus ici, *He no longer works here.*
When speaking quickly, the French often drop the **ne**. Try not to!
Always remember: two parts **ne... rien**; **ne... pas**, *nothing, doesn't*;
ne... jamais, *never*; **ne... plus**, *no longer, no more.*

Remember to read your Assimil every day. Only by constant contact can you pick up a language naturally and efficiently.

43

Quarante-troisième leçon

▶

Que faites-vous dans la vie ?

1 De nos jours [1], il y a une grande variété
   d'emplois ;
2 on peut devenir ingénieur ou informaticien,
   médecin ou avocat par exemple.
3 Ces dernières [2] professions nécessitent
   plusieurs_années d'études supérieures
4 à l'université ou dans_une grande école [3].
5 D'autres préfèrent devenir journaliste ou
   publicitaire.
6 Et n'oublions pas les_artisans tels [4] que le
   menuisier, le plombier ou le maçon.

🗨 Pronunciation
*1 ... varee-aytay ... 2 ... anzhenyeur ... anformatiseeah, medsan
... avoka ... 3 ... dairneeair ... nessesseet plyoozee-eur zanay
... 5 ... zhoornaleest ... pyooblissitair 6 ... layzarteezohn tel ...
menweezeeay plombeeay ... massohn*

📁 Notes
1 de nos jours (lit. "of our days"), *nowadays*; dans le passé (or, more ele-
   gantly: jadis *[zhadeess]*) - *in the past*; dans le futur (or dans l'avenir),
   in the future.
2 dernier, *last, latest.* Voici les dernières nouvelles, *Here is the latest
   news.* Le dernier avion est à onze heures vingt, *The last plane is at
   11.20,* but ce dernier (or ces derniers, ces dernières), *the latter.* Ce premier, *the former* (there is also a feminine form: cette première.)

43

Forty-Third Lesson

What do you [do] in *(the)* life?

1 Nowadays, there is a wide variety of jobs;
2 one can become [an] engineer or [a] computer specialist, [a] doctor or [a] lawyer, for example.
3 These latter professions necessitate several years of higher *(superior)* studies
4 at *(the)* university or at a *grande école*.
5 Others prefer to become journalist[s] or advertiser[s].
6 And [let's] not forget the craftsmen *(artisans)* such [as] the joiner, the plumber or the builder *(mason)*.

3 **les grandes écoles** are top-flight engineering colleges and business schools that play a special part in French life. For further details, see lesson 105, §1.

4 **tel** (f. **telle**; pl. **tels**, **telles**) means *such*; followed by a list of examples it means *such as*: **Des actrices célèbres telles que Nicole Douly**, *Famous actresses such as Nicole Douly*. We will look at other meanings later on.

7 Certaines personnes [5] ne peuvent pas
supporter [6] de travailler à l'intérieur

8 dans des_usines, des_ateliers ou des bureaux,

9 alors elles peuvent devenir représentant, ou
même chauffeur de taxi.

10 Et malheureusement, il y a ceux qui ne
trouvent pas de travail [7], les chômeurs [8].

Définition d'une administration

11 Une administration est_un service où ceux qui
arrivent en retard

12 croisent ceux qui partent en avance. □

*7 sairten ... 8 ... daizyoozeen ... 9 ... peuv ... 10 ... se kee ...
shohmeur 12 ... krwahz ... part ...*

Notes

5 une **personne** is <u>always</u> feminine, even if the person is a man. (This can take a little getting used to!)

6 Je ne peux pas le (la) **supporter**, *I can't stand him (her).* **Est-ce que vous supportez le froid ?**, *Can you put up with the cold?*

***

▶ Exercice 1 – Traduisez

❶ Que font-ils ? – Il est ingénieur et son frère est informaticien. ❷ Et que fait sa femme ? – Elle est au chômage. ❸ Il a un travail très intéressant : il est avocat. ❹ Je ne supporte pas le froid. ❺ Ça nécessite beaucoup de travail.

7 Certain persons cannot stand to work inside *(at the interior)*
8 in factories, workshops or offices,
9 so they can become representative[s], or even taxi driver[s].
10 And, unfortunately, there are those who [can] do not find a job – the unemployed.

Definition of an administration

11 An administration is a department where those who arrive late
12 cross those who leave early.

---

7 Note how the partitive article **du** changes in a negative expression: **Il a trouvé du travail**, *He has found work.* ≠ **Il n'a pas trouvé de travail. Il a trouvé un travail** (or **un emploi**), *He has found a job.* **Travailler**, *to work.* Two other work-related words are **une œuvre**, *a work of art* and **les travaux**, *construction works.*

8 **un chômeur**, *an unemployed person.* **Être au chômage**, *to be unemployed.* Why **les chômeurs**? Because we are speaking about them as a group.

***

Answers to Exercice 1
❶ What do they do? – He is an engineer and his brother is a computer specialist. ❷ And what does his wife do? – She is unemployed. ❸ He has a very interesting job: he is a lawyer. ❹ I can't stand the cold. ❺ It necessitates a lot of work.

Exercice 2 – Complétez

❶ We call those who cannot find work "unemployed".
On appelle .... ne trouvent pas de travail les
"........".

❷ There are doctors and lawyers. The latter are often very rich.
Il y a des .... et des .... Ces .... sont
souvent très riches.

❸ You can become [an] artisan and have work.
On peut .... artisan et avoir ....

44

Quarante-quatrième leçon

▶ M. Duclos accueille [1] un client

1 M. Duclos est cadre [2] dans_une grande société [3]
pétrolière.

2 Aujourd'hui il est_à l'aéroport de Roissy pour
accueillir un client [4] suisse.

🗨 Pronunciation
... *akeuy* ... *kleeohn* **2** ... *ohzhourdwee* ... *eye-ropor* ... *akeuyeer*
... *sweess*

📖 Notes

1 rencontrer, *to meet* someone (or something), *to come across* them. **Une
rencontre**, *a meeting, an encounter*; **une réunion**, *a business meeting*.
accueillir (j'accueille, vous accueillez) means *to greet* or *welcome*
someone. It is a tricky word, both to spell (**uei**) and pronounce – the
[euy] sound does not exist in standard English. Listen carefully to the
recording. In public buildings, **Accueil** means *Reception*.

❹ I can't stand this person.
Je ne peux pas .... personne.

❺ Those who arrive late cross those who leave early.
... ... arrivent ... ... croisent ... ... partent ..
... .

Answers to Exercice 2

❶ – ceux qui – chômeurs ❷ – médecins – avocats – derniers – ❸ –
devenir – du travail ❹ – supporter cette – ❺ Ceux qui – en retard
– ceux qui – en avance

44

Forty-Fourth Lesson

Mr Duclos meets a client

1   Mr Duclos is [an] executive in a large oil firm.
2   Today, he is at the airport of Roissy to meet a Swiss
    client.

2   **Un cadre** is literally *the frame of* a painting. In a business context,
    un cadre is broadly speaking a member of middle management. The
    cadre system is fairly complex, so suffice it to say that the word is used
    in opposition to a manual or clerical worker. We translate it as *execu-
    tive* here.

3   **une société**, *a society*, in the socio-cultural sense, or, more commonly,
    a company, *a firm*. The business names of most French companies
    terminate with the initials SA or SARL, **société anonyme**, *public limited
    company*, or **société anonyme à responsabilité limitée**, *private limited
    company*.

4   **un client** (**une cliente**) is used both for *a customer* and *a client*.

3   Il l'attend devant la sortie de la douane.

4   "Le vol Air France deux mille huit cent
     soixante-sept en provenance de Genève

5   vient d'arriver [5] à la porte numéro six".

6   M. Duclos cherche parmi la foule des gens qui
     sortent,

7   mais il ne reconnaît personne [6]. Attendez...

8   Là-bas, l'homme en costume gris avec un
     magazine sous le bras...

9 – Ça doit_être lui, se dit M. Duclos. Je vais me
     présenter.

10   Il avance vers l'homme et, tendant [7] la main, lui
     dit :

11 – Permettez-moi de me présenter, je suis M.
     Duclos de la société IPF [8]

12 – Je ne comprends pas le français, dit l'homme
     avec un fort accent allemand.   ☐

🔊 4 ... *deu meel weesson swassohnt set* ... 5 ... *vyehn dareevay* ...
6 ... *sort* 8 ... *brah* 9 ... *sa dwataitr* ... 10 ... *tohndohn ... man* ... 11 ...
ee-pay-ef 12 ... *for aksohn* ...

🔲: Notes

5   *Je viens, I am coming / I come.* The verb can be used as an
     auxiliary in the idiomatic construction **venir de** meaning *"have just"*: **Je viens de
     manger**, *I have just eaten.* **Nous venons d'arriver**, *We have just arrived.*

6   **Je n'ai vu personne**, *I saw nobody.* Remember, we always need the
     double negative in French. **Personne n'est là**, *Nobody is there.* **Il n'aime
     personne**, *He doesn't like anybody.*

3 He [is] waiting [for] him in front of the exit of *(the)* customs.

4 "Air France flight 2867 *(coming)* from Geneva

5 has just arrived at *(the)* gate *(door)* No. 6.

6 Mr Duclos looks among the crowd of people who come out,

7 but he does not recognize anybody. Wait [a minute]...

8 Over there, the man in [the] grey suit with a magazine under his *(the)* arm...

9 – That must be him, says [to] himself Mr Duclos. I will *(am going)* introduce *(present)* myself.

10 He goes *(advances)* towards the man and, holding [out] his *(the)* hand, says to him:

11 – Allow me to introduce myself. I am Mr Duclos of *(the company)* IPF.

12 – I do not understand French, says the man with a strong German accent.

PRÉSENTEZ-MOI À VOTRE SOEUR.

7 tenir, *to hold*; tendre, *to hold out*. je tends, tu tends, il/elle tend, nous tendons, vous tendez, ils/elles tendent. Tendez votre assiette, *Hold out your plate*. Past participle: tendu.

8 This is a formal way of introducing oneself; a more "relaxed" phrase would be, Bonjour, je m'appelle Duclos.

▶ Exercice 1 – Traduisez

❶ Il a un magazine sous le bras. ❷ Vous venez d'arriver ?
– Oui, j'arrive de Genève. ❸ Je ne reconnais personne...
Attendez ! Ça doit être lui. ❹ Présentez-moi à votre sœur.
❺ L'homme en costume bleu avance vers la porte. ❻ J'ai
rencontré un ami en vacances.

***

Exercice 2 – Complétez

❶ Do you recognize anyone? – No, no one.
............-vous quelqu'un ? – Non, ...

❷ We have just arrived and we are tired.
Nous .... et nous sommes ....

❸ My brother is an executive in a large company.
Mon frère est ..... dans une grande ....

❹ Wait for me in front of the exit.
.... devant la ....

45

Quarante-cinquième leçon

▶ ## M. Duclos trouve son client

1 M. Duclos est perplexe...
2 Derrière lui, une voix dit :
  – Vous me cherchez, peut_-être ?
3 Je suis Marcel Chavan. Heureux de vous
  connaître.

💬 Pronunciation
1 ... pairpleks **3** ... shavohn

Answers to Exercice 1

❶ He has a magazine under his arm. ❷ You have just arrived? – Yes, I've come from Geneva. ❸ I don't recognize anybody... Wait! That must be him. ❹ Introduce me to your sister. ❺ The man in a blue suit goes towards the door. ❻ I met a friend on holiday.

***

❺ You must be Mr Duclos. Allow me to introduce myself.

Vous .... M. Duclos. Permettez-moi de ....

Answers to Exercice 2

❶ Reconnaissez – personne ❷ – venons d'arriver – fatigués ❸ – cadre – société ❹ Attendez-moi – sortie ❺ – devez être – me présenter

45

Forty-Fifth Lesson

Mr Duclos finds his client

1 Mr Duclos is puzzled...
2 Behind him, a voice says:
  – You're looking for me perhaps?
3 I am Marcel Chavan. Pleased to meet you *(Happy to know you)*.

4 – Enchanté [1]. Je suis Michel Duclos de la...

5 – Je sais, répond le Suisse avec un sourire ironique.

6 – Euh... Voulez-vous [2] me suivre ? Nous‿allons chercher ma voiture.

7 Les deux‿hommes se dirigent vers les‿ascenseurs.

8 – J'espère que vous‿avez fait bon voyage.

9 – Oui, ce n'était pas mal, quoique [3] je n'aime pas l'avion.

10 – Voulez-vous aller tout de suite à votre hôtel

11 ou voulez-vous passer au bureau d'abord ?

12 – Non, je veux déposer mes‿affaires d'abord. □

4 onshontay ... 5 ... eeroneek 7 ... deereezh ... layzasonseur 9 ... kwake ... 10 ... toot-sweet ... 12 ... daypozay mayzaffair ...

Notes

1 This exchange illustrates the formal greetings made by two people meeting for the first time. **Enchanté** is not as flowery as it sounds: it simply means *Delighted to meet you*. In an informal context, you could simply respond with **Bonjour** or **Bonsoir**, depending on the time of day.

Young people, close acquaintances – and some TV personalities attempting to be laid back – say **Salut !** *[salyoo]*.

4 – Delighted. I am Michel Duclos of *(the)*...

5 – I know, replies the Swiss with an ironic smile.

6 – Um... will you *(do you want to)* follow me? We are going to get *(look for)* my car.

7 The two men go *(direct themselves)* towards the lifts.

8 – I hope you had *(made)* a good journey.

9 – Yes, it wasn't bad, although I don't like planes *(the plane)*.

10 – Do you want to go immediately to your hotel

11 or do you want to go *(pass by)* to the office first?

12 – No, I want to drop off my things *(affairs)* first.

2 In this dialogue, we see the two uses of **Voulez-vous...** The literal meaning (lines 10 & 11) is clear: it is asking for a preference; the polite use (line 6) is a way of introducing a suggestion or a request and is the equivalent in English of *Will you...?* or *Would you mind...?*

3 **quoique** *[kwahke]* or **bien que**: both mean *although*. They are followed by a subjunctive, a "mood" of verb used when the content of the following clause is supposed or doubted. We will have plenty of opportunity to discover the subjunctive mood later on.

▶ Exercice 1 – Traduisez

❶ Il veut aller tout de suite à son hôtel. ❷ Voulez-vous bien me suivre, s'il vous plaît ? ❸ Je suis Michel Duclos. – Heureux de vous connaître. ❹ Je veux déposer mes affaires d'abord. ❺ Il n'a pas fait bon voyage, il était malade.

***

Exercice 2 – Complétez

❶ Although I don't like planes, it wasn't bad.
.... je n'aime pas ...., ce .. était pas mal.

❷ I'm Marcel Chavan. – Pleased to know you.
Je suis Marcel Chavan. – ....

❸ The two men go towards the lift.
Les deux hommes .... l'ascenseur.

46

Quarante-sixième leçon

▶ ## À l'hôtel

1   Les deux‿hommes arrivent devant l'entrée [1] de l'hôtel de Meaux.

2   C'est‿un hôtel quatre étoiles situé non loin des Champs-‿Élysées.

🗨 Pronunciation
1 ... lontray ... otel de mow 2 ... katraytwal ... lwan ... shonzayleezay

Answers to Exercice 1

❶ He wants to go straight to his hotel. ❷ Would you follow me, please? ❸ I am Michel Duclos. – Pleased to meet you. ❹ I want to drop off my things first. ❺ He didn't have a good trip, he was ill.

***

❹ Do you want to go immediately to the hotel?
   . . . . aller . . . . à l'hôtel ?

❺ Will you open the window, please?
   . . . . la fenêtre, s'il vous plaît ?

Answers to Exercice 2

❶ Quoique – l'avion – n' – ❷ – Enchanté ❸ – se dirigent vers –
❹ Voulez-vous – tout de suite – ❺ Voulez-vous ouvrir –

46

Forty-Sixth Lesson

At the hotel

1 The two men arrive in front of the entrance of the Hotel de Meaux.

2 It is a 4-star hotel situated not far from the Champs-Élysées.

Note

1 **l'entrée**, *the entrance*, can also mean *the lobby* or *the entrance hall*; **la sortie**, *the exit*; **sortie de secours**, *emergency exit*. (On a restaurant menu **l'entrée** is usually *the appetizer*, the dish with which you "enter" the meal.)

3 La première chose qu'ils voient ² est_un panneau marqué "Complet",

4 mais_ils ne s'inquiètent pas parce que M. Chavan a réservé sa chambre.

5 Ils s'approchent de la réception et le Suisse s'adresse à la réceptionniste :

6 – Bonjour, madame ; j'ai une chambre réservée au nom de Chavan.

7 – Une minute, s'il vous plaît. Quel nom avez-vous dit ? Je ne trouve rien.

8 Oh pardon. Voilà. Une chambre avec salle de bains réservée pour trois nuits.

9 C'est la chambre trois cent un (301) au troisième étage. Voilà le chasseur.

10 Merci ³ madame ; je préfère porter ma valise moi-même ⁴.

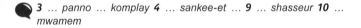

3 ... panno ... komplay 4 ... sankee-et ... 9 ... shasseur 10 ... mwamem

Notes

2 il voit *[eel vwa]* is singular; ils voient *[eel vwa]* is the plural but both are pronounced the same. Notice carefully the pronunciations of all of these plural verbs (or better still, listen to the recordings).

3 Be careful! **merci** means not only *thank you* but also *no thank you*! If, at a table, you are offered something which you wish to take, you would say **s'il vous plaît**; **merci** would be a refusal. Many a foreigner has missed out on second helpings because of this particularity! (Alternatively, you can always nod your head vigorously...)

3   The first thing which they see is a sign marked "No Vacancy" *(Full up)*,

4   but they don't worry because Mr Chavan has reserved his room.

5   They approach *(themselves of)* the reception and the Swiss addresses *(himself to)* the receptionist:

6 – Good morning madam, I have a room reserved in *(at)* the name of Chavan.

7 – One minute please. What name did you say *(have you said)*? I don't find anything *(nothing)*.

8   Oh, pardon. Here. A room with bathroom reserved for three nights.

9   It is *(the)* room 301 on the third floor. Here is the page-boy.

10   [No] Thank you madam; I prefer to carry my suitcase myself.

4   Like *myself, yourself*, etc. **moi-même, toi-même**, etc. are emphatic pronouns used to stress the "doer" of an action. **Si vous voulez du café, préparez-le vous-même,** *If you want coffee, make it yourself.* More later.

11 – Vous_êtes sûr, monsieur ? L'ascenseur est_en
panne [5] ! ☐

Note

5 Literally "broken down". **Une panne** is a *breakdown* (mechanical, elec-
trical, etc.). You will see the **en panne** sign on lifts, vending machines,
cars, etc. You may also see **Hors service**, which means that a machine
is not in use, but it is basically another way of saying the same thing!

***

Exercice 1 – Traduisez

❶ Ils voient une affiche "Complet", mais ils ne s'inquiètent
pas. ❷ J'ai une chambre réservée au nom de Duclos. ❸ Mais
je ne trouve rien ! ❹ Une minute, s'il vous plaît ! ❺ Voulez-
vous des carottes ? – Merci, je n'ai plus faim.

***

Exercice 2 – Complétez

❶ My car has broken down. Can you help me?
   Ma voiture est . . . . Pouvez-vous m'aider ?

❷ It is room 301.
   C'est la chambre . . . .

❸ The room is reserved in the name of Chavan.
   . . chambre est . . . . de Chavan.

11 – You're sure, sir? The lift is not working!

> **Tomber en panne**, *to break down*. And since French is a logical lan-
> guage, **dépanner** means *to repair a breadown*, and **un dépanneur** is a
> *repair man*. (In Quebec, **un dépanneur** is an all-night grocery store that
> "helps you out" when you run out of milk, matches, etc.)

***

Answers to Exercice 1

❶ They see a "No Vacancy" sign but they don't worry. ❷ I have a room reserved in the name of Duclos. ❸ But I can't find anything! ❹ One minute please! ❺ Do you want some carrots? – No thank you; I'm no longer hungry.

***

❹ Don't worry; there's no problem.
    Ne vous .... pas ; il n'. .... de problème.

❺ She is arriving at 9.30. – You are sure of that?
    Elle arrive à .... heures .... – Vous .. êtes ... ?

Answers to Exercice 2

❶ – en panne – ❷ – trois cent un ❸ La – réservée au nom – ❹ – inquiétez – y a pas – ❺ – neuf – et demie – en – sûr

47

Quarante-septième leçon

Pas si vite [1]

1 Devant une boîte de nuit, les gens font patiemment la queue,

2 attendant leur tour [2] malgré la pluie.

3 Tout_à coup un jeune homme arrive, bouscule quelques personnes

4 et se dirige résolument vers le début de la queue.

5 Une énorme main le saisit par le col de sa veste.

6 – Dites donc, le resquilleur [3] ! Vous_allez faire la queue comme tout le monde...

Pronunciation
1 ... bwat de nwee ... passeeamoh ... keu 2 ... malgray ... 3 tootakoo ... booskyool ... 5 ... sayzee ... 6 ... reskeeyeur ...

Notes

1 As in English, **vite**, *fast*, is both adjective and adverb. You can either say **conduire rapidement** or **conduire vite** for *to drive quickly, to drive fast*.

2 We regularly stress the importance of learning the gender at the same time as you learn a noun. Here is a good example of why: **un tour**, *a turn, a tour*. **C'est mon tour**, *It's my turn*; **le Tour de France**, *the Tour of France bicycle race*: a major annual sporting event. However **une tour** means *a tower*: **La Tour Montparnasse**, *The Montparnasse Tower*. Do try and memorise the gender of new words!

47

Forty-Seventh Lesson

Not so fast

1 In front of a night club (night box), (the) people are patiently queuing (make patiently the queue),

2 waiting their turn despite the rain.

3 Suddenly (All a blow) a young man arrives, jostles a few people

4 and goes resolutely towards the beginning of the queue.

5 An enormous hand seizes him by the collar of his jacket.

6 – Hey, queue-jumper! You are going to queue up like everybody...

3 Here, and in the next line, we meet our first slang words: **resquiller** (which some say is a national pastime...), means *queue-jumping*, or slipping into a cinema, bus, etc. without paying; **un resquilleur** (**une resquilleuse**) is the person who does it. **Dites-donc** means something like: *Hey you!*

7 ou bien... Le costaud [4] n'a pas besoin de terminer sa phrase !

8 – C'est comme vous voulez, monsieur, répond le jeune homme,

9 mais si je ne passe pas maintenant,

10 vous_allez tous [5] attendre longtemps...

11 La sono est_en panne et je suis le dépanneur ! □

*7 ... kostoh ... **10** ... voo ... tooss ...*

Notes

4 costaud as an adjective means *strong*, *hefty*, or *large*, and **un costaud** (no feminine) describes such a person. L'**argot**, *slang*, is widely used in everyday speech, in the popular press and on TV. However, a non-native speaker should beware of using slang unless he or she is reasonably fluent – and is sure of the meaning and impact of the words used. We'll

***

Exercice 1 – Traduisez

❶ Faites la queue ici, s'il vous plaît. **❷** Nous attendons tous notre tour. **❸** Malgré la pluie, je vais au cinéma ce soir. **❹** Vous n'avez pas besoin de tous ces vêtements. **❺** C'est comme vous voulez, monsieur.

***

Exercice 2 – Complétez

❶ The queue-jumper never queues up.

Le .... ne .... la queue.

❷ Do like everybody else!

Faites comme .... !

❸ Fortunately he's hefty; this suitcase is heavy!

Heureusement qu'il est ....; cette valise est lourde !

7 or else... The hefty *(man)* doesn't need to finish his
sentence!

8 – It's as you like, sir, answers the young man,

9 but if I don't get through *(pass)* now,

10 all of you *(you all)* are going to wait *(a)* long time.

11 The sound system is broken *(down)* and I'm the
repair man!

help you get a feel for the words you can use and those you'd best
avoid. Meanwhile, **costaud** is perfectly acceptable!

5 Remember that when **tous** is a pronoun, it is pronounced *[toos]*.

***

Answers to Exercice 1

❶ Queue up here please. ❷ We are all waiting our turn. ❸ Despite the
rain, I'm going to the cinema this evening. ❹ You don't need all those
clothes. ❺ It's up to you, sir.

***

❹ Despite the price, I'm going to buy it.
...... le prix, je vais ....

❺ The Tour of France passes in front of the Eiffel Tower.
.. .. de France passe devant .. .. Eiffel.

Answers to Exercice 2

❶ – resquilleur – fait jamais – ❷ – tout le monde ❸ – costaud –
❹ Malgré – l'acheter ❺ Le Tour – la tour –

48

Quarante-huitième leçon

Quelques expressions idiomatiques

1 – Ne faites pas de bruit ; je suis en train [1]
d'enregistrer !
2 – Qu'est-ce que c'est que ce machin ? [2]
– C'est pour écrire à l'envers [3].
3 – Lequel de ces deux pulls voulez-vous ?
– Ça m'est égal.
4 – Ce n'est pas la peine de crier ; je suis sourd
comme un pot.
5 – J'espère qu'il a l'habitude de voyager beaucoup
s'il accepte cet emploi.

Pronunciation
*1 ... ooonrezheestray 2 ... ma-shahn ... alonvair 3 ... pyool ... 4 ...
pa la pen ... poh 5 ... labeetyood ...*

Notes

1 We said earlier that the present tense in French translates both English
present tenses (I work; I am working). If, however, we wish to insist upon
the present aspect of an action – "I'm in the middle of..." etc., we add
être en train de before the verb: **Je suis en train d'écrire**, *I am busy
writing.*

Forty-Eighth Lesson

Note: *Because idioms are impossible to translate literally, we have tried where possible to give an English equivalent.*

A few idiomatic expressions

1 – Don't make any noise; I'm busy recording!
2 – What on earth is that thing?
   – It's for writing backwards.
3 – Which of these two sweaters do you want?
   – I don't mind.
4 – It's useless shouting: I'm as deaf as a post.
5 – I hope he's used to travelling a lot if he takes that job.

2 **machin** and its bed-fellow **truc** – both masculine – are real life-savers: they mean **thingammy-bob**, **whatname**, etc. and can fill in for any word missing from your vocabulary until you learn the correct one. Memorise them now!

3 à l'envers, *backwards* (for direction, not education); à l'endroit, *the right way around*. **You're wearing it back to front**, *Vous le portez à l'envers*.

6 – Passe-moi un coup de fil [4] si tu as le temps.

7 – Est-ce que je peux vous poser une question ?
   – Allez-_y [5].

8 – Qu'est-ce qu'il y a ? Vous_êtes malade ?

9   Il vaut mieux être riche et en bonne santé

10   que pauvre et malade !   □

6 ... koodefeel ... **7** ... allayzee **9** ... voh myeu ...

Exercice 1 – Traduisez
❶ Mon fils me passe un coup de fil tous les mardis. ❷ Nous sommes en train d'apprendre le français. ❸ Elle a l'habitude de faire la cuisine : elle a une grande famille. ❹ Vous êtes prêt ? Bien, allez-y ! ❺ Votre pull est à l'envers !

**

Exercice 2 – Complétez
❶   Which of these two wines do you want? – I don't mind.
   ...... de ces deux vins voulez-vous ? – Ça ....

❷   It's useless insisting: I haven't got any more money.
   Ce n'est .... d'insister ; je n'ai .... d'argent.

❸   He gave me a ring last week.
   Il m'a ...... un .... la semaine dernière.

6 – Give me a ring if you have time.
7 – Can I ask you a question?
   – Go ahead.
8 – What's up? Are you sick?
9 It's better to be rich and healthy *(in good health)*
10 than poor and sick!

Notes

4 un fil *[feel]* is *a wire*. The plural, of course, has an unpronounced **s**: des fils *[feel]*. <u>Do not confuse this</u> with: un fils *[feess]*, *a son* (plural des fils *[feess]*). Obviously, the context is of capital importance! un coup de fil, *a phone call* (*a buzz* or *a ring*).

5 **Allez-y** is a very useful expression that can be used whenever you want someone to go ahead and do an action: cross the road, walk in front of you, start eating, etc. It is best translated as *Go on*, *Go ahead*.

***

Answers to Exercice 1
❶ My son rings me every Tuesday. ❷ We are busy learning French. ❸ She is used to cooking: she has a large family. ❹ Ready? Well, go ahead! ❺ Your jumper is on back to front!

***

❹ What on earth is that thing? – I don't know.
   Qu'est- . . . . que ce . . . . . .? – Je ne sais pas.

❺ It's better to be rich than poor.
   Il . . . . être riche . . . pauvre.

Answers to Exercice 2
❶ Lequel – m'est égal ❷ – pas la peine – plus – ❸ – passé – coup de fil – ❹ – ce que c'est – machin – ❺ – vaut mieux – que –

Quarante-neuvième leçon

Révision – Revision

1 Who... Which... / *Qui... Que...* (continued)

We have already seen that **qui** and **que** are used to express *which, that, who(m)*, etc. depending on whether the relative is the subject (**qui**) or object (**que**) of the sentence.
We also know the compound relatives **ce qui** and **ce que**.
Now we have a plural form:
ceux qui – ceux que:
Ceux qui veulent venir, dépêchez-vous !, *Those who* (subject) *want to come, hurry up!*
Prenez ceux que vous voulez et laissez le reste, *Take those that you want and leave the rest.*

2 Must, *Devoir*

devoir: **je dois** *[dwah]*, **tu dois**, **il/elle doit**, **nous devons**, **vous devez**, **ils/elles doivent** *[dwahv]*.
This verb expresses the idea of *must*, *to have to*.
It is generally followed by an infinitive.
Nous devons partir, *We must leave.*
Il ne doit pas boire, *He mustn't drink.*
Ça doit être eux, *That must be them.*
The past participle is **dû**. Note the circumflex (^) over the **u**, to distinguish the part participle (**dû**) from the partitive article (**du**). The circumflex does not alter the pronunciation.
Elle a dû partir means either *She had to leave* or *She must have left*. Another simplification. (**devoir** means also *to owe*).

Forty-Ninth Lesson

49

3 To be worth, *Valoir*

Another common and idiomatic verb is **valoir**, *to be worth*. It is usually found in these forms:

Ça vaut très cher, *It is worth a lot*;

Ils ne valent rien, *They are worth nothing*;

and in these idioms:

Est-ce que ça vaut la peine ?, *Is it worth the trouble?*

Il vaut mieux partir, *You had better leave.*

Est-ce qu'il vaut mieux acheter un appartement ou en louer un ?, *Is it better to buy an apartment or to rent one?*

We will gradually see more and more such idioms whenever they crop up naturally.

The "second wave"

So far, your studying has been passive – all we have asked you to do is to read, understand and let the feel of the language sink in. Tomorrow the active phase begins: it will add about five minutes to your daily study. Here is what we want you to do:

When you have been through lesson 50 in the usual way, go back to lesson 1. After listening to the French text again and reading through it aloud, cover it up and try to reproduce it from the translation opposite. Check through afterwards. Lesson 51 will send you back to lesson 2 and so on.

This is the way to consolidate and develop your knowledge, going from the receptive stage to the reproductive stage until finally you reach – in your own time – the creative, or generative stage.

But, whatever you do, make sure you are enjoying yourself!

50

Cinquantième leçon

Une lettre

1 Chers maman et papa, Me voici à la fin de mes vacances dans le Midi ¹.

2 J'ai fait beaucoup de choses et j'ai rencontré plein de ² gens.

3 Avant-_hier, j'ai visité la Camargue ³. Quelle merveille !

4 J'ai même essayé de monter à cheval...

5 Malheureusement, le résultat n'était pas brillant !

6 Hier, j'ai téléphoné à Oncle Jacques, qui vous_embrasse,

7 et j'ai acheté plein de cadeaux pour vous.

8 Malheureusement, j'ai oublié d'apporter mon_appareil photo ⁴ ;

Pronunciation
1 ... me vwassee ... 2 zhay fay ... zhay ronkontray ... 3 avonteeyair ... veezeetay ... kamarg ... mervay 4 ... essayay ... 5 ... rayzoolta ... etay ... breeyohn 6 eeyair ... telefohnay ... 8 ... oobleeyay ... apparay ...

Notes

1 Remember (lesson 24, note 1) that **le Midi** is not, as one would expect, the middle of France, but the *south*! **Un accent du Midi**, *a southern accent*, but **il est midi**, *it is 12.00 midday*.

2 A colloquial way of saying **beaucoup de**, *a lot of*. It is invariable. **J'ai plein de travail en ce moment**, *I've tons of work at the moment*. **On a rencontré plein de gens**, *We met loads of people*.

Fiftieth Lesson

A letter

1 Dear Mum and Dad, Here I am near the end of my holiday(s) in the

2 I have done many things and I have met loads of people.

3 [The day] before yesterday, I *(have)* visited the Camargue. What [a] marvel!

4 I *(have)* even tried to ride *(mount to)* a horse...

5 Unfortunately the result wasn't brilliant!

6 Yesterday, I *(have)* phoned *(to)* Uncle Jack, who sends his love *(kisses you)*,

7 and I *(have)* bought loads of presents for you.

8 Unfortunately I *(have)* forgotten to take my camera.

J'AI MÊME ESSAYÉ DE MONTER À CHEVAL.

3 **La Camargue** is a beautiful, wild region of lakes and marshes on the Mediterranean coast to the east of Montpellier. It is famous for its white ponies and its gypsy heritage.

4 There is a series of words in French that we call "false friends"; they look like English words but mean something different. **Une caméra** is a good example: it means *a movie camera. A camera* is **un appareil photo**. For more detailed analysis – and more examples – see lesson 105.

9 j'ai emprunté celui de Michel, mais_il n'a pas marché.

10 Donc j'ai acheté des cartes postales, c'est mieux [5] que rien.

11 Je sais que cette lettre n'est pas très longue

12 mais au moins, ça prouve que j'ai pensé à vous.

13 Je vous_embrasse bien fort.
    Paul   ☐

🗨 **9** ... *ompruntay* ... *marshay* **10** ... *ashtay* ... **12** ... *ponssay* ...

***

▶ Exercice 1 – Traduisez

❶ C'est une carte postale, mais c'est mieux que rien. ❷ Hier, nous avons visité la Camargue. ❸ Vous n'avez pas acheté trop de cadeaux, j'espère. ❹ Elle a oublié son appareil photo... ❺ ... mais elle a emprunté celui de son cousin.

***

Exercice 2 – Complétez

❶ I've done loads of things and I've bought a lot of presents.
   J'ai fait .... choses et j'ai ...... beaucoup de ....

❷ My brother played better than me.
   ... frère a .... que moi.

❸ I phoned Uncle Jack, who sends his love.
   J'............. Oncle Jacques qui vous ....

❹ The holidays are approaching their end.
   ..... la fin ....

9 I (have) borrowed Michel's (the one of Michel), but it
   did not (has not) work.
10 Thus I (have) bought postcards; it's better than nothing.
11 I know that this letter isn't very long
12 but at least it proves that I (have) thought of you.
13 All my love (I kiss you very strong).
   Paul

Note

5 We have already come across this word: it is an irregular comparative
of **bien**. **Il joue bien**, *He plays well*; **elle joue mieux que lui**, *she plays
better than him*. Don't forget that French uses **bien** for *good*.

***

Answers to Exercice 1

❶ It's a postcard, but it's better than nothing. ❷ Yesterday we visited
the Camargue. ❸ You haven't bought too many presents, I hope.
❹ She forgot her camera, ❺ but she borrowed her cousin's.

***

❺ I forgot my pen, so I borrowed Michel's.
   J'........ mon stylo, donc j'.. .... de Michel.

Answers to Exercice 2

❶ – plein de – acheté – cadeaux ❷ Mon – joué mieux – ❸ – ai
téléphoné à – embrasse ❹ Voici – des vacances ❺ – ai oublié – ai
emprunté celui –

***Please spend the extra time necessary to do this "second wave";
it's worth the effort!***

Second wave: 1st Lesson

51

Cinquante et unième leçon

R.S.V.P. [1]

1 – Et maintenant, quelques questions : où est Paul ?

2 – Qu'est-ce qu'il a fait avant-_hier ? [2]

3 – Est-ce qu'il a visité Montpellier ?

4 Quand_est-ce qu'il a téléphoné à Oncle Jacques ?

5 Est-ce qu'il a pris des photos ? Pourquoi ?

6 Qu'est-ce qu'il a essayé de faire en [3] Camargue ?

7 À qui est-ce qu'il écrit ?

8 – Quelle dure journée aujourd'hui au bureau !

9 Nous_avons travaillé comme quatre.

10 – Vous devez_être épuisé !

11 – Pas tellement [4]. Nous sommes huit_au bureau ! □

 Pronunciation

*air ess vay pay **3** … monpeleeyay **4** konteske … **10** … aypweezay*

Notes

1   If you have received a formal invitation, you will know these letters **Répondez S'il Vous Plaît**, *Please Reply*. When writing informally, the French often abbreviate **s'il vous plaît** to **svp**.

2   As with the present tenses, we are showing the less formal (i.e. spoken) way of forming questions. When this has become almost automatic, we will introduce the more elegant form.

51

Fifty-First Lesson

R.S.V.P.

1 – And now, a few questions: Where is Paul?
2 – What did he do [the day] before yesterday?
3 – Did he visit Montpellier?
4 When did he phone *(to)* Uncle Jack?
5 Did he take [any] photos? Why [not]?
6 What did he try to do in [the] Camargue?
7 Who is he writing to?
8 – What [a] hard day today at the office!
9 We worked like four.
10 – You must be exhausted!
11 – Not too much. There are eight of us *(we are 8)* in the office!

---

3 la **Camargue**, *the Camargue*; la **Bretagne**, *Brittany*, but we say: **Elle va en Bretagne tous les ans**, *She goes to Brittany every year*. **Nous prenons nos vacances en Normandie**, *We take our holidays in Normandy*. When you are in a region or going to a region, you replace the definite article (**le**, **la**) by **en**. For administrative purposes, France is divided into 22 regions and 100 areas called **départements** *(m.)*. But, as in most countries, the geographical and political areas do not always coincide. So la **Camargue**, for example, is in the Rhône delta in the South of France. But it is not a region in the political sense of the term. Anyone who spends any time in France will quickly come to appreciate the importance of regional identity.

4 Il fait **tellement** chaud !, *It is so hot!* **Aimez-vous le champagne ? – Pas tellement**, *Do you like champagne? – Not so* ("much"). **Il a tellement d'argent qu'il est malheureux**, *He has so much money that he is unhappy*.

▶ Exercice 1 – Traduisez

❶ Est-ce que vous avez visité la Normandie ? ❷ Est-ce qu'il a essayé ce chapeau ? ❸ À qui est-ce que vous avez parlé au téléphone ? ❹ Quelle dure journée ! Je suis épuisé ! ❺ J'ai tellement de travail aujourd'hui !

Exercice 2 – Complétez

❶ Last year, we visited Brittany.
L'année dernière, nous . . . . Bretagne.

❷ Have you brought your photos?
. . . . vous . . . . vos photos ?

❸ They have bought a house in Normandy.
Ils . . . . une maison . . Normandie.

❹ We must leave the day after tomorrow.
Nous . . . . . . partir . . . .

❺ When did the film begin?
. . . . le film . commencé ?

52

Cinquante-deuxième leçon

⏺ ## Un entretien d'embauche

1 – Eh bien, M. Lopez, vous voulez travailler pour nous ?

2 – Oui, c'est ça. Je n'ai pas d'emploi actuellement [1].

🗩 Pronunciation
… ontretyen dombohsh 2 … omplwa …

Answers to Exercice 1

❶ Have you visited Normandy? ❷ Has he tried this hat? ❸ To whom did you speak on the phone? ❹ What a hard day! I'm exhausted! ❺ I have so much work today!

Answers to Exercice 2

❶ – avons visité la – ❷ Est-ce que – avez apporté – ❸ – ont acheté – en – ❹ – devons – après-demain ❺ Quand est-ce que – a –

Second wave: 2nd Lesson

52

Fifty-Second Lesson

A job interview *(hiring)*

1 – Well, Mr Lopez, you want to work for us?
2 – Yes, that's right. I don't have a job at the moment.

] Note

1 Another "false friend": **actuellement** means *now*, *at the moment*. The adjective is **actuel** (f. **actuelle**), *current*, *present*. We have seen that **les actualités** means the news (i.e. "current events"). Our word *actually* is **en effet** (and is much less used than in English).

3 – Alors dites-moi : qu'est-ce que vous avez fait jusqu'à maintenant ?

4 – Oh, j'ai fait beaucoup de métiers dans ma vie.

5 J'ai conduit [2] des camions, j'ai joué du piano dans un cabaret...

6 – Oui, très intéressant, mais est-ce que vous avez travaillé dans la haute couture ?

7 – Ben, en quelque sorte [3]. Mais j'ai aussi construit [4] des maisons.

8 J'ai vendu [5] des glaces aux Esquimaux...

9 – Sans doute. Mais dans la haute couture ?

10 – Vous tenez [6] absolument à le savoir ?
    – Bien sûr !

11 – Eh bien, quand j'étais en prison, j'ai repassé des chemises !   □

3 ... *zhooska* ... **4** ... *meteeyay* ... **5** ... *kondwee* ... *zhooay* ... *kabaray* ... **6** ... *owt kootyoor* **7** ... *konstrwee* ... **8** ... *owzeskeemow* **11** ... *repassay* ...

Notes

2 conduire, *to drive*; je conduis, tu conduis, il/elle conduit, nous conduisons, vous conduisez, ils/elles conduisent *[kondweez]*. Past participle: conduit.

3 en quelque sorte is a very useful expression meaning: *in a certain way, in a manner of speaking*.

4 construire, *to build* conjugated like conduire.

3 – Well, tell me: what have you done up to now?

4 – Oh, I have done many jobs in my life.

5   I have driven lorries, I have played *(of)* the piano in a cabaret...

6 – Yes, very interesting, but have you worked in *(the high)* fashion?

7 – Well, in a manner of speaking. But I have also built houses.

8   I have sold ice-creams to Eskimos...

9 – Without doubt. But in *(the high)* fashion?

10 – You insist absolutely on knowing?
    – Of course!

11 – Well, when I was in prison, I ironed shirts!

5 vendre, past participle: **vendu**. rendre, *to give back*, **rendu**, etc.

6 tenir, *to hold*. je tiens, tu tiens, il/elle tient, nous tenons, vous tenez, ils/elles tiennent *[tyen]*. Past participle: **tenu**. This idiomatic construction (followed by **à**) means: *to insist on*, *to hold on to*... Il tient à le faire, *He insists on doing it*. Elle y tient comme à la prunelle de ses yeux, *She treasures it/him/her*. (This is an almost literal translation of the English idiom "It's the apple of her eye".) Vous tenez absolument à savoir ?, *You really want to know?*

▶ Exercice 1 – Traduisez

❶ Ils ont construit de nouveaux immeubles là-bas. ❷ Qu'est-ce que tu fais actuellement ? ❸ Êtes-vous poète ? – En quelque sorte, j'écris des slogans *[slowgohn]* publicitaires. ❹ Vous tenez absolument à y aller ? ❺ Racontez-moi une histoire. ❻ Il a fait beaucoup de métiers.

***

Exercice 2 – Complétez

❶ What has he done already?
Qu'est- . . . .il . déjà .... ?

❷ He doesn't like his present job.
Il n'aime pas . . . .

❸ When I was in prison, I ironed shirts.
Quand j'. . . . . .. prison, j'ai repassé des . . . .

53

Cinquante-troisième leçon

▶ ## Encore le passé !

1 – Regardez ce que j'ai trouvé ! Une carte de crédit !
2 – Ça alors ! J'en_ai justement perdu une !

***

3 – Est-ce que vous_avez vu ¹ le nouveau film de Blanchard ?
4 – Non, je voulais ² le voir mais je n'ai pas_encore eu le temps.

🗣 Pronunciation
4 ... voolay ... pazonkhor yoo ...

Answers to Exercice 1

❶ They have built some new blocks of flats over there. **❷** What are you doing at the moment? **❸** Are you a poet? – In a manner of speaking. I write advertising slogans. **❹** You really want to go there? **❺** Tell me a story. **❻** He has done a lot of jobs.

***

❹ It's undoubtedly very interesting.
C'est très intéressant . . . .

❺ She has never driven a car.
Elle n'. . . . . de voiture.

Answers to Exercice 2

❶ – ce qu' – a – fait **❷** – son emploi actuel **❸** – étais en – chemises
❹ – sans doute **❺** – a jamais conduit –

Second wave: 3rd Lesson

53

Fifty-Third Lesson

The past again!

1 – Look what I've found! A credit card!
2 – There's a thing! It just so happens *(justly)* that I have lost one!

***

3 – Have you seen the new film by *(of)* Blanchard?
4 – No, I wanted to see it but I haven't yet had the time.

Notes

1 voir, *to see*. Past participle: vu.

2 voulais is the "imperfect" tense of vouloir, *to want*. We'll see it in greater detail later on.

5 – Qu'est-ce qu'il y a ? Tu as le cafard [3] ?

6 – Oui ; ce matin, j'ai reçu [4] ma feuille d'impôts ;

7   hier, j'ai reçu deux factures, un relevé [5] d'électricité

8   et mon relevé de banque : je n'ai plus un sou [6].

***

9 – Est-ce qu'ils_ont fini leur repas ? Je veux débarrasser la table.

10 – Ils_ont commencé il y a [7] deux_heures à peu près,

11   mais ils n'ont pas_encore pris le dessert [8]. □

5 ... *kafar* **6** ... *foy dampoh* **7** ... *relevay* ... **11** ... *dayssair*

: Notes

3   **un cafard** is literally *a cockroach*! Anyone who has ever been infested with roaches knows how depressing it can be. Hence **avoir le cafard** means *to be down in the dumps*. **Ses films me donnent le cafard**, *His/Her films really depress me.*

4   **recevoir**, *to receive*. **je reçois, tu reçois, il/elle reçoit, nous recevons, vous recevez, ils/elles reçoivent** *[reswahv]*. Past participle: **reçu.**

5   **une facture** or **une addition** both mean *bill* or *invoice* (the latter is especially used for restaurant bills), **un relevé** is a word used for electricity, gas or phone bills – or, as in line 8, *a bank statement.*

Another word for a bill, generally used in hotels, is **la note** *[nott]*. **Voulez-vous me préparer la note, s'il vous plaît ?**, *Woud you prepare my bill, please?* All three words have two things in common: they are all feminine – and they all mean that you have to pay!

5 – What's the matter? [Are you] down in the dumps?

6 – Yes. This morning I got *(received)* my tax-form;

7 yesterday, I received two bills, an electricity bill

8 and my bank statement: I haven't got a bean.

***

9 – Have they finished their meal? I want to clear the table.

10 – They began about two hours ago,

11 but they haven't yet had *(taken the)* dessert.

6 **un sou** is an ancient French coin, which no longer exists. Interestingly, the Latin root of **sou** – *solidus* – is the same word that gave the English their "solidi" in the pre-decimal currency system (£.s.d.). Today, **le sou** is used in familiar language to mean *money*. **Il est près de ses sous**, *He is close to his money* (i.e. miserly). **Je n'ai pas un sou**, *I haven't a penny*. Another way of saying **je n'ai pas un sou** would be **je suis fauché**, meaning *I'm broke* (from the verb **faucher**, *to reap*).

7 We know **il y a** meaning *there is* or *there are*. If we find it before a measure of time, it means *ago*. **Je l'ai vu il y a cinq minutes**, *I saw it* ("him") *5 minutes ago*. Notice it must be placed before the noun.

8 **prendre**, *to take*. Past participle: **pris**.

▶ Exercice 1 – Traduisez

❶ J'en ai perdu un il y a deux minutes. ❷ Qu'est-ce qu'elle a ? – Elle a le cafard. ❸ Est-ce que vous avez fini votre repas ? ❹ Non, je n'ai pas encore pris le dessert. ❺ Elle n'a pas encore eu le temps de le voir. ❻ Ils ont débarrassé la table il y a un quart d'heure.

***

Exercice 2 – Complétez

❶ He is broke; he hasn't got a bean!
Il est fauché *[foshay]*; il .. a ..... /un ... !

❷ Is that a credit card? I have lost one.
C'est une ....? J'......... une.

❸ I always wanted to see that film.
J'ai toujours ..... voir ce film.

❹ I haven't seen it/him yet.
Je .. l'..... encore ...

54

Cinquante-quatrième leçon

▶ ## Une mauvaise rencontre

1   Un jour, à Lille, M. Le Clerc va faire des courses [1].

2   Au marché, il rencontre un_étranger [2] – un grand_homme [3] habillé en noir.

💬 Pronunciation
1 ... koors 2 ... etronzhay ... grontom abeeyay ...

🗂 Notes

1   **faire des courses**, *to go shopping* (usually in the market). **Une course** is also *a race*.

Answers to Exercice 1

❶ I lost one of them two minutes ago. ❷ What's the matter with her? – She's down in the dumps. ❸ Have you finished your meal? ❹ No, I haven't yet had dessert. ❺ She hasn't yet had time to see it/him. ❻ They cleared the table a quarter of an hour ago.

***

❺ This morning, I received two bills and my bank statement.
Ce matin, ... deux .... et mon ...... de banque.

Answers to Exercice 2

❶ – n' – pas le – sou ❷ – carte de crédit – en ai perdu – ❸ – voulu – ❹ – ne – ai pas – vu ❺ – j'ai reçu – factures – relevé –

Second wave: 4th Lesson

54

Fifty-Fourth Lesson

An unfortunate (bad) encounter

1 One day in Lille, Mr Le Clerc goes shopping.
2 At the market, he meets a stranger – a tall man dressed in black.

2 **un étranger** has two meanings: *a stranger* (someone you don't know) and *a foreigner*. The context should help you determine which of the two is meant. **Étrange** (adj.), *strange, unusual*.

3 **grand** means *big*, but applied to a person, can also mean *tall*. For a building, we would say **haut** *[oh]*.

3 L'étranger lui dit :
– Mais que faites-vous ici, M. Le Clerc ?

4 – Qui êtes-vous ? dit notre homme.
– Je suis la Mort.

5 Terrifié [4], M. Le Clerc rentre à la maison, fait sa valise

6 et dit à sa femme :
– J'ai rencontré la Mort.

7 Je pars pour Toulouse. Adieu [5] chérie !

8 Mme Le Clerc est furieuse [6] : elle croit à [7] une mauvaise plaisanterie.

9 Alors elle va au marché et trouve le grand étranger.

10 – Pourquoi avez-vous effrayé mon mari ?

11 La Mort lui répond :
– Eh bien, madame, je suis surpris :

12 j'ai vu votre mari à Lille, mais j'ai rendez-vous avec lui

13 ce soir... à Toulouse. □

7 ... adyeu ... 8 ... krwa ... plezontree

Notes

4 The past participle is also used as an adjective, in which case it will naturally agree. If we were talking about Mrs Le Clerc, we would write **terrifiée** (the pronunciation does not alter).

5 This way of saying goodbye has an air of finality, i.e. the next time we see each other it will be with *God* (**Dieu**). In some parts of France, it is colloquially used to replace the usual *Au revoir !*

3 The stranger says to him:
– But what are you doing here, Mr Le Clerc?
4 – Who are you? says our man.
– I am Death.
5 Terrified, Mr Le Clerc goes back to his house, packs *(does)* his case
6 and says to his wife:
– I met Death.
7 I'm leaving for Toulouse. Goodbye darling!
8 Mrs Le Clerc is furious; she believes it is a bad joke.
9 So she goes to the market and finds the tall stranger.
10 – Why did you frighten my husband?
11 Death replies:
– Well, madam, I am surprised:
12 I saw your husband in Lille but I have [a] meeting with him
13 this evening... in Toulouse.

6 *m.* furieu**x**.

7 **croire**, *to believe*; je crois, tu crois, il/elle croit, nous croyons, vous croyez, ils/elles croient *[krwah]* – Past participle: **cru**. Note that French uses: **Je crois** where English says: *I think so.* **Croire en quelqu'un**, *to believe in someone*, i.e. *to trust, to have faith in him/her.* **Croire en quelque chose**, *to believe something be true.*

▶ Exercice 1 – Traduisez

❶ Elle a vu son mari au marché et elle est surprise. ❷ Est-ce qu'il vient demain ? – Je crois. ❸ Il rentre à la maison et fait sa valise. ❹ J'ai rendez-vous avec lui à dix heures et demie. ❺ C'est un grand homme habillé en noir.

***

Exercice 2 – Complétez

❶ She has met Death and she is terrified.
   Elle a ……… la Mort et elle est ……….

❷ Do you believe in God?
   Est-ce que vous …… … Dieu ?

❸ I'm leaving in five minutes to do the shopping.
   Je …. dans cinq minutes pour …… …… ………

55

Cinquante-cinquième leçon

… mais il a surtout bu

1 L'autre soir, M. Zitoun a assisté à un cocktail ¹ au bureau.

🗣 Pronunciation
1 … koktel …

📖 Note

1 Three examples (lines 1, 2 and 4) of how English words are taken directly into French – a trend definitely frowned upon but seemingly inevitable. Loan words are generally assigned the masculine gender, and plurals

Answers to Exercice 1

❶ She saw her husband at the market and she is surprised. ❷ He is coming tomorrow? – I think so. ❸ He goes back to the house and packs his suitcase. ❹ I have a meeting with him at 10.30. ❺ He's a tall man dressed in black.

***

❹ But what are you doing here?
Mais que ......-.... ici ?

❺ This story is a little strange.
..... histoire est un peu ....

Answers to Exercice 2

❶ – rencontré – terrifiée ❷ – croyez en – ❸ – pars – faire les courses ❹ – faites-vous – ❺ Cette – étrange

Second wave: 5th Lesson

55

Fifty-Fifth Lesson

... but above all he drank

1 The other evening, Mr Zitoun went to *(attended at)* a cocktail [party] at the office.

are formed by simply adding an **s**. Be careful! Sometimes, the way a loan word is used in French bears little relation to its original English meaning. For example, **un smoking** is *a dinner suit* or *dinner jacket*. **Un cocktail** is not a drink, but *a cocktail party* or, usually, *a reception* or *drinks party*. Other "approximate" usages include **un parking**, *a car park*, **un shampooing**, *a shampoo* and **un meeting**, *a political rally* (see lesson 80).

2   Il a mangé quelques petits sandwichs et des canapés

3   mais_il a surtout bu ² !

4   Il a bu quatre grands whiskys

5   et ensuite il a vidé une bouteille de champagne !

6   À dix_heures, il a décidé de rentrer chez lui.

7   Il a laissé sa voiture et il a pris un taxi.

8   Arrivé devant sa maison, il a réalisé qu'il n'avait ³ pas ses clefs ⁴.

9   Alors il a voulu entrer par la fenêtre, mais, étant_un peu ivre,

10   il n'a pas pu ⁵ : il a cassé un carreau.

11   Tout_à coup, quelqu'un a ouvert la fenêtre en haut

12   et a crié :
      – Mais qu'est-ce que vous faites, Bon Dieu ?

13   C'était la maison de son voisin !   ☐

2 … sondweesh … 3 … byoo 4 … weeskee 5 … veeday … 8 … navay … klay 9 … eevr 10 … pyoo … karroh 11 … on oh 13 setay …

Notes

2   boire, *to drink*; je bois, tu bois, il/elle boit, nous buvons, vous buvez, ils/elles boivent *[bwahv]*. Past participle: **bu**. Une boisson, *a drink*.

3   We have already seen j'**étais**, il **était**, *I/he was*, j'**avais**, il **avait**, *I/he had*. This is the imperfect tense, which we will look at in detail later. Note how these two forms are used in this text.

2 He ate a few small sandwiches and some canapés
3 but above all he drank!
4 He drank four large whiskies
5 and afterwards he emptied a bottle of champagne!
6 At 10.00 p.m. he decided to go back home.
7 He left his car and *(he)* took a taxi.
8 Arriving *(arrived)* in front of his house, he realised that he didn't have his keys.
9 So he wanted to enter through *(by)* the window but, being a little drunk,
10 he couldn't: he broke a [window]-pane.
11 Suddenly, someone opened the window above *(on high)*
12 and shouted:
  – But what are you doing, for God's sake *(good God)*?
13 It was his neighbour's house!

---

4 une clef, *a key*, is sometimes written une clé (pl. des clés); this does not change the meaning. **Fermer à clef**, *to lock. To unlock* is simply ouvrir. As in English, la clef can be used figuratively: C'est l'homme clé de l'entreprise, *He's the key person in the company.*

5 pouvoir, *to be able*; je peux, tu peux, il/elle peut, nous pouvons, vous pouvez, ils/elles peuvent. Past participle: pu.

▶ Exercice 1 – Traduisez

❶ Pouvez-vous assister à la réunion* ce soir ? ❷ Ils ont bu trois bouteilles de champagne ! ❸ Il n'avait pas ses clefs et il n'a pas pu entrer. ❹ Étant un peu ivre, il a cassé un carreau. ❺ Nous avons laissé notre voiture et nous allons prendre un taxi.

*la réunion: *the meeting*

***

Exercice 2 – Complétez

❶ They wanted to go in through the window.
Ils .... entrer ... la fenêtre.

❷ He heard a voice; it was his neighbour.
Il a entendu une voix *[vwa]* ; .... son ....

❸ He ate but, above all, he drank.
Il . ..., mais il a ....

56

Cinquante-sixième leçon

Révision – Revision

1 Which... / What..., *Quel/le...*

We know that **quel/quelle**, etc. means *which* (**Quelle chaîne veux-tu regarder ?**, *What channel do you want to watch?*). But it can also be used in an exclamatory form: **Quel homme intelligent !**, *What an intelligent man!*
Quelle ville merveilleuse !, *What a wonderful city!*
Quels acteurs magnifiques !, *What magnificent actors!*
or, if the adjective is implied, we can simply say: **Quel homme ! Quelle ville ! Quels acteurs !**
Notice that no indefinite article is used. Also, like any adjective,

Answers to Exercice 1

❶ Can you come to the meeting this evening? ❷ They drank three bottles of champagne! ❸ He didn't have his keys and he could not get in. ❹ Being a little drunk, he broke a window pane. ❺ We have left our car and we are going to take a taxi.

***

❹ She realized that she didn't have her keys.
Elle . . . . qu'elle n' . . . . . pas . . . clefs.

❺ They can come when they like.
Ils . . . . venir . . . . . ils veulent.

Answers to Exercice 2

❶ – ont voulu – par – ❷ – c'était – voisin ❸ – a mangé – surtout bu ❹ – a réalisé – avait – ses – ❺ – peuvent – quand –

Second wave: 6th Lesson

56

Fifty-Sixth Lesson

quel must agree with its noun. (This only makes a difference in pronunciation when the following noun is plural and begins with a vowel, in which case we liaise: **Quels_acteurs** *[kelzakteur]*.)
Be careful: the exclamation *What?!*, indicating surprise or disbelief, is **Quoi ?**

2 Yet, *Encore*

encore, with a negative verb, means *yet*:
Je ne l'ai pas encore vu, *I haven't seen it/him yet.*
Elle n'a pas encore fini, *She hasn't finished yet.*
However, in the interrogative, the word disappears: whereas English says: *Has she finished yet?*, French would say: **Est-ce qu'elle a fini ?**
Est-ce que vous l'avez vu ?, *Have you seen it yet?*

To be more emphatic, in English, we use *still* instead of *yet*: *She still hasn't finished* (i.e. and she started some time ago). French translates this idea with **toujours**: **Elle n'a toujours pas fini !**, *She still hasn't finished!*

Il ne m'a toujours pas payé !, *He still hasn't paid me!*

Notice that **encore** comes <u>after</u> **pas** and **toujours** comes <u>before</u> it. (To revise another use of **encore**, see lesson 20).

3 Present participle

The *present participle* (**participe présent**) is formed by taking the first person plural of the verb and replacing **-ons** by **-ant**.

donner	–	donnons	–	donnant	*giving*
finir	–	finissons	–	finissant	*finishing*
vendre	–	vendons	–	vendant	*selling*

The participle can be used
• as an adjective – in which case it must agree with the noun:
Quelle ville charmante !, *What a charming town!*
• or as part of a verb, in which case it is invariable.
Étant un peu surprise, elle a cassé..., *Being a little surprised, she broke...*

Often, we put **en** before the present participle to get the idea of *while*, *on*, etc. (This usage is often left untranslated in English.)
Elle descend la rue en chantant, *She goes down the road singing.*
Il se coupe en se rasant, *He cuts himself (while) shaving.*
Be careful of the English construction: *I saw him going upstairs.*
The subject is not the person who is climbing the stairs: to avoid any possible ambiguity in French, we express the second action by an infinitive:
Je l'ai vu monter les escaliers.
We heard him singing: **Nous l'avons entendu chanter.**

Special note: With verbs like *to lie*, **s'étendre**, *to hang*, **pendre**, and *to sit*, **s'asseoir**, French uses the past participle where English uses the present: **Je l'ai vu assis par terre**, *I saw him sitting on the floor.*

Perhaps you have noticed that we have given you very few rules about writing French – especially accentuated letters. You already know the difference, for example, between **à** – the preposition (*to*, *at*, etc.) and **a** – the verb (*has*) or between the preposition **sur** (*on*) and the adjective **sûr**. Rest assured: there's method in our madness! Firstly, we want to stimulate your intuition and secondly, there are more important things to worry about for the time being. We will address the issue of writing in due course.

Meanwhile, work regularly and do the second wave...

Second wave: 7th Lesson

57

Cinquante-septième leçon

Deux bonnes réponses

1 Un homme est_assis dans_un train ¹, une pipe à la bouche.
2 Un contrôleur lui dit :
 – Vous ne pouvez pas fumer ici !
3 – Je ne fume pas, répond l'homme calmement.
4 – Mais vous_avez une pipe à la bouche ! s'écrie le contrôleur.
5 – D'accord. J'ai aussi des chaussures aux pieds,
6 mais je ne marche pas !

***

7 Visitant la Sorbonne ², un touriste voit une bibliothèque ³ très impressionnante.
8 Au-dessus de la porte est_inscrit : "Bibliothèque Félix Fournier".

Pronunciation
4 … saykree …8 … fayleeks fourneeyay

Notes
1 Be careful how you pronounce this word. The closest we can come to this "nasal" vowel sound (which we have already encountered in **le pain**, *bread*) is to pronounce an English word like *tram* or *pan* without voicing the final consonant. As a general rule, always double-check the pronunciation of words that are the same as in English by listening carefully to the recordings.
2 Established in 1257, the Sorbonne (the name comes from its founder, Robert de Sorbon) is one of the oldest and most prestigious universities

57

Fifty-Seventh Lesson

Two good answers

1 A man is sitting in a train, a pipe in his *(the)* mouth.

2 An inspector says [to] him:
  – You can't smoke here!

3 – I'm not smoking, replies the man calmly.

4 – But you have a pipe in your *(the)* mouth! cries the inspector.

5 – OK. I also have shoes on my *(the)* feet,

6 but I'm not walking!

***

7 Visiting the Sorbonne, a tourist sees an impressive library.

8 Above the door is engraved *(inscribed)*: "Félix Fournier Library".

---

in the world. Although the main buildings are still in the Latin Quarter of Paris – so called because instruction at La Sorbonne was originally given in Latin – there are several new faculties located in different parts of Paris.

3 **une bibliothèque**, *a library*. In a house, it is a **bookcase** – or the room that contains it. A "false friend": **une librairie**, *a bookshop*; **un libraire**, *a bookshop owner*; **un bouquin** *[bookan]* is a slang word for a book.

Along the banks of the River Seine in Paris are dozens of second-hand book sellers, each with their little stall. They are known as **les bouquinistes** *[bookeeneest]*.

Note: When telling stories, French prefers the present tense to the past. This is called **le présent historique** and gives added force to the narrative, bringing incidents right up to the present moment. (It also makes our life simpler!) This device is often used in popular fiction, but almost never in newspapers.

9 – Je ne connais pas cet_auteur : qu'est-ce qu'il a écrit ?

10 – Son guide sourit et lui répond :
   – Un gros chèque !   □

9 … setohteur … 10 … groh shek

***

▶ Exercice 1 – Traduisez

❶ Visitant la Sorbonne, ils ont vu un bâtiment impressionnant. ❷ Si vous voulez acheter mon livre, allez dans une librairie. ❸ Il a des chaussures aux pieds et un chapeau sur la tête. ❹ Passez-moi un coup de fil demain. – D'accord. ❺ L'affiche est au-dessus de la porte.

Exercice 2 – Complétez

❶ You can *(may)* smoke if you want.
   Vous ...... fumer si vous ....

❷ I don't know this author; what did he write?
   Je .... auteur ; qu'est-ce qu'il ...... ?

❸ He smiles and answers *(him)*: – A cheque.
   Il ...... et .... : – Un chèque.

❹ Put the book back in my bookcase.
   Remettez le livre dans ....

❺ He was seated, a pipe in his mouth.
   Il .... , une pipe ... bouche.

9 – I don't know this author; what did he write?
10 – His guide smiles and replies *(to him)*:
– A fat cheque!

***

Answers to Exercice 1
❶ Visiting the Sorbonne, they saw an impressive building. ❷ If you want to buy my book, go to a bookshop. ❸ He has shoes on his feet and a hat on his head. ❹ Give me a ring tomorrow. – OK. ❺ The poster is above the door.

Answers to Exercice 2
❶ – pouvez – voulez ❷ – ne connais pas cet – a écrit ❸ – sourit – lui répond – ❹ – ma bibliothèque ❺ – était assis – à la –

IL A DES CHAUSSURES AUX PIEDS ET UN CHAPEAU SUR LA TÊTE.

Second wave: 8th Lesson

58

Cinquante-huitième leçon

Un peu de tourisme

1 Saint-Jean-aux-Bois est_un ravissant petit village qui se trouve
2 à cinquante kilomètres de Paris en pleine forêt [1].
3 Vous sortez de l'autoroute et vous prenez la N 31 (trente et un) [2] ;
4 ensuite, vous prenez une petite route bordée d'arbres
5 et vous_entrez dans le village au bout de [3] trois kilomètres.
6 Vous passez d'abord devant un étang et tout de suite

Pronunciation
*1 sahn zhon ow bwa … raveessohn … veelazh … 2 … foray …
3 … oh-toh-root … enn trentayuhn 4 … borday … 5 … oh boo …
6 … aytohn … tootsweet*

Notes
1 We know that **plein** means *full* (*empty*, **vide**). But when used in expressions with **en**, it means *"right in the middle of"*, etc. **En plein désert**, *in the middle of the desert*; **en pleine rue**, *right out in the road* (notice the agreement with a feminine noun); **en plein air**, *in the open air*.
2 French roads are designated by a number and an initial letter. France has an extensive road network organised around a system of toll motorways. **Une autoroute**, *a motorway* e.g. **A6**. Next in importance, we have **la route nationale**: e.g. **la N 10**, then comes **la départementale**:

Fifty-Eighth Lesson

A little tourism

1 St-Jean-aux-Bois is a delightful *(ravishing)* little village which is situated *(finds itself)*

2 *(at)* 50 km from Paris in the middle of a *(full)* forest.

3 You get off the motorway and you take the N 31;

4 next you take a tiny *(a little)* road lined [with] *(of)* trees

5 and you enter *(in)* the village at the end of 3 km.

6 You pass first in front of a pond and straight away

e.g. **la D 603**. Smaller roads include **C (communal)** and **V (vicinal)**. **une carte routière**, *a road map*. Notice the difference between **la rue**, *the street* and **la route**, *the road*.

3 **le bout** *[boo]*, *the end*, i.e. *the tip* or *extremity*. To talk about the end of a film or a story, we use the word **la fin** *[fa]*. **Au bout de trois ans**, *after* ("at the end of") *three years*. **Les toilettes sont au bout du couloir**, *The toilets are at the end of the corridor*. **Allez au bout de la rue**, *Go to the end of the street*.

7 vous_arrivez devant la mairie et la place du marché.
8 Il faut_aller d'abord au syndicat d'initiative ⁴
9 pour savoir ⁵ ce qu'il y a à visiter.
10 Ensuite, une visite à l'église s'impose ⁶ :
11 elle date du xɪvᵉ siècle et elle est splendide.
12 Comme la plupart ⁷ des_églises en France, elle est catholique.
    (à suivre)   □

8 ... *sandeeka deeniseeateev* 10 ... *sampohz* 12 ... *plyoopar* ...

Notes
4 le syndicat d'initiative is similar to *a tourist office* (see lesson 111).

***

Exercice 1 – Traduisez
❶ Vous passez devant la mairie et vous arrivez à la place du marché. ❷ Il faut aller tout de suite au syndicat d'initiative, ❸ pour savoir ce qu'il y a à visiter. ❹ Une visite à l'église s'impose. ❺ Il est assis en plein soleil.

***

Exercice 2 – Complétez
❶ Go to the end of the road and turn left.
   Allez . . . . la rue et tournez . . . .

❷ His/Her house is situated in the middle of the forest.
   . . maison est . . . . . . en . . . . . . forêt.

❸ I want to know what there is to do here.
   Je . . . . savoir . . . . à faire ici.

7 you arrive in front of the town hall and the market place.

8 You must go first to the tourist office

9 to find out what there is to visit.

10 After, a visit to the church is called for:

11 it dates from the 14th century and it is splendid.

12 Like *(the)* most *(of)* churches in France, it is Catholic. *(continued)*

---

5 **savoir**, *to know* something; **je sais, tu sais, il/elle sait, nous savons, vous savez, ils/elles savent.** Past participle (irreg.): **su. Pour savoir,** *to find out*.

6 **imposer**, *to impose*; **imposant**, *imposing*. The reflexive form, used to describe an object, means *"is called for"*, *"is necessary"*. **Le champagne s'impose !**, *Champagne is called for!*

7 **la plupart des gens**, *most people*. **La plupart des gens dans la rue**, *Most of the people in the street*.

***

Answers to Exercice 1

❶ You pass in front of the town hall and you arrive at the market place. ❷ You must go straight away to the tourist office, ❸ to find out what there is to visit. ❹ A visit to the church is called for. ❺ He is sitting right in the sun.

***

❹ Most of the churches here are Catholic.

. . . . **églises ici sont catholiques.**

❺ You must visit the cathedral: it is splendid.

. . . . **visiter la cathédrale :** . . . . **est splendide.**

Answers to Exercice 2

❶ – au bout de – à gauche ❷ Sa – située – pleine – ❸ – veux – ce qu'il y a – ❹ La plupart des – ❺ Il faut – elle –

Second wave: 9th Lesson

59

Cinquante-neuvième leçon

Un peu de tourisme (suite)

1 Nous sommes toujours dans notre joli village
2 et nous venons de visiter l'église Sainte-Marie [1].
3 Nous_allons maintenant faire un petit tour dehors
4 pour admirer le beau jardin public avec sa pelouse,
5 ses rosiers et ses_arbres en fleurs.
6 Maintenant, si ça vous dit [2], on peut visiter le musée
7 où l'on [3] peut voir toute l'histoire de St-Jean-aux-Bois...
8 Ah bon ? Vous n'êtes pas amateurs [4] de musées ?

Pronunciation
3 ... de-or 5 ... rohzeeyay ... 6 ... myoozay 8 ... ama-teuh ...

Notes
1 Used before a name, **saint** is considered as an adjective, and must therefore agree: Saint-Jean *[sahn zhon]* but Sainte-Marie *[sant maree]*, abbreviated respectively to **St** and **Ste**.
2 **Est-ce que cela (ça) vous dit ?**, *Does that tempt you?* **Mmm, une glace ! Ça me dit !**, *Mmm, an ice-cream! I'd love one!* **Ça ne me dit rien du tout**, *That really doesn't tempt me*. Remember, idioms are impossible to translate: we attempt to give you the closest equivalents.

Fifty-Ninth Lesson

A little tourism (continued)

1 We are still in our pretty village
2 and we have just visited the church of St Mary.
3 We are now going to walk around *(make a little tour)* outside
4 to admire the beautiful public garden with its lawn,
5 its rose bushes and its trees in bloom*(s)*.
6 Now, if you feel like it, we *(one)* can visit the museum
7 where we *(one)* can see all the history of St. Jean-aux-Bois...
8 Oh really? You're not partial *(a liker of)* to museums?

3 The **l** is only here for emphasis, to avoid the two vowels **ou on**. However, in spoken French, it would seem overly formal. Watch out for it in written French.

4 **amateur** comes from the verb **aimer** and means *"someone who likes/ loves"*. **Rémi est un amateur d'art**, *Rémi is an art lover*. It can be used to translate the idea of *to be fond of* or *to have a taste for*. **Elle est amateur de chocolat**, *She's fond of chocolate*. The second meaning of **amateur** is the same as in English. (Note that a *lover*, in the amatory sense, is **un amant**.)

9 Quoi alors ? Ah, ça y est [5] ! J'ai compris.

10 Nous continuons alors notre promenade, contournant le poste de police [6],

11 et nous nous dirigeons vers la place du marché ;

12 et voici le vrai but de notre voyage : l'Auberge des Bois. □

🗨 *11 … direeezhon vair … 12 … byoot …*

Notes

5 Another idiom, an exclamation uttered when something has been understood, realised, etc. Had Archimedes been French, *Ça y est !* would have been his *Eureka!*

***

▶ Exercice 1 – Traduisez

❶ Ça y est ! Il a enfin compris ! ❷ Vous contournez le jardin public. ❸ Nous allons faire un petit tour dehors, d'accord ? ❹ Nous pouvons visiter le musée, est-ce que ça vous dit ? ❺ Nous sommes toujours à la leçon cinquante-neuf.

***

Exercice 2 – Complétez

❶ Go out now? That really doesn't tempt me.
   Sortir maintenant ? Ça . . . . du tout.

❷ We admired the beautiful lawn and the rose bush.
   Nous . . . . la belle pelouse et le rosier.

❸ That's it! I've found the answer!
   . . . . ! J'ai . . . . . la réponse !

9 What then? Ah, so that's it! I've understood.

10 We continue, therefore, our walk, going around the police-station,

11 and we go *(direct ourselves)* towards the market place;

12 and here is the real goal of our journey: l'Auberge des Bois.

6 The French police system is based on a national force (**la police nationale**) divided into various divisions. A separate division, **les CRS**, is deployed in riot situations. There is also a para-military force, **les gendarmes** (lit. "people with arms"). A division of the army, they are responsible for law and order and road safety. Depending on its size, a community will have **un poste de police**, *police station*, or **un commissariat**, *main police station*. **Les gendarmes** are based in **une gendarmerie**.

***

Answers to Exercice 1

❶ That's it! He has understood at last! ❷ You walk around the public garden. ❸ We are going for a walk outside, OK? ❹ We can visit the museum, do you feel like it? ❺ We're still at lesson 59.

***

❹ I've just told you that it doesn't interest me.

Je …… .. vous dire que ça ne m'intéresse pas.

❺ We can visit the garden if that interests you.

…… .. visiter le jardin si ……… …….

Answers to Exercice 2

❶ – ne me dit rien – ❷ – avons admiré – ❸ Ça y est – trouvé – ❹ – viens de – ❺ On peut – ça vous dit

Second wave: 10th Lesson

Soixantième leçon

Prendre le train

1 Catherine Farina doit_assister à [1] un colloque à Strasbourg et pense prendre le train.

2 Elle appelle le service de renseignements de la SNCF [2].

3 – Bonjour, pouvez-vous m'indiquer [3] les_horaires des trains pour Strasbourg s'il vous plaît ?

4 – Bien sûr, madame. Quand souhaitez-vous partir ?

5 – Je dois être là-bas le vendredi 21 vers quatorze heures

6 et je veux rentrer assez tôt le dimanche soir.

7 – Alors vous n'avez que [4] deux trains. Il y a un train direct qui quitte Paris à neuf_heures et qui arrive à Strasbourg à treize heures,

---

Pronunciation
*1 … kolok … strazboor … 2 … ronsaynemohn … ess-en-say-eff
4 … soo-etay-voo …*

Notes

1 Remember, **assister à** (with the preposition) means *to attend* (an event): **Quarante mille personnes ont assisté à la finale de la Coupe**, *40,000 people attended the cup final*. The verb is sometimes used (without the preposition) to mean *to assist someone*, although we would generally use **aider**, *to help*. In technical French, **assisté** is used in compound words to mean *aided*, e.g. **conception assistée par ordinateur (CAO)**, *computer-aided design*.

60

Sixtieth Lesson

Taking *(to take)* the train

1 Catherine Farina has to go to a conference in Strasbourg and thinks about taking *(to take)* the train.

2 She calls the SNCF information service.

3 – Good morning. Can you tell me the times of trains to Strasbourg, please?

4 – Of course, madam. When do you want to leave?

5 – I have to be there on Friday 21 around 2 pm

6 and I want to return fairly *(quite)* early [on] Sunday evening.

7 – In that case *(well)*, you have only two trains. There's a direct train that leaves Paris at 9 am and that arrives at Strasbourg at 1 pm,

---

2 Created on the eve of the second world war, **la Société Nationale des Chemins de Fer Français (la SNCF)** is the state-run railway board.

3 The verb **indiquer** is used when asking for directions, information, etc. in a formal register. For example, **Pouvez-vous m'indiquer les toilettes, s'il vous plaît ?**, *Could you tell me where the toilets are, please?* is more formal than **Où sont les toilettes ?**

4 We know how to use **seulement** to mean *only*: **Il y a seulement deux trains.** Here's another way, with **ne... que**: **Il n'y a que deux trains.** There is no difference in meaning between the two forms. **J'ai seulement une semaine de vacances** OR **Je n'ai que deux semaines de vacances**.

8 ou bien un_autre à dix_heures, mais avec un changement. Il faut_attendre une demi-heure.

9 – Combien coûte le voyage ?

10 – Vous voulez un_aller simple ou un_aller-retour [5]? Première ou deuxième classe ?
– Deuxième classe. Aller-retour.

11 – Avez-vous une réduction – famille nombreuse, moins de vingt-cinq_ans, par exemple ?
– Non.

12 – Préférez-vous fumeur ou non-fumeur ?
– Toutes ces questions !

13 – Si vous préférez, vous pouvez faire la réservation par ordinateur et payer par carte de crédit.

14 – C'est très_efficace.

15 – Oui, la SNCF s'est beaucoup modernisée [6] depuis dix_ans. ☐

🗩 *8 … foht-atendreu … 13 … kaht de craydee*

🗔 Notes

5 un billet aller simple, *a single ticket*; un billet aller et retour (or aller-retour), *a return ticket*. In everyday conversation, we generally drop the billet (as in English: un aller simple, *a single*). deuxième and second *[segohnd]* have exactly the same meaning. However, second is used when there are no more than two: Marguerite était la seconde femme d'Édouard I, *Marguerite was the second wife of Edward I* (i.e. he had only two wives) whereas deuxième means the second of a longer series: Marguerite était la deuxième femme de Jean ; ensuite il a épousé Hélène, *Marguerite was Jean's second wife; afterwards, he married Helen*. In practice, deuxième is the more common.

8   or another at 10 pm, but with a change. You have to wait a half hour.

9 – How much is the trip?

10 – Do you want a single or a return? First or second class?

– Second class return.

11 – Are you entitled to [do you have] a reduction – large family, or under-25, for example?

– No.

12 – Do you prefer smoking or non-smoking?

– All these questions!

13 – If you like, you can make the reservation by computer and pay by credit card.

14 – That's very efficient.

15 – Yes, the SNCF has modernised *(itself)* a lot in the past [since] 10 years.

6   We have already seen how most verbs form their past tense with **avoir** + past participle. But for reflexive verbs (those with **se** before the infinitive), we use **être** preceded by the relative pronoun. **Je me suis levé à midi**, *I got up at noon.* **Il s'est blessé**, *He injured/hurt himself.* **Vous vous êtes rasé ce matin ?**, *Did you shave this morning?* You'll be happy to know that there are no exceptions!

Note, too, that the participle must agree with the subject of the verb – here **la SNCF**. So, **La société s'est modernisée**. For the time being, don't worry about this problem of agreement. Just familiarise yourself with the basic rule.

▶ **Exercice 1 – Traduisez**

❶ Pouvez-vous m'indiquer les horaires des vols pour Hanovre ? ❷ Dépêchez-vous, nous n'avons que dix minutes avant le départ du train. ❸ Elle m'attend à la gare. ❹ Voulez-vous un aller simple ou un aller-retour ? – Un aller-retour, s'il vous plaît. ❺ Nous voulons rentrer assez tôt.

***

Exercice 2 – Complétez

❶ I've only got three weeks holiday this year.

. . . . trois semaines . . . . cette année.

❷ He got up at 4 o'clock and shaved in the dark.

Il . . . . à quatre heures et . . . . dans le noir.

❸ She got up three hours later.

Elle . . . . trois heures plus tard.

61

Soixante et unième leçon

Location de voiture

1 – Mais après tout, c'est peut-être plus pratique d'y ¹ aller en voiture, se dit Catherine.

🗎 Note

1 The **y** replaces the indirect object, here: Strasbourg. Notice that we don't generally translate it: Tu ne vas plus à Joigny ? – Si, j'y vais en

Answers to Exercice 1

❶ Can you tell me the times of flights to Hanover? ❷ Hurry up, we've got only 10 minutes before the train leaves. ❸ She's waiting for me at the station. ❹ Do you want a single or a return? – A return, please. ❺ We want to come back fairly early.

***

❹ I've got to go attend a conference in Strasbourg.

Je . . . . un colloque . Strasbourg.

❺ You have to wait for an hour.

. . . . heure.

Answers to Exercice 2

❶ Je n'ai que – de vacances – ❷ – s'est levé – s'est rasé – ❸ – s'est levée – ❹ – dois assister à – à – ❺ Il faut attendre une –

Second wave: 11th Lesson

61

Sixty-First Lesson

Car rental

1 – But after all, perhaps it's more practical to go *(there)* by car, Catherine says to herself.

fin de semaine, *You're not going to Joigny any more? – Yes, I'm going (there) at the end of the week.*

2 Elle téléphone aux renseignements ² et obtient plusieurs numéros de téléphone d'agences de location.

3 – Merci d'avoir appelé Hervis Location. Laurent à votre service ³.

4 – Bonjour, je désire louer une voiture pour me rendre à Strasbourg.

5 – Bien sûr, madame. Quelle catégorie de voiture désirez-vous ?

6 – Euh, je ne sais pas. Pouvez-vous me donner quelques_explications, s'il vous plaît ?

7 – Eh bien, ça va de la catégorie A, qui correspond aux petites voitures, jusqu'à la catégorie E, les voitures haut de gamme ⁴.

Pronunciation
2 … obtyenh … azhohns … 4 … dayzeer … 5 … dayzeeray … 7 … oh de gamm

Notes

2 One complication in English is our difference between countable and uncountable nouns (for example, we can say "the news" but not "a new"). This does not exist in French: **un renseignement**, *a piece of information*; **les renseignements**, *information*. In this context, **les renseignements**, *directory enquiries*. If you want to find a telephone number, but don't want to speak to anyone, you can look it up in an online directory, **un annuaire** (or even in a paper one if you can find it). As in many countries, business numbers are listed in *the Yellow Pages*, **les Pages Jaunes**.

2 She calls directory enquiries *(Information)* and gets
 several phone numbers for *(of)* car rental agencies.

3 – Thank you for calling Hervis Location. Laurent at
 your service.

4 – Good morning. I want to rent a car to go *(take myself)*
 to Strasbourg.

5 – Of course, madam. What category of car do you
 want?

6 – Um, I don't know. Could you give me some
 explanations, please?

7 – Well, it goes from category A, which corresponds to
 small cars, to Category E, top-of- the-range cars.

3 Businesses generally answer the telephone by giving the name of the
 company followed by **Bonjour**, spoken with a rising intonation (listen
 to Exercise 1). Increasingly, however, service companies are adopting the
 Anglo-American habit of thanking the caller and asking how they can
 be of service.

4 **une gamme**, *a range* (of products); **haut de gamme** *[oh-de-gam]*, *top
 of the range*; **bas de gamme** *[bah-de-gam]*, *bottom of the range*. (Both
 expressions can be used idiomatically to mean, respectively, *top class*
 and *cheap*.)

8 – Une petite me convient ⁵ parfaitement. Quelles sont vos conditions ? ⁶

9 – Vous partez combien de temps ?

10 – Du vendredi au dimanche.

11 – Si ça vous_intéresse, venez à l'agence avec votre permis de conduire et une carte de crédit. Simple, n'est-ce pas ⁷ ?

12 – Laissez-moi réfléchir et je vous rappellerai jeudi ou vendredi.

13 – Bien sûr, madame, mais n'oubliez pas que nous_avons beaucoup de demande en fin de semaine. □

🗨 **8** … kohnvyenh … **12** … rap-el-eray …

📑 Notes

5 **convenir** is a very useful verb for social situations. It basically means *to suit*. **Est-ce que mardi vous convient ou préférez-vous jeudi ?**, *Does Tuesday suit you, or do you prefer Wednesday?* To which you could reply: **Mardi me convient parfaitement** or *Mardi ne me convient pas du tout*. (Note that **convenir** is the source of our word *convenience*.)

However, when you want to say that, for instance, an item of clothing or a colour suits someone, you would use the verb **aller**: **Le bleu vous va bien**, *Blue suits you*. **Ce chapeau ne vous va pas du tout**, *That hat doesn't suit you at all*.

***

▶ Exercice 1 – Traduisez

❶ Société Française de Gaz, bonjour. – Bonjour. M. Suzzoni, s'il vous plaît. ❷ J'espère que cette chambre vous conviendra ? – Elle me convient parfaitement. ❸ Ces lunettes ne te vont pas du tout. Mais pas du tout ! ❹ Prenez le forfait, ça revient beaucoup moins cher. ❺ Nous avons toujours beaucoup de monde en fin de semaine.

8 – A small car suits me perfectly. What are your rates *(conditions)*?

9 – How long are you going for?

10 – From Friday to Sunday.

11 – If you're interested, come to the agency with your driver's licence and a credit card. Simple, isn't it?

12 – Let me think about it *(reflect)* and I'll call you back Thursday or Friday.

13 – Of course, madam. But don't forget that we get a lot of demand at the end of the week.

6 In a commercial context, **les conditions** means *the terms* of a purchase (think of our expression *terms and conditions*). **J'ai pu avoir d'excellentes conditions,** *I was able to get excellent terms.* You would ask the question **Quelles sont les conditions ?** when you are enquiring about hotel rooms, car rentals – in fact, anything that may involve certain conditions!

7 This expression, pronounced *[ness-pah]*, corresponds to our "tag" questions like *isn't it?*, *don't they?*, etc. It is <u>invariable</u>: **Il fait chaud, n'est-ce pas ?**, *It's hot, isn't it?*; **Vous venez, n'est-ce pas ?**, *You're coming, aren't you?*; **Tu l'as vue, n'est-ce pas?**, *You saw her, didn't you?* Note, however, that **n'est-ce pas** is used much less frequently than our tag questions. Moreover, in certain situations, it may be considered as somewhat "precious".

***

Answers to Exercice 1

❶ Société Française de Gaz, good morning. – Good morning. Mr Suzzoni, please. ❷ I hope that this room will suit you? – It suits me perfectly. ❸ Those eye-glasses don't suit you at all. And I mean not at all! ❹ Take the all-in price, it works out much cheaper. ❺ We are always busy at the end of the week.

Exercice 2 – Complétez

❶ You saw her, didn't you?
Vous . . . . , ... ?

❷ How long are you going for?
Tu . . . . ?

❸ If you are interested, come to the office.
Si . . . . bureau.

❹ I'll call you back towards the end of the week.
Je . . . .

62

Soixante-deuxième leçon

Ne soyons ¹ pas trop sérieux

1 Un homme baratine ² une jolie serveuse
  dans‿un restaurant :
2 – N'y a-t-il pas trois petits mots que
  vous‿aimeriez entendre ?
3 – En‿effet, répond la fille : "Gardez la monnaie".

***

4 Un Breton fête la naissance de l'enfant de sa
  sœur.
5 – Patron, servez une tournée générale : c'est moi
  qui paie.

Pronunciation
*1 ... barateen ... 2 neeyateelpa ... emereeyay ... 4 ... fet ...
nessonss ...*

❺ I need some information: what are your terms?

J'ai besoin . . . . : . . . . **vos**

. . . . **?**

Answers to Exercice 2

❶ – l'avez vue, n'est-ce pas **❷** – pars combien de temps **❸** – ça t'intéresse, viens au – **❹** – vous rappellerai en fin de semaine **❺** – d'un renseignement : quelles sont – conditions

Second wave: 12th Lesson

62

Sixty-Second Lesson

Let's not be too serious

1 A man [is] chatting up a pretty waitress in a restaurant:

2 – Are there not three little words that you would like to hear?

3 – In fact [there are] replies the girl: "Keep the change."

***

4 A Breton [is] celebrating the birth of his sister's child.

5 – Landlord, drinks all round (*a general round*): It's on me (*it is me who pays*).

Notes

1 This is the subjunctive form of **être**. It is used where English would say *Let us...* (which, in fact, is also the subjunctive). **Soyez heureux**, *Be happy*. More about the subjunctive later.

2 **baratiner** is a popular expression which means *to chat up, to turn on the charm*. You can say: **Baratin !** to dismiss an unctuous phrase, in much the same way as we say *Rubbish!* or *Baloney!* in English.

6 Ma sœur vient d'accoucher !
7 Le patron du bistrot ³ lui demande :
– C'est_un garçon ou une fille ?
8 Le Breton se tait ⁴ brusquement.
– J'ai oublié de demander ;
9 je ne sais pas si je suis oncle ou tante ⁵.

***

10 Pendant un entretien ⁶, un journaliste ose demander à une actrice pulpeuse :
11 – Qu'est-ce que vous portez ⁷ la nuit ?
12 Réponse :
– Du Chanel numéro cinq !   □

🗣 **6** … dakooshay **7** … beestroh … **8** … se tay brooskemohn

---

□ Notes

3 A slang word for **café**. The origin comes from Cossack officers encamped in Paris in 1814. Finding Parisian waiters too slow, they would yell in Russian "Bistro, bistro!", or "Quickly, quickly!". And the word has stuck.

Un bistrot is also a family-style restaurant serving simple, hearty cuisine. In the 1980s, some owners of high-class restaurants serving elaborate **grande cuisine** opened their own **bistrots**, going back to their roots in classic French cuisine. The trend reflects a deep attachment to a simpler, more rural way of life.

4 **se taire**, *to shut up*; je me tais, tu te tais, il/elle se tait, nous nous taisons, vous vous taisez, ils/elles se taisent. Past participle: tu. **Taisez-vous !**, *Shut up!*

6 My sister has just given birth!

7 The landlord of the café asks him:

– Is it a boy or a girl?

8 The Breton suddenly shuts up:

– I forgot to ask [it];

9 I don't know if I am [an] uncle or [an] aunt.

***

10 During an interview a journalist dares ask a voluptuous actress:

11 – What do you put on at night?

12 Reply:

– Chanel number 5!

5 **les parents** means *parents* and *relatives*. Other relatives are: **un cousin** *[koozan]* (f. **une cousine**); **un grand-père**, *a grandfather*; **une grand-mère**, *a grandmother*: **les grands-parents**, *grandparents*; (notice that **grand** agrees with **parents** but not with **mère**); **un beau-père**, *a father-in-law*; **une belle-mère**, *a mother-in-law*: (**les beaux-parents**).

6 "franglais" (see Lesson 55, note 1) prefers **une interview** and the (hideous) verb **interviewer** *[anterviouvay]*. Notice that we can say **un journaliste** or **une journaliste**, the noun remaining unchanged.

7 **porter**, *to carry*, also means *to wear*. **Il porte un costume pour aller au bureau**, *He wears a suit to go to the office*.

▶ Exercice 1 – Traduisez

❶ L'homme a commencé à baratiner la jolie serveuse ❷ qui lui a répondu "Taisez-vous !". ❸ Vous avez des frères ou des sœurs ? – En effet. J'ai un frère et une sœur. ❹ Patron, ce n'est pas moi qui paie ! ❺ Qu'est-ce que vous portez quand vous allez à l'opéra?

***

Exercice 2 – Complétez

❶ The grandmother and the grandfather are the grandparents.
La .... et le .... sont les ....

❷ My cousin has just had a child!
Ma .... avoir un enfant !

❸ Isn't there something you want to hear?
N' .... pas quelque chose ... vous voulez entendre ?

63

Soixante-troisième leçon

Révision – Revision

1 *Falloir*

falloir, *to be necessary*, *to have to*, is what we call an "impersonal verb" and it takes a little while to master. First, in the present, it is only found in the third person singular form **il** (<u>never</u> **elle**) **faut**.
Pour faire une omelette, il faut trois œufs *[euh]*, *To make an omelet, you need* ("one needs") *three eggs*.
Il faut beaucoup de patience pour apprendre le chinois, *You need a lot of patience* (or: *a lot of patience is necessary*) *to learn Chinese*. The problem here is that English dislikes impersonal forms like *one* and usually either attributes an imaginary *you* or constructs

Answers to Exercice 1

❶ The man began to chat up the pretty waitress ❷ who answered "Shut up!" ❸ Have you (any) brothers or sisters? – Indeed. I have one brother and one sister. ❹ Landlord, I'm not paying! ❺ What do you put on you when you go to the opera?

***

❹ You are Breton, aren't you? – I am indeed.
    Vous êtes Breton .... **pas ? – En** ....

❺ Jacques! Be serious, please!
    Jacques ! ..... **sérieux, s'il vous plaît !**

Answers to Exercice 2

❶ – grand-mère – grand-père – grand-parents ❷ – cousine vient d' – ❸ – y a-t-il – que – ❹ – n'est-ce – effet ❺ – Soyez –

Second wave: 13th Lesson

63

Sixty-Third Lesson

a passive form, making it difficult to convey the "impersonal", empirical feeling of **il faut**.
Je ne veux pas manger ça ! – Il faut manger !, *I don't want to eat that! – You must eat!* (i.e. it is necessary that you do so).
Est-ce qu'il faut un visa pour visiter la Chine ?, *Do you need ("is it necessary") a visa to visit China?*
Enough for now. We will look at more complex forms later.

2 Have just done..., *Vient de...*

The immediate past form *have just done...* is expressed in French by the idiomatic construction **venir de...** + infinitive:
Il vient de partir, *He has just left.*
Nous venons de manger, *We have just eaten.*

With reflexive verbs, the idiom comes before the reflexive pronoun:
Elle vient de se lever, *She has just got up*.
Je viens de me laver les mains, *I have just washed my hands*.

3 No prepositions

Ah, ces maudites prépositions ! (*Ah, those damned prepositions!*)
Here's a mnemonic to help you remember some of the most commonly used verbs that don't take a "post-position": CAPERED – this stands for:

64

Soixante-quatrième leçon

▶

Bonne route !

(À l'agence de location)
1 – Bonjour, madame. Puis-je vous aider ?
   – Je vous ai téléphoné il y a deux jours à propos d'une ¹ location pour ce week-end.
2 – Je me souviens. Vous vous rendez en province ², n'est-ce pas ?
3 – Absolument. Il me faut une petite voiture, avec votre forfait week-end.

🗨 Pronunciation
1 … pweezh … apropoh … 2 … provants ness-pa 3 … forfay …

📖 Notes
1 **à propos de**, *about*. The expression is synonymous with **au sujet de** (see lesson 15, line 6). **Je vous appelle à propos de votre annonce.** Basically, **le propos** is the subject of an enquiry, conversation, etc. **Il veut vous voir. – À quel propos ?**, *He wants to see you. – What about?* (Note that we have the same expression in formal English – apropos of, etc.)

Chercher, *to look for*
Attendre, *to wait for*
Payer, *to pay for*
Écouter, *to listen to*

Regarder, *to look at*
Espérer, *to hope for*
Demander, *to ask for*

See? No preposition after these verbs (with, of course, the odd exception, which we'll see later).

Second wave: 14th Lesson

64

Sixty-Fourth Lesson

Have a good trip (*Good road*) !

(At the rental agency)
1 – Good morning, madam. Can I help you?
  – I called you two days ago about a rental for this weekend.
2 – I remember. You're going to the provinces, aren't you?
3 – That's right (*Absolutely*). I need a small car, with your all-in weekend rate.

2 **la province**, *the provinces*. Since France has a legacy of centralization, **la province** refers to anything that is not Paris (and can sometimes be used condescendingly...). Notoriously, traffic reports on the radio will tell you that **L'autoroute est bouchée dans le sens Paris-province**, *The motorway is jammed heading out of Paris* (i.e. towards the rest of France!). Note the preposition **en**: **Ils habitent en province. Je vais en province.** Be careful not to confuse **la province** *[provans]* with **la Provence** *[provons]*, that stunningly beautiful and atmospheric region in the south of France.

4 – Bien sûr, madame. Mais d'abord quelques petites formalités et vous êtes en route.

5 Il me faut votre permis de conduire et une carte de crédit.

6 Votre nom et adresse ?
– Catherine Farina, ça s'écrit F-A-R-I-N-A [3] ; 31, rue Damrémont, 75018 Paris.

7 – Avez-vous un contact ou un numéro de téléphone à Strasbourg ?

8 – Non. Enfin, si [4]. Je descends [5] à l'hôtel de Colmar.

9 – Très bien. Voulez-vous une assurance complémentaire ?
– Non merci.

10 – Alors mettez vos initiales dans les cases A et B et signez en bas, s'il vous plaît.

11 Voici donc votre contrat et les clés de la voiture. C'est la Peugeot [6] verte en face.

🗣 **5** … permee … **6** … eff-a-air-ee-en-a **10** … kaz … **11** … klay …

Notes

3 Don't forget to practise spelling words out loud. Choose five words on this page and say each letter aloud. Repeat the exercise several times, getting a little faster each time.

4 You use **si** when you want to contradict something you have just said. It means "No; yes"! **Connaissez-vous strasbourg ? – Non. Si, j'y suis allé une fois**, *Do you know Strasbourg? – No. I mean, yes. I've been there once*. The **enfin** simply adds a little emphasis.

4 – Of course, madam. But first a few formalities, and
then you're on [your] way.

5 I need your driver's licence and a credit card.

6 Your name and address?

– Catherine Farina, that's spelt F-A-R-I-N-A, 31, rue
Damrémont, 75018 Paris.

7 – Do you have a contact or a phone number at
Strasbourg?

8 – No. Well, actually yes. I'm staying at the Hôtel de
Colmar.

9 – Fine. Do you want additional insurance?

– No thanks.

10 – Then initial boxes A and B and sign at the bottom,
please.

11 Here's your [rental] agreement and the car keys. It's
the green Peugeot opposite.

5 An idiomatic use of **descendre** (lit. "to go down"), used for hotels: **Il
descend toujours au George V quand il visite Paris**, *He always stays
at the George V hotel when he visits Paris.*

6 Remember that *a car* is feminine (**une voiture**), so even if you use the
name of the marque, you must still make the adjective agree: **une
Renault grise**, *a grey Renault.*

12 Avez-vous besoin d'une carte ⁷ routière ?
   – Non merci, je connais ⁸ bien la région.
13 – Alors, je vous souhaite bonne route ⁹.   □

12 … ray-zhohn

7 Since **une carte** has several meanings (*a card, a menu, a map*), we often stipulate what kind of **carte** we are referring to: **une carte routière**, *a road map*; **une carte de visite**, *a business card*; **une carte de crédit**, *a credit card*; **une carte postale**, *a postcard*.

8 **connaître**, *to know* (a person, a place, a date, etc.); **je connais, tu connais, il/elle connaît, nous connaissons, vous connaissez, ils/elles connaissent.** Past participle: **connu.** Remember that French makes a distinction that is missing in English. We use the verb **savoir** to refer to the fact of knowing something (i.e. to have knowledge). **Je sais où il habite**, *I know where he lives* (i.e. I have that knowledge). BUT **Je**

***

▶ Exercice 1 – Traduisez
❶ Est-ce vrai que Gisèle habite en province ? – Non, idiot ! Elle habite en Provence. ❷ Il me faut absolument parler au directeur. – À propos de quoi ? ❸ Connaissez-vous la région ? – Non. Enfin, si, un petit peu. ❹ Il me faut votre permis de conduire et une carte de crédit, s'il vous plaît. ❺ Savez-vous où je peux trouver une carte routière ?

***

Exercice 2 – Complétez
*(Choose between **connaître** and **savoir**, putting the verb in the correct form.)*
❶ Do you know where he lives?
    . . . . où il habite ?

❷ Do you know his/her address? (Use the familar form.)
    . . . . son adresse ?

❸ I know why she's unhappy.
    Je . . . . elle est triste.

12   Do you need a road map?
– No thanks, I know the region well.
13 – Then, have a good trip *(I wish you a good road)*.

connais son adresse, *I know his (her) address*. Although this distinction can sometimes be hard to establish, here are two rules of thumb: a) **savoir** never means to know a person; b) it can be followed by **où**, **comment** or **pourquoi**.

9   The French are always wishing each other a "*good*" something or other! You know the ritual **Bon appétit** before a meal, but you will also come across **Bon week-end**, **Bon dimanche**, **Bonnes vacances**, **Bon voyage**, **Bon retour** (*Have a safe journey back*), **Bon courage** (a useful one, this: *Hang on in there!*). Sometimes, this well-wishing can border on the ridiculous: in a certain category of restaurant you may get not only **Bon appétit** with the starter, but also **Bonne continuation** with the main course and **Bonne fin de repas** with the dessert. Not to mention **Bonne fin de soirée** when you leave...

***

Answers to Exercice 1

❶ Is it true that Gisèle lives in the provinces? – No, you idiot! She lives in Provence. ❷ I really need to talk to the manager. – What about? ❸ Do you know the region? – No. Well actually yes, a little bit. ❹ I need your driver's licence and a credit card, please. ❺ Do you know where I can find a road map?

***

❹   They know the way very well.
Ils / . . . . très bien la route.

❺   I know how to get there.
Je . . . . y aller.

Answers to Exercice 2

❶ Savez-vous – ❷ Connais-tu – ❸ – sais pourquoi – ❹ – Elles connaissent – ❺ – sais comment –

Second wave: 15th Lesson

65

Soixante-cinquième leçon

La tour Eiffel

1   Gustave Eiffel est né en 1832 (mille huit cent trente-deux) à Dijon.
2   Il est devenu ingénieur très jeune.
3   Il a toujours voulu construire quelque chose d'extraordinaire [1] ;
4   donc il est venu à Paris en 1886 (mille huit cent quatre-vingt-six)
5   pour la Grande Exposition, où son projet pour une tour a gagné le premier prix [2].
6   La construction a commencé en 1887 (mille huit cent quatre-vingt-sept) et a duré deux ans.
7   La tour est construite en fer et mesure trois cent vingt mètres de haut [3].

Pronunciation
1 goostav effel … nay … meel weesohn trohnt deu … 2 … anzhaynyeur … 3 … konstrweer … 5 … pree 7 … fair …

Notes
1   Notice that we use the partitive article **de** in such expressions as quelque chose de grand, *something big*; quelque chose d'intéressant, *something interesting*; Qu'est-ce que vous voulez boire ? – Quelque chose de chaud, *What do you want to drink? – Something hot.*

65

Sixty-Fifth Lesson

The Eiffel Tower

1 Gustave Eiffel was born in Dijon in 1832.
2 He became [an] engineer [when he was] very young.
3 He always wanted to construct something *(of)* extraordinary;
4 so he came to Paris in 1886
5 for the Great Exhibition, where his plan for a tower won the first prize.
6 The construction began in 1887 and lasted two years.
7 The tower is constructed of *(in)* iron and measures 320 m. in height.

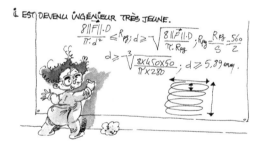

2 **un prix** *[pree]* (pl. **des prix**) means either *a price* or *a prize*; **gagner un prix**, *to win a prize*; **payer le prix**, *to pay the price*; **gagner** also means *to earn money*. **Combien est-ce qu'il gagne ?**, *How much does he earn?*

3 **six mètres de haut**, *six meters high*. Once again the (untranslated) partitive article. **Deux mètres de large**, *two meters wide*; **vingt centimètres de long**, *twenty centimetres long*; **la hauteur** *[ohteur]*, *the height*; **la longueur**, *the length*; **la largeur**, *the width*; **la profondeur**, *the depth*.

8   Il y a trois étages et une antenne de télévision tout en haut.

9   Heureusement, depuis 1965 (mille neuf cent soixante-cinq) l'ascenseur hydraulique a été remplacé par un ascenseur électrique.

10   En 1923 (mille neuf cent vingt-trois), un journaliste est descendu du troisième étage en bicyclette !

11   La construction de la tour a coûté six millions et demi de francs.

12   Elle appartient maintenant à la ville de Paris ⁴

13   et attire chaque année plus de trois millions de visiteurs.

14   Gustave Eiffel est mort en 1923 (mille neuf cent vingt-trois). ☐

🗨 *9 … ee-drol-eek … **10** … beeseeklet*

***

▶ Exercice 1 – Traduisez

❶ Si on va au cinéma, je veux voir quelque chose de drôle. ❷ Sa tour a gagné le premier prix à l'exposition. ❸ La boîte fait un mètre de haut et soixante-dix centimètres de large. ❹ Il a toujours voulu être ingénieur. ❺ Il y a une antenne de télévision tout en haut.

8 There are three floors and a television aerial right at the top.

9 Fortunately, since 1965 the hydraulic lift has been replaced with an electric lift.

10 In 1923, a journalist went down from the third floor by bicycle!

11 The tower cost six and a half million francs to construct.

12 It now belongs to the city of Paris

13 and draws more than three million visitors a *(each)* year.

14 Gustave Eiffel died in 1923.

] Note

4 We already know that **une ville** means both *town* and *city*. In the Middle Ages, the word **une cité** existed to describe what we today call *a city*. It still exists today but is used either to designate the old, historical part of some towns (and cities!) – **Provins et sa cité médiévale**, *Provins and its medieval Old Town* – or in compound nouns like "**une cité-dortoir**" (*dormitory town*) or "**une cité-jardin**", *garden city*. We'll see a couple of special uses later on.

***

Answers to Exercice 1

❶ If we go to the cinema, I want to see something funny. ❷ His tower won first prize in the exhibition. ❸ The box is 1 metre high and 70 cm wide. ❹ He has always wanted to be an engineer. ❺ There is a television aerial right at the top.

Exercice 2 – Complétez

❶ He became a teacher at the age of 20.

Il .... professeur . l'..... vingt ans.

❷ She earns a good salary.

Elle ..... un bon salaire.

❸ His father died two years ago.

Son père .... il y a deux ans.

66

Soixante-sixième leçon

La promenade du dimanche

1   La famille Launay a bien déjeuné ce dimanche
2   et les enfants viennent de mettre les assiettes
    dans le lave-vaisselle
3   pendant que ¹ les parents font une petite sieste ;
4   maintenant, ils vont se promener ² dans les bois.
5   Ils s'apprêtent ³ à partir quand, tout à coup...
6   Valérie :
    – Oh, ça y est. Il pleut ...!

🗨 Pronunciation

2 ... vessel 4 ... bwa

📑 Notes

1   **pendant trois ans**, *for three years*; **pendant la guerre**, *during the war*; **pendant que**, *while*. **Pendant que je lis**, *While I am reading*. (Don't confuse **pendant** with **cependant**, which means *however*.)

4 This book belongs to my mother-in-law.
   Ce livre .... ma belle-mère.

5 The film lasted two hours.
   Le film . .... deux heures.

Answers to Exercice 2
1 – est devenu – à – âge de – **2** – gagne – **3** – est mort – **4** –
appartient à – **5** – a duré –

Second wave: 16th Lesson

66

Sixty-Sixth Lesson

The Sunday walk

1 The Launay family has eaten well this Sunday
2 and the children have just put the plates in the
    dishwasher
3 while the parents [are] taking *(doing)* a little nap;
4 now, they are going for a walk in the woods.
5 They [are] getting ready to leave when, suddenly...
6 Valérie:
    – Oh, that's it. It [is] raining!

2 marcher, *to walk*; se promener, *to go for a walk* (for pleasure); il s'est
promené, *he went for a walk*; une marche, *a walk* (as opposed to a
drive, etc.)

3 Vous êtes prêt ?, *Are you ready?*; s'apprêter à, *to get ready*.

7 Pierre :
– Ça ne fait rien. Je vais chercher nos imperméables et nos bottes.

8 – Bon. À qui est [4] ce manteau ?
Jean :
– C'est le mien.

9 Pierre :
– Voilà le tien, Valérie. Et tes bottes. À qui sont celles-là ?

10 Valérie :
– Ce sont les miennes, je crois. Pierre :
– D'accord ; et voilà les tiennes, Jean.

11 Tout le monde est prêt ? Bon. On y va [5]. □

🗣 **7** … ampairmayabl … **8** … myehn **9** tyehn … **10** … myenn … tyenn … **11** … pray …

📋 Notes

4 À qui est ce manteau ?, *Whose is this coat?* À qui appartient ce chapeau ?, *Whose hat is this?* À qui sont ces lunettes ?, *Whose glasses are these?* One easy way to remember the À qui... ? construction is to think of the formal English interrogative: *To whom does this... belong?* À moi, *To me* (mine); à lui, à elle, *to him, to her*.

***

▶ Exercice 1 – Traduisez
❶ Il s'est promené dans les bois dimanche. ❷ Pendant que les parents font une sieste, ❸ les enfants remplissent le lave-vaisselle. ❹ Je n'ai pas d'argent ! – Ça ne fait rien. C'est moi qui paie. ❺ À qui sont ces bottes ? – À Jean. ❻ Prêt ? Bon. On y va !

7 Pierre:
– That doesn't matter. I will *(am going)* fetch our raincoats and our boots.
8 – Good; whose is this coat?
Jean:
– It's mine.
9 Pierre:
– Here is yours, Valérie. And your boots. Whose are those *(there)*?
10 Valérie:
– They are mine, I think.
Pierre:
– OK; and here are yours, Jean.
11 Everybody is ready? Good. Let's go.

JE N'AI PAS D'ARGENT !

5 We have seen that **Allons...** means *Let's go...* if it is followed by another verb. **Allons voir s'il est là**, *Let's go and see if he is there*. But if we want to say: **Let's go! Let's be off!**, we usually say *On y va !*

***

Answers to Exercice 1

❶ He went for a walk in the woods on Sunday. ❷ While the parents are having a nap, ❸ the children fill the dishwasher. ❹ I haven't got any money! – It doesn't matter. I'm paying. ❺ Whose are these boots? – John's. ❻ Ready? Good. Let's go.

Exercice 2 – Complétez

❶ I will fetch the raincoats; it is raining.
   Je vais .... les imperméables ; il ......

❷ The children have just finished the lesson.
   Les enfants .... terminer la leçon.

❸ Whose is this mobile phone? – It's mine.
   .... ce téléphone portable ? – C'est ... .

67

Soixante-septième leçon

L'optimiste et le pessimiste

1   La bouteille est à moitié pleine...
    – La bouteille est à moitié vide !
2   *(Au Nouvel An)*
    Bonne année !
    – Un an de moins à vivre [1] !
3   "Après la pluie vient le beau temps"
    – Quel temps de chien ! [2]
4   Enfin les premiers beaux jours !
    – Une hirondelle ne fait pas le printemps.
5   Ah ! Un mois de vacances au soleil !
    – La rentrée [3] va être triste et dure.

Pronunciation
4 ... eerondel ... prahntohn

Notes

1   We have already seen the difference between **un matin** and **une ma-**
    tinée. Here we have a similar pair of words: **un an** and **une année**.
    It is easier to make the following generalisation: **une année** refers to
    the duration of the year whereas **un an** is a statistic (i.e. *one year*). We
    say: **pendant l'année** – *during the year*, but **deux (trois...) ans** – *two*

❹ Whose are these boots? – They're yours (familiar form).

. . . . **ces bottes ? – Ce sont** . . . .**.**

❺ Where is mine? (masc. sing.) – Here it is.

Où . . . .**? – Le** . . . . . .**.**

Answers to Exercice 2

❶ – chercher – pleut ❷ – viennent de – ❸ À qui est – le mien ❹ À qui sont – les tiennes ❺ – est le mien – voilà

Second wave: 17th Lesson

67

Sixty-Seventh Lesson

The optimist and the pessimist

1 The bottle is *(at)* half full...
   – The bottle is *(at)* half empty!
2 *(At the new year)*
   Happy New Year *(Good year)*!
   – One year less to live!
3 After the rain comes the fine weather.
   – What terrible weather!
4 At last the first fine days!
   – One swallow doesn't make summer *(spring)*.
5 Ah! One month of holidays in the sun!
   – The return [is] going to be sad and hard.

(three...) years. **Le Nouvel An** – *The New Year*. **Il a soixante-quinze ans** – *He is 75 years old*. Rather than try to LEARN rules, we suggest you memorize a few examples.

2 An idiom meaning *What terrible weather!* (although what a dog has to do with it...). You can also say: **Il tombe des cordes**, *It's pouring down*. (**une corde** = *a rope*)

3 From the verb **rentrer**, *to go* ("come") *back*. **La rentrée** is the period in September when children go back to school and their parents to work after the summer break (see lesson 110).

6 Le vin va être très bon cette année !
  – Les prix vont augmenter.
7 Cette leçon est facile...
  – Attendez demain !
8 Quelle différence y a-t-il entre un homme politique et un miroir ?
9 Les miroirs, eux [4], réfléchissent [5] sans parler [6],
10 alors que [7] les hommes politiques parlent sans réfléchir.   □

🗣 **6** ... owgmontay **8** ... eeyateel ... **9** ... reflesheess ...

📑 Notes

4 Another idiomatic turn of phrase: we repeat the tonic pronoun to lend emphasis to the thing(s) or person (s) in question: **Étienne est étudiant**, *Étienne is a student*, **mais Pierre, lui, est ingénieur**, *but Pierre, he's an engineer*. In English, we achieve the same effect by adding the pronoun.

5 réfléchir: je réfléchis, tu réfléchis, il/elle réfléchit, nous réfléchissons, vous réfléchissez, ils/elles réfléchissent. Past participle: réfléchi.

   les verbes réfléchis: *reflexive verbs*. The verb means *to reflect* (for mirrors or people).

                              ***

▶ Exercice 1 – Traduisez
❶ La salle était à moitié vide. **❷** Le prix du vin a beaucoup augmenté. **❸** Il a donné la réponse sans réfléchir. **❹** Quelle différence y a-t-il entre "un an" et "une année" ? **❺** Il a travaillé pendant trente ans. **❻** Le vin va être très bon l'année prochaine.

6 The wine will be very good this year!
  – The prices [are] going to increase.
7 This lesson is easy...
  – Wait for tomorrow!
8 What difference is there between a politician *(political man)* and a mirror?
9 Mirrors *(them)* reflect without speaking,
10 whereas politicians speak without reflecting.

6 **sans parler**, *without talking*. The infinitive is always used after **sans**. (You'll also come across the expression **sans parler de** which is equivalent to our "not to mention". **Ils ont deux chiens, trois chats et six lapins – sans parler de trois cochons d'Inde**, *They've got two dogs, three cats and six rabbits, not to mention three guinea pigs*.)

7 **alors**, *well, so* etc. **Alors que**, *whereas*. (Another expression with the same meaning is **tandis que** *[tondeeke]*.)

***

Answers to Exercice 1
❶ The hall was half empty. ❷ The price of wine has increased a lot. ❸ He gave the answer without thinking. ❹ What difference is there between "un an" and "une année"? ❺ He worked for 30 years. ❻ The wine is going to be very good next year.

Exercice 2 – Complétez

❶ What terrible weather! – Wait for next year.

Quel ..... de .....! – Attendez l'.... ....•

❷ Pierre isn't working at the moment, but Marie, *(she)* is working very hard.

Pierre ne travaille pas en ce moment mais Marie, ...,
travaille très ....

❸ The cup is half-full.

La tasse est . ...•

68

Soixante-huitième leçon

Le corps humain

1   Le corps de l'homme et de la femme est composé de trois parties :

2   la tête, le tronc et les membres.

3   La tête est d'habitude [1] couverte de cheveux [2],
sinon on est chauve.

4   Les yeux [3], les sourcils, le nez, la bouche et le menton

5   forment le visage, beau ou laid !

Pronunciation

... *kor yooma* **2** ... *trohn* ... *mombr* **3** ... *sheveu* ... *showv* **4** *layzyeu*
... *soorsee* ... *mohntohn* **5** ... *lay*

Notes

1   une habitude, *a habit;* s'habituer à, *to get used to.* Elle s'habitue à la
vie en France, *She is getting used to life in France.* avoir l'habitude,
to be used to. J'ai l'habitude de parler en public, *I'm used to public
speaking.* d'habitude, *usually.*

❹ Jeanne isn't coming! – One person less.
   Jeanne ne vient pas ! – Une personne . . . .

❺ They always talk without thinking *(reflecting)*.
   Ils . . . . toujours . . . .

Answers to Exercice 2
❶ – temps – chien – année prochaine ❷ – elle – dur ❸ – à moitié
pleine ❹ – de moins ❺ – parlent – sans réfléchir

Second wave: 18th Lesson

68

Sixty-Eighth Lesson

The human body

1 The body of a *(the)* man and of a *(the)* woman is
  composed of three parts:
2 the head, the trunk and the limbs.
3 The head is usually covered with hair, if not you are
  (one is) bald.
4 The eyes, the eyebrows, the nose, the mouth and the
  chin
5 form the face, beautiful or ugly!

---

2 **un cheveu**, *a hair*; **des cheveux**, *hair*. Whereas English says: **Your hair
is long**, the French more logically say: *Vos cheveux sont longs*. **Couper
les cheveux en quatre**, *to split hairs* ("cut them in 4!").

la tête est couverte: Remember that the past participle is an adjective and, as such, must agree: **les mains sont couvertes; le corps est
couvert**.

3 **un œil** *[oy]*; **des yeux** *[yeu]* is one of the few irregularly pronounced
plurals in French. Three others are: **un œuf, des œufs** *[euh]*, *eggs*; **un
bœuf, des bœufs** *[beu]*, *oxen*; **un os, des os** *[oh]*, *bones*.

6 Entre la tête et le tronc, il y a le cou.
7 Le tronc porte généralement deux bras et deux jambes.
8 Il y a d'autres usages pour ces mots que nous venons de voir :
9 par exemple, on parle d'un tronc d'arbre ou des membres d'un gouvernement.
10 La Bible nous apprend : 4 œil pour œil, dent pour dent.
11 Et si vous n'aimez pas ça, vous pouvez toujours faire la tête 5 ! □

🗨 **10** ... beebl ... oy ... dohn ...

📁 : Notes

4 There are two verbs that are easily confused: *to teach* is **enseigner**: **Elle enseigne l'histoire**, *She teaches history*.

To learn is **apprendre**; but often French uses **apprendre** to mean both. **Il apprend le français aux étrangers**, *He teaches French to foreigners*. Although not incorrect, this use of **apprendre** can be off-putting, so make a mental note and stick to **enseigner** for *to teach*. Remember, too, that the generic word for *a teacher* is **un enseignant**.

***

▶ Exercice 1 – Traduisez
❶ Il n'a pas envie d'y aller ; regardez sa tête ! ❷ D'habitude, je bois du café le matin. ❸ J'apprends ma leçon tous les soirs. ❹ Il n'a pas l'habitude de ce nouvel ordinateur. ❺ Elle est grande, belle et elle a des cheveux blonds.

6 Between the head and the trunk there is the neck.

7 The trunk usually has *(carries)* two arms and two legs.

8 There are other uses for these words which we have just seen:

9 For example, we talk *(one talks)* of a tree trunk, or of the members of a government.

10 The Bible teaches us: [an] eye for [an] eye [and a] tooth for [a] tooth.

11 And if you don't like that you can always pull *(make the)* a face!

5 Il fait la tête: faire la tête, *to sulk, to mope, to pull a long face.* Ne fais pas la tête!, *Don't sulk!* La tête is also used idiomatically for a person's expression – usually one of surprise or discomfiture. Il a fait une drôle de tête quand il a appris la nouvelle, *You should have seen his expression when he heard the news.*

***

Answers to Exercice 1

❶ He doesn't want to go; look at his expression! ❷ Usually I drink coffee in the morning. ❸ I learn my lesson every evening. ❹ He is not used to this new computer. ❺ She is tall, beautiful and she has blond hair.

Exercice 2 – Complétez

❶ The committee is composed of twenty members.

Le comité … … … … de vingt … … … .

❷ He's our teacher; he teaches us history.

C'est notre professeur ; il … … … … l'histoire.

❸ In Canada, one speaks French and English.

Au Canada, .. parle .. français et ..anglais.

69

Soixante-neuvième leçon

Le corps humain (suite)

1 Les bras se plient aux coudes et aux poignets.
2 Ils sont terminés par les mains, formées de cinq doigts, dont le pouce
3 est un des plus utiles. Les doigts se terminent par les ongles.
4 Les jambes se plient aux genoux et aux chevilles.
5 D'habitude, on se tient debout ¹ sur ses ² pieds

Pronunciation

1 … kood … pwanyay 2 … dwa … pooss 4 … plee … zhenoo … shevee

Notes

1 When in English we say: *she is standing over there*, the word *"standing"* is a supplementary piece of information – the main idea is that the person <u>is</u> over there. This is how we treat the situation in French: **Elle est**

❹ Usually the head is covered with hair.

.... la tête est .... de ....

❺ There are other words to say that.

Il . . d'...... mots pour dire cela.

Answers to Exercice 2

❶ – est composé – membres ❷ – nous enseigne – ❸ – on – le – l' –
❹ D'habitude – couverte – cheveux ❺ – y a – autres –

Second wave: 19th Lesson

69

Sixty-Ninth Lesson

The human body (continued)

1 The arms bend *(themselves)* at the elbows and at the wrists.

2 At the end are *(they finish themselves by)* the hands, formed of five fingers of which the thumb

3 is one of the most useful. The fingers finish by the nails.

4 The legs bend at the knees and at the ankles.

5 Usually, one stands *(holds oneself up)* on one's feet

là-bas. If we really wish to know if the person is sitting, standing, lying, etc. we must add the necessary adverb: **Elle est debout là-bas**, *She is over there, standing.* **Se mettre debout**, *to stand up*; **se tenir debout**, *to be standing.*

2 **On se tient debout sur ses pieds**, *One stands on one's feet.* **On a sa réputation**, *One has one's reputation.* Remember that on is much less formal than *"one"* in English and is often translated either by a passive construction or by an imaginary *you, we.*

deux cent soixante-douze • 272

6 et on dort couché ³ sur le dos.

7 Les gens peuvent être grands ou petits, gros ou maigres.

8 Nous espérons en tout cas que vous êtes en bonne santé.

9 Si vous avez faim et que vous êtes très pressé,

10 vous pouvez manger sur le pouce ⁴ et si vous avez besoin d'aide,

11 vous pouvez demander un coup ⁵ de main – et si on vous le refuse,

12 on dit qu'on vous a tourné le dos. □

6 … doh **7** … groh … megr **8** … sontay **11** … koo …

Notes

3 We already saw that French considers **couché, assis, pendu,** etc. as past participles (the initial action having been accomplished) whereas English treats them as present participles. **Il est assis en plein soleil,** *He is sitting right in the sun.*

4 An idiom **manger sur le pouce,** *to have a quick bite to eat.* Where? In **un snack,** *a snack-bar,* **un self,** *a self-service restaurant* or **un fast-food** (!). As you can see, culinary imports work both ways!

***

Exercice 1 – Traduisez

❶ Elle est assise là-bas. **❷** Nous espérons que vous êtes en bonne santé. **❸** Je n'ai pas le temps ; je suis très pressé. **❹** Vous avez cinq doigts dont un qui s'appelle "le pouce". **❺** Donne-moi un coup de main, s'il te plaît. **❻** Je lui ai demandé de l'argent et il m'a tourné le dos.

6 and one sleeps lying on one's back.

7 People can be large or small, fat or thin.

8 We hope, in any case, that you are in good health.

9 If you are hungry and *(that)* you are *(very hurried)* in a hurry,

10 you can have a quick snack and if you need help,

11 you can ask for a hand – and if one refuses you,

12 we say that one has turned one's back [on] you.

5 One of the most common words to be found in French idiomatic expressions: **un coup** literally means *a blow* (we know, in English, **a coup d'État**). **Donnez-moi un coup de main**, *Give me a hand*. We already know **un coup de fil**, *a phone call*; **donner un coup de poing**, *to punch*; **un coup de fusil**, *a gunshot* and the famous **coup de foudre**, *love at first sight*.

***

Answers to Exercice 1

❶ She is sitting over there. ❷ We hope you are in good health. ❸ I don't have time; I'm in a hurry. ❹ You have five fingers, one of which is called "the thumb". ❺ Give me a hand, please *(fam. form)*. ❻ I asked him for money and he turned his back on me.

Exercice 2 – Complétez

❶ Three people, two of whom were children, were injured.
   Trois personnes, ... deux enfants, étaient blessées.

❷ I received six letters, three of them were from abroad.
   J'ai reçu six lettres .... trois de l' ....

❸ He's the man about whom I spoke to you.
   C'est l'homme .... je vous ....

70

Soixante-dixième leçon

Révision – Revision

1 Past tense with *être*

Some verbs form their past tense not with **avoir** + past participle, but with **être** + past participle. (We have already come across this peculiarity with reflexive verbs: **Il s'est couché à huit heures**, *He went to bed at 8.00*.)

Here is a list of the verbs which take **être** in the past. All except one concern movement.

Most denote a change in position and form opposite pairs:

aller, *to go*; **venir**, *to come*; **arriver**, *to arrive*; **partir**, *to leave*; **entrer**, *to enter*; **sortir**, *to go out*; **monter**, *to go up*; **descendre**, *to go down*; **retourner**, *to return*; **tomber**, *to fall*.

All compounds of these verbs begin with **re-**: e.g. **revenir**, *to come back*; **rentrer**, *to go back in*, etc. Three of them denote a change of state:

naître, *to be born*; **devenir**, *to become*; **mourir**, *to die*, and, just to be perverse: **rester**, *to remain*.

Read the following passage:

Jean came to the house at nine o'clock. He went to the front door. He went in and went up to the first floor. Nobody. He went downstairs and went out the back door. He returned and went back

❹ They turned their back on me.

. . . . le dos.

❺ She sleeps lying on her back.

Elle dort . . . . sur . . dos.

Second wave: 20th Lesson

_____

70

Seventieth Lesson

*inside. His father was born in this house, he became famous and
he died there: he fell from a window. Jean stayed for ten minutes
then he left.*

Try and depict the situation – even if it is a little far-fetched! Now
go back over it in your mind and read the translation:

Jean est venu **à la maison à neuf heures. Il est** allé **à la porte principale. Il est** entré **et il est** monté **au premier étage. Personne. Il
est** descendu **et il est** sorti **par la porte de derrière. Il est** retourné
et il est rentré. **Son père est** né **dans cette maison ; il est** devenu
célèbre et il y est mort : **il est** tombé **d'une fenêtre. Jean est** resté
dix minutes et puis il est parti.

Since the past participle in these cases is an adjective, it must agree
with its subject.

Elle est descendue, *she went down*; **ils sont partis**, *they* (m.) *left*;
elles sont sorties, *they went out* (as always, if the subject includes
both genders, we choose the masculine: **Jean et Marie sont restés**,
Jean and Marie stayed).

For the moment, this detail should not bother us too much since
(a) it generally does not change the pronunciation and (b) we will
return to written French later on.

2 Numbers and dates

mille	a thousand
un million	a million
trois mille neuf cent vingt-deux	3,922
un million neuf cent mille	1,900,000
trois mille personnes	3,000 people,

but
deux millions de **personnes,** d'**euros,** etc.

For dates, **mille** is often written **mil** (no difference in pronunciation); a date is treated simply as a number: 1625, *one thousand, six hundred and twenty five,* **mil six cent vingt-cinq.** 1982, *one thousand nine hundred and eighty two,* **mil neuf cent quatre-vingt-deux.** How do we say the following dates: 1945 1863 1495 1787 1960 2000 2008 (Answers at the end of the lesson).

3 Possessive pronoun

The possessive pronoun, like the possessive adjective (**mon, ma, mes,** etc.) agrees with the **gender** of the object possessed (not, as in English, with the possessor). Here are the pronouns:
le mien, la mienne, les miens, les miennes (*mine*)
le tien, la tienne, les tiens, les tiennes (*your* fam.)
le sien, la sienne, les siens, les siennes (*his/hers*)
le nôtre, la nôtre, les nôtres (*ours*)
le vôtre, la vôtre, les vôtres (*yours* – polite or plural)
le leur, la leur, les leurs (*theirs*).

This list might appear daunting but a closer look will show you that in fact it is very regular and easy to remember.

4 *Dont*

dont is a very useful relative which expresses the English ideas of: *of whom, of which, whose.*
Look at these examples:
les gens dont vous parlez, *the people of whom you are speaking;*

la femme dont la voiture est dehors, *the woman whose car is outside*; **la maison dont les fenêtres sont cassées**, *the house the windows of which are broken*.

Do you notice that **dont** always follows the noun to which it relates? Look again at the word order:
le chef dont j'aime la cuisine, *the chef whose cooking I like*.

We obviously do not expect you to learn all these rules and lists by heart straight away. Look at the examples given in the texts and try, with this extra information, to extend your knowledge.

Answers to dates
1945 **mil** (or **mille**) **neuf cent quarante-cinq**
1863 **mil** (or **mille**) **huit cent soixante-trois**
1495 **mil** (or **mille**) **quatre cent quatre-vingt-quinze**
1787 **mil** (or **mille**) **sept cent quatre-vingt-sept**
1960 **mil** (or **mille**) **neuf cent soixante**
2000 **deux mille**
2008 **deux mille huit**

Second wave: 21st Lesson

71

Soixante et onzième leçon

Une déception

1 – Anne, est-ce que c'est vrai que les Français aiment bien manger ?

2 – Mais oui. Cela fait partie ¹ de nos qualités (ou de nos défauts) !

3 Mais pourquoi tu me poses cette question ?

4 – Avant de venir en France, tout le monde m'a dit :

5 "Ah, vous verrez, en France, on mange bien ;

6 vous mangerez des spécialités, des produits frais,

7 vous goûterez à des petits vins de pays, et tout et tout ²."

8 Mais ça fait trois jours que je suis‿ici ³

9 et, aux Champs‿-Élysées, par exemple, je n'ai vu que

10 des fast-food ou des pizzerias… pas très typiques !

🗨 Pronunciation

2 … kalitay … dayfoh 3 … powz … 5 … veray … 6 … monzheray … prodwee fray 7 … gooteray … payee ay tooaytoo 10 … fest … peetzeria …

 Notes

1 cela (ça) fait partie de, *that is part of* ("one of"); une partie, *a part*; une partie de cartes, *a game of cards* (not a card-game); **a party**: *une fête*. Ça fait partie des traditions, *That's one of the traditions*.

71

Seventy-First Lesson

A disappointment

1 – Anne, is it true that the French like to eat well?
2 – But of course. That is part of our qualities (or of our faults)!
3 But why [do] you ask me this question?
4 – Before coming *(to come)* to France, everybody told me:
5 "Ah, you will see, in France, they eat well;
6 you will eat specialities, fresh produce,
7 you will taste *(at)* "little country wines" and so on.
8 But I have been here for three days
9 and on *(at)* the Champs-Élysées for example, I have seen only
10 fast food *(outlets)* or pizzerias... not very typical!

2 We can say **et cetera** (etc.) *[etseterah]* or **et ainsi de suite**, at the end of a phrase for *and so on, and so forth*. The expression **et tout et tout** is a more familiar way of expressing the same idea.

3 An idiomatic construction: **Ça fait deux ans qu'il est mort**, *He has been dead for two years*; **Ça fait trois mois qu'il étudie le français**, *He has been studying French for three months*.

Notice this use of the present tense, which we will see in greater detail when we look at *for* and *since*.

11 – Oui, mais le prix du mètre carré [4] y est
tellement_élevé [5]

12 que seuls les restaurants "industriels" sont
rentables.

13 Mais ne t'en fais pas [6], mon touriste affamé,

14 demain, je t'emmènerai dans_un vrai
restaurant français.

◻

🗨 **11** … elevay **14** … tomeneray …

📂 : Notes

4 **un carré**, *a square shape*, **un rond** *[rohn]*, *a round shape*, **une racine
carrée**, *a square root*; **un bâtiment rond**, *a round building*. Obviously,
surface area is given in *square meters*, **mètres carrés**. When describing
the size of a house or flat, we give the number of square meters. **Il
habite un cinquante mètres carrés dans le centre de Lyon**, *He lives in
a 50 sq. m. (flat) in the centre of Lyons*.

***

▶ Exercice 1 – Traduisez

❶ Il fait partie du gouvernement. ❷ En France, on mange
bien. ❸ Ça fait deux semaines que je travaille très dur.
❹ Les prix en Suisse sont très élevés, mais les salaires sont
élevés aussi. ❺ Il n'a vu que des restaurants industriels.

11 – Yes, but the price of a *(the)* square meter is so high there

12 that only "industrial" restaurants are profitable.

13 But don't worry, my starving tourist,

14 tomorrow I will take you to a real French restaurant.

IL FAIT PARTIE DU GOUVERNEMENT.

5 We say **haut**, *high*, for a building (see lesson 54, note 3), but **élevé** (lit. "raised") for prices: **un prix bas**, *a low price*; **un niveau élevé**, *a high level*.

6 **s'inquiéter**, *to worry* (oneself); **Je m'inquiète**, *I am worried*; **Ne vous inquiétez pas**, *Don't worry*. **Ne vous en faites pas** (fam. *Ne t'en fais pas*) is a colloquial way of saying the same thing.

***

Answers to Exercice 1

❶ He is part of the government. ❷ In France, they eat well. ❸ I have been working very hard for two weeks. ❹ Prices in Switzerland are very high, but salaries are high too. ❺ He only saw industrial restaurants.

❶ Don't worry; it's not difficult.
Ne vous . . . .; ce n'est pas dur.

❷ We went to Paris and we saw only tourists.
Nous . . . . à Paris et nous . . avons vu . . . des touristes.

❸ It's one of his faults, you know.
Ça . . . . ses défauts, tu sais.

72

Soixante-douzième leçon

▶ ## Le lendemain, dans un grand ¹ restaurant

1 – Cette carte ! ² Quelle merveille ! Je n'ai jamais vu une chose pareille ³ !

🔊 Pronunciation
1 ... mairvay ... paray

📰 Notes

1 **grand** has a much wider meaning than just *big* or *large*: **la grande majorité des gens**, *the vast majority of people*; **un grand vent**, *a high wind*; **un grand vin**, *a great wine*; **un grand restaurant**, *a high-class* or *luxury restaurant*. Thus, the English equivalent of **grand** varies according to the context. Also, note the expression **grand-chose**: **Ça ne vaut pas grand-chose**, *It's not worth much*. **Je n'ai pas vu grand-chose**, *I didn't see much*. As you can see, **grand-chose** has many of the same uses as **beaucoup**.

❹ Only industrial restaurants are profitable.

..... les restaurants industriels sont ....

❺ He has been trying to do it for two weeks.

Ça .... deux semaines qu'il essaye de le faire.

Answers to Exercice 2

❶ – en faites pas – **❷** – sommes allés – n' – que – **❸** – fait partie de
– **❹** Seuls – rentables **❺** – fait –

Second wave: 22nd Lesson

Seventy-Second Lesson

The next day at a high-class restaurant

1 – This menu! What [a] marvel! I have never seen
anything like it!

2 In a restaurant, **le menu** means a *fixed price menu* (which we call, in English (!), "table d'hôte"); **la carte** is *the menu* – the list of dishes and their prices; **manger à la carte** is to choose from the menu rather than take the fixed-price meal. Some bistros now offer **un menu-carte** (!). This is basically a fixed price menu with several choices for each dish.

3 **C'est toujours la même chose = C'est toujours pareil**, *It's always the same.* **Pareil** (f. **pareille**) is both an adjective and an adverb. As an adjective it is used in the same way as **même**: **Elle en a une exactement pareille**, *She has one exactly the same*; or as **comme ça**. **Je n'ai jamais vu une chose comme ça**, *I have never seen anything like that*; **Je n'ai jamais entendu une chose pareille**, *I have never heard anything like that*; **avec un temps comme ça, avec un temps pareil**, *with weather like that*, (with such weather); or as an adverb: **Ils s'habillent pareil**, *They dress alike.* Naturally, being an adverb and not an adjective in this example, **pareil** does not agree with the subject.

2 – Oui, c'est_impressionnant... et ce cadre [4]. Quel luxe !

3 – Dis-moi, Anne, qu'est-ce que c'est que ce machin-là [5] :

4 "Cardinal de l'océan avec son_accompagnement de diamants du Périgord" ?

5 – Je suppose que c'est tout simplement un homard avec des truffes.

6 – Ah bon... ? Heu, dis-moi, Anne, tu es bien une femme moderne ?

7 Tu me dis toujours que tu vis avec ton_époque [6], n'est-ce pas ?

8 – Mais oui, et j'en suis fière ; mais où veux-tu en venir [7] ?

9 – Heu, voilà... Je propose que chacun [8] paye sa part de l'addition. D'accord ?

10 – Mais bien sûr ! Maintenant, tu pourras manger tranquillement !

□

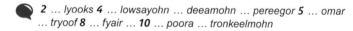

2 ... lyooks **4** ... lowsayohn ... deeamohn ... pereegor **5** ... omar ... tryoof **8** ... fyair ... **10** ... poora ... tronkeelmohn

Notes

4 We saw one particular meaning of **un cadre** in lesson 44, note 2. Here's another common usage: **un cadre luxueux**, *luxurious surroundings*, or *décor*.

5 See lesson 48, note 2.

6 Although **époque** is feminine, we use **ton** instead of **ta** to avoid having two vowels together (in the same way as we say **mon amie**); **ta carte de crédit**, but **ton amie**.

2 – Yes, it's impressive... and the surroundings. What luxury!

3 – Tell me, Anne, what on earth is this thing:

4 "Cardinal of the ocean with its accompaniment of diamonds of the Périgord"?

5 – I suppose it's quite simply a lobster with truffles.

6 – Oh really? Um, tell me, Ann, you are really a modern girl?

7 You always tell me that you live with your age *(epoch)*, don't you?

8 – Of course, and I am proud of it; but what are you getting at?

9 – Um, well... I propose that each one pays his part of the bill, OK?

10 – But of course! Now you will be able to eat in peace!

7 Another idiom: **Je ne sais pas où il veut en venir,** *I don't know what he's getting at, what he's leading up to.* **Où veux-tu en venir ?,** *Where are you getting at?* i.e. Get to the point.

8 **chacun** (fem. **chacune**) means: <u>each one</u>. **Chacun des plats est cher,** *Each of the dishes is expensive.* **Chacune des sœurs est belle,** *Each ("one") of the sisters is beautiful.* **Ils m'ont donné chacun dix euros,** *Each ("one") gave me ten euros.* or <u>everyone</u>: **comme chacun sait,** *as everyone knows;* **chacun son tour,** *everyone in turn,* and the old saying **Chacun pour soi et Dieu pour tous !,** *Everyone for himself and God for ("us") all!*

▶ Exercice 1 – Traduisez

❶ Je ne vois pas où vous voulez en venir. ❷ Ton amie est très belle ! – La tienne aussi ! ❸ Chacun sait que ce n'est pas vrai. ❹ Je n'ai jamais entendu une chose pareille. ❺ C'est une fille moderne et elle en est fière. ❻ Tu prends le menu ou tu manges à la carte ?

***

Exercice 2 – Complétez

❶ Your ring is pretty; I have one the same.
Ta bague est jolie ; j'.. ai une ....

❷ Each one pays his part, OK?
...... paye sa part, d'...... ?

❸ She went to the opera but she didn't see much.
Elle .... à l'opéra mais elle n'a pas ....

73

Soixante-treizième leçon

▶ **Oh, les beaux jours !**

1 – C'était comment la France avant la guerre, grand-père ?

2 – Oh tu sais, c'était bien différent de maintenant !

3 Nous n'étions pas_aussi riches et nous n'avions pas_autant de ¹ belles choses,

🗨 Pronunciation

1 setay ... gair grohnpair *2* ... deefairohn ... *3* ... netiohn ... owtohn ...

Answers to Exercice 1

❶ I don't see what you are getting at. ❷ Your (girl)friend is very beautiful! – Yours too! ❸ Everyone knows that it isn't true. ❹ I have never heard anything like it. ❺ She is a modern girl and she is proud of it. ❻ Are you taking the "table d'hôte" or are you choosing from the menu?

**

❹ Tomorrow is Monday; you will be able to go to the bank.
Demain, c'est ..... ; tu .... aller à la banque.

❺ What on earth is that thing there?
Qu' ...-.. que c'est ... ce ....-là ?

Answers to Exercice 2

❶ – en – pareille ❷ Chacun – accord ❸ – est allée – vu grand-chose
❹ – lundi – pourras – ❺ – est-ce – que – machin –

Second wave: 23rd Lesson

73

Seventy-Third Lesson

Happy days!

1 – What was France like *(How was France)* before the war, grandfather?

2 – Ah, you know, it was really different than now!

3 We weren't as rich and we didn't have as many beautiful things

] Note

1 **autant de**, *as much/many* **que**, *as*. Il n'y a pas autant de neige que l'année dernière, *There is not as much snow as last year*. Il a autant de vêtements que moi, *He has as many clothes as me*. If we omit the noun, we also drop the **de**: Il en a autant que moi, *He has as much/many* ("of them") *as me*. J'en ai autant que lui, *I have as much/many as him*.

4 mais je pense que nous vivions mieux qu'aujourd'hui.

5 Mon père avait un grand jardin et il cultivait [2] tous nos légumes,

6 et moi et mes copains [3] travaillions pour un fermier

7 qui nous donnait des œufs frais et du lait qui était encore tiède [4].

8 On ne mangeait pas beaucoup de viande à cette époque.

9 Mais il y avait autre chose : les gens étaient plus aimables.

10 Ils se connaissaient tous et ils se parlaient [5].

🔊 *4 … veeviohn … 5 … avay … koolteevay … 6 … kopan traveyiohn … fairmeeyay 7 … dayzeuh … tyed 8 … mohnzhay … 10 … tooss …*

Notes

2 un homme cultivé, *a cultured man*; cultiver des légumes, etc., *to grow vegetables, etc.* (lesson 40, line 10). Those familiar with the work of Voltaire probably know Candide's famous maxim: **Il faut cultiver son jardin**, *We must work in our garden*. The verb **grandir**, *to grow*, is intransitive: **Son fils a grandi**, *His son has grown*.

3 A very common slang word for a (male) friend. Used by a woman, it can also mean *boyfriend*. **Elle a le même copain depuis quatre ans**, *She's been with the same guy for four years*. The feminine form is **une copine**. An old slang word, **un pote** (*a buddy*), was revived by the anti-racist movement in the 1990s and used in the slogan: **Touche pas à mon pote**, *Don't touch my buddy*, which has entered the language as a catch-phrase. Note that the Canadians, often influenced by their English-speaking neighbours to the south, talk about **mon chum**!

4 but I think that we used to live better than today.

5 My father had a big garden and he used to grow all our vegetables

6 and me and my mates used to work for a farmer

7 who [would] give us fresh eggs and milk which was still warm.

8 We didn't use to eat much meat at that time.

9 But there was something else: people were more likeable.

10 They used to know each other and they used to speak [to] each other.

4 **tiède**, *warm* or *lukewarm*, depending on the context. One commonly held view is that **les Anglais boivent de la bière tiède**, *The English drink ("luke") warm beer*. Used figuratively, **tiède** is equivalent to *tepid*; **un accueil tiède**, *a tepid ("half-hearted") welcome*. And, in the same way that **tiède** means *warm* or *lukewarm*, **frais** can mean either *fresh* or *cool*: **une boisson fraîche**, *a cool drink*; **des œufs frais**, *fresh eggs*.

(Incidentally, be careful of taps in French-speaking countries: "C" stands, not for Cold but for **Chaud** – the opposite! "F": *froid*.)

5 This is what we call a "reciprocal verb". **Il se regarde dans le miroir**, *He looks at himself in the mirror* (reflexive verb); but **Ils se regardent**, *They look at each other* ("or one another"). **Elle se connaît**, *She knows herself* (i.e. qualities and faults), but **Vous vous connaissez, n'est-ce pas ?**, *You know each other, don't you?*

11 Puis, il y a eu la guerre et les_hommes sont partis... [6]

12 Et les_enfants étaient mieux_élevés que de nos jours !

13 Ils ne s'endormaient pas pendant que leur grand-père leur parlait [7] !   ☐

13 ... sondormay ...

Notes

6 Notice the change in tense in this sentence. All the other imperfect verbs describe habitual actions in the past but both the arrival of the war and the departure of the men were two specific incidents.

***

▶ Exercice 1 – Traduisez

❶ Nous étions plus heureux mais nous n'avions pas grand-chose. ❷ Nous vivions mieux qu'aujourd'hui. ❸ Je crois qu'ils se connaissent bien. ❹ Mes copains et moi pouvons vous donner un coup de main. ❺ Cet enfant est très bien élevé. ❻ La bière en Angleterre est tiède !

***

Exercice 2 – Complétez

❶ Their father told them to take their things.

.... père .... a dit de prendre ..... affaires.

❷ He used to grow vegetables but he didn't eat meat.

Il .... des légumes mais il ne .... pas de viande.

❸ They looked at each other for ten minutes before recognising each other.

Ils ...... regardés pendant dix minutes avant de .. reconnaître.

11   Then there was the war and the men left...
12   And children were better brought-up than today!
13   They didn't use to fall asleep when their grandfather talked to them!

Accordingly, we use the past tense. **Il parlait au téléphone quand nous sommes arrivés**, *He was speaking on the phone when we arrived*.

7   **leur grand-père... leur**, here, is the possessive adjective; **leur parlait**, *spoke to them*, is a personal pronoun. No difference in either spelling or pronunciation; but only the possessive can take an **s**. **Pierre et Jean ont pris leurs affaires**, *Peter and John took their things*. But **Je leur ai donné leurs affaires**, *I gave them their things*.

***

Answers to Exercice 1

❶ We were happier but we didn't have very much. ❷ We used to live better than today. ❸ I think they know each other well. ❹ My mates and me can give you a hand. ❺ This child is very well brought-up (*i.e. well-mannered*). ❻ The beer in England is lukewarm!

***

❹   When I entered, he was reading a book.
    Quand je ...., il lisait un livre.

❺   There was something else, people were more likeable.
    Il y ..... autre chose, les gens .... plus aimables.

Answers to Exercice 2

❶ Leur – leur – leurs – ❷ – cultivait – mangeait – ❸ – se sont – se – ❹ – suis entré – ❺ – avait – étaient –

Second wave: 24th Lesson

74

Soixante-quatorzième leçon

Le grand écran

1 – Madame, mademoiselle, monsieur, bonsoir et bienvenue à notre soirée cinéma.

2 Aujourd'hui nous_avons le plaisir d'accueillir l'acteur Alain Belon [1].

3 Merci d'être venu [2], Alain. Alors vous_avez eu une vie fabuleuse, n'est-ce pas ?

4 – Oui, en_effet. Très variée. Et j'ai toujours été très_apprécié.

5 Quand j'étais_à l'école, tout le monde m'aimait_énormément.

6 Il faut dire que j'étais très doué [3] et que j'avais la cote avec [4] les filles.

7 Puis, à l'armée, les_autres gars [5] me respectaient.

🗨 Pronunciation
2 … akeuyeer … 6 … dooay … kot … 7 … ga …

Notes

1 accueillir quelqu'un, *to welcome somebody*. Bienvenue ! (or **Soyez le bienvenu !**), *Welcome!* Notice that when used with **le**, bienvenue loses the final "e". Je vous en prie, *You're welcome, Don't mention it*.

2 Notice the difference between the French and the English construction: **Merci d'avoir pensé à moi**, *Thank you for thinking of me*. **Merci de l'avoir acheté**, *Thank you for buying it*. **Merci d'être venu**, *Thank you for coming* (Remember our verbs conjugated with **être**, lesson 70.)

Seventy-Fourth Lesson

The big screen

1 – Ladies and gentlemen, good evening and welcome to our movie night.

2 Today, we have the pleasure of welcoming the actor Alain Belon.

3 Thank you for coming, Alain. Well, you have had a fabulous life, haven't you?

4 – Yes, indeed. Very varied. And I have always been greatly appreciated.

5 When I was at school, everybody liked me enormously.

6 It must be said that I was very clever and I was popular with girls.

7 Then, in the army, the other guys respected me.

---

3 **un don**, *a gift* (either material or talent); **doué** (**douée**) literally means *gifted*, but is often used simply to mean *clever*. **Il est doué pour ça**, *He's good at that*. **Qu'est-ce qu'elle est douée !**, *She's really bright!*

4 **Il a la cote**, *He is very successful* (with people) (slang). **Un diplôme très coté**, *a prized diploma*. In stock exchange language, **la cote** is the official list of quoted companies.

5 Notice the pronunciation *[ga]*. This slang word means *guy* or *bloke*. It is generally used by men to mean *the guys*, *the lads*. **Salut, les gars !**, *Hi, guys!* Another common slang word is **un type**. (You may also hear **un mec**, but this is overly familiar.) Referring to a woman, the equivalent to **un type** is **une nana**, but once again we are straying into the realms of familiarity. Our advice? Stick to standard usage until you feel really at home in French, try **un type**.

8 J'ai quitté l'armée après la guerre – ils m'ont demandé de rester –

9 et là, j'ai rencontré Brigitte Charlot, avec qui j'ai commencé ma brillante carrière.

10 J'ai d'abord été cascadeur, mais ensuite comme je suis si beau,

11 Jules Bassin m'a sorti[6] des figurants, et me voilà aujourd'hui.

12 – Et quelle est la qualité que vous préférez chez[7] les gens ?

13 – Mmm... La modestie. ☐

9 ... breeyont ...

Notes

6 Il est sorti – *He went out*, but if **sortir** is used transitively (i.e. with a direct object), it is conjugated with **avoir**. Elle a sorti un mouchoir de sa poche – *She took a handkerchief from her pocket*. Elle est descendue – *She came down*. But Il a descendu les valises – *He brought down the suitcases*.

***

Exercice 1 – Traduisez

❶ Vous avez eu une carrière très intéressante, n'est-ce pas ? **❷** Elle a sorti toutes les vieilles lettres. **❸** Jean est un pianiste très doué. **❹** Il a toujours été comme ça. **❺** Quelle qualité aimez-vous chez votre mari ? **❻** Il faut dire que ce n'était pas à moi.

8 I left the army after the war – they asked me to stay –

9 and then *(there)* I met Brigitte Charlot, with whom I began my brilliant career.

10 I was first a stunt man but afterwards, as I am so handsome,

11 Jules Bassin took me out of the extras, and here I am today.

12 – And what *(is the)* quality that you prefer in people?

13 – Mmm... Modesty.

7 **Ce que j'aime chez lui, c'est son honnêteté** – *What I like in him is his honesty.* **Ce qui me plaît chez eux, c'est leur humour [youmour]** – *What I like about them is their humour.* This use of **chez** to attribute qualities (or vices) to people is very common.

***

Answers to Exercice 1

❶ You have had a very interesting career, haven't you? ❷ She took out all the old letters. ❸ John is a very gifted pianist. ❹ He has always been like that. ❺ What quality do you like in your husband? ❻ It must be said that it wasn't mine.

Exercice 2 – Complétez

❶ Thank you for staying; I want to talk to you.
Merci d' .... ; je veux vous parler.

❷ We brought down the three boxes yesterday.
Nous .... les trois cartons .....

❸ We have had a marvellous day.
Nous .... une journée ....

75

Soixante-quinzième leçon

▶

Une consultation efficace

1 Le docteur Azoulay est non seulement médecin,
mais un peu psychiatre ¹ aussi.
2 Un jour, un_homme entre dans son cabinet
3 en se plaignant de maux ² de tête affreux.
4 – Alors, dit le docteur, ça dure depuis combien de
temps ³ ?

🔊 Pronunciation
1 … pseekeeatr … 2 … kabeenay 3 … playniohn … mow …

◧ Notes

1 Be careful of the pronunciation of all those words that come from
Greek and begin with **ps** – or **pn** –: the **p** is sounded along with the
following consonant: **la pneumonie** *[peuneumoany]*, *pneumonia*; **un
psychologue** *[pesseekolog]*, *a psychologist*. (In fact the **p** is not quite
as strong as our figurative pronunciation suggests. Listen closely to the
recording, if you have them.)

❹ He asked me to leave.
   Il . . . . de . . . .

❺ The other guys respected me enormously.
   Les autres . . . . me . . . . énormément.

Second wave: 25th Lesson

──────────────────────────────── **75**

Seventy-Fifth Lesson

An efficient consultation

1 Doctor Azoulay is not only [a] doctor, but a little [of a] psychiatrist, too.
2 One day a man comes into his surgery
3 complaining of awful headaches.
4 – Well, says the doctor, how long has this being going on?

2 un mal de tête, *a headache* – (des maux de tête). J'ai mal à la tête, *I have a headache*. **Est-ce que vous avez mal ?**, *Does it hurt?* **Faire mal** is *to hurt someone*. Le dentiste m'a fait mal, *The dentist hurt me*.

3 Another great simplification: the present perfect continuous tense (have + been + doing) is expressed by the present tense, with both *for* and *since* being translated by **depuis**. Je suis ici depuis dix minutes, *I have been here for ten minutes*. Elle vit à Paris depuis août, *She has been living in Paris since August*. Je vous aime depuis mon enfance, *I have loved you since my childhood* (we can't say "have been loving" in English).

5 – Oh, depuis que je suis_au monde. Enfin, depuis
    quelques_années.
6 – Et vous_avez mal maintenant ?
    – Oh que ⁴ oui, docteur.
7   J'ai terriblement ⁵ mal depuis... oh, depuis dix
    minutes.
8 – Qu'est-ce que vous faites comme travail ?
    – Je suis guitariste dans un groupe de hard-rock.
9 – Et où habitez-vous ?
10 – J'habite à côté de l'aéroport d'Orly depuis cinq
    ou six_ans.
11   Le docteur a compris depuis longtemps ⁶. Il se
    lève
12   et va à un placard d'où il sort une énorme scie.
13 – Bon, on va examiner votre cerveau, pour voir...
14 – Ce n'est pas la peine, docteur, je me sens
    mieux ⁷ depuis deux minutes. Au revoir !   □

🗨 **7** *... tereeblemohn ...* **8** *... ard rok* **9** *... abeetay ...* **10** *... eyeropor*
... 12 ... see 13 ... servoh ...

Notes

4 The **que** merely adds emphasis: *Oh, yes really!*; **Oh que non !**, *Not at all!*

5 **Elle parle terriblement bien l'anglais**, *She speaks pretty amazing
    English*. **Terriblement** is a fairly polite way to say *very* or *really*. Our
    rocker would probably have said **vachement** (lit. "cow-ly" – see lesson
    81). However, we'd advise you not to imitate him. It's considered
    familiar. **Il joue vachement bien !**, *He plays bloody well!*

5 – Oh, since I have been in the world. Well, for several years.

6 – And does it hurt now?

– Yes, and how, doctor!

7 It has been hurting like mad for ... oh, for ten minutes.

8 – What is your job?

– I'm a guitarist in a hard rock band.

9 – And where do you live?

10 – I have been living next to the Airport of Orly for five or six years.

11 The doctor understood a long time ago. He gets up

12 and goes to a cupboard from which *(where)* he takes out an enormous saw.

13 – Good. We are going to examine your brain to see...

14 – Don't trouble yourself, doctor. I have been feeling much better for two minutes. Goodbye!

6 Il est parti depuis dix minutes (lit. "he has been left for ten minutes") can only be translated in English by *He left ten minutes ago*. Il l'a perdu depuis deux semaines, *He lost it two weeks ago*. In this case (i.e. with the verb in the past tense, not the present), depuis can be replaced by il y a: Il l'a perdu il y a deux semaines.

7 se sentir, *to feel* (i.e. one's physical condition). Elle se sent malade, *She's feeling sick*. Je me sens mieux, *I feel better*.

Exercice 1 – Traduisez

❶ Qu'est-ce que vous faites comme travail ? ❷ Vous sentez-vous mieux ? – Oui, depuis hier, merci. ❸ Il aime ça depuis qu'il est au monde. ❹ Vous avez mal maintenant ? – Oh que oui ! ❺ Il est non seulement psychiatre, mais aussi psychologue.

***

Exercice 2 – Complétez

❶ I have been working at Michelin for two years.

Je .... chez Michelin ...... deux ans.

❷ The flat has been empty since last month.

L'appartement ... vide ...... le mois dernier.

❸ She lost her dog four days ago.

Elle ...... son chien ...... quatre jours.

76

Soixante-seizième leçon

Détendons-nous

1 Après un concert donné par l'orchestre
symphonique de Paris, un spectateur –
2 sans doute pas très futé [1] – passe un petit mot
au chef d'orchestre :
3 – "Je ne veux pas paraître rapporteur, monsieur,

Pronunciation
2 ... fyootay ...

Answers to Exercice 1

❶ What is your job? ❷ Do you feel better? – Yes, since yesterday, thank you. ❸ He has liked that since he has been in the world (since he was born). ❹ Does it hurt now? – Yes, and how! ❺ He is not only a psychiatrist but a psychologist, too.

***

❹ How long has this been going on?
   Ça .... depuis .... de ..... ?

❺ He came in complaining of headaches.
   Il .... se plaignant de .... de tête.

Answers to Exercice 2

❶ – travaille – depuis – ❷ – est – depuis – ❸ – a perdu – depuis – ❹ – dure – combien – temps ❺ – est entré en – maux –

Second wave: 26th Lesson

76

Seventy-Sixth Lesson

Let's relax

1   After a concert given by the Paris symphony
    orchestra, a spectator –
2   no doubt not very bright – passes a note *(little word)*
    to the conductor *(orchestra chief)*:
3 – "I don't want to appear [a] tell-tale, sir,

Note

1   futé means *sharp, bright, smart*. **Futé comme un renard,** *As cunning as a fox*.

4   mais je crois utile de vous signaler que
       l'homme qui joue de la grosse caisse ²

5   ne frappe que lorsque ³ vous le regardez".

***

6 – Ma femme voulait une nouvelle voiture pour
       Noël,

7   alors je lui ai offert ⁴ un collier de perles.

8   Je sais ce que tu vas dire, mais tu comprends,

9   on ne fabrique pas_encore de fausses Citroën ⁵.

***

10 Jean-Alphonse Fontaine était_arriviste à tel
       point

11 que lorsqu'il entrait derrière vous dans_une
       porte à tambour,

12 il réussissait ⁶ quand même à en sortir le
       premier !

***

13 – Méfie-toi de ce dragueur ⁷ ! C'est_un vrai
       nouveau riche,

14 et je te préviens qu'il est beaucoup plus
       nouveau que riche !   □

🗣 *4 … growss kess 5 … lorske … 7 … offair … koleeyay … pairl 9 …
fowss … 11 … tomboor 12 … rayoosseessay …*

Notes

2 **une caisse** is either a *packing-case* or a *cash desk*. **Payez à la caisse**, *Pay at the cash desk*. **La grosse caisse**, *the bass drum*. Remember that the verb **jouer** takes the partitive **du** or **de la** when referring to an instrument. **Il joue aux échecs**, *He plays chess*, but **elle joue du clavecin**, *She plays the harpsichord*.

3 **lorsque** basically means the same as **quand**, *when*. It is generally used (as here) when two actions coincide.

4 **offrir**: j'offre, tu offres, il/elle offre, nous offrons, vous offrez, ils/elles offrent. Past participle: **offert**, means *to offer* but is also used to mean,

4 but I think it useful to point out [to] you that the man who plays (of) the bass drum
5 only hits when you look at him."

***

6 – My wife wanted a new car for Christmas,
7 so I gave her a pearl necklace.
8 I know what you [are] going to say, but you see (understand),
9 they don't yet make false Citroëns.

***

10 Jean-Alphonse Fontaine was a social climber to such an extent
11 that when he went in behind you in a revolving door
12 he succeeded all the same in coming out (of it) first!

***

13 – Beware of that wolf! He's a real nouveau-riche,
14 and I warn you that he is much more "new" than "rich"!

to give a present: **Il lui a offert une belle bague,** *He gave her/him a beautiful ring.*

5 Remember that proper names usually do not take an s in the plural: **Les Fontaine**, *the Fontaines*; **les Renault**, *the Renaults*, etc.

6 **réussir**; je réussis, tu réussis, il/elle réussit, nous réussissons, vous réussissez, ils/elles réussissent. Past participle: **réussi**, *to succeed in.* **J'ai réussi à le trouver,** *I succeeded in finding it/him.* **Réussir un examen,** *to pass an exam*; **une réussite,** *a success.*

7 A prime slang word: **draguer** (lit. "to dredge!") means *to chase the opposite sex, to chat up*; **un dragueur**, *a "wolf".*

▶ Exercice 1 – Traduisez

❶ La machine ne marche que lorsque vous appuyez ici.
❷ Je lui ai offert un beau cadeau. ❸ Il en sort toujours le
dernier. ❹ Méfiez-vous de cet homme ! C'est un dragueur !
❺ Je vous préviens que c'est très difficile.

***

Exercice 2 – Complétez

❶ I know what you are going to say, but it's not true *(false)*.
Je sais . . . . . tu . . . ., mais c'est faux.

❷ He is undoubtedly not very bright.
Il n'est . . . . pas très . . . . . .

❸ They didn't succeed in opening it.
Ils n' . . . pas . . . . l'ouvrir.

77

Soixante-dix-septième leçon

Révision – Revision

1 The future tense

As well as expressing a future idea by using **aller** + infinitive (**je vais
voir**, etc.), we can use the future tense.
This is formed by simply adding the verb endings of the present
tense of **avoir**: **-ai**, **-as**, **-a**, **-ons**, **-ez**, **-ont** to the infinitive of the verb:
donner: **je donnerai**, **il donnera**, **ils donneront**.
finir: **tu finiras**, **vous finirez**, **nous finirons**.
For verbs like **vendre**, we drop the final **e**. Thus:
je vendrai, **tu vendras**, **il vendra**, **nous vendrons**, **vous vendrez**,
ils vendront.

Answers to Exercice 1

❶ The machine only works when you push here. ❷ I gave him/her a beautiful present. ❸ He always comes out of it last. ❹ Beware of that man! He's a wolf! ❺ I warn you that it's very difficult.

***

❹ He is rich to such an extent that he has four houses.
Il est riche . . . . il a quatre maisons.

❺ They are much more"new" than "rich".
Ils sont beaucoup . . . . nouveaux . . . riches.

Answers to Exercice 2

❶ – ce que – vas dire – ❷ – sans doute – futé ❸ – ont – réussi à – ❹ – à tel point qu' – ❺ – plus – que –

Second wave: 27th Lesson

77

Seventy-Seventh Lesson

It is as simple as that! All verbs take these endings; however, a few irregular verbs change their stems. Remember the following which are the most common:
aller: j'irai, etc.
avoir: j'aurai, etc.
être: je serai, etc.
pouvoir: je pourrai, etc.
faire: je ferai, etc.

Here are some examples:
Ils finiront dans dix minutes, *They will finish in ten minutes*.
Elle vendra sa voiture la semaine prochaine, *She will sell her car next week*.

Je vous le donnerai demain, *I'll give it to you tomorrow*.
Il sera si content de te voir, *He will be so happy to see you*.
Vous n'aurez pas de problème, *You won't have any problems*.
Nous serons là à partir de dix heures, *We will be there from 10.00 onwards*.

As you can see, this use is almost exactly the same as in English.

Remember that: *Will you follow me?* is **Voulez-vous me suivre ?** etc.

2 The imperfect tense

Whereas the past tense describes completed actions in the past (he went, I saw, we bought, etc.), the imperfect tense describes a constant state or continuous action in the past.
Look at these examples:
Nous cultivions nos légumes, *We used to grow our vegetables*.
Ils travaillaient pour un fermier, *They used to work for a farmer*.
Elle allait à la campagne toutes les semaines..., *She would go to the country every week...* **quand elle était jeune**, *when she was young*.

We form the imperfect tense by replacing the **-ons** of the first person plural of the present by **-ais, -ais, -ait, -ions, -iez, -aient**:
cultiver – cultivons (present) – **cultivions** (imperfect).
(**être** is an exception, but notice that the endings are still the same: **j'étais, tu étais, il était, nous étions, vous étiez, ils étaient**.)
Il était heureux, *He was happy*.
Le soleil brillait et les oiseaux chantaient dans les arbres, *The sun was shining and the birds were singing in the trees*.

You can see that the "translation" of the imperfect depends on whether we are talking about a state, a continuous action or a habitual action in the past. A single tense conveys all three ideas.

For the time being, just get the feel of the imperfect as it is used in the lessons.

Have you noticed how much simpler French verb tenses are than their English counterparts?

Just to demonstrate what we mean, look at this table of equivalents:

Le présent **(je regarde)**	present simple (*I look*) present continuous (*I am looking*) present emphatic (*I do look*) present perfect continuous (*I have been looking*)
Le passé composé **(j'ai regardé)**	past simple (*I looked*) present perfect (*I have looked*)
L'imparfait **(je regardais)**	past continuous (*I was looking*) past frequentative (*I used to look*)
Le futur **(je regarderai)**	future simple (*I will look*) future continuous (*I will be looking*)

Second wave: 28th Lesson

78

Soixante-dix-huitième leçon

La femme est la patronne

1 Jean et Mireille font l'inventaire de leur magasin de vêtements :

2 – M. Bon, ici j'ai vingt-deux jupes gris clair [1], taille trente-huit...

3 – J. Oui, mais attends. Michelle en [2] a commandé une, n'est-ce pas ?

4 – M. Je la lui ai donnée la semaine dernière. On peut continuer ?

5 – J. D'accord.
– M. Après, nous_avons dix chemisiers en soie, dix_écharpes...

6 – J. Stop ! [3] Dix ? J'en_ai douze. Où sont les deux_autres ?

7 – M. Mais tu ne te souviens de rien ! Les deux Japonais ! Je leur en_ai vendu deux hier !

Pronunciation
1 ... meeray ... 2 ... zhyoop ... tie ... 5 ... swa deezaysharp

Notes

1 Composite adjectives of colour remain invariable after nouns: **un chapeau bleu ciel**, *a sky-blue hat*; **deux écharpes bleu marine**, *two navy-blue scarves*. Remember: **clair**, *light*; **foncé**, *dark* (for colours).

2 Notice the use of **en** in this lesson. It is added to the sentence to replace the noun just referred to. (Don't bother translating it.) Try and see how it is inserted to "balance" the sentence.

78

Seventy-Eighth Lesson

The woman is the boss

1 Jean and Mireille are taking the inventory of their clothes-shop:

2 – **M.** Right, here, I have twenty-two light-grey skirts, size 38...

3 – **J.** Yes, but wait. Michelle ordered one, didn't she?

4 – **M.** I gave it to her last week. Can we continue?

5 – **J.** OK.
  – **M.** After we have ten *(in)* silk blouses, ten scarves...

6 – **J.** Stop! Ten? I have twelve. Where are the two others?

7 – **M.** But you don't remember anything! The two Japanese! I sold them two yesterday!

3 We know **arrêter** for *to stop*. But there is also a French verb **stopper** (which is taken from English) and means *to stop abruptly*. It is most commonly found in the exclamation **Stop !**

Also, **faire de l'auto-stop**, *to hitch-hike*; **un auto-stoppeur**, *a hitch-hiker*.

8 – **J.** Ça va alors. Ensuite il y a quarante collants ⁴ et...

9 – **M.** Qu'est-ce qu'il y a ?
   – **J.** Je ne trouve pas mon crayon.

10 – **M.** Mais je te l'ai passé tout_à l'heure ⁵. Ah, le voilà, sous l'escabeau ⁶ !

11 – **J.** Tu sais, je suis un peu fatigué ; on peut s'arrêter deux minutes, s'il te plaît ?

12 – **M.** Je te l'ai déjà dit : on s'arrêtera quand_on_aura fini – et pas avant.

13 – **J.** Qu'est-ce que tu es dure comme patronne, alors ! ⁷   □

🔊 *8 ... kollahn ... **10** ... eskaboh*

🗂 Notes

4 **collant** comes from the verb **coller**, *to stick*. **Un collant** is a pair of tights (*panty-hose*) – in the same way that **un pantalon** is a pair of trousers. This singular/plural difference with English only applies to "nether garments".

***

▶ Exercice 1 – Traduisez

❶ Qu'est-ce que vous êtes gentil, alors ! ❷ L'échelle ? Je la lui ai prêtée hier. ❸ Mais tu ne te souviens de rien ! ❹ Stop ! Il y a une voiture qui vient ! ❺ Il en a commandé un avant-hier. ❻ Zut alors !

8 – **J.** That's alright then. Next, there are forty pairs of tights and...

9 – **M.** What's the matter?

– **J.** I can't *(don't)* find my pencil.

10 – **M.** But I gave *(passed)* it to you earlier. Ah, there it is, under the step-ladder!

11 – **J.** You know, I'm a little tired; can we stop *(ourselves)* two minutes, please?

12 – **M.** I already told you we will stop *(ourselves)* when we *(will)* have finished and not before.

13 – **J.** What a hard boss you are!

5 **Je l'ai vu tout à l'heure,** *I saw him a little while ago.* **Je le verrai tout à l'heure,** *I will see him soon.* The meaning depends on whether the verb in the phrase is past or future. **À tout à l'heure** (as a parting salutation) means *See you later.*

6 **un escabeau,** *a step-ladder;* **une échelle,** *a ladder.* Ladders are often used by **les pompiers,** *the firemen.*

7 **alors !** is often added to exclamations to make them more emphatic: **Qu'est-ce que je suis content, alors !,** *I'm really happy!* **Zut alors !,** *Damn!*

***

Answers to Exercice 1

❶ How kind you are! ❷ The ladder? I lent it to him yesterday. ❸ But you don't remember anything! ❹ Stop! There is a car coming! ❺ He ordered one the day before yesterday. ❻ Bloody hell!

Exercice 2 – Complétez

❶ We will stop when we have finished.
On s'........ quand on ....

❷ A scarf? I sold her one yesterday.
Une écharpe ? Je .... vendu une hier.

❸ Your pencil? I passed it to you a little while ago.
Ton crayon ? Je ...... passé .... l'...... .

79

Soixante-dix-neuvième leçon

La politique

1 La semaine prochaine, les Français voteront pour élire un nouveau président.

2 Ces_élections présidentielles ont lieu [1] tous les sept_ans [2].

3 Tous ceux qui ont plus de dix-_huit_ans ont le droit de voter.

Pronunciation
2 ... lyeu ... 3 ... drwa ...

Notes
1 **La réunion aura lieu mardi prochain**, *The meeting will take place next Tuesday*. **Elle a eu lieu il y a dix jours**, *It took place ten days ago*. Be careful: the expression **prendre place** resembles to "to take place", but it means *to take a seat*. **Prenez place, je vous en prie**, *Please take a seat* (a very formal usage).

❹ I have twelve *(of them).* Where are the two others?

   J'.... douze. Où sont les deux ...... ?

❺ When he phones me, I will tell you.

   Quand il me .... je vous le ....

Answers to Exercice 2

❶ – arrêtera – aura fini ❷ – lui en ai – ❸ – te l'ai – tout à – heure ❹ – en ai – autres ❺ – téléphonera – dirai

Second wave: 29th Lesson

79

Seventy-Ninth Lesson

Politics

1 Next week, the French will vote to elect a new president.

2 These presidential elections take place every seven years.

3 All those who are older *(have more)* than 18 have the right to vote.

LA SEMAINE PROCHAINE, LES FRANÇAIS VOTERONT POUR ÉLIRE UN NOUVEAU PRÉSIDENT.

2 **toutes les dix minutes**, *every ten minutes* (**minute** is feminine). **tous les jours**, *every day*; **à toute heure**, *at any time*; **un sur deux**, *one in two*.

trois cent quatorze • 314

4 L'élection se passe en deux temps [3] ou "tours", comme on les_appelle.

5 Au premier tour il y a souvent une dizaine [4] de candidats,

6 mais ce sont les deux qui ont_obtenu le plus de voix [5]

7 qui peuvent se présenter au deuxième tour.

8 Donc, il y a deux semaines, les candidats se sont présentés

9 et les_électeurs leur ont donné leurs voix.

10 Maintenant il ne reste qu'un candidat de droite et un de gauche.

11 Lequel va être choisi ? Nous n'en savons rien [6],

12 mais nous vous rappelons ce dicton, qui dit :

13 "Le capitalisme est l'exploitation de l'homme par l'homme,

14 alors que le socialisme, c'est le contraire !" ☐

*5 … kondeedah **6** … plyoos … vwa **12** … deektohn …*

Notes

3 **en deux (trois…) temps**, *in two (three…) phases, steps*. **Dans un premier temps**, *initially, firstly*. Dans un premier temps, nous allons examiner les candidatures, *Firstly, we'll examine the candidacies.*

4 **dix**, *ten*; **une dizaine**, *about ten*; **vingt**, *twenty*; **une vingtaine**, *about twenty* (and thus for all multiples of ten). L'homme avait la quarantaine, *The man was about forty years old*. Be careful of **une douzaine**, *a dozen*; **une quinzaine (de jours)**, *a fortnight*. Another word derived from a number is **le quinquennat**: it refers to the five-year term of the French president under the Fifth Republic.

4 The election happens in two phases or "rounds" as they are called.

5 At the first round, there are often about ten candidates,

6 but it is *(these are)* the two who have obtained the most votes

7 that can stand *(present themselves)* at the second round.

8 So, two weeks ago, the candidates stood

9 and the voters gave them their votes.

10 Now, there remains only one candidate of [the] right and one of [the] left.

11 Which one is going to be chosen? We have no idea,

12 but we remind you [of] this saying which says:

13 "Capitalism is the exploitation of man by man

14 whereas socialism *(it)* is the opposite"!

---

5 une voix (pl. des voix), *a voice.* Une voix grave, *a deep voice;* une voix aiguë *[aygyoo], a high voice;* **une voix** also means *a vote.*

6 Je n'en sais rien is a synonym for Je n'en ai aucune idée. Both mean: *I have no idea.* Je lui ai demandé mais il n'en savait rien, *I asked him but he had no idea.*

▶ Exercice 1 – Traduisez

❶ C'est lui qui a le plus de succès. ❷ Ceux qui ont plus de soixante ans ne doivent pas travailler. ❸ Le débat a eu lieu à dix heures et demie. ❹ Je leur ai donné mon opinion. ❺ Nous vous rappelons qu'il est interdit de fumer.

***

Exercice 2 – Complétez

❶ Which do you want? – I have no idea.

.... veux-tu ? – Je n'.......... .

❷ The exhibition takes place every six years.

L'exposition ..... tous ....

❸ The one who obtains the most votes wins.

..... qui obtient .... voix gagne.

80

Quatre-vingtième leçon

Les sondages

1 Pendant la période des_élections, il y a beaucoup de sondages

2 qui donnent parfois des résultats curieux...

3 – Pardon, monsieur, voulez-vous répondre à quelques questions, s'il vous plaît ?

4 Pour qui avez-vous l'intention de voter ?

– Aucune [1] idée.

🗨 Pronunciation

4 ... ohkyoon ...

Answers to Exercice 1

❶ It is he who has the most success. ❷ Those who are older than sixty do not have to work. ❸ The debate took place at 10.30. ❹ I gave them my opinion. ❺ We remind you that it is forbidden to smoke.

***

❹ About ten candidates stood *(presented themselves)*.
   Une .... candidats ....

❺ This article is expensive, whereas this one is cheap.
   ... article est cher .... celui-ci est bon marché.

Answers to Exercice 2

❶ Lesquels – en sais rien ❷ – a lieu – les six ans ❸ Celui – le plus de – ❹ – dizaine de – se sont présentés ❺ Cet – alors que –

Second wave: 30th Lesson

80

Eightieth Lesson

Opinion polls

1 During the period of the elections, there are many opinion polls
2 which sometimes give curious results...
3 – Excuse me, sir, will you answer *(to)* a few questions, please?
4 For whom *(have)* do you intend to vote?
   – No idea.

] Note

1 aucun (aucune) is more absolute than pas de. **Vous n'avez pas d'opi-nion**, *You have no opinion*. **Vous n'avez aucune opinion**, *You have no opinion at all*. **Aucune idée**, i.e. **Je n'ai aucune idée**, *I haven't the slightest idea*. **Je n'ai aucun ami**, *I have no friends whatsoever*.

5 – Y a-t-il un candidat dont vous avez entendu
parler ² davantage ³ ?
   – Non.

6 – À qui ⁴ pensez-vous quand on vous dit
"président" ?
   – À personne.

7 – De quoi ⁴ parlez-vous avec vos amis ?
   – Je n'en ai pas.

8 – Y a-t-il un meeting ⁵ auquel vous avez
l'intention d'assister ?
   – Aucun.

9 – Bon. Je dois noter que vous n'avez aucune
opinion politique. Au revoir, dit le sondeur.

10   Derrière lui, il entend la voix de l'homme qui
marmonne :

11 – Qu'est-ce qu'ils sont bêtes ⁶, ces sondages !   □

 8 … ohkel … ohkeun

 : Notes

  2 **entendre parler**, *to hear of* (i.e. reputation). **Est-ce que vous avez entendu parler de ce livre ?**, *Have you heard of this book?* **J'en ai entendu parler**, *I have heard of it/him/her* (depending on what precedes the
sentence).

  3 *more than* is **plus que**; (Important: pronounce the **s** of **plus** in this
construction.) **Je l'aime plus que l'autre**, *I like it/him/her more than
the other*; but: **Je l'aime davantage**, *I like it/him/her more*. **Davantage**
is used if there is no comparison and is usually found at the end of a
clause.

  4 **à qui, à quoi, de qui, de quoi**, etc. We know the rules for **qui** and **que**.
The preposition must always accompany the relative. Modern English
has a tendency to push the preposition to the end of the sentence. *The
man* ("that") *I talk to*. In French, we must say: **L'homme à qui je parle**. It

5 – Is there one candidate of whom you have heard
   (speak) **more?**
   – **No.**
6 – **Of** *(To)* **whom do you think when someone says
   "President"?**
   – *(To)* **Nobody.**
7 – **Of what do you talk with your friends?**
   – **I haven't any.**
8 – **Is there a rally which you intend to attend?**
   – **None.**
9 – **Good. I must note that you have no political opinion
   at all. Goodbye, says the pollster.**
10 **Behind him, he hears the voice of the man muttering**
   *(who mutters)***:**
11 – **How stupid these opinion polls are!**

is not at all as formal as its literal translation in English. Moreover, there
is no alternative form. Remember: preposition and relative together.

5 In politics, English has provided French with a couple of loan words;
un meeting is *a rally, a political gathering;* **un leader** needs no translation; neither does the following noun: **Aucun des deux hommes n'a
imposé son leadership sur son parti,** *Neither man has asserted his...
leadership over his party.*

6 **Qu'est-ce qu'il fait chaud !,** *How hot it is!* **Qu'est-ce que j'ai soif !,** *How
thirsty I am!* Although this use of **Qu'est-ce que...** as an exclamatory
phrase is grammatically incorrect, it is very common.

▶ Exercice 1 – Traduisez

❶ Est-ce que tu as des idées pour un cadeau ? – Aucune ! ❷ Ils me donnent les résultats demain. ❸ À qui pensez-vous ? – À mon copain Georges. ❹ C'est une chose à laquelle je ne pense jamais. ❺ Qu'est-ce que vous êtes bête ! ❻ Y a-t-il quelque chose que vous voulez ?

***

Exercice 2 – Complétez

❶ For whom are you going to vote? – No idea at all.

.... allez-vous voter ? – ...... idée.

❷ What do you talk about with your friends?

.... parlez-vous avec ... amis ?

❸ Those are ideas which I have heard (of).

Ce sont des idées .... j'ai ....•

81

Quatre-vingt-unième leçon

▶

L'argot

1 – Oh ! là, là ! Que c'est dur de trouver un appart !

2 Je fais les petites_annonces depuis un mois et je n'ai rien trouvé

3 jusqu'à ¹ présent. Dur, dur !

▢ Notes

1 **jusqu'à**, *until*, can be used for distance as well as time. **Jusqu'à dix heures**, *until 10.00*; **jusqu'au bout de la rue**, *to the end of the road*.

Answers to Exercice 1

❶ Do you have any ideas for a present? – Not at all! **❷** They will give me the results tomorrow. **❸** Who are you thinking about? – About my friend Georges. **❹** It's a thing which I never think about. **❺** How daft you are! **❻** Is there anything you want?

***

❹ It is the type of meeting which I never attend.
C'est le genre de réunion à .... je n'....... jamais.

❺ Do you intend to go there?
Est-ce que vous .... l'......... d'y aller ?

Answers to Exercice 2

❶ Pour qui – Aucune – **❷** De quoi – vos – **❸** – dont – entendu parler **❹** – laquelle – assiste – **❺** – avez – intention –

Second wave: 31st Lesson

81

Eighty-First Lesson

Slang

1 – Oh dear, how hard it is to find an apartment!
2 I have been looking at (*I do*) the small ads for a
month and I haven't found anything
3 up to now. It's a hard life!

4 – Qu'est-ce que tu cherches ?
  – Oh, un grand studio ou un truc ² comme ça,
5   mais tout_est vachement cher ³. Bon, tu as ton loyer ⁴,
6   mais en plus, il faut payer une caution
7   et si tu passes par une agence, il faut aussi compter des frais ⁵ d'agence !
8   J'en_ai vu un qui était chouette ⁶ mais je n'avais pas assez de fric ⁷.
9 – En plus ce n'est pas le bon ⁸ moment. Il vaut mieux attendre
10   les grandes vacances, quand tout le monde s'en va ;

Pronunciation
4 … tryook … 5 … vashmohn … lwoyay 6 … kohseeyohn 7 … fray … azhonss 8 … shwet …

Notes

2 We have already seen **un truc**, *a thingamy*. In this lesson we hear two young people using a lot of **argot**, *slang*. In an (unconscious) attempt to combat the formalism of their language, the French replace many words by slang equivalents, which do not have the same connotations as their "literal" translations in English (for example, **un appart**, short for **appartement**, line 1, does not have a commonly used direct equivalent in English). We want you to recognize such slang words and expressions. After contact with French people, you will get to know when to use them (and when to avoid them). This you can't learn from a book. So read our notes, and keep your ears open (we will put an asterisk before slang words).

3 *vachement, an adverb which amplifies (like **très**); **vachement dur**, *bloody hard*, etc. (see lesson 75, note 5).

4 – What [are] you looking for?
– Oh, a large studio or something like that,
5 but everything's so bloody expensive. OK, you have your rent,
6 but on top you also have to pay a deposit
7 and if you go through *(by)* an agency, you have to count agency fees on top!
8 I saw one which was lovely, but I didn't have enough cash.
9 – What's more, it's not the right moment. It is better to wait [for]
10 the *(big)* holidays when everyone goes away;

4 un loyer, *a rent*; louer, *to rent*; un locataire, *a tenant*. We've already seen une voiture de location, *a rental car*.

5 des frais, *charges*, *expenses*; frais bancaires, *bank charges*; frais de déplacement, *travel expenses*. As in English, les frais is always used in the plural.

6 *chouette (lit. "owl!"), *great*, *wonderful*, *lovely*, etc.

7 *le fric, *money*, *bread*, *cash*, etc. This is the most common of around twenty expressions.

8 bon also means *right*: Vous n'avez pas le bon numéro, *You don't have the right number*. Cette pièce n'est pas la bonne, *This part is not the right [one]*.

11   et là, avec un peu de veine [9], tu trouveras
      quelque chose.
12 – Oh et puis, j'en_ai marre [10] ! Allez, on va boire
      un pot [11] et parler d'autre chose.   □

11 ... ven ... 12 ... poh ...

Notes

9 avoir de la veine – *to be lucky*; *un veinard – a lucky devil*; *Pas de
veine ! – Out of luck!*

10 *en avoir marre (de)*, *to be fed up (with)*. Il en a marre de son travail,
He is fed up with his job. Note that en is always used in this expression.

***

Exercice 1 – Traduisez
❶ Il n'a jamais de fric, celui-là ! ❷ Son appart est chouette,
mais il est vachement cher. ❸ J'en ai marre d'écouter la
même chanson ! ❹ Bon, tu as ton loyer, mais il y a la caution
en plus. ❺ Il n'est pas là pour le moment. Il est allé boire
un pot avec Jean.

***

Exercice 2 – Complétez
❶ Agency fees have to be counted on top!
   Il ... ... des frais d'agence ... !

❷ Do you have another key? This one is not the right one.
   Vous n'avez pas une autre clef ? ...- là n'est pas la
   ... .

❸ We have been doing this exercise for a quarter of an hour.
   Nous ... cet exercice ... un ... d'heure.

11 and there, with a bit of luck, you'll find something.

12 – Oh and anyway, I'm fed up! Come on, we'll go for a drink and talk about something else *(of other thing[s])*.

11 *boire or **prendre un pot**, *to go for a glass, for a drink*.
All the slang words in this lesson are in common use. However, until you have a little more hands-on experience of speaking French, we suggest you make do with recognising them. (We give some more examples of common idioms in Lesson 110.)

***

Answers to Exercice 1

❶ He's never got any cash, that one! ❷ His/Her flat is lovely but it's bloody expensive! ❸ I'm fed up with listening to the same old song! ❹ OK, you have your rent, but there's the deposit on top. ❺ He's not here for the moment. He's gone for a drink with Jean.

***

❹ It's better to wait for tomorrow to be sure.

Il . . . . attendre demain pour être sûr.

❺ Everybody is going away on holiday.

. . . . s'. . . . en vacances.

Answers to Exercice 2

❶ – faut compter – en plus ❷ – Celle – bonne ❸ – faisons – depuis – quart – ❹ – vaut mieux – ❺ Tout le monde – en va –

Second wave: 32nd Lesson

82

Quatre-vingt-deuxième leçon

Un voyage à Beaune

1 – Je veux partir ce week-end, dit un jour Mme Froment à son mari.

2 N'importe où [1], mais je veux partir ! J'en_ai marre de Paris !

3 – Tiens ! On peut aller à Beaune. Comme ça, les_enfants verront [2] les_Hospices,

4 et nous pourrons acheter du vin pour notre cave. Qu'en penses-tu ?

5 – Superbe ! Je veux partir maintenant ! Tout de suite !

6 – Ne sois [3] pas bête ! Tu sais bien qu'entre huit_heures et neuf_heures, c'est l'heure de pointe,

7 et toutes les routes sont bloquées. Attendons un peu,

Pronunciation

... bown **2** ... namportoo ...**3** ... layzosspees **4** ... kahv konponstyoo **6** ... swa ... pwant

Notes

1 n'importe is a useful expression for the notion *anyhow, anywhere*, etc. n'importe où, *anywhere...*; n'importe quand, *at any time...*; n'importe comment, *in any way...*; n'importe qui, *anybody...*; n'importe quel jour, *any day* (i.e. no restrictions). **N'importe qui peut venir,** *Anybody can come.* **Choisissez une carte, n'importe laquelle,** *Choose a card, any one.* (See also lesson 105, § 2.)

82

Eighty-Second Lesson

A trip to Beaune

1 – I want to leave this weekend, said one day Mrs Froment to her husband.

2 Anywhere, but I want to leave! I'm fed up with Paris!

3 – Hold on! We can go to Beaune. Like that, the children will see the almshouses

4 and we will be able to buy some wine for our cellar. What do you think?

5 – Superb! I want to leave now! Straight away!

6 – Don't be silly. You know [very] well that between 8.00 and 9.00 it's the rush hour,

7 and all the roads are blocked. Let's wait a bit,

NE SOIS PAS SI PRESSÉ !

2 voir, *to see*, in the future tense is: **je verrai, tu verras, il verra, nous verrons, vous verrez, ils verront**. **On peut y aller ? – On verra**, *Can we go? – We'll see.*

3 This is the **tu** form of **soyez**, the subjunctive of **être**. It is used as an imperative.

8 et on partira vers onze heures. Comme ça, on_évitera les_embouteillages.

9 – Où est-ce qu'on va dormir ?⁴ Tes_amis sont toujours là-bas ?

10 – Non, mais on choisira un hôtel dans le guide Michelin⁵,

11 n'importe lequel⁶, ils sont tous bons. Et si on ne trouve rien à Beaune même,

12 on_ira ailleurs⁷. Allez ! Appelle les_enfants et préparons nos_affaires. □

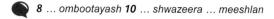 *8 … ombootayash* **10** *… shwazeera … meeshlan*

Notes

4 **dormir** is the physical act of sleeping, **se coucher** is *to go to bed*. **Une chambre à coucher**, *a bedroom*.

5 **le guide Michelin** – a popular tourist guide which lists places of interest, hotels and restaurants. Another popular hotel and restaurant guide is the Gault et Millau.

***

Exercice 1 – Traduisez

❶ Ne sois pas si pressé ! ❷ Tu sais bien que c'est l'heure de pointe. ❸ On pourra éviter les embouteillages si on part maintenant. ❹ Je veux lire un journal. N'importe lequel. ❺ Si on ne trouve rien, on ira ailleurs.

8 and we will leave around 11.00. That way, we'll avoid the traffic jams.

9 – Where are we going to sleep? Your friends are still there?

10 – No, but we'll choose a hotel from *(in)* the Michelin Guide,

11 any one, they are all good. And if we don't find anything in Beaune itself,

12 we will go elsewhere. Come on! Call the children and let's get our things together *(ready)*.

6 n'importe **lequel**, *any one*, <u>but</u> n'importe **qui**, *anyone*, *anybody* (person).

7 ailleurs, *elsewhere*. **D'ailleurs...** (at the beginning of a sentence), *Moreover...*

***

Answers to Exercice 1

❶ Don't be in such a hurry! ❷ You know very well that it's the rush hour. ❸ We will be able to avoid the traffic jams if we leave now. ❹ I want to read a newspaper. Any one. ❺ If we don't find anything, we will go elsewhere.

Exercice 2 – Complétez

❶ Anybody has the right to go in.
N'.......... a le ..... d'entrer.

❷ He was fed up with Paris, so he left for somewhere else.
Il en ..... marre de Paris, donc il ... parti ....

❸ We will see our friends and the children will be able to play.
Nous .... nos amis et les enfants .... jouer.

83

Quatre-vingt-troisième leçon

Voyage à Beaune (suite)

1 À onze‿heures, la voiture chargée [1] d'enfants et de valises,
2 les Froment partent pour Beaune. À la porte d'Orléans [2]
3 ils prennent l'autoroute du Sud. Il n'y a pas trop de monde.
4 Il fait‿un temps magnifique et tout le monde est‿heureux.

Notes

1 We saw in lesson 81 that **les frais** meant *charges*. Here is another "false friend" **charger**, *to load*. **Ce fusil est chargé**, *This gun is loaded*. **Ils ont chargé le camion**, *They loaded the lorry*.

2 There are 22 entrances into Paris, called **portes**, *gates*. They all lead off from a circular expressway called **le boulevard périphérique**.

❹ I want to see you. Tell me a day. At any time.
Je veux vous voir. Dites-moi un jour. N'........ ....

❺ What do you think *(of it)*? – Don't be silly!
Qu'.. ......- ..? – Ne .... pas bête !

Second wave: 33rd Lesson

──────────────────────────────── 83

Eighty-Third Lesson

Trip to Beaune (continued)

1 At 11.00, the car laden with children and suitcases,
2 the Froments leave for Beaune. At the Porte
   d'Orléans
3 they take the southern motorway. There are not too
   many people.
4 The weather is magnificent and everybody is happy.

IL EST TRÈS FACILE À RECONNAÎTRE.

5 Ils s'arrêtent à une station-service pour faire le
   plein d'essence [3] et se dégourdir les jambes.

6 Bientôt, ils_arrivent en Bourgogne.

7 C'est facile à reconnaître à cause des vignobles
   qui couvrent les collines.

8 Ils prennent la sortie de Beaune et s'arrêtent au
   péage [4].

9 M. Froment cherche sa carte de crédit.

10 L'ayant trouvée [5], il paie,

11 et la famille continue son chemin [6] vers le
    centre-ville.   □

Pronunciation
6 ... boorgoyn

Notes

3 Be careful at petrol stations in France! l'essence (m.), *petrol*, but **gas oil**
   or **gazole** is *diesel fuel*. Some people confuse one for the other – but
   only once! We see in line 5 how to say *fill the tank*, **faire le plein**. Most
   service stations are self-service, but if you do have an attendant, you ask
   for **Le plein, s'il vous plaît**. **Le pétrole**, *mineral oil*; **l'huile**, *oil* (for cars,
   for cooking, etc.).

4 **un péage** is both *a toll* and *a tollbooth*. **Un pont à péage**, *a toll bridge*;
   payer un péage, *to pay a toll*. All motorways in France are tollroads.

***

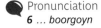
Exercice 1 – Traduisez

❶ Ayant fait un peu de chemin, il s'est arrêté. ❷ Elle s'en va
demain pour la Bourgogne. ❸ Il est très facile à reconnaître.
❹ On a passé dix minutes à chercher la sortie. ❺ Il n'y a
jamais trop de monde à cette heure. ❻ Le plein, s'il vous
plaît.

5 They stop at a service station to fill up with petrol and stretch their legs.

6 Soon, they arrive in Burgundy.

7 It is easy to recognize because of the vineyards which cover the hills.

8 They take the exit for (*of*) Beaune and stop at the toll booth.

9 Mr Froment looks for his credit card.

10 Having found it, he pays,

11 and the family continues its way towards the town centre.

---

5 **ayant** is the present participle of **avoir**. It is used either as part of a verbal phrase: **Ayant un peu d'argent, il est allé au restaurant**, *Having a little money, he went to a restaurant*; or as an auxiliary: **Ayant demandé à un policier, il a continué son chemin**, *Having asked a policeman, he continued on his way*. (For a brief explanation of the "agreement" of the past participle, see lesson 84.)

6 **un chemin** literally means *a path* or *lane*. However, it can be used figuratively to mean *way* or *road*. **Tous les chemins mènent à Rome**, *All roads lead to Rome*. **Je vais lui demander le chemin**, *I am going to ask him/her the way*. **Ce chemin mène à la gare**, *This road leads to the station*. **Nous sommes sur le bon chemin**, *We are on the right road*. **Le chemin de fer**, *the railway*. We find this term in the national railway authorities of France (SNCF), Belgium (SNCFB) and Switzerland (CFF). **Le chemin des_écoliers** – ("the schoolboy's road"): the longest possible way round! **Désolé pour mon retard – j'ai pris le chemin des écoliers**, *Sorry I'm late – I took the long way round*.

***

Answers to Exercice 1

❶ Having gone a little way, he stopped. ❷ She is leaving tomorrow for Burgundy. ❸ He is very easy to recognize. ❹ We spent ten minutes looking for the exit. ❺ There are never too many people at this time. ❻ Fill it up, please.

Exercice 2 – Complétez

❶ I'm going to stretch my legs.
Je vais . . . .

❷ We will stop before arriving.
Nous nous . . . . avant d' . . . .

❸ I spent ten years working for him.
J'ai . . . . . dix ans à . . . . pour lui.

Quatre-vingt-quatrième leçon

Révision – Revision

1 Pronoun order

We have already a good notion of the order of pronouns before verbs. We know that personal pronouns come before the verb (**il me parle**, **je lui donne**, etc.), unless we are using the imperative mood (**donnez-moi**, **téléphonez-moi**, etc.). But what happens when we have a more complex sentence with several pronouns?

Subject	Indirect object	Direct object	Indirect object	
je	me			
tu	te	le	lui	verb
il/elle	se	la		or
nous	nous			auxiliary
vous	vous	les	leur	
ils/elles				

It's not as bad as it looks!

❹ Can you show me the way to the town centre?
.... m'indiquer le ...... pour le ......-..... ?

❺ He looked for his credit card. Having found it, he paid the toll.
Il a cherché .... L'............, il a payé ..
......

Answers to Exercice 2
❶ – me dégourdir les jambes ❷ – arrêterons – arriver ❸ – passé
– travailler – ❹ Pouvez-vous – chemin – centre-ville ❺ – sa carte de
crédit – ayant trouvée – le péage

Second wave: 34th Lesson

84

Eighty-Fourth Lesson

If you memorise this table, you will always know in what order the
pronouns come. For example, *I gave it to him*. We need subject +
direct object + indirect object + auxiliary which gives us: **Je le lui
ai donné**.
She told me it: **Elle me l'a dit**.
Will you send them to us?: **Voulez-vous nous les envoyer ?**
Look back at the table and check.
These "mental gymnastics" take a little time to master, but if you
make an effort to remember the order, you will find that, very soon,
you can form sentences automatically – and correctly!
(We can expand this table by adding **y** and **en** to it. See lesson 88.)

You have probably noticed that, in the past tense, the past participle changes form depending on what is in front of it. The basic
rule that governs this is:
(a) verbs conjugated with **être** agree with their subject,
(b) verbs conjugated with **avoir** agree with the nearest preceding
direct object.
For the time being, we ask you simply to remember the rule. We
do not intend to expand on it yet; and since the pronunciation of
the past participle does not change, it is something that needs not
worry us for the moment.

2 *Quand, dès que* + future tense

Quand il viendra, je vous le dirai, *When he comes, I will tell you*.
In such a construction, French puts both verbs into the future tense
(which is logical since neither action has yet taken place!). So, after
quand (lorsque), and **dès que (aussitôt que)**, the following verb is
in the future tense.
Dès que le courrier arrivera, je vous l'apporterai, *As soon as the
mail arrives, I will bring it to you*.
(Notice the order of the pronouns, too.)
So, where English uses the present perfect (when he has finished...),
the French puts the auxiliary in the future: **dès qu'il aura fini**.
Quand vous l'aurez lu, donnez-le moi, *When you have read it, give
it to me*.

Being able to manipulate such constructions automatically is a
question of reflex – which means practice. Memorise one or two of
the model sentences and try and invent new, short ones based on
them. You will be surprised how quickly it becomes second nature.

3 Reflexive verbs

French uses reflexive verbs (e.g. **se laver**) more extensively than
English. Some verbs change their meaning depending on whether
they are reflexive or not. Here are six very common ones. To help
memorise them, think of the word ABROAD:

Aller, *to go*	**s'en aller**, *to go away, to leave*
Battre, *to beat*	**se battre**, *to fight*
Rappeler, *to remind*	**se rappeler**, *to remember*
Occuper, *to occupy*	**s'occuper (de)**, *to look after*
Attendre, *to wait for*	**s'attendre à**, *to expect*
Demander, *to ask*	**se demander**, *to wonder*.

Here are a few examples:
Il est allé en Espagne, *He went to Spain*.
Ils s'en vont en vacances, *They are going on holiday*.
La France a battu la suisse, *France beat Switzerland*.
Les supporters se sont battus, *The supporters fought ("each other")*.

Rappelez-moi votre nom, *Remind me of your name.*
Elle ne se rappelle pas cette histoire, *She does not remember this story.*
Of course there are others – but we don't want to do everything at once.

4 Compound relatives *lequel, laquelle* etc.

We know how to use **quel**, **quelle**, etc.
Now, look at these "compound relatives", (i.e. preposition + a relative pronoun): **lequel**, **laquelle** (**lesquels**, **lesquelles**).
Laquelle de ces deux collines ?, *Which of these two hills?*
Lesquelles de ces cartes de crédit... ?, *Which of these credit cards?*
(i.e. you can have more than one).

We can also use the above relatives in the affirmative form:
un homme avec lequel je travaille, *a man with whom I work.*
une société dans laquelle il a des actions, *a company in which he has shares.*

If the verb we are using takes the preposition **à** (e.g. **penser à**), we use: **auquel**, **à laquelle** (**auxquels**, **auxquelles**).
C'est une solution à laquelle j'ai déjà pensé, *It's a solution I have already thought of.*

We sometimes find **duquel**, **de laquelle** (**desquels**, **desquelles**), *of which*, *of whom*, but **dont** is more common; or **de qui** if there is a preposition before the preceding noun:

C'est un homme duquel on dit du bien	*He is a man*
C'est un homme dont on dit du bien	*who is highly*
C'est un homme de qui on dit du bien	*spoken of.*

We don't wish to swamp you with details but to show you how, from one simple rule you have already mastered, other more complex forms can be assembled. Remember that there is an enormous difference between "complex" and "complicated".

Seconde Wave: 35th Lesson

85

Quatre-vingt-cinquième leçon

Une visite à Beaune (fin)

1 Les Froment sont_arrivés à Beaune à
   trois_heures dix,
2 et ils se sont précipités [1] pour visiter
   les_Hospices.
3 Ces bâtiments, aux toits polychromes [2], datent
   du quinzième siècle ;
4 ils sont toujours habités [3], mais_aujourd'hui il
   n'y a ni malades ni mendiants [4],
5 seulement des personnes du troisième âge [5].
6 Une fois la visite finie, ils se sont rendus
   dans_une cave
7 pour déguster du vin et pour en_acheter.

Pronunciation
3 ... twa poleekrom dat ...

Notes

1 **Je suis pressé,** *I am in a hurry.* **Dépêchez-vous,** *Hurry up!* **se précipiter,**
   to rush. **Elle s'est précipitée dans ses bras,** *She rushed into his arms.*
   (Notice the "agreement" of the past participle, which takes an **s** with the
   plural subject **ils**.)

2 **La fille aux cheveux blonds,** *The girl with blond hair.* **Au, à la,** indicates
   a physical property. (Polychromatic is the adjective applied to a certain style of roofing found in Burgundy which used red, gold and green
   tiles.)

3 Be careful of this "false friend": **habiter,** *to live in*; **une maison habitée,**
   an inhabited house; **une maison inhabitée,** *an uninhabited house*; **un**
   habitant, *an inhabitant.*

Eighty-Fifth Lesson

A visit to Beaune (end)

1   The Froments arrived at Beaune at 3.10,
2   and they rushed to visit the almhouses.
3   These buildings, with their polychromatic roofs, date from the 15th century,
4   they are still inhabited but today there are neither sick [people] nor beggars,
5   only senior citizens.
6   Once the visit [was] finished they went *(rendered themselves) (in)* to a cellar
7   to taste wine and to buy some.

CE ROMAN EST FRANCHEMENT MAUVAIS.

4   **Je n'ai ni argent, ni amis,** *I have neither money nor friends.* Don't forget that the verb must be negative as well: **Il ne veut ni manger ni boire,** *He doesn't want to eat or drink.* **Vous pouvez prendre soit du cuir soit du plastique,** *You can take either leather or plastic.* **Je peux vous voir soit aujourd'hui, soit après-demain,** *I can see you either today or the day after tomorrow.* (Another form of *either... or* is **ou... ou** instead of **soit... soit**), **ou du cuir ou du plastique.**

5   **le troisième âge** is an euphemism for elderly people. Similarly, in English, we transformed *"old age pensioners"* into *"senior citizens".*

8 – Qu'est-ce que tu penses de celui-ci ?

   – Il est franchement mauvais.

9 – Et celui-là n'est pas fameux [6] non plus.

   – Et ce Côtes-de-Beaune [7] ?

10 – Beurk ! C'est le pire de tous !

   – Moi, je trouve qu'il n'est pas mauvais.

11 – D'accord. Commande-le toi-même et moi, je le paierai [8].

12   Après cet_épisode hautement culturel, M. Froment a décidé

13   de chercher un petit_hôtel sympathique pour y coucher.

14   Mais, n'ayant rien trouvé ni à Beaune, ni dans les_environs,

15   ils sont repartis pour Paris à huit_heures.   ☐

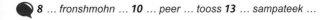 **8** … fronshmohn … **10** … peer … tooss **13** … sampateek …

Notes

6   *Famous* is **célèbre**; **fameux** is a familiar way of saying *first rate, great*. **Il est fameux, ton vin !**, *Your wine is really great!* **Pas fameux**, *not up to much*, or for a person, *not good at*. **Je ne suis pas fameux en_maths**, *I'm not good at maths*.

7   **la côte**, *the coast*. **La Côte d'Ivoire**, *Ivory Coast*. The word is often found in wine names, indicating which region the wine comes from*: **Le Côtes-de-Nuits**, **le Côtes-de-Beaune**, etc. (To see how accents sometimes affect pronunciation, skip back to lesson 74, line 6, and listen to the word **la cote** *[kot]*. Now listen to **côte** with the circumflex *[koht]*. It takes a little training, but your ear – and in this case your palate! – will soon make the difference.)

8 – What do you think of this one?
  – It's downright *(frankly)* bad.
9 – And this one isn't wonderful either.
  – And this Côtes-de-Beaune?
10 – Yuk! It's the worst of all!
  – *(Me)*, I find *(that)* it isn't bad.
11 – OK, order it yourself and *(me)*, I will pay [for] it.
12 After this highly cultural episode, Mr Froment decided
13 to look [for] a little, nice hotel to sleep in *(there)*.
14 But, having found nothing either in Beaune or in the surroundings,
15 they left again for Paris at 8.00.

---

* the gender changes since **le vin** is masculine. Another subtlety: When Bourgogne and Bordeaux refer to the regions, they take an initial capital. When they refer to the wines, they take a lower case (see exercise 1, No. 2).

8 **payer quelque chose**, *to pay for something*; **payer quelqu'un**, *to pay someone*. We can write either **je paie, tu paies, il paie, ils paient**, or **je paye, tu payes, il paye, ils payent** (**nous payons** and **vous payez** are the only possible forms with these pronouns). This is true for other verbs ending in **-ayer** like **bégayer**, *to stammer*, **rayer**, *to cross out*.

▶ Exercice 1 – Traduisez

❶ J'habite à Paris. – Paris même ou les environs ? ❷ C'est un bourgogne ou un bordeaux ? – Ni l'un ni l'autre. ❸ Ce roman est franchement mauvais. – Celui-ci est pire. ❹ Regarde ! Là-bas, c'est le président lui-même ! ❺ Une fois le repas fini, il est reparti chez lui. ❻ Beurk ! Pas fameux, ton vin !

***

Exercice 2 – Complétez

❶ Neither my wife nor I can come.
   .. ma femme .. moi .. pourrons venir.

❷ He pays them, as usual, two months late.
   Il les .... d'........ avec deux mois de retard.

❸ She rushed to see him.
   Elle s'............ pour le voir.

86

Quatre-vingt-sixième leçon

▶ ## À l'école primaire

1   L'institutrice ¹ s'adresse à ses élèves à la fin de
    la leçon :

Note

1   un instituteur (une institutrice) works in une école primaire, *a primary school*; un élève, *a pupil*; un lycéen (-éenne), *a high school pupil* (see lesson 110).

Answers to Exercice 1

❶ I live in Paris. – Paris itself or the surroundings? ❷ It is a burgundy or a bordeaux? – Neither one nor the other. ❸ This novel is downright bad. – This one is worse. ❹ Look! Over there, it's the President himself! ❺ Once the meal was finished, he left again for his house. ❻ Yuk! Your wine isn't up to much!

***

❹ The almhouses welcomed either beggars or sick people.
Les Hospices accueillaient .... des mendiants .... des
....

❺ They told us it themselves.
Ils ...... ont dit ....

Answers to Exercice 2

❶ Ni – ni – ne – ❷ – paie comme – habitude – ❸ – est précipitée – ❹ – soit – soit – malades ❺ – nous l' – eux-mêmes

Second wave: 36th Lesson

Eighty-Sixth Lesson

At the primary school

1   The teacher addresses (herself to) her pupils at the
    end of the lesson:

2 – Eh bien, les_enfants, je vous_ai appris les temps ² de tous les verbes.

3 Vous connaissez le présent, le passé, le futur et l'imparfait.

4 J'espère que vous_avez bien compris ? Voyons...

5 Chloé, si je te dis ³ "Je me suis lavé, tu t'es lavé, il s'est lavé,

6 nous nous sommes lavés, vous vous_êtes lavés, ils se sont lavés", qu'est-ce que c'est ?

7 – Ben, mademoiselle, c'est dimanche !

8 – Passons_à autre chose. Benoît, nous_avons parlé de sens ⁴ civique et de l'écologie.

9 Alors, qu'est-ce qu'on fait d'une voiture qui est trop vieille,

10 qui est rouillée et dont_on ne veut plus ?

11 – On la vend à mon père, mademoiselle ! ⁵

***

12 – Aïe ! Qu'est-ce que j'ai mal au genou ! dit le cancre.

13 – Un peu de migraine, je suppose ? dit son professeur.

☐

Pronunciation
*2 ... too ... 8 ... sohnss ... **10** ... rooyay ... **13** ... meegren ...*

Notes

2 **un temps**, in a grammatical sense, is *a verb tense*.

3 Primary school teachers use the **tu** form when addressing their pupils, who reply with the **vous** form.

4 **le sens** *[sohnss]*, *the sense, the feeling of*. **Il n'a pas le sens de l'humour**, *He has no sense of humour*. The word can also mean "direction" and we find it in the expression: **une rue à sens unique** (lit. "one direction"), *a one-way street*.

2 – Well, children, I have taught you the tenses of all the verbs.

3 You know the present, the past, the future, and the imperfect.

4 I hope you have really *(well)* understood ? Let's see...

5 Chloé, if I say to you: "I have washed, you have washed, he has washed,

6 we have washed, you have washed, they have washed"; what is it?

7 – Ehm, miss, it's Sunday!

8 – Let's go on *(pass)* to other things. Benoît, we have spoken of civic pride *(sense)* and the environment.

9 So what do people *(one)* do with a car which is too old,

10 which is rusty and *(of)* which one wants no longer?

11 – They sell it to my father, miss!

***

12 – Ouch! *(How)* my knee hurts! says the dunce.

13 – A slight *(little of)* migraine, I suppose ? says his teacher.

5 Notice how we translate **on** in this exchange. The pronoun here refers to people in general, a habit or custom shared, and we translate it accordingly. Yet another example of how **on** is widely used in everyday French.

▶ Exercice 1 – Traduisez

❶ Passons à autre chose, si vous voulez bien. ❷ Quel jour sommes-nous ? – C'est mardi. ❸ Qu'est-ce que j'ai mal à la tête ! ❹ Je me suis adressé au bureau de renseignements. ❺ Qu'est-ce qu'on fait de ce vieux meuble ?

***

Exercice 2 – Complétez

❶ What do you say in French when you're unhappy?
Qu'est-ce qu'.. dit .. français quand .. est malheureux ?

❷ She explained it to me but I didn't really understand.
Elle ..... expliqué, mais je n'ai pas .... compris.

❸ A car which is old and which one no longer wants.
Une voiture qui est vieille et ...... ne veut .....

87

Quatre-vingt-septième leçon

▶ ### Faites attention à "faire"

1 Voici quelques_exemples de l'emploi du verbe "faire" :

2 – Il fait bon ici. Il ne fait ni trop chaud ni trop froid.

3 – Je crois que je vais faire une petite sieste.

4 – Excusez-moi de vous faire attendre.

5 – Si je rentre trop tard, mes enfants vont faire des_histoires.

Answers to Exercice 1

❶ Let's go on to something else, if you please. ❷ What day is it? – It's Tuesday. ❸ I've got a terrible headache! ❹ I asked at the information office. ❺ What do we do with this old piece of furniture?

***

❹ He taught it to us last week.
   Il ...... a appris la semaine dernière.

❺ We will talk about it next year.
   Nous en .... l'année prochaine.

Answers to Exercice 2

❶ – on – en – on – ❷ – me l'a – bien – ❸ – dont on – plus ❹ – nous l' – ❺ – parlerons –

Second wave: 37th Lesson

_____

87

Eighty-Seventh Lesson

Be careful with "to do/to make"

1   Here are a few examples of the use of the verb "to do/to make":
2 – It's nice here. It is neither too hot nor too cold.
3 – I think that I will go for a little nap.
4 – Excuse me for making you wait.
5 – If I go back too late, my children will make a fuss.

6 – Ne fais pas l'idiot ! Tu m'as fait peur avec tes bêtises [1].

7 – Le fromage n'était pas_assez "fait" ; en revanche [2], le poisson l'était trop.

8 – J'ai fait une gaffe monumentale ! Je croyais que c'était sa femme !

9 – Ce tableau faisait deux mille au marché. Je l'ai payé mille.

– On vous_a refait ! [3]

10 – Si tu leur téléphones maintenant, tu feras d'une pierre deux coups.

11 L'habit ne fait pas le moine.

12 – Il a gagné au loto mais il a perdu son ticket. Faut le faire [4] ! ☐

Pronunciation

7 … *revonsh* … **10** … *koo* **11** *labee* … *mwan*

Notes

1 We know that **bête** means *stupid*. **Une bêtise** is *a stupid action*. **Cet enfant ne fait que des bêtises**, *This child is always doing stupid things*.

2 **en revanche**, *on the other hand, to make up for it*. **Il n'est pas très beau, mais en revanche, il est très intelligent**, *He's not very handsome, but, to make up for it, he's very intelligent*. **Nous ne sommes pas pour l'idée, mais en revanche, nous ne la critiquons pas**, *We are not for the idea, but, on the other hand, we don't criticize it*. **Par contre** is widely used instead of **en revanche**, but this is frowned upon by purists.

6 – Don't be an idiot! You frightened me with your idiocies.

7 – The cheese wasn't ripe *("done")* enough; on the other hand, the fish was too *(much)*.

8 – I made a monumental blunder! I thought she was his wife!

9 – This painting cost *(made)* 2,000 in the market. I paid 1,000 [for] it.
 – You were had *(done)*!

10 – If you phone them now, you will kill two birds with one stone *(make of one stone two blows)*.

11 The clothes don't make the monk *(i.e. appearances are not everything)*.

12 – He won *(at)* the loto but lost his ticket! That takes some doing *(It is necessary to do it)*!

3 The idiom is very similar to the English. So is the alternative. **On vous a eu !**, *You have been had!*

4 This is an exclamation of astonishment: *That takes some doing!* It can be used either pejorative – as here – or as a compliment. **Elle parle quatre langues couramment. Faut le faire !**, *She speaks four languages fluently. That takes some doing!*

▶ Exercice 1 – Traduisez

❶ Il a fait d'une pierre deux coups. ❷ Je crois qu'il fait une sieste. ❸ Excuse-nous de te faire attendre. ❹ Quelle gaffe ! Tu ne fais que des bêtises ! ❺ Combien fait ce tableau ? ❻ On t'a eu, mon pauvre ami.

***

Exercice 2 – Complétez

❶ It was very hot in India.
Il .... très chaud en Inde.

❷ He frightened me!
Il ... . peur !

❸ We are going to go for a little walk.
On ... . une petite ....

❹ They won four times. That takes some doing!
Ils ... . quatre fois. .... !

88

Quatre-vingt-huitième leçon

▶ ## Le petit écran ¹

1 De plus en plus, la télévision prend␣une place majeure dans notre vie, qu'on le veuille ou non ².

2 Les téléviseurs ³ sont partout : presque tous les foyers en possèdent au moins un,

🗣 Pronunciation
1 ... veuy ... 2 ... fwayay ...

🔲 Notes

1 See our remark on metonymy in lesson 38, note 1. **Le petit écran** is a substitute expression for *television*.

2 **veuille** is the subjunctive of **vouloir**. We'll look at the subjunctive in greater detail later. For the time being, just remember this expression

Answers to Exercice 1

❶ He killed two birds with one stone. ❷ I think he's having a nap.
❸ Excuse us for making you wait. ❹ What a blunder! You're always
doing stupid things! ❺ How much is this painting? ❻ You've been
had, my poor friend.

***

❺ They made me wait.
Ils ..ont ....

❻ It's not very big but, to make up for it, it's very robust.
Ce n'est pas très grand mais .... c'est très solide.

Answers to Exercice 2

❶ – faisait – ❷ – m'a fait – ❸ – va faire – promenade ❹ – ont gagné
– Faut le faire ❺ – m' – fait attendre ❻ – en revanche –

Second wave: 38th Lesson

88

Eighty-Eighth Lesson

The small screen

1 More and more, television is taking a major place in
our life, whether we like it or not.
2 TV sets are everywhere: almost all households have
at least one,

qu'on le veuille ou non, *whether you/we/one like(s) it or not*. Il sera
embauché, qu'on le veuille ou non, *He'll get the job, whether we like
it or not*. Listen carefully to the pronunciation *[veuy]*.

3 le téléviseur (no short form) always means *the TV set*. Although la
télévision (and the familiar short form la télé) generally refers to the
medium of TV, the words are sometimes used to refer to the set. The
context will make things clear.

3 et le nombre de chaînes augmente d'année en année : avec le câble et le satellite, on peut‿en recevoir jusqu'à deux ou trois cents.

4 En France, la "télé" – comme on dit – est financée en partie par la publicité [4],

5 et dans le cas des chaînes publiques, par la redevance audiovisuelle.

6 Côté [5] émissions, il y en‿a pour tous les goûts.

7 Une soirée typique commencera avec un jeu et une série, suivis du journal et de la météo [6].

8 On‿enchaîne avec un divertissement ou un téléfilm – ou peut-‿être une soirée thématique.

9 Certaines chaînes proposent des films inédits [7] à la télévision, qu'on peut‿acheter à la séance avec une télécommande.

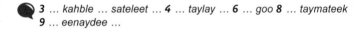

3 ... kahble ... sateleet ... 4 ... taylay ... 6 ... goo 8 ... taymateek 9 ... eenaydee ...

Notes

4 **la publicité** (often shortened to **la pub** in everyday speech) translates two notions in English: *advertising* and the broader word *publicity*. Much in vogue is the word **la communication**, which means *public relations*, but which in its basic form is a synonym for advertising.

5 **le côté**, *the side*. **Du côté droit, la tour Eiffel, du côté gauche, le Trocadéro**, *On the right, the Eiffel Tower, on the left, the Trocadéro*. In line 6, we use **côté** idiomatically – without the article – to mean *As for...* **L'hôtel est très sympa. Côté cuisine, c'est superbe**, *The hotel is great. As for the cooking, it's fabulous*. In such constructions, **côté** is always used to start a sentence in apposition.

6 Two commonly contracted nouns: **le journal télévisé** (sometimes abbreviated to **le JT** and pronounced *[le zhee-tay]*) is more simply referred

3 and the number of channels increases from year to year: with cable and satellite, we can receive up to two or three hundred.

4 In France, the "telly", as we call it, is financed partly by advertising,

5 and in the case of the public channels, by the [audiovisual] licence.

6 In terms of programmes, there is something for every taste.

7 A typical evening will begin with a game and a series, followed by the news and weather [forecast].

8 We continue with an entertainment [show] or a telefilm or possibly a themed evening.

9 Some channels offer first-run features *(unpublished on TV)* on a pay-per-view basis *(which can be bought per showing with the remote control)*.

to as **le journal**. This is usually followed by **le bulletin météorologique**, shortened to **la météo**. Notice the shift in gender; this is due to the fact that **météo** is assumed to be the short form of **la météorologie**, *the science of meteorology*. You see how important it is to learn the gender of a noun?!

7 **inédit** literally means *unpublished* from the verb **éditer**, *to publish* (**un éditeur** = *a publisher*). It can be taken in the broader sense, as it is here, **un film inédit à la télé**, *a film that hasn't been shown on the box before*. And in an even broader interpretation, it means anything that is novel, and hence surprising: **un spectacle inédit**, *a surprising show*.

10 Mais il y a ceux qui ne supportent pas [8] le petit écran.

11 Comme cette femme qui confie à son amie :
– Mon fils regarde tellement la télé

12 que si tu lui dis : Viens regarder ce magnifique coucher de soleil,

13 il te demande : C'est sur quelle chaîne ? □

11 … konfee … fees … 12 … kooshay de solay

***

Exercice 1 – Traduisez

❶ Inutile de discuter. Il viendra qu'on le veuille ou non.
❷ Viens vite regarder cette émission ! C'est hilarant. ❸ Je veux regarder la météo. C'est sur quelle chaîne ? ❹ Son livre est inédit en France. ❺ Je ne supporte pas la télé.

***

Exercice 2 – Complétez

❶ Televisions are everywhere. Every household has at least one.
Les .... sont partout. Tous les foyers ....
au moins un.

❷ How many channels? We can receive twenty.
Combien de chaînes ? .... vingt.

❸ The hotel is great. As for the cooking, it's great.
L'hôtel est .... c'est superbe.

❹ The number of visitors increases every year.
Le nombre de visiteurs ....

10   But there are those who can't stand the television
         (small screen).
11   Like the woman who confides to her friend:
   –   My son watches so much TV
12   that if you say to him: Come and look at this
         beautiful sunset,
13   he [will] ask you: What channel's it on?

] Note

8   In addition to the literal meaning of *to support*, **supporter** also means
        to tolerate. The verb is generally found in the negative form, e.g. **Je ne
        peux pas supporter...**, *I can't stand...* A variant: **Je ne supporte pas...**
        Je n'irai jamais en Égypte. Je ne supporte pas la chaleur, *I'll never go
        to Egypt. I can't stand the heat.*

***

Answers to Exercice 1

❶ No point arguing about it. He'll come whether we like it or not.
❷ Come quickly and watch this programme! It's hilarious. ❸ I want
to watch the weather forecast. What channel is it on? ❹ His/Her book
has never before been published in France. ❺ I can't stand the telly.

***

❺ Television, or the telly, as we call it, is financed by advertising.
   **La télévision, .. "........", ..., est financée par la
   publicité.**

Answers to Exercice 2

❶ – téléviseurs – en possèdent – ❷ – On peut en recevoir – ❸ – très
sympa – Côté cuisine – ❹ – augmente d'année en année ❺ – ou "la
télé", comme on dit –

Second wave: 39th Lesson

89

Quatre-vingt-neuvième leçon

Le Tour de France

1 Cette célèbre course cycliste a beaucoup changé depuis sa création en mille neuf cent trois.

2 À cette époque, le Tour ne comptait que six_étapes,

3 tandis qu'aujourd'hui, il en compte plus de vingt.

4 Et aussi, à son_origine, le Tour ne quittait pas la France, alors que

5 de nos jours, les coureurs se rendent_en Espagne, en Belgique, aux Pays-Bas [1]...

6 L'année dernière, cent cinquante participants, venus de partout [2], ont couru.

7 Le Belge, Robet, a porté le maillot jaune [3] pendant trois jours de suite,

8 et le Français Moutet l'a porté pendant quinze jours [4].

Prononciation
1 … krayaseeohn 2 … seezaytap 3 tondee … 5 … payee ba 7 … maïyoh …

Notes
1 We say en **Italie**, en **Pologne** (*to Italy, Poland*) etc., but aux **Pays-Bas** (*to the Netherlands*), aux **États-Unis**, etc., because these latter are plural groups (like _the_ Seychelles, les **Seychelles**, _the_ Carribean, les **Caraïbes**, etc.).

89

Eighty-Ninth Lesson

The Tour of France

1 This famous cycle race has changed a lot since its creation in 1903.
2 At that time, the Tour included *(counted)* only six stages,
3 whereas today it includes *(counts)* more than 20.
4 And also, at its beginning *(origin)*, the Tour did not leave France, whereas
5 nowadays *(of our days)* the racers go to Spain, to Belgium, to the Netherlands ...
6 Last year, 150 participants *(come)* from all over raced.
7 The Belgian, Robet, wore the yellow jersey for three consecutive days
8 and the Frenchman Moutet wore it for two weeks.

---

2 **partout**, *everywhere, all over.* Il y a des affiches partout, *There are posters everywhere*; des musiciens venus de partout, *musicians from all over.* **Nulle part**, *nowhere, anywhere* (negative). Je n'en _ai trouvé nulle part, *I couldn't find any anywhere.*

3 **un maillot de bain**, *a swimming costume*; **un maillot de corps**, *a (man's) vest*; **le maillot jaune** ("the yellow jersey") is the singlet worn by the leading cyclist at each stage of the **Tour de France**.

4 The French say **quinze jours** where the English would say *two weeks*. **Une quinzaine**, *a fortnight.*

9 Il ne l'a perdu qu'une fois, lors d' ⁵une étape contre la montre.

10 La dernière étape – l'entrée triomphale dans Paris – était passionnante :

11 Le Français et le Belge se sont disputé ⁶ la première place pendant douze kilomètres,

12 puis le Français a crevé ⁷ et a dû s'arrêter.

13 Voilà pourquoi le Tour de France a été gagné par un étranger. ☐

 9 ... lor ...

Notes

5 **lors de**, *pendant, during*. **Lors d'un séjour aux États-Unis** = Pendant un séjour aux États-Unis, *During a stay in the USA*. **Lors de** is more formal than **pendant**.

6 **se disputer**, *to argue*. **Les deux chauffeurs se sont disputés**, *The two drivers argued*. However, when followed by a direct object, the meaning changes – to fight over, to struggle for – and so does the past participle. **Ils se sont disputé la première place**, *They were neck and neck*.

***

Exercice 1 – Traduisez

❶ Il vient de rentrer d'un séjour aux Pays-Bas et il est crevé. ❷ Ils ont dû vendre leur voiture. ❸ Il a porté le maillot jaune pendant quinze jours de suite. ❹ Ne nous disputons pas ; ça n'en vaut pas la peine. ❺ Lors d'un séjour en Europe, il s'est rendu deux fois en Espagne. ❻ Il l'a perdu en mille neuf cent neuf.

9 He only lost it once, during a stage against the clock *(watch)*.

10 The last stage – the triumphal entry into Paris – was very exciting:

11 The Frenchman and the Belgian were neck and neck for 12 km,

12 when the Frenchman had a puncture and had to stop.

13 That's why the Tour of France was won by a foreigner.

ILS ONT DÛ VENDRE LEUR VOITURE.

(We'll discuss the agreement of the past participle in lesson 91 and also later on.) **Une dispute**, *an argument* (a heated exchange); **un argument**, *an argument* (a series of reasons).

7 **un pneu** *[peneuh]* **crevé**, *a punctured tire*. **Il a crevé sur l'autoroute**, *He had a puncture on the motorway*. We also find the word used in a very frequent idiom: **Je suis crevé !**, *I'm worn out!* (see lesson 101, note 8).

***

Answers to Exercice 1

❶ He has just returned from a stay in the Netherlands and he is worn out. ❷ They had to sell their car. ❸ He wore the yellow jersey for two weeks running. ❹ Let's not argue; it's not worth it. ❺ During a stay in Europe, he went to Spain twice. ❻ He lost it in 1909.

Exercice 2 – Complétez

❶ They came from all over to race.
Ils .... de .... pour courir.

❷ We won three times running.
Nous avons ..... trois fois ....

❸ She has changed a lot since the last time I saw her.
Elle a beaucoup changé ...... la dernière fois ... je
l'.. vue.

90

Quatre-vingt-dixième leçon

Avez-vous bien lu ?

1 Quand le Tour de France a-t-il été créé [1] ?
2 Combien y avait-_il d'étapes à l'origine ?
3 Combien y en_ [2] a-t_-il aujourd'hui ?
4 Dans quels pays les coureurs se rendent_-ils [3] ?
5 Pendant combien de temps le Français a-t-il
porté le maillot jaune ?
6 Quand l'a-t-_il perdu ? Comment s'appelait-_il ?
7 Pourquoi le Français s'est-_il arrêté ?

***

8 – Je suis_en train de lire un bouquin [4]
passionnant !

Pronunciation
1 ... kray-ay 4 ... rondeteel 6 ... sapelayteel 8 ... bookan ...

Notes
1 A difficult verb to pronounce: **créer** *[kray-ay]*; je **crée** *[kray]*, tu **crées**,
il **crée**, nous **créons**, vous **créez** *[kray-ay]*, ils **créent**. Past participle:

❹ He has won the stage; he will wear the yellow jersey tomorrow.
Il a gagné l'étape ; il ……. le maillot jaune demain.

❺ They looked for it but they couldn't find it anywhere.
Ils l'ont cherché mais ils ……. trouvé ……. …….

Answers to Exercice 2
❶ – sont venus – partout – ❷ – gagné – de suite ❸ – depuis – que – ai
– ❹ – portera – ❺ – ne l'ont – nulle part

Second wave: 40th Lesson

90

Ninetieth Lesson

Have you read carefully *(well)*?

1 When was the Tour de France created?
2 How many stages were there at the beginning?
3 How many *(of them)* are there today?
4 To *(In)* which countries do the racers go?
5 For how long did the Frenchman wear the yellow
   jersey?
6 When did he lose it? What was his name?
7 Why did the Frenchman stop?

***

8 – I am in the middle of reading a fascinating book!

créé. We are now studying the more elegant – correct – form, where we
replace **est-ce que** by an inversion.

2 The **en** replaces the noun **étapes** we saw in line 2.

3 Here, and in lines 6 and 7 (**rendent-ils**, **s'appelait-il**, **s'est-il**), the **t** at the
end of the verb permits the liaison with the following vowel.

4 See lesson 57, note 3.

9   Il y a un tel suspense ! On ne sait pas si ça va finir bien

10   ou en catastrophe !

11 – J'espère que tu me le prêteras quand tu l'auras fini.

12   Je suppose que c'est‿un roman policier ?

13 – Pas du tout. C'est‿un livre de cuisine !   ☐

*9 ... syoospenss ... **10** ... katastroff ... **12** ... poleeseeyay ...*

***

▶ Exercice 1 – Traduisez

❶ Je te le prêterai dès que je l'aurai fini. **❷** L'année dernière, il y avait trois employés*, aujourd'hui, il y en a vingt. **❸** Ce bouquin est vraiment passionnant. **❹** Qu'est-ce que tu es en train de lire, là ? **❺** Comment s'appelait ton ami allemand ?

* un(e) employé(e), *an employee*

***

Exercice 2 – Complétez

❶   Le Tour de France a été créé en 1903.
        Quand le Tour de France ...... été .... ?

❷   Il y avait vingt étapes.
        Combien y .... d'étapes ?

❸   Il l'a porté pendant deux jours.
        Pendant .... de temps .... porté ?

❹   Il l'a perdu lors d'une étape contre la montre.
        Quand l'...... perdu ?

9 It's full of *(There is such a)* suspense! One doesn't know if it's going to finish well

10 or in catastrophe!

11 – I hope that you will lend it to me when you *(will)* have finished.

12 I suppose that it's a crime *(police)* novel?

13 – Not at all. It's a cookery *(kitchen)* book!

***

Answers to Exercice 1

❶ I will lend it to you as soon as I have finished it. **❷** Last year, there were three employees, today there are twenty. **❸** This book is really fascinating. **❹** What are you busy reading there? **❺** What was your German friend's name?

***

❺ Le Français s'est arrêté parce qu'il a crevé.
   Pourquoi le Français s' .... ?

Answers to Exercice 2

❶ – a-t-il – créé **❷** – avait-il – **❸** – combien – l'a-t-il – **❹** – a-t-il – **❺** – est-il arrêté

Second wave: 41st Lesson

91

Quatre-vingt-onzième leçon

Révision – Revision

1 Disjunctive pronouns

moi-même, *myself*
toi-même, *yourself*
nous-mêmes, *ourselves*
vous-même(s), *yourself, yourselves*
lui/elle-même, *him/herself*
eux-mêmes, **elles-mêmes**, *themselves*

As in English, these disjunctive pronouns add emphasis to a verb.
Je le ferai, *I will do it.*
Je le ferai moi-même, *I will do it myself.*

In French railway stations, you will see signs telling you: **Compostez votre billet vous-même**, *Punch your own ticket* ("your ticket yourself"). This means you have to date-stamp your ticket before boarding the train.
by yourself is **seul(e)**. **Faites-le seul**, *Do it yourself, alone.*
Soi-même is used when the subject is an indefinite pronoun like **on**; **tout le monde**, **personne**, etc.
On composte son billet soi-même, *One punches one's own ticket* ("one's ticket oneself"). And we have seen that **même** can also be added to a proper noun: **Paris même**, *Paris itself*; **la ville même**, *the town itself.*

2 Disjunctive pronouns (continued)

In lesson 84, we saw a table of pronouns and their order before a verb. We can add **en** + **y** to this list but, so as not to make life too hard, let's remove the subject pronouns (**je**, **tu**, **il**, etc.), taking it for granted that they always come first.

Ninety-First Lesson

This then gives us:

me			
te			
	le		
se		**lui**	
	la	**y**	**en**
nous		**leur**	
	les		
vous			

This is like a football team, with five forwards, three halves, two backs, goalkeeeeper and a referee!

Let's put this into practice: *I will speak to him about it* – **Je + lui + en +** verb (**parlerai**).

He will answer it tomorrow: **Il y répondra demain**.

She will drive you there: **Elle vous y conduira**.

If you retain this (playing) order, you will have no problem putting pronouns in the right place.

en + y are a little elusive: basically both replace a noun (or a pronoun) in a sentence – much as English uses *one + ones* – (*I want a cigarette. – I haven't got one*) – to avoid repeating the object noun. Let's look at some examples:

Vous allez à Paris ? – Oui, j'y vais, *Are you going to Paris? – Yes, I am ("going there")*.

Je dois y rester, *I must stay here ("there")*.

Est-ce qu'il va au bureau ?, *Is he going to the office?*

Oui, il y va tous les jours, *Yes, he goes ("there") every day*.

And some idiomatic uses:

On y va !, *Let's go!*

Vous y êtes ?, *Do you follow ("an explanation")?*

Pensez-y !, *Think it over!*

Ça y est !, *That's it!*

en expresses quantity, but only the expression of quantity itself is translated (i.e. the number, weight, etc.).

J'en connais plusieurs, *I know several.*

Combien de cigarettes fumez-vous ? – J'en fume dix par jour, *How many cigarettes do you smoke? – I smoke ten a day.*

En voulez-vous deux ou trois ?, *Do you want two or three?* – **Il n'en manque qu'un**, – *Only one is missing.*

In fact, it is easier for us to learn to place **en** than it is for a French person to learn whether or not to translate it into English!

When we use a numeral pronoun (i.e. *one of them*, *several*, etc.), we do not use **en**:

Quatre d'entre eux parlent le français, *Four of them speak French.*

Deux d'entre nous sont fatigués, *Two of us are tired.*

Plusieurs ont acheté des actions, *Several bought shares.*

***

92

Quatre-vingt-douzième leçon

Aux Armes, Citoyens ! [1]

1 Parmi tous les jours fériés [2] dont‿on bénéficie en France,

🗨 Pronunciation
1 parmee ... dont-ohn ...

📑 Notes

1 Aux armes, citoyens, **Formez vos bataillons** (*To Arms, Citizens! Form your batallions!*) is the stirring chorus to the French national anthem, **La Marseillaise**. Composed as a battle anthem by Rouget de Lisle in 1792, it was first sung in Paris by the Marseilles batallion, hence the name.

Just a couple of examples of the agreement of the past participle in the past tense. We know that in verbs conjugated with **être**, the participle agrees with the subject; and with **avoir**, it agrees with the nearest preceding direct object – if there is one.

J'ai acheté des pommes (no preceding direct object), but: **Les pommes que j'ai achetées.**

Il a trouvé les livres, but **Les livres qu'il a trouvés.**

Je l'ai vu, *I saw him/it* (masculine object); **Je l'ai** vue, *I saw her/it* (feminine object).

There is no agreement when the preceding object is indirect (to them, etc.).

Elle leur a donné un cadeau, *She gave them* (ind.) *a present.*

Don't worry unduly about this rule. For the time being, we are less worried about writing correct French than speaking it.

Second wave: 42nd Lesson

92

Ninety-Second Lesson

To Arms, Citizens!

1   Among all the public holidays that we enjoy in France,

The rest of the words are suitably martial. (A reggae version made in the 1980s by the late singer Serge Gainsbourg caused a public outcry.)

2   **un jour férié** is a *public holiday*, either religious or civil. Remember that, because of France's Roman Catholic origins, some holidays are referred to by their religious names rather than their dates (15 August is often called **l'Assomption**, *the Assumption*).

2 – le premier de l'an, la Pentecôte, le quinze
août, le premier mai, le onze novembre, et
cetera –,

3 il y en_a un qui tient une place particulière
dans le cœur de tout Français :

4 Il s'agit ³ du 14 juillet, la fête nationale.

5 Cette fête commémore le début de la
Révolution en mil ⁴ sept cent quatre-vingt-neuf
(1789)

6 et plus_exactement la prise de la Bastille,

7 cette terrible prison ⁵ qui symbolisait le pouvoir
de la monarchie.

8 Ce jour-là, une foule de vingt mille Parisiens,
à la recherche d'armes, a pris la forteresse
d'assaut.

9 Ayant libéré les prisonniers ⁶ et tué le
gouverneur,

10 les révolutionnaires ont proclamé le
gouvernement de la Commune de Paris.

Pronunciation
*2 … pohnt-kot … kanzoot … etsetera 4 eel sazhee … 7 … tayreeble
… monarshee 8 … dassoh 9 ayohn … tyou-ay …*

Notes

3 We'll discuss this awkward verb (**s'agir de**) in greater detail later on.
Basically, it is an impersonal verb that refers to the subject of the sentence. It can often be omitted when translating: **Je vais vous parler
d'une fête religieuse : il s'agit de la Pentecôte**, *I'll tell you about a
religious holiday: Whitsun.*

4 Remember that we can also say **dix-sept cents**… And in line 11, **mil
huit cent**…

5 We know that adjectives generally come after the noun they qualify,
with the exception of a handul of short ones: **petit/grand; bon/mauvais;**

2 – New Year's Day, Whitsun, 15 August, 1 May, 11 November, etc. –

3 there is one that holds a very special place in the heart[s] of every French [person].

4 It is 14 July, the national holiday.

5 This holiday commemorates the beginning of the Revolution in 1789

6 and, more precisely, the taking of the Bastille,

7 that terrible prison that symbolised the power of the monarchy.

8 On that day, a crowd of 20,000 Parisians, in search of weapons, stormed the fortress *(took the fortress by assault).*

9 Having freed the prisoners and killed the governor,

10 the revolutionaries proclaimed the government of the Commune of Paris.

CHAQUE ANNÉE A LIEU UNE GRANDE FÊTE POPULAIRE.

jeune/vieux; beau and joli (note that, with the exception of the last two, these adjectives form opposing pairs). However, sometimes we place the adjective <u>before</u> the noun to add emphasis.

There is no hard-and-fast rule for this, so just pay attention and note the context. For example, **Ils avaient une maison somptueuse,** *They had a gorgeous house* can be made even more emphatic by changing the place of the adjective and putting the stress on it (listen to the recording): **Ils avaient une somptueuse maison.**

6 For the record, two madmen, four forgers and a nobleman jailed for debauchery...

11 Plus de cent_ans après – en mille huit cent
quatre-vingt-huit, plus_exactement –

12 la date du quatorze juillet était_adoptée
comme fête nationale.

13 Depuis, chaque année, a lieu une grande
kermesse [7] populaire

14 avec des défilés, des feux d'artifice et des bals
partout en France. ☐

Pronunciation
14 … dayfeelay … feu-darteefees …

***

Exercice 1 – Traduisez
❶ Ils habitent une somptueuse maison en Bretagne.
❷ Ayant acheté son billet, il est monté dans le train.
❸ Chaque année a lieu une grande fête populaire. ❹ Voici
un air que vous connaissez tous : il s'agit de *La Marseillaise*.
❺ Parmi les dates-clés dans l'histoire de la France, citons
732, 1431, 1789, 1848 et 1914.

Exercice 2 – Complétez
❶ Of all the public holidays that we get, one is particularly important:
..... tous les jours fériés ...... bénéficie, ... qui
est particulièrement important :

❷ it is the National Holiday.
. . . . la fête nationale.

❸ It commemorates the Revolution, or more precisely the taking
of the Bastille.
Elle .... la Révolution, ou .... la ..... de
la Bastille.

11 Over 100 years later – in 1888 more precisely –
12 the date of 14 July was adopted as the national holiday.
13 Since *(Then)*, each year, a great popular celebration takes place
14 with parades, fireworks and dances all over France.

Note

7 You'll often come across **une kermesse** in towns and villages all over France. Originally a religious celebration feast day (it comes from the Flemish for "church feast"), the word is now used for all kinds of celebrations, from a village fête to a full-blown fair.

***

Answers to Exercice 1

❶ They live in a gorgeous house in Brittany. ❷ Having bought his ticket, he got onto the train. ❸ Each year, a great popular festival takes place. ❹ Here's a tune you all know: it's the Marseillaise. ❺ Among all the key dates in the history of France, let's mention 732, 1431, 1789, 1848 and 1914.

❹ Having freed the prisoners and killed the governor, they proclaimed the Commune.

. . . . les prisonniers et . . . le gouverneur, ils ont . . . . la Commune.

❺ et, juste pour changer, listez les paires d'adjectifs qui se placent devant le nom (essayez de ne pas relire la note 5 !)

. . . . . / . . . . . ; . . . / . . . . ; . . . . . / . . . . . ; . . . . / . . . .

Answers to Exercice 2

❶ Parmi – dont on – il y en a un – ❷ il s'agit de – ❸ – commémore – plus exactement – prise – ❹ Ayant libéré – tué – proclamé – ❺ petit/grand; bon/mauvais; jeune/vieux; beau/joli

Second wave: 43rd Lesson

93

Quatre-vingt-treizième leçon

Le savoir-faire

1   Dans son compartiment, M. Delmont attend le départ.
2   Dès que ¹ le train démarre, il sort un cigare et il l'allume.
3   Un des passagers dans le compartiment lui dit :
    – Je vous prie ² d'éteindre ³ ce cigare.
4   Vous_êtes dans_un compartiment non-fumeurs. Sinon, j'appellerai le contrôleur.
5   – Appelez qui vous voudrez ⁴, répond M.Delmont.
    Fâché, l'homme part à la recherche du contrôleur.
6   Il le trouve, et tous les deux reviennent dans le compartiment.
7   Le contrôleur est sur le point de parler, quand M. Delmont lui coupe la parole ⁵ :

Pronunciation
2 dayke … 3 … aytandr …

Notes

1   **dès que** or **aussitôt que**. Both expressions mean *as soon as*. Remember that in a sentence like: *I will tell you as soon as I receive it*, we must put the second verb into the future tense: **Je vous le dirai quand je le recevrai**.

2   **Je vous prie de…** (see also line 8) is a formal, polite way of introducing a request. In everyday language, we would simply say: **Éteignez ce cigare, s'il vous plaît** (**Je vous_en prie**, *Don't mention it*).

Ninety-Third Lesson

Know-how

1 In his [railway] compartment, Mr Delmont [is] waiting [for] the departure.

2 As soon as the train starts, he takes out a cigar and he lights it.

3 One of the passengers in the compartment says [to] him:
  – Please, put out that cigar.

4 You are in a non-smoking compartment. If not, I'll call the inspector.

5 – Call whom you like, replies Mr Delmont. Angry, the man leaves in search of the inspector.

6 He finds him, and the two come back to the compartment.

7 The inspector is on the point of speaking *(to speak)* when Mr Delmont butts in *(cuts his word)*.

---

3 **éteindre**, *to put out*: **j'éteins, tu éteins, il éteint, nous éteignons, vous éteignez, ils éteignent**. Past participle: **éteint**. An awkward conjugation. The only other commonly-used verb that is so conjugated is **peindre**, *to paint*.

4 **Venez quand vous voudrez** (lit. "Come when you will like") is a more elegant way of saying: **Venez quand vous voulez**. **Allez où vous voudrez**, *Go where you like*.

5 There are two ways of saying *a word* in French: **un mot** and **une parole**. The first is used for the grammatical unit, the second for what is behind the word itself: **J'ai donné ma parole**, *I gave my word*. **Les paroles de cette chanson sont de Prévert**, *The words of this song are by Prévert*. **M. Delmont a pris la parole**, *Mr Delmont took the floor* (i.e. began to speak).

8 – Je vous prie de demander son billet à ce
monsieur.

9 Le voyageur tend ⁶ son billet et le contrôleur
s'exclame :

10 – Mais vous voyagez en première classe avec un
billet de seconde ⁷ !

11 Venez avec moi. Vous‿aurez une amende !

12 Quand‿ils sont partis, un‿autre passager
demande à M. Delmont :

13 – Dites-moi, comment avez-vous su que l'autre
n'était pas‿en règle ⁸?

14 – C'était facile. Son billet dépassait de sa poche

15 et j'ai vu qu'il était‿identique au mien !   □

Pronunciation
9 … tohn … **10** … segond

: Notes

  6 tendre, *to hold out, to stretch*, conjugates like **vendre**. (Note that the adjective **tendre** means *tender*: **un baiser tendre**, *a tender kiss*.) **La main tendue**, *hand outstretched*; **détendre**, *to relax*; **Détendez-vous !**, *Relax!* (However, Franglais has gained ground yet again: **relax** has <u>almost</u> become a French word.)

  7 See lesson 60, note 5.

8 – Please, ask the gentleman for his ticket *(ask the ticket to this sir)*.

9 The traveller holds out his ticket and the inspector exclaims:

10 – But you [are] travelling *(in)* first class with a second-[class] ticket!

11 Come with me. You will be fined *(have a fine)*!

12 When they have *(are)* left, another passenger asks Mr Delmont:

13 – Tell me, how did you know that the other [guy] was not "legal"?

14 – It was easy. His ticket was sticking out of his pocket

15 and I saw that it was identical to mine!

8 une **règle**, *a rule*. **Votre passeport n'est pas en règle**, *Your passport is not in order*. **En règle** is a common piece of legalese, generally indicating that one's situation, papers, etc. are not in order. Thus, **régler** means *to put in order*, *to adjust*. Remember, **régler des comptes**, *to settle accounts*; **un règlement**, *a payment*. (Notice once again the use of the historic present.)

▶ Exercice 1 – Traduisez

❶ Dès qu'il sera parti, j'éteindrai la lumière. ❷ Ma voiture ne démarre pas quand il fait froid. ❸ Venez quand vous voudrez ; nous vous attendrons. ❹ Il m'a tendu la main et m'a dit : Bonjour ! ❺ Quand l'avez-vous su ? – Hier soir.

***

Exercice 2 – Complétez

❶ The two women came back into the living-room.
Les deux femmes ... ... le salon.

❷ He left in search of the inspector.
Il ... ... à la ... ... contrôleur.

❸ She always interrupts him *(butts in)*.
Elle lui ... ... toujours ... ...

❹ Hurry up! We're on the point of leaving.
Dépêche-toi ! Nous sommes ... ... partir.

94

Quatre-vingt-quatorzième leçon

Stéréotypes

1 – Les Français – selon eux – sont des gens débrouillards [1], indisciplinés, cultivés.

💬 Pronunciation
1 ... daybrooyar ... andeeseepleenay ...

Answers to Exercice 1

❶ As soon as he leaves, I will turn out the light. ❷ My car doesn't start when it's cold. ❸ Come when you like; we will wait for you. ❹ He held out his hand to me and said: Good morning! ❺ When did you know? – Yesterday evening.

***

❺ We would ask you to put out your cigarettes.

Nous vous ...... d'........ vos cigarettes.

Answers to Exercice 2

❶ – sont revenues dans – ❷ – est parti – recherche du – ❸ – coupe – la parole ❹ – sur le point de – ❺ – prions – éteindre –

Second wave: 44th Lesson

____

94

Ninety-Fourth Lesson

Stereotypes

1 – The French – according to them – are resourceful, undisciplined, [and] cultured people.

🗋 Note

1 le brouillard *[brooyar], fog.* Se débrouiller (lit. "to get out of the fog") means *to get by.* Il se débrouille bien en français, *He gets by well in French.* Un débrouillard (a high compliment in French) is *a canny, resourceful person* who gets out of difficulties with ease.

trois cent soixante-dix-huit • 378

2 Les‿Anglais sont *fair-play* [2], un peu froids et pragmatiques.

3 Les‿Allemands sont disciplinés, mélomanes, martiaux...

4 Ce sont là des stéréotypes qui influencent notre façon de penser,

5 mais‿aussi notre façon de parler. Nous disons, par exemple,

6 "filer à l'anglaise" [3] pour "partir discrètement" ;

7 quelqu'un qui a trop bu est "saoul comme un Polonais" [4].

8 Une personne que l'on‿attaque systématiquement est‿une "tête de Turc" [5] !

9 Si l'on ne gagne pas beaucoup d'argent, on dit "ce n'est pas le Pérou" [6] !

10 Et si l'on parle mal le français – ce qui n'est pas votre cas –,

11 on dit qu'on parle comme une "vache espagnole" [7].

 *3 ... marseeoh 6 feelay ... 7 ... soo ...*

Notes

2 Yes! That's how you say *fair-play* in French. An attempt was made to introduce **le franc-jeu** but **le fair-play** (il est très fair-play) has resisted all attempts to dislodge it. (Being a foreign word there is no agreement of the adjective.)

3 It is interesting how countries who have a long mutual history attribute different vices and virtues to each other: **filer à l'anglaise** is... *to take French leave*!

2 The English are fair *(-play)*, a little cold and pragmatic.

3 The Germans are disciplined, music-loving, martial...

4 These are *(here)* all stereotypes which influence our way *(fashion)* of thinking

5 but also our way of talking. We say for example

6 "to slip away in the English manner" for "to leave discreetly";

7 someone who has drunk too much is "[as] drunk as a Pole".

8 A person whom one attacks systematically is a "Turk's head" [whipping boy].

9 If one doesn't earn much money, one says: "It isn't Peru"!

10 And if one speaks French badly – which is not [at all] your case,

11 one says that he speaks like "a Spanish cow"!

---

4 Not as racist as it sounds! Emperor Napoleon, mortified that his officers could not take their drink as well as his squadron of Polish lancers, exhorted them to "be drunk, but like the Poles", i.e. capable of fighting nonetheless. Unfortunately, the origin of the expression has been lost. So be careful!

5 This was the name of a "test-your-strength" machine at funfairs and by transference refers to anyone who is pushed around or bullied.

6 Peru was always the fabled land of gold and wealth. **C'est pas le Pérou** (the **ne** is dropped in familiar speech), *I won't get rich this way!*

7 The origin of this picturesque expression has in fact nothing to do with cows. The original expression was **parler comme un Basque l'espagnol** (the Basques were supposed to speak poor Spanish). Years of use have transformed **Basque** to **vache** – and popular wisdom has left it that way.

12   L'Allemagne est faite pour y voyager, l'Italie
        pour y séjourner,

13   l'Angleterre pour y penser

14   et la France pour y vivre.
        D'Alembert   □

***

▶ Exercice 1 – Traduisez

❶ Elle se débrouille en quatre langues : l'italien, l'allemand,
l'anglais et le polonais. ❷ Il a beaucoup trop bu. ❸ On le
critique tout le temps ; c'est une vraie tête de Turc. ❹ Il
a été beaucoup influencé par son père. ❺ Vous gagneriez
deux fois plus si vous preniez cet emploi. ❻ C'est pas le
Pérou !

Exercice 2 – Complétez

❶ France is *(made)* to live in.
   La France … …… pour . vivre.

❷ Do you know Italy? – I have stayed there.
   – ……….-vous l'Italie ? – J'. … séjourné.

❸ I like his way of speaking very much.
   J'aime beaucoup sa …… .. …….

❹ They left very discreetly; they "took French leave"!
   Ils …… …… très discrètement ; ils …… … à
   ……… !

❺ According to them, he's a Polish composer.
   …… …, c'est un compositeur ……….

12 Germany is *(made)* to travel in, Italy to stay in,
13 England to think in
14 and France to live in.
       D'Alembert

***

Answers to Exercice 1

❶ She gets by in four languages: Italian, German, English and Polish.
❷ He has drunk far too much. ❸ He's always criticized. He's a real
whipping boy. ❹ He was very much influenced by his father. ❺ You
would earn twice as much if you took that job. ❻ I won't get rich like
that!

Answers to Exercice 2

❶ – est faite – y – ❷ Connaissez – y ai – ❸ – façon de parler ❹ – sont
partis – ont filé – l'anglaise ❺ Selon eux – polonais

Second wave: 45th Lesson

95

Quatre-vingt-quinzième leçon

Joindre l'utile à l'agréable

1 Aujourd'hui nous verrons des_expressions pratiques ¹ qui vous_aideront en voyage.

2 D'abord, des_expressions de politesse (dont vous connaissez déjà un bon nombre).

3 – Excusez-moi de vous déranger... Pouvez-vous me dire... ?

4 Je voudrais savoir... Pourriez-vous m'aider... ?

5 C'est très gentil... Vous_êtes bien_aimable...

6 – Merci beaucoup.
   – Je vous_en prie (ou : – De rien).

7 – Est-ce que cette place est prise ? Est-ce que ça vous gêne si... ?

8 – Allez-_y. Ça ne fait rien. C'est sans_importance. Ce n'est pas grave.

9 – Je ne l'ai pas fait exprès ². Je suis désolé. Excusez-moi.

🗣 Pronunciation
9 ... *ekspray*

📔 Notes

1 **pratique**, *practical*. Notice the spelling. **Pratiquer** means *to practise* a religion, rules, etc. **C'est un catholique pratiquant**, *He's a practising Catholic*; or for a sport where English would use *do* or *play*: **Elle pratique la natation**, *She goes swimming* ("regularly"). There are several

95

Ninety-Fifth Lesson

Mixing business with pleasure
(Join the useful to the agreeable)

1 Today we will see some practical expressions which will help you when travelling *(in travel)*.
2 First, polite expressions (of which you know already a good number).
3 – Excuse me for disturbing you ... Can you tell me...?
4 I would like to know... Could you help me...?
5 It's very kind... You're very kind...
6 – Thank you very much. – Don't mention it.
7 – Is that seat taken? Does it disturb you if...?
8 – Go ahead. It doesn't matter. It's not *(without)* important. It doesn't matter/isn't serious.
9 – I didn't do it on purpose. I'm [very] sorry. Excuse me.

ways of saying *to practise* (i.e. to rehearse): **Elle essaye son français**, *She is practising her French. That exercise is good practice*: **Cet exercice est un bon entraînement.**

2 **exprès**, *on purpose*, should not be confused with **express**, **un train express**, *an express train*. (Also, the pronunciation is different. The final s sound is not voiced in **exprès**.) **Garçon ! Deux express !**, *Waiter! Two expressos!* (coffees). **Elle est venue exprès pour me voir**, *She came especially to see me.*

10 – Bon_appétit ! Ça a l'air très bon. C'était
      délicieux.
11 – Pardon ? Voulez-vous répéter [3], s'il vous plaît ?
      Je n'ai pas_entendu.
12 – Au revoir. Bon retour. À bientôt.
13   On ne peut pas_être poli tout le temps,
      cependant...
14 – Allez-vous-_en !
      – Fichez-moi la paix !
      – Taisez-vous !   □

14 ... feeshay mwa ... tezay ...

Note

3 Remember that using such a sentence will probably cause the person
to whom you are speaking to do just that: repeat without making any
effort to slow down or use different words. A phrase like: **Dites-le autre-
ment**, *Say it in another way*, is rather unconventional, but very useful.
Other "survival expressions" are: **Parlez plus lentement**, *Speak more*

***

Exercice 1 – Traduisez
  ❶ Parlez plus fort, s'il vous plaît. Je ne vous entends pas.
  ❷ Est-ce que ça vous dérange si j'ouvre la fenêtre ? – Allez-y.
  ❸ Pourriez-vous m'aider à traduire le menu ? ❹ Au revoir et
  bon retour. À bientôt. ❺ Pouvez-vous me dire où se trouve la
  rue Cambon ? ❻ Désolé, je ne sais pas. – Ce n'est pas grave.

10 – Bon appétit ! [Enjoy your meal]! This looks very
good. It was delicious.

11 – Pardon ? Would you repeat please? I didn't hear.

12 – Goodbye. Get home safely. See you soon.

13 One cannot be polite all the time, however...

14 – Go away!
   – Get lost!
   – Shut up!

slowly; **Parlez plus fort**, *Speak louder*. Also, when you lack confidence
in a foreign language, your voice tends to become a hoarse whisper!
Say what you want to say out loud (as you have been practising with
this method). At least that way, if you make mistakes, people can hear
you and correct you.

***

Answers to Exercice 1

❶ Speak louder please. I can't hear you. **❷** Would it disturb you if
I open the window? – Go ahead. **❸** Could you help me to translate
the menu? **❹** Goodbye and get home safely. See you soon. **❺** Can
you tell me where the rue Cambon is? **❻** I'm sorry, I don't know. – It
doesn't matter.

Exercice 2 – Complétez

❶ I will see if it will help me.
Je ...... si ça m'.......

❷ Some expressions of which you know a good number.
Des expressions .... vous .... un ....

❸ Eat some; I bought it specially for you.
Mangez- .. ; je l'ai acheté ...... pour vous.

96

Quatre-vingt-seizième leçon

Les taxis [1]

1 Si vous_êtes pressé et que vous n'avez
   pas_envie de prendre les transports en
   commun, vous pouvez toujours prendre un taxi.
2 Dans la plupart des grandes villes, on_en
   trouve facilement – sauf quand_il pleut !
3 On peut se rendre à une station [2] ou héler une
   voiture dans la rue.

Pronunciation
3 … aylay …

Notes
1 **un taxi** usually means *a taxi*; however, the word is often used as an
   abbreviated form of **un chauffeur de taxi**, *a taxi driver*. **Son père a fait
   le taxi à Paris pendant quarante ans**, *His/Her father was a taxi driver in
   Paris for 40 years*.

❹ Could you tell me the time, please?

...... - .... me dire l'heure, s'il vous plaît ?

❺ We would like to know how much that costs.

Nous .... savoir combien ça coûte.

Answers to Exercice 2

❶ – verrai – aidera ❷ – dont – connaissez – bon nombre ❸ – en
– exprès – ❹ Pourriez-vous – ❺ – voudrions –

Second wave: 46th Lesson

96

Ninety-Sixth Lesson

Taxis

1 If you are in a hurry and you do not want to take
public transport, you can always take a taxi.

2 In most large cities, they can be easily found...
except when it is raining!

3 You can go to a [taxi] rank or wave one down *(hail a
car)* in the street.

2 **une station de taxi,** *a taxi rank* (remember that *a railway station* is **une
gare** – see line 6).

4 Quant_aux tarifs, vous payez la prise en charge ³, plus une somme pour chaque fraction d'un kilomètre par la suite.

5 Mais attention ! Ces tarifs sont majorés ⁴ le soir, le dimanche ou les jours fériés.

6 – Taxi !
– Bonjour. Vous_allez où ?
– À la gare de Lyon.
– Alors montez.

7 – Y a-t_-il beaucoup de circulation ?
– Il y a toujours trop de voitures. C'est la faute du gouvernement. Il faut_interdire les voitures privées.
– Et que ferait_-on, alors ?

8 – Ben voyons ⁵, on prendrait les taxis, évidemment !

9 *(Le taxi est pris dans_un embouteillage monstre, et le client s'impatiente.)*

10 – Dites donc, lance le chauffeur, si vous_êtes si pressé, j'ai une excellente idée.
– Vous connaissez un raccourci ?

🗨 *5 … mazhoray … 7 … ferey-tohn … 8 bahn vwayohn …*

📭 Notes

3 prendre en charge is one of a handful of catch-all verbs that are very popular in French. It basically means *to be taken in charge* – often financially – and can be used in many situations: **Les soins sont pris en charge par la Sécurité Sociale**, *The [medical] treatment is covered by the social security system*; **Le coût est pris en charge par la société**, *The expense is charged to the company*, etc. In the case of a taxi, **la prise en charge** is *the flagfall*, i.e. the money you pay the driver for taking you on board.

4 As for the fares, you pay the flagfall plus a certain sum per kilometer after that.

5 But be careful! These fares [are] increased in the evening, [on] Sundays and (or) public holidays.

6 – Taxi!
– Good morning. Where are you going?
– To the Gare de Lyon (station).
– Hop in.

7 – Is there much traffic?
– There are always too many cars. It's the government's fault. Private cars must be banned.
– And what would we do in that case?

8 – What do you think? You'd take taxis, of course!

9 (The taxi is stuck in a huge traffic jam, and the passenger (client) gets impatient.)

10 – Hey, says the driver, if you're in a hurry, I've an excellent idea.
– You know a short-cut?

---

4 majorer means to increase a price by adding a surcharge. In some cafés, you will see the sign: **Les consommations sont majorées à partir de minuit**, which tells you that you'll pay more for your drink after midnight. Such an increase is called **une majoration**. However, the fact of simply putting up a price (a manufacturer, shopkeeper, etc.) is **augmenter le prix**: **Les prix ont augmenté de deux pour cent cette année**, *Prices have risen by 2% this year*.

5 One of an arsenal of interjections that the French are so fond of! **Ben voyons** is similar to our rhetorical question: *Well, what do you think?* See also **Dites-donc**, in line 10, which could be translated as *Hey*. Although you'll rarely use such expressions, it's useful to recognize them.

trois cent quatre-vingt-dix • 390

11 – Non, mieux que ça. Vous me réglez la somme au compteur,

12 vous me donnez un bon pourboire pour me remercier du tuyau... [6]

13 et vous continuez votre trajet à pied. □

12 ... *twee-yo*

***

▶ Exercice 1 – Traduisez

❶ Il ne prend jamais les transports en commun. ❷ Quant aux tarifs, les prix sont majorés à partir de minuit. ❸ Que ferait-on ? – Ben voyons, c'est évident. ❹ Dites donc, si vous êtes si impatient, prenez le métro ! ❺ Je lui ai donné un pourboire et j'ai continué à pied.

***

Exercice 2 – Complétez

❶ The patient is taken care of by the social security system.
Le malade est .... la Sécurité sociale.

❷ Private cars must be banned.
. . .. les voitures privées.

❸ They are in a hurry and they don't want to take the bus.
... ... et ils .... de prendre le bus.

❹ As for the fares, they go up. – When? – From midnight.
.... tarifs, ils sont majorés. – .....? – ....
minuit.

11 – No, better than that. You pay what's *(the sum)* on the meter,

12 you give me a good tip to thank me for the advice...

13 and you continue your journey on foot.

Note

6 **un tuyau** literally means *a pipe for water*, *gas*, etc. **Les tuyaux sont bouchés**, *The pipes are blocked* (note the irregular plural). In slang, however, it means *a piece of useful information*, *a tip*. **Il m'a donné un bon tuyau pour mes vacances**, *He gave me a good tip for my holidays*. By the way, don't confuse this type of "tip" with the one the driver asked for: **un pourboire** is *a gratuity*, literally money with which to buy a drink (**pour** + **boire**).

***

Answers to Exercice 1

❶ He never takes public transport. ❷ As for the fares, they go up from midnight onwards. ❸ What would we do? – What do you think? It's obvious. ❹ Hey, if you're so impatient, take the metro! ❺ I gave him a tip and continued on foot.

***

❺ I've got a great idea. – You know a short cut? – No, better than that.

J'ai une excellente idée. – Vous connaissez ..

.... ? – Non, ...

Answers to Exercice 2

❶ – pris en charge par – ❷ Il faut interdire – ❸ Ils sont pressés – n'ont pas envie – ❹ Quant aux – Quand – À partir de – ❺ – un raccourci – mieux que ça

Second wave: 47th Lesson

97

Quatre-vingt-dix-seiptième leçon

 Un pot-pourri d'expressions idiomatiques

1 – Ça y est ! Elle pleure. Tu as encore mis les pieds dans le plat !

2 – S'il continue à étudier comme ça, il risque [1] de réussir [2] son_examen.

3 – Mais_il ne travaille pas du tout ! Il fait semblant [3].

4 – Je ne peux pas continuer. J'en_ai ras le bol [4] !

5 – Ce type-là, je ne peux pas le voir en peinture.
   – Moi non plus [5].

6 – Au moins, elle dit ce qu'elle pense. Elle ne tourne pas autour du pot.

Pronunciation
*1 sa-yay … plah **4** … ralbol*

Notes

1 **risquer**, *to risk*, does not always imply danger. It means that something will very probably happen; **Ils risquent de passer tout_à l'heure**, *They'll probably come by later*.

2 Remember our "false friends"? **Avoir** ou **passer un examen**, *to sit an exam*; **réussir à un examen**, *to pass an exam*. (**Rater un examen**, *to fail an exam*.)

3 Another "false friend": *to pretend*, **faire semblant (de)**. **Il fait semblant de dormir**, *He is pretending to sleep*. **Ne faites pas semblant !**, *Don't pretend!* The verb **prétendre** means *to claim, to state*. (We find it in this sense in English when we talk of the "pretender" (claimant) to the throne.)

97

Ninety-Seventh Lesson

A "pot-pourri" of idiomatic expressions

1 – There! She's crying! You've put your foot in it *(in the plate)* again!

2 – If he continues studying like that, he'll probably get his exam.

3 – But he's not working at all! He's pretending.

4 – I can't continue. I'm fed up!

5 – I can't stomach that bloke.
  – Neither can I.

6 – At least she says what she thinks. She doesn't beat *(turn)* around the bush *(pot)*.

4 ras is an adjective found in compound expressions, where it usually indicates the edge or the lip of something (container, etc.). **Il a rempli mon verre à ras (bord)**, *He filled my glass to the brim*. The idiom in sentence 4, one of the most common uses of **ras**, means that one's bowl is full to the brim, i.e. that it cannot take any more. Think of the English expression: fed up. (**un pull ras du cou**, *a crew neck sweater*).

5 **Je l'aime beaucoup. – Moi aussi.** (*So do I; Me too*). **Il n'en veut pas. – Elle non plus.** (*Neither does she*). **Ils sont Allemands. – Eux aussi**; *They are German. – So are they*.

7 – Jeudi étant férié, je vais faire le pont [6]. À lundi !

8 – On n'arrive pas à le joindre. Tu crois qu'il est sorti ?

9 – Vous_êtes au courant ? [7] Ils_ont enfin réussi à vendre leur maison.

10 – On_a eu son message, mais on ne sait pas ce qu'il veut dire [8]. □

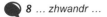 *8 ... zhwandr ...*

Notes

6 un jour férié is *a public one-day holiday*. If this falls on a Thursday or a Tuesday, many people "make the bridge", i.e. take off the Friday or the Monday to form a 4-day weekend. (A Wednesday-to-Friday holiday is sometimes called **un viaduc**!) **Le pont de l'Ascension**, *the long weekend on Ascension Day* (the last Thursday of May).

***

Exercice 1 – Traduisez

❶ Arrête de crier comme ça ! J'en ai ras le bol ! **❷** Ne tournez pas autour du pot comme ça ; **❸** dites-nous ce que vous voulez dire ! **❹** Je ne sais pas pourquoi, mais il ne peut pas me voir en peinture. **❺** J'ai réussi à le joindre hier. **❻** Allez, à lundi !

7 – Thursday being a holiday, I'm going to have a long weekend. [See you] on Monday!

8 – We can't manage to get in touch with (*join*) him. Do you think he's gone out?

9 – Have you heard the news? They finally succeeded in selling their house.

10 – We had his message but we don't know what it means.

---

7 être au courant de, *to be in the know; to know the news*. **Se mettre au courant de quelque chose**, *to find out about something*. **Tu es au courant ? Il a démissionné**, *Have you heard? He's resigned.*

8 **Qu'est-ce que ce mot veut dire ?**, *What does this word mean?* **Qu'est-ce que tu veux dire par là ?**, *What do you mean by that?* **Le sens d'un mot**, *the meaning of a word.*

***

Answers to Exercice 1

❶ Stop shouting like that! I'm fed up! ❷ Don't beat around the bush like that; ❸ tell us what you mean! ❹ I don't know why, but he can't stomach me. ❺ I was able to get in touch with him yesterday. ❻ OK. See you on Monday!

Exercice 2 – Complétez

❶ They pretended to know nothing.
Ils . . . . de ne rien savoir.

❷ Did you know? We weren't able to find him.
Tu . . . . ? Nous n'avons . . . . . le trouver.

❸ Do you know what she means?
Vous savez . . . . ?

❹ I will take a long weekend if Thursday is a holiday.
Je . . . . . le pont si jeudi est . . . . . .

98

Quatre-vingt-dix-huitième leçon

Révision – Revision

1 The conditional

There is one more important tense that we have to study: the conditional *(I would...)*. It is simple in both construction and use. We form it by adding the endings for the imperfect (**-ais, -ais, -ait, -ions, -iez, -aient**) to the stem of the future.
Look at the two following examples:

donner	je donnerais	tu donnerais
	il donnerait	nous donnerions
	vous donneriez	ils donneraient

finir	je finirais	tu finirais
	il finirait	nous finirions
	vous finiriez	ils finiraient

The tense is used in much the same way as in English. Let us accept that the auxiliary in English is *would* and that *should* is the conditional form of *must*. We usually find the conditional in a

❺ I like this. – Me too. – But not that. – Neither do I.
J'aime ceci. – ... ... – Mais pas ça. – ... ...

Answers to Exercice 2
❶ – ont fait semblant – **❷** – es au courant – pas pu – **❸** – ce qu'elle veut dire **❹** – ferai – férié **❺** – Moi aussi – Moi non plus

Second wave: 48th Lesson

98

Ninety-Eighth Lesson

construction with *if*...
If you left now you would arrive on time.
But instead of using the past tense after *if*, we must use the imperfect: **Si vous partiez** (imp.) **maintenant, vous arriveriez** (cond.) **à l'heure.**
Never use the conditional after **si**. The main confusion that beginners make is due to the similarity between these two tenses. Remember that the conditional endings are added to the future stem.
Si j'avais (imp.) **son numéro, je l'appellerais**, *If I had his/her number, I would call him/her.*
He would tell you if he knew, **Il vous le dirait** (condit.) **s'il le savait** (imp.).

A major use of the conditional – as in English – is to convey politeness: *Could you tell me...?, I would like to know*, etc.
For this, we must look at two irregular conditionals:
vouloir → je voudrais
(the remainder of the conjugation follows the normal rule)
pouvoir → je pourrais

and, of course, our auxiliaries **être** and **avoir**:

être → je serais, etc.

avoir → j'aurais, etc.

Pourriez-vous me dire... ?, *Could you tell me...?*

Je voudrais savoir..., *I would like to know...*

We know already that *Would you (close the window)?* is translated by: **Voulez-vous (fermer la fenêtre ?)**

There are a few minor differences in usage which we will not worry about for the moment.

(You will probably have realized that, between the first person singular future – **je partirai** – and the first person singular conditional – **je partirais** –, the only difference is a silent **s**. You will have to live with this slight drawback: if you remember the construction **Si...** imperfect... conditional, life will be much easier!)

2 The subjonctive

Il faut que j'achète: **achète** is subjunctive.

The subjunctive is not a tense but a mood. Up to now we have seen tenses in the indicative mood – i.e. they indicate real actions and definite events. Using the subjunctive mood suggests doubt, hypothesis or condition (if you like, the verb in the subjunctive is "joined" to another verb on which its existence depends).

Let us straight away make the difference between when we must use a subjunctive (after certain conjunctions or certain verbs) and when using subjunctive adds nuance and depth to the sentence. The latter category is a subject of debate – and sometimes error – even among well-educated French speakers.

To form the subjunctive we add the endings **-e**, **-es**, **-e**, **-ions**, **-iez**, **-ent** to – in most cases – the stem of the third person plural present:

donner	je donne	tu donnes
	il donne	nous donnions
	vous donniez	ils donnent

When you are sure of this, check in the grammatical appendix for the verbs **boire**, **devoir**, **prendre**, **recevoir**, **tenir** and **venir** where

there is a slight difference. We must also learn **être** and **avoir**.
être: **je sois, tu sois, il soit, nous soyons, vous soyez, ils soient**
avoir: **j'aie, tu aies, il ait, nous ayons, vous ayez, ils aient**.
(Other major irregular verbs are: **aller, faire, pouvoir, savoir, vouloir**.)

There is also an imperfect subjunctive which is so infrequently used in everyday French that we will not bother with it.
When must the subjunctive be used? Look at this sentence in English: *I demand that he be found*. *be* is a subjunctive. It depends on: I demand... and is "sub-joined" to it by *that*.
In French we often express this by the impersonal form **il faut que**...

Any verb following this construction must be put into the subjunctive (the two verbs are "sub-joined" by the word **que**).
Il faut que vous soyez à l'heure, *You must be on time*.
Il faut que je vous parle, *I must talk to you*.
Il faut que vous finissiez à huit heures, *You must finish at 8.00*.

Likewise if I impose my will on someone – *I want him/her to come early* –, I say: **Je veux que** and a subjunctive: **Je veux qu'il/elle vienne tôt**.
He wants me to tell him the secret: **Il veut que je lui dise le secret**.

Do you see how, in both cases, the second idea is dependent on a first verb expressing command or desire? And that the two ideas are "sub-joined" by the relative **que**?

Enough for now. (If you want a list of more conjunctions which must be followed by the subjunctive, check in the grammatical appendix.)
Since the aim of this first volume is to allow you to understand everyday conversation and to express yourself, we have deliberately omitted further discussion of the subjunctive. As long as you can recognize the mood, and have an idea of when it is used, we consider this sufficient for now.

Seconde wave: 49th Lesson

99

Quatre-vingt-dix-neuvième leçon

In the last two weeks of our course, we will be translating the French text much more idiomatically than we have done so far. So we'll only

Le travail

1 Jean-Michel et Claude habitent à Vannes en Bretagne, une belle ¹ région dans l'ouest de la France.

2 Claude est_institutrice ². Elle travaille dans_une petite école à une trentaine de kilomètres de Vannes.

3 Jean-Michel, lui, est_ingénieur informaticien. Mais il y a trois mois, la société pour laquelle il travaillait a fermé ses portes

4 et Jean-Michel s'est retrouvé ³ au chômage. Depuis, il cherche du travail.

5 – Encore une lettre de refus ! Ça fait la quatrième depuis le début du mois.

Pronunciation :
You reached a level where you don't need our "figurative" pronunciation any more (except in really special cases). Listen extra carefully to the recordings, if you have them.

Notes
1 We've already learned that adjectives generally come before the noun they qualify. Three of the most common are **beau** (f. **belle**), **grand** (f. **grande**) and **petit** (f. **petite**): **un grand projet**, **une petite calculatrice**, *a large project, a small* (i.e. pocket) *calculator*.

Ninety-Ninth Lesson

use our system of [ ] and ( ) brackets when really necessary. Our aim is to encourage overall understanding rather than a word-by-word equivalence.

Work

1 Jean-Michel and Claude live in Vannes in Brittany, a beautiful region in western France.

2 Claude is a primary school teacher in a small school about 30 kms from Vannes.

3 As for Jean-Michel, he is a computer engineer. But the company he used to work for closed down three months ago

4 and Jean-Michel was made redundant *(found himself unemployed).* Since then, he has been looking for work.

5 – Another letter of refusal! That's the fourth one since the beginning of the month.

IL N'A PAS TELLEMENT ENVIE DE CHANGER DE MÉTIER.

2 **un professeur**, *a teacher*. The world is used generically, including for university professors. The official name for *a school teacher* (primary and secondary) is **un professeur des écoles**. (The former term for *a primary teacher*, **un instituteur / une institutrice** is sometimes used by older people.)

3 Remember the reflexive form: **il s'est retrouvé**: *he found himself.*

quatre cent deux •402

6 Cette fois-ci, paraît-_il, je suis trop qualifié. Tu vois, maintenant les boîtes ⁴ embauchent les jeunes avec bac plus trois, qui sont moins chers.

7 Évidemment, avec mon diplôme d'ingénieur et mes dix_années d'expérience, je suis presque trop vieux déjà.

8 – Ne te tracasse ⁵ pas, chéri. Ça ne fait que trois mois que tu cherches. Tu trouveras bientôt, j'en suis sûre.

9 – Au point où j'en suis, je suis prêt à accepter n'importe quel petit boulot ⁶. À la limite, je donnerais des cours de maths.

10 – Tu dis n'importe quoi. De toute façon, tu détestes l'enseignement.

11 – Là, tu as tort. J'aime assez donner des cours. En tout cas, j'aime bien les jeunes.

12 Je n'aime pas l'idée d'abandonner mon métier, mais qu'est-ce que tu veux ? Ce que je ne peux pas accepter, c'est de ne rien faire.

13 – Pas question ⁷ d'abandonner ton métier. Si besoin est, on peut quitter la région. Je n'en_ai pas tellement envie, mais s'il le faut…

14 – Bon, pas de précipitation. Attendons encore un peu. □

Notes

4 We saw in lesson 44 that the usual word for *a company* is **une entreprise** or **une société** (the latter is often found as part of the company name – **SFR, Société Française du Radiotéléphone** – or in the initials that follow it: **SA, société anonyme**, *public limited company*; **SARL, société anonyme à responsabilité limitée**, *private limited company*). However, in familiar language, people use **la boîte** (lit. "box"). **Ma boîte m'envoie en Bretagne**, *My company's sending me to Brittany*. There is no real equivalent in English.

6 This time, it seems that I'm too qualified. You see, companies now are looking for young people straight out of university (with three years' higher education), because they're cheaper.

7 Naturally, with my engineering qualifications and ten years' experience, I'm almost too old already.

8 – Don't get het up about it, darling. You've only been looking for three months. You'll find something soon, I'm sure.

9 – It's got to the point where I'm ready to accept any odd job. If it came to it, I'd give maths lessons.

10 – You're talking nonsense. Anyway, you hate teaching.

11 – You're wrong about that. I quite like giving lessons. In any case, I like young people.

12 I don't like the idea of giving up my job, but what do you expect? The one thing I can't stand is doing nothing.

13 – There's no question of you giving up your job. If need be, we can move away from the region. I don't particularly want to, but if we have to…

14 – Well, let's not rush into things. Let's wait a little longer.

---

5 se tracasser is a synonym for s'inquiéter, *to worry*. It can also be used transitively.

6 Just as people talk familiarly about their boîte, they also speak of their boulot (pronounced *[booloh]*) or job. Again, there is no common equivalent in English. In this context, however, un petit boulot is *a subsistence-level job*, sometimes referred to as… un job.

7 This is an emphatic (and colloquial) form of Il n'est pas question de: *There is no question of…* An alternative form: Abandonner ton métier est hors de question: *Abandoning your job is out of the question.*

▶ Exercice 1 – Traduisez

❶ Serge est bibliothécaire. Nathalie, elle, est assistante sociale. ❷ Depuis la fermeture de l'usine, il cherche du travail. ❸ Ça fait trois mois qu'elle est au chômage. ❹ Je n'aime pas l'idée de quitter la Bretagne. ❺ Il n'a pas tellement envie de changer de métier.

***

Exercice 2 – Complétez

❶ He works in a factory about fifty kilometers from Vannes.
Il travaille dans une usine située . . . .
. . . . Vannes.

❷ That's the third letter since the beginning of the month.
. . . . . . la troisième lettre . . . . . . le début du mois.

❸ She found herself out of work.
Elle . . . . au chômage.

100

Centième leçon

▶ ### Admettons...

1 Six mois plus tard, Jean-Michel n'a toujours rien trouvé.
2 Les_emplois se font rares [1] dans la région, et il est maintenant complètement découragé.

◻ : Note

1 **se faire rare** is not the equivalent of the English expression "to make oneself scarce", of which it is the literal translation. It means *to become*

Answers to Exercice 1

❶ Serge is a librarian. As for Nathalie, she's a social worker. ❷ Since the factory closed, he has been looking for a job. ❸ She's been unemployed for three months. ❹ I don't like the idea of leaving Brittany. ❺ He doesn't really want to change professions.

***

❹ You're talking nonsense. You know that you hate teaching.
Tu . Tu sais très bien que tu ....

❺ You're wrong there. We can leave Brittany if needs be.
.., tu ... On peut quitter la Bretagne.

Answers to Exercice 2

❶ – à une cinquantaine de kilomètres de – ❷ Ça fait – depuis –
❸ – s'est retrouvée – ❹ – dis n'importe quoi – détestes l'enseignement
❺ Là – as tort – si besoin est

Second wave: 50th Lesson

___

100

Hundredth Lesson

Possibly so

1 Six months later, Jean-Michel has still not found anything.
2 Jobs are getting hard to find in the region, and he is now completely disheartened.

hard to find: **Les techniciens expérimentés se font rares,** *It's becoming hard to find experienced technicians.* **L'argent se fait rare,** *Money's getting tight.*

3 – Dis, chérie, tu te souviens de ce que tu as dit l'autre jour ? Qu'on pourrait éventuellement quitter la région ?

4 – Oui mais je préférerais l'éviter si je peux.

5 – Je comprends, mais regarde ² : ça fait maintenant neuf mois que je cherche, et toujours rien !

6 Je suis sûr que je trouverais du boulot ³ à Paris.

7 – Admettons ⁴. Mais on n'aurait pas du tout la même qualité de vie là-bas qu'ici.

8 À Paris, il y la pollution, la circulation, le bruit – la foule, quoi. Et n'oublie pas que le coût de la vie ⁵ est plus_élevé.

9 – Je te l'accorde, mais il faut aller là où il y a du travail.

10 C'est vrai que la vie est plus chère à Paris, mais les salaires y sont plus_élevés aussi.

11 Et puis, on n'est pas obligés d'habiter Paris même ⁶. On peut chercher quelque chose en grande banlieue, si ça te dit ⁷.

⊓ Notes

2 Remember that the second person singular form (**tu**) of **-er** verbs loses the **s** when used in the imperative: **tu regardes** BUT **Regarde !** The pronunciation does not change.

3 As we saw (lesson 99, note 6), **un boulot** is a familiar word for a job. It can also mean *work*. **Il y a autre chose que le boulot dans la vie**, *There's more to life than work*. **Jean a du boulot pour moi**, *Jean has some work for me*.

4 Note these two different ways of conceding a point but arguing back. The first, **admettons**, is invariable: **Vous dites qu'il est très pauvre. Admettons, mais il a quand même trois voitures**, *You say he's very*

3 – Darling, remember what you said the other day? That we might possibly leave the region?

4 – Yes, but I'd prefer to avoid it if I can.

5 – I understand, but look. I've been looking for nine months now, and still nothing!

6 I'm sure I would find work in Paris.

7 – Possibly so. But we would have nothing like the same quality of life there as we do here.

8 Paris means pollution, traffic, noise – in short, crowds. And don't forget that the cost of living is higher.

9 – I agree with you, but you've got to go where the work is.

10 True, life is more expensive in Paris, but wages are higher, too.

11 And after all, we don't have to live in Paris itself. We can look for something in the outer suburbs if you want.

poor. *Let's say that he is. But he still owns 3 cars.* The second (line 9) can be used with **tu** and **vous**: **Paris est très cher, je te/vous l'accorde. Mais les salaires sont plus élevés**, *I agree that Paris is very expensive, but wages are higher*.

5 **la vie** means both *life* and *living* (lines 7 and 8). **Elle a eu une vie extraordinaire**, *She's had an extraordinary life.* **Il gagne bien sa vie**, *He earns a good living* (lit. "life").

6 Remember that **même** can be added to a noun to mean *itself, proper.* **Est-ce qu'elle habite Lyon même ou en banlieue ?** *Does she live in Lyons itself or in the suburbs?*

7 Lit. "if it says to you", i.e. *if you would like.* A common expression. **Ça te dit d'aller voir l'exposition au musée d'Orsay ?**, *How about going to see the exhibition at the Orsay Museum?* You can answer **Ça me dit** or, *if you don't feel like it*, **ça ne me dit rien.** (**Dire** is in the third person singular (**dit**) because the subject is **ça**.)

12 – Tu ne penses pas que tu brûles les_étapes[8]?
     Attendons encore un petit peu.
13 – Je ne vois pas d'autre solution.
   – Ne t'en fais pas.[9] Tout_ira bien.
14 Tout_est bien qui finit bien.   □

Notes

8 We know **une étape**: *a stage* (of a sporting event, a process, etc.). **La dernière étape du Tour de France se passe aux Champs-Élysées**, *The last stage of the Tour de France takes place on the Champs-Élysées*. The expression **brûler les étapes** (lit. "burn the stages") means *to cut corners* or *to do something in haste*. Moreover, we have a similar sporting expression in English: *to jump the gun*.

9 **s'en faire** is another expression (see lesson 99, note 5) for *to worry*. It is generally found in the imperative form: **Ne t'en fais pas / Ne vous en faites pas !**, *Don't worry about it!*

***

Exercice 1 – Traduisez
❶ Je n'ai toujours rien trouvé. **❷** Tu n'auras pas du tout la même qualité de vie. **❸** Elle préférerait l'éviter si elle peut. **❹** Je vous l'accorde, mais le coût de la vie est très élevé. **❺** Ne brûle pas les étapes.

***

Exercice 2 – Complétez
❶ Jobs are becoming few and far between in this region.
Les emplois . . . . dans cette région.

❷ Let's say that it's true. But don't forget that there's a lot of pollution.
. . . . Mais . . . . beaucoup de
pollution.

❸ The *(cost of)* living is more expensive, but wages are higher, too.
La vie . . . . , mais . . . . sont . . . .
aussi.

12 – Don't you think you're jumping the gun? Let's wait a bit longer.

13 – I can't see any other solution.
  – Don't worry, everything will be fine.

14 All's well that ends well.

***

Answers to Exercice 1

❶ I still haven't found anything. ❷ You won't have anything like the same quality of life. ❸ She would prefer to avoid it if she can. ❹ I take your point, but the cost of living is higher. ❺ Don't jump the gun.

***

❹ You can look for something in the suburbs if you feel like it.

Vous .... quelque chose .... si ....

❺ Don't worry. I'm sure you can do it.

.... Je suis sûr que vous .. êtes capable.

Answers to Exercice 2

❶ – se font rares – ❷ Admettons – n'oublie pas qu'il y a – ❸ – est plus chère – les salaires y – plus élevés – ❹ – pouvez chercher – en banlieue – ça vous dit ❺ Ne vous en faites pas – en –

Second wave: 51st Lesson

101

Cent unième leçon

La candidature

1 Ayant pris la décision de quitter la Bretagne, Jean-Michel se met_activement à la recherche d'un emploi dans la région parisienne.

2 Tous les jours, il achète les grands quotidiens et scrute ¹ attentivement les_offres d'emploi.

3 Il consulte aussi les_annonces disponibles sur le Minitel ². Il y a l'embarras du choix, mais peu d'offres qui l'intéressent vraiment.

4 Et puis un jour, il tombe sur l'annonce suivante : "SSII ³ recherche informaticien(ne) expérimenté(e) (H/F). Diplômé(e) grande école ou institut ingénierie. Connaissances multimédia obligatoires ⁴.

Notes

1 **scruter**, *to scan* or *to examine* (a document, etc.). We can recognise the English word "to scrutinise". One particular form of scrutiny is *the electoral ballot*, known as **le scrutin**. **On élit le président par voie de scrutin**, *The chairman is elected by ballot*.

2 Minitel is the name of the public videotext service introduced in the 1980s. A precursor to the World Wide Web, it was used to find practical information (train times, phone numbers, etc.). The system does not exist anymore.

101

One Hundred and First Lesson

The application

1 Having made the decision to leave Britanny, Jean-Michel energetically sets about looking for a job in the Paris area.
2 Every day, he buys the principal daily newspapers and carefully examines the job advertisements.
3 He also looks at the ads *(available)* on the Minitel. He is spoiled for choice, but few offers are really interesting.
4 And then one day he comes acoss the following ad: IT services company seeks experienced computer specialist (male or female). Business school or engineering school graduate. Knowledge of multimedia vital.

3 **société de service et ingénierie informatiques**, *computer services company*. As we have already seen, French loves acronyms and initials, even going so far as to make nouns from them (e.g. **un cégétiste**: *a member of the CGT trade union*). As to pronunciation, when two vowels are repeated (here, II), they are pronounced as double I. So, **SSII** is pronounced *[ess-ess-deuzee]*. Listen to the recording.

4 Equal-opportunity legislation bars discrimination in job applications, which must be worded to apply to both men and women. The pronunciation of **expérimenté** and **diplômé** is the same in the masculine and the feminine. Note the telegraphic style of the advertisement (**Connaissances multimédia** instead of **Connaissances en multimédia**, etc.).

5 Libre de suite. Anglais indispensable. Adresser C.V. et lettre de motivation au DRH, Société Toutvu, Les_Ulis [5]."

6 – Ça y est. Ça correspond parfaitement à mon profil. Et en plus, le poste [6] est_à pourvoir tout de suite.

7 Jean-Michel s'installe à son_ordinateur, charge l'application de traitement de texte et se met_à écrire :

8 "Messieurs, en réponse à votre annonce parue hier, j'ai l'honneur de poser ma candidature au poste d'informaticien.

9 Diplômé de l'ENSEA, j'ai dix_ans d'expérience en informatique.

10 Je vous prie de bien vouloir trouver ci-joint mon C.V., qui vous fournira de plus_amples renseignements sur mon parcours [7] professionnel.

11 Dans l'espoir que vous voudrez bien considérer favorablement ma candidature, je vous prie de croire, messieurs, à l'assurance de mes sentiments distingués."

12 Jean-Michel attend le retour de Claude avec impatience pour partager la bonne nouvelle.

: Notes

5 As we have seen, English speakers find the French **u** hard to pronounce. (It is similar to the English "ew" in *yew*.) The problem is compounded when the vowel sounds *[ou]* and *[u]* are in close proximity, as in the name of this company. Listen carefully to the recording and try to imitate the speaker.

5 Free straight away. English vital. Send CV and covering letter *(of motivation)* to head of personnel, Toutvu Co., Les Ulis.

6 – That's it. It matches my [career] profile exactly. What's more, the post is free right away.

7 Jean-Michel sits down at his computer, loads the word processing program and starts typing

8 "Sirs, In reply to your advertisement yesterday, I wish to apply for the post of computer specialist.

9 A graduate of the ENSEA, I have 10 years' experience in IT.

10 I enclose my CV, which provides more information about my career path.

11 I hope my application will interest you. Yours faithfully,"

12 Jean-Michel waits impatiently for Claude to return so that he can share the good news.

OUF, JE N'EN PEUX PLUS, JE SUIS CREVE.

6 Another example of why it is vital to learn the gender of a noun. **Le poste**, *the job* (in the sense of opening, vacancy), **la poste**, *the post office*. The expression **le poste (est) à pourvoir** is a formal way of saying *the vacancy ("is") to be filled*.

7 **un parcours** is literally *a journey* or *a route*. But it is commonly used to mean a career path, professional experience, etc. **Ce soir, un documentaire sur le groupe Indochine et son parcours,** *Tonight a documentary on the group Indochine and its history.*

13 Elle rentre vers six_heures et, épuisée après sa longue journée, s'affale dans un fauteuil.

14 – Ouf, je suis crevée [8] ! Qu'est-ce que tu as fait de ta journée ?

15 – Devine ? J'ai trouvé une offre d'emploi qui semble parfaite pour moi et j'ai envoyé ma candidature. Croisons les doigts. □

Note

8 Another difficult pronunciation. Listen carefully to the recording. **Crever** literally means *to puncture*. **Un pneu crevé**, *a flat tire*. However, in familiar language, **Je suis crevé** is equivalent to *I'm whacked*.

***

Exercice 1 – Traduisez

❶ Il y a l'embarras du choix, mais rien qui les intéressait vraiment. ❷ Ça y est. Ça correspond parfaitement à son profil. ❸ Ouf, je n'en peux plus. Je suis crevé. ❹ Qu'est-ce qu'elle a fait de sa journée ? ❺ Croisons les doigts.

***

Exercice 2 – Complétez

❶ I enclose details about my career.

Je . . . .- . . . . . . les
renseignements sur . . . . professionnel.

❷ Yours truly.

Je . . . . , messieurs, à . . . . de mes
. . . .

❸ Having decided to look for work, he buys all the national dailies.

. . . . la décision . . . . du travail, il achète . . . .
les . . . .

13   She gets back at around 6 pm and, exhausted after her long day, collapses into an armchair.

14 – Phew, I'm whacked! What did you get up to today?

15 – Guess? I found a job offer that seems perfect for me and I sent off an application. Let's keep our fingers crossed.

***

Answers to Exercise 1

❶ They were spoiled for choice, but nothing really interested them. ❷ That's the one. It matches his career profile perfectly. ❸ Phew, I''ve had it. I'm worn out. ❹ What did she get up to today? ❺ Let's keep our fingers crossed.

***

❹ Exhausted after a long day's work, he collapses into an armchair.
……. après … … …… ……… .. ….…, il ……… dans un fauteuil.

❺ They await for him *(her)* to return so that they can tell him *(her)* the good news.
… ……… … …… pour lui raconter la bonne nouvelle.

Answers to Exercise 2

❶ – vous prie de bien vouloir trouver ci-joints – mon parcours – ❷ – vous prie de croire – l'expression – sentiments distingués ❸ Ayant pris – de chercher – tous – grands quotidiens ❹ Épuisé – une longue journée de travail – s'affale – ❺ Ils attendent son retour –

Second wave: 52nd Lesson

102

Cent deuxième leçon

Une réponse

1 Après une semaine passée sur des charbons_ardents ¹, Jean-Michel reçoit enfin une lettre de la société Toutvu :

2 – "Monsieur,
Nous avons pris connaissance de votre candidature, qui a retenu toute notre attention.

3 Nous souhaitons vous rencontrer afin d'en ² parler en détail.

4 Aussi ³ nous vous_invitons à prendre rendez-vous avec M. François Fauconnier, notre directeur des ressources_humaines.

5 Dans cette attente, nous vous prions d'agréer, monsieur, l'expression de nos sentiments distingués."

6 – Enfin ! Mais je ne dois pas trop me réjouir à l'avance. Après tout, ça n'est qu'un_entretien ⁴ ...

Pronunciation
(1) Listen carefully to the difference between the *[ou]* and *[u]* sounds in Toutvu.

Notes
1 le charbon, *coal*. In this expression, **ardent** means *hot* think of "an ardent lover". So **sur des charbons ardents** literally means "on burning coals". In the figurative sense, it is equivalent to *on tenterhooks*.

102

One Hundred and Second Lesson

An answer

1 After a week on tenterhooks, Jean-Michel finally receives a letter from Toutvu.

2 – "Sir,
we read your application with great interest.

3 We would like to meet you in order to discuss it in detail.

4 Therefore, we invite you to contact Mr François Fauconnier, our personnel director.

5 Yours faithfully,"

6 – At last! But I mustn't look forward to it too much. After all, it's only an interview...

2 **afin de** is a more formal way of saying **pour** for *in order to*. In a formal register, a statement like **Je veux la rencontrer pour parler de son projet**, *I want to meet her to talk about her plan*, would be expressed **Je souhaite vous rencontrer afin de**, etc. (Think of the English expression *To that end...*).

3 Another formal usage. We have seen **aussi** meaning *also*. At the <u>beginning</u> of a sentence, it means *therefore* or *thus*. **Aussi, nous pensons que vous êtes l'homme qu'il nous faut**, *Thus, we think you are the man we need*.

4 **un entretien**, *an interview*, or *talk* with someone. Used formally and informally. **Suite à notre entretien téléphonique d'hier**, *Further to our telephone conversation yesterday...* Also, remember lesson 62, note 6: the word for a media interview is... **une interview** (pronounced virtually the same as in English).

7 Trois jours plus tard, Jean-Michel prend le TGV [5] pour gagner Paris. À la gare Montparnasse, il prend le métro pour se rendre au siège [6] de Toutvu.

8 – Bonjour monsieur, puis-je [7] vous‿aider ?

9 – Bonjour, je m'appelle Bellon, Jean-Michel [8]. J'ai rendez-vous avec M. Fauconnier.

10 – Monsieur Bellon... en effet. À neuf [9] heures et quart. Asseyez-vous, je vous‿en prie. Je l'appelle tout de suite.

***

11 Un homme va voir un vieux copain [10] qui est devenu ministre.

Notes

5 le train à grande vitesse, universally known as the **TGV** [tay-zhay-vay], is the name of France's high-speed train system. Launched in 1984, these sleek bullet trains have been highly successful with the general public, slashing journey times and bringing most areas of France within fast, easy reach of major cities. Broadly, TGV fares are the same as those charged for ordinary trains, but in certain cases, there is *an additional fee*, **un supplément**. Before boarding most trains in France (TGV or not), passengers must *date-stamp*, **composter** their tickets in special machines located at the head of the platform.

6 un siège, *a seat*. **Prenez un siège en attendant**, *Take a seat while you wait*. Figuratively, it is used for parliamentary seats (**Le parti a trois cents sièges à l'Assemblée**, *The party has 300 seats in the National Assembly*) and corporate seats: **La société a son siège en province**, *The company's headquarters are in the provinces*.

7 Three days later, Jean-Michel takes the highspeed train for Paris. At Montparnasse Station, he takes the metro to the headquarters of Toutvu.

8 – Good morning sir, may I help you?

9 – Good morning, my name's Jean-Michel Bellon. I have an appointment with Mr Fauconnier.

10 – Mr Bellon, yes indeed. At 9.15. Please take a seat. I'll call him straight away.

***

11 A man goes to see an old friend who has become a minister.

MON PÈRE A COMMENCÉ EN BAS DE L'ÉCHELLE.

7 We know that, in formal usage, we generally invert the verb and pronoun in the interrogative form. (**Est-ce que vous voulez...?** → **Voulez-vous...?**). When we do this with the first person singular of **pouvoir**, *can*, we do not use **peux** but **puis**. Thus **Est-ce que je peux** → **Puis-je** *[pweezh]*. This is a formal usage.

8 In certain formal situations, the French have a disconcerting habit of announcing the surname before the first name. It's not a rule, just usage. But be prepared!

9 Listen carefully to the pronunciation: *[neuv eur]*.

10 **un copain** = an informal word for *a friend*. Sometimes used to mean *boyfriend*. **Le copain de Marie l'a quittée**, *Marie's boyfriend has left her*. Feminine: **une copine** (see lesson 73, note 3).

12 – Dis donc, je t'ai rendu beaucoup de services dans le passé. Maintenant, il faudrait me renvoyer l'ascenseur [11].

13 Peux-tu trouver un boulot pour mon fils, qui est un bon à rien ?

14 – Bien sûr, répond le ministre. Je peux l'embaucher demain comme directeur de cabinet [12].

15 – C'est trop.
   – D'accord, je le prends comme directeur de la communication.

16 – Non, il faut qu'il commence en bas de l'échelle. Tu n'as pas‿un simple poste de coursier, par exemple ?

17 – Si tu veux, mais il y a un problème. Pour ce genre d'emploi, il faut qu'il ait‿ [13] un diplôme d'ingénieur...

□

Notes

11 In English, when someone returns a favour, they scratch our back. In French, they "send back the lift". **Dis donc, il est temps de me renvoyer l'ascenseur**, *Hey, [I've scratched your back]; now you scratch mine*.

***

▶ Exercice 1 – Traduisez

❶ Elle a reçu une réponse ? – Pas encore. Elle est sur des charbons ardents. ❷ Elle prend le train pour se rendre à Paris et le métro pour gagner son bureau. ❸ Puis-je vous aider ? – Nous avons rendez- vous avec Monsieur Julliard. ❹ Dis donc, il faudrait me renvoyer l'ascenseur. ❺ Mon père a commencé en bas de l'échelle.

12 – Listen here, I've done you lots of favours in the past. Now it's time to pay me back.

13 Can you find a job for my good-for-nothing son?

14 – Of course, answers the minister. I can employ him tomorrow as director of *(my)* private office.

15 – That's too much.

– OK, I'll take him on as director of public relations.

16 – No, he's got to start on the bottom *(rung)* of the ladder. Haven't you got an ordinary job as a messenger, for example?

17 – If you want. But there's a problem. For that kind of job, he'll need to be a graduate engineer…

12 In France, every senior minister has **un cabinet**, or *a private office*. **M. Legal est le chef de cabinet du ministre de la culture**, *Mr Legal is head of the private office of the arts minister*.

13 See lesson 98, note 2: The present subjunctive of **avoir** is **que j'aie, que tu aies, qu'il/elle ait, que nous ayons, que vous ayez, qu'ils aient**. As regards pronunciation, **aie, aies, ait** and **aient** *[ay]* are almost indistinguishable; **ayons** = *[ay-ohn]* and **ayez** = *[ay-ay]*.

***

Answers to Exercice 1

❶ Has she received an answer? – Not yet. She's on tenterhooks. ❷ She takes the train to Paris and the metro to her office. ❸ May I help you? – We have a meeting with Mr Julliard. ❹ Listen here, it's your turn to scratch my back. ❺ My father started out on the bottom rung of the ladder.

Exercice 2 – Complétez

❶ We must have a good excuse.

Il . . . . une bonne excuse.

❷ I've done you a lot favours. Now, it's time [you have to] scratch my back.

Je . . . . beaucoup de . . . . : maintenant il faudrait . . . .

❸ After all, it's only an interview.

. . . . , ça . . . . entretien.

103

Cent troisième leçon

L'entretien d'embauche

1 – Monsieur Bellon ? François Fauconnier ¹. Je suis le directeur des ressources_humaines de Toutvu. Venez vous_asseoir.

2 Nous_avons été très_impressionnés par votre C.V. Parlez-moi un peu de votre expérience dans le multimédia.

3 – Euh, j'ai toujours été fasciné par les technologies de pointe ². Je suis convaincu qu'elles vont révolutionner notre façon de travailler.

4 – Pour ma part, je pense que vous_avez raison. Mais tout le monde ne pense pas comme vous ³.

Notes

1 In a formal introduction, some people prefer simply to announce their names rather than go through the rigmarole of **Permettez-moi de me présenter, je m'appelle...** This can be disconcerting at first, but you soon get used to it. Compared with English, French is still a relatively formal language, and automatic use of a stranger's first name is not commonplace. But times are changing!

❹ Can I help you (informal)?

.... je .... vous aider ?

❺ Can I help you (formal)?

.... vous aider ?

Answers to Exercice 2

❶ – faut que nous ayons – **❷** – vous ai rendu – services – me renvoyer l'ascenseur **❸** Après tout – n'est qu'un – **❹** Est-ce que – peux – **❺** Puis-je –

Second wave: 53rd Lesson

103

One Hundred and Third Lesson

The job interview

1 – Mr Bellon? [I'm] François Fauconnier. I'm the personnel director of Toutvu. Come and sit down.

2   We were very impressed by your CV. Tell me a little about your experience with multimedia.

3 – Um, I've always been fascinated by advanced technologies. I'm convinced they're going to revolutionise the way we work.

4 – As far as I'm concerned, I agree with you. But not everybody thinks like you.

2   **de pointe** (lit. "of the point") is used as an adjective to indicate the culminating point of an activity. The two most common uses are **la vitesse de pointe (d'une voiture)**, *the top speed* ("of a car") and **les industries/technologies de pointe**, *advanced industries/technologies*. Unfortunately, you will find it difficult to avoid media references to **les industries hi-tech**...

3   Note the difference with the English construction: **Tout le monde ne pense pas comme vous**, *Not everybody thinks like you*.

5 – À mon avis, il ne faut pas revenir en arrière.
Voilà pourquoi je travaille depuis longtemps
avec Internet.

6 Maintenant, je considère que je me débrouille [4]
pas mal... euh, je veux dire, je suis_à même
de [5]...

7 – Je vous_en prie. Ici nous sommes_assez
informels. Ou "relax", si vous préférez.

8 À propos du poste, il s'agit d'un poste de cadre
à plein temps. Le candidat retenu sera amené à
se déplacer à l'étranger quatre ou cinq fois par
an.

9 Il dirigera une équipe de recherches composée
de huit personnes.

10 Alors, au niveau du salaire, quelles sont vos
prétentions ? Pardon. Combien voulez-vous
gagner ?

11 – Euh, vous savez, je ne connais pas trop les
salaires pratiqués à Paris.

12 Dans mon_ancien travail, je gagnais trois mille
euros sur treize mois [6].

Notes

4 With its derivatives, **se débrouiller** is virtually a vocabulary in itself. The
basic meaning is *to get by*. **Parlez-vous russe ? – Je me débrouille**,
Do you speak Russian? – I can get by. We'll see other uses later on.
Pronunciation: Beware the *[ou-ee]* diphthong: *[zhe me day-brou-ee]*.

5 – In my opinion, we can't *(mustn't)* go backwards. That's why I've been working with [the] Internet for a long time.

6 Now I reckon I get by quite well... um, I mean I am fully capable of...

7 – Please, we're quite informal here. Or "laid back", if you prefer.

8 About the job, it's a full-time position at executive level. The candidate we choose will be required to travel abroad four or five times a year.

9 He'll direct a research team made up of eight people.

10 Now, in terms of salary, what remuneration do you require? I'm sorry, how much do you want to earn?

11 – Um, you know, I'm not too familiar with salaries in Paris.

12 In my old job, I earned three thousand euros with an extra month's bonus.

L'ENTRETIEN D'EMBAUCHE

5 Jean-Michel has lapsed into informal language and is trying to move back up the register.

6 Wages and salaries in France are generally calculated on a monthly basis, except in certain sectors that have been influenced by Anglo-Saxon business practices. In many cases, salaries include a bonus equivalent to an extra month's pay, i.e. "over thirteen months". **Le treizième mois**, *the year-end bonus*.

13 – Avec les_avantages en nature, je pense que nous pouvons_arriver un peu au-dessus.

14 – Permettez-moi de dire que je suis très_intéressé par le poste. Est-ce qu'il y a d'autres candidats ?

15 – Il faut que je voie [7] encore une personne cet_après-midi. Nous vous ferons part [8] de notre décision sous huit jours. Au revoir. □

Notes

7 Subjunctive. Note how, in line 5, we used **il faut** with an infinitive, thus avoiding the subjunctive altogether. This is only possible when using the impersonal form. The subjunctive takes a little getting used to, but you'll soon pick it up naturally if you repeat each line aloud.

***

▶ Exercice 1 – Traduisez

❶ Salut, Jean-Michel. Viens t'asseoir. **❷** À mon avis, vous avez raison. **❸** Au niveau du salaire, combien est-ce que vous voulez gagner ? **❹** Y a-til d'autres candidats? **❺** Il se débrouille pas mal en russe.

***

Exercice 2 – Complétez

❶ We have received four wedding invitations.
Nous .... quatre .....-.... de mariage.

❷ As far as he's concerned, he's convinced that she's wrong.
...., il est convaincu .... tort.

❸ Not everyone thinks the same as me.
.... comme moi.

13 – With perks, I think we'll manage to exceed that slightly.

14 – May I say that I'm very interested in the job. Are there any other candidates?

15 – I have to see one more person this afternoon. We'll let you know our decision within a week. Goodbye.

8 faire part de quelque chose is a formal way of saying *to let someone know* (i.e. to make them a part of it). One common derivative is **un faire-part** (a formal notification): **Tiens, on a reçu un faire-part de mariage d'Hélène**, *Look, we have received a wedding announcement from Helen*. (In this case, **le faire-part** is probably an invitation.) There is no plural form: **des faire-part**.

***

Answers to Exercice 1

❶ Hi, Jean-Michel. Come and sit down. ❷ As far as I'm concerned, you're right. ❸ In terms of salary, how much do you want to earn? ❹ Are there any other candidates? ❺ He gets by quite well in Russian.

***

❹ I must see the director in person.

   Il ... ... le directeur en personne.

❺ We must not go back*(wards)*.

   Il .. .. en ....

Answers to Exercice 2

❶ – avons reçu – faire-part – ❷ Pour sa part – qu'elle a – ❸ Tout le monde ne pense pas – ❹ – faut que je voie – ❺ – ne faut pas retourner – arrière

Second wave: 54th Lesson

Cent quatrième leçon

Félicitations !

1 Encore une semaine d'angoisse ¹ pour Jean-Michel, qui commence à perdre espoir. Et puis, lundi matin…

2 – Allô ², M. Bellon ?
– Lui-même ³.
– Ici François Fauconnier. Je ne vous dérange pas ?
– Pas du tout.

3 – Je vous_appelle pour vous_annoncer notre décision de vous_embaucher comme chef d'équipe.

4 Allô ? Vous êtes toujours là ?
– Absolument. Je suis ravi, je…

5 – Dois-je ⁴ comprendre que vous acceptez ?
– Et comment ! Je veux dire, oui, j'accepte volontiers.

Notes

1 Naturally, you recognise the English word *anguish*. However, **l'angoisse** is not quite as strong. It means *fear* or *anxiety*. **Il vit dans l'angoisse**, *He's permanently anxious*. It is commonly used as an exclamation: **Une lettre du fisc. L'angoisse !**, *A letter from the tax office. I dread to think!*

2 Remember that **Allô** is only used for phone conversations. It can be used when you answer a call or if you cannot hear the person at the other end (line 4).

One Hundred and Fourth Lesson

Congratulations!

1   Another week of anxiety for Jean-Michel, who
is beginning to lose hope. And then, on Monday
morning...

2 – Hello, Mr Bellon?
– Speaking.
– This is François Fauconnier. I hope I'm not disturbing
you?
– Not at all.

3 – I'm calling to tell you that we have decided to hire
you as project manager [team leader].

4   Hello? Are you still there?
– Absolutely. I'm delighted, I...

5 – Am I to take it that you accept?
– And how! I mean, yes, I accept willingly.

---

3   Literally "himself". **Regarde, c'est le Premier ministre lui-même !**,
Look, it's the prime minister himself (in the flesh, etc.). On the phone,
however, you can use it instead of **Oui**, rather like we say *Speaking*. **M.
Chérel ? – Lui-même**, *Mr Chérel? – Speaking*. A woman would answer
Elle-même.

4   Formal: *Am I to understand*, etc. Pronounced *[dwazh]*. A more common
usage would be in questions like **Dois-je venir tout de suite ?**, *Must I
come right now?* or, when asking for the bill in a café, **Combien vous
dois-je ?**, *How much do I owe you?* In all cases, it is more elegant than
est-ce que je dois.

6 – Très bien. Vous commencerez à la fin de la semaine. Nous vous_envoyons votre contrat par la poste. Bienvenue chez Toutvu.

7 – *(Plus tard.)*
Chéri ? Je suis de retour. Mais pourquoi as-tu mis ton manteau ? Où va-t-on ? ⁵

8 – Au restaurant, pour fêter la bonne nouvelle. J'ai décroché le boulot chez Toutvu !

9 – Félicitations ! Qu'est-ce que je suis contente ⁶ !

10 – *(Au restaurant.)*
Bonsoir madame, bonsoir monsieur. Voici la carte. Désirez-vous prendre l'apéritif ?

11 – Deux coupes de champagne, s'il vous plaît. Ce soir, on fait la fête ⁷ !

12 – Puis-je prendre votre commande ⁸ ?
– On commencera avec un plateau de fruits de mer ⁹ pour deux.

Notes

5 A more elegant way of saying **Où est-ce qu'on va ?**, *Where are we going?*

6 Listen carefully to the recording. Using **qu'est-ce que** before an exclamation adds emphasis. **Qu'est-ce qu'on est bien ici !**, *Isn't it wonderful here?* The more elegant form is **Que je suis contente !**, *How happy I am / I'm so happy!*

7 **fêter**, *to celebrate*. **Il est né un 29 février, donc il fête son anniversaire le 28**, *He was born [on] the 29th of February, so he celebrates his birthday [on] the 28th*. But it can also mean *to party*. **Ce soir, on fait la fête !**, *Tonight, we're having a party!* Another useful word (?) is **un fêtard**, *a party-goer*. The word can be admiring or disapproving, depending on the age of the person who uses it…

6 – Very well. You'll start at the end of the week. We are sending your contract by post. Welcome to Toutvu.

7 – *(Later)*
Darling? I'm home. Why have you got your coat on? Where are we going?

8 – Out for dinner *(To the restaurant)* to celebrate the good news. I got the job at Toutvu!

9 – Congratulations. Oh, I'm so happy!

10 – *(At the restaurant)*
Good evening madam, good evening sir. Here's the menu. Would you like a drink before dinner?

11 – Two glasses of champagne, please. Tonight's a celebration!

12 – May I take your order?
   – We'll start with a seafood platter for two.

8 We've seen **Dois-je**; now meet **Puis-je** *[pweezh]*, also a formal usage. In a lower register, we would say **Est-ce que peux prendre votre commande ?** or even **Je prends votre commande ?**

9 As usual, French is more poetic than English when describing food. Compare **les fruits de mer** (lit. "fruit of the sea") with our prosaic *seafood*.

13   Ensuite, pour moi, la sole meunière. Et toi ?
     – Je ne suis pas très poisson. [10] Je prendrai plutôt une côte de bœuf.

14 – Et une bouteille de pernand-vergelesses 87.
    – Très bien, monsieur.

15 – À ta santé, mon chéri.

16   Il y a juste une chose. Il faut maintenant que je trouve un travail à Paris, moi aussi [11] !   □

Notes

[10] Instead of saying **Je n'aime pas beaucoup le poisson** (viande, etc.), some people have a habit of saying **Je ne suis pas très poisson** (lit. "I'm not very fish"). Not to be recommended.

***

▶ Exercice 1 – Traduisez

❶ Bonjour, ici François Fauconnier. Je ne vous dérange pas, j'espère ? – Pas du tout. ❷ Allô, Jean ? Tu viens ce soir ? – Absolument. ❸ Où est-ce qu'on va ? – Ce soir, on fait la fête ! ❹ Il a décroché le boulot. Que je suis contente pour lui ! ❺ Combien vous dois-je ? – Beaucoup !

***

Exercice 2 – Complétez

❶ Where are going this evening? – To a restaurant to celebrate my birthday.
. . . . ce soir ? – Nous allons au restaurant . . . . mon anniversaire.

❷ I'll have fish, too – Very good, madam.
. . . . du poisson, ..., madame.

❸ Can I take your order? – Must I order right now?
. . . .-. . . . . votre commande ? – . . . .-. . . . . tout de suite ?

13 Then I'll have the sole meunière. And you?
  – I'm not too fond of fish. I'd rather have a prime rib of beef.
14 – And a bottle of pernand-vergelesses 87.
  – Very good, sir.
15 – Your health, my darling.
16 There's just one thing. Now I have to find a job in Paris, too!

11 We often add **moi aussi, vous aussi**, etc. to the end of a statement for emphasis. So, **Il parle le russe aussi** can be made more emphatic thus: **Il parle le russe, lui aussi**. Equivalent to *He, too, speaks Russian* – but much less formal.

***

Answers to Exercice 1

❶ Good morning, this is François Fauconnier. I hope I'm note disturbing you? – Not at all. **❷** Hello, Jean? Are you coming this evening? – Absolutely. **❸** Where are we going? – Tonight we're celebrating! **❹** He got the job. I'm so happy for him! **❺** How much is that? – A lot!

***

❹ He called me to announce his decision.
  Il .... décision.
❺ How happy we are to be here this evening!
  .... contents d'être ici ce soir !

Answers to Exercice 2

❶ Où va-t-on – pour fêter – **❷** Je prendrai – moi aussi – Très bien – **❸** Puis-je prendre – Dois-je commander – **❹** – m'a appelé pour annoncer sa – **❺** Que nous sommes –

Second wave: 55th Lesson

105

Cent cinquième leçon

Révision – Revision

1 A few facts about the French educational system

Although the French educational system has changed radically over the past decades – and continues to do so – its cornerstone is still **le baccalauréat**. Universally referred to as **le bac**, this secondary-school graduation diploma is the key to further education. A well-known catch phrase is **Passe ton bac d'abord** (*Take your "bac" before you do anything else*). Remember that **passer un examen** is *to take an exam* and **réussir un examen** is *to pass* it. Passing **le bac** allows a young person to go to university or other forms of higher education. These include university (**les universités** (f.) and **les instituts techniques universitaires** (m.) or **IUT** (university-level technical institutes). A person's level of higher education is generally measured in the number of years' study after **le bac**. So potential employers, for example, will advertise for someone with **bac plus trois** (three years of higher education, equivalent to a bachelor's degree in the UK system), **bac plus quatre** (master's) or even **bac plus sept** (Ph.D).

An alternative to the university system are **les grandes écoles** (lit. "major schools"), a select group of engineering and business schools that are a passport to the upper echelons of corporate and political life. One of the most prestigious of these is **l'École polytechnique** or just **Polytechnique**, whose graduates are referred to as **les polytechniciens** (or, more cryptically, **les X**). But arguably the best known of **les grandes écoles** is the **École nationale d'administration** or **l'ENA**, the training ground of France's elite. Most senior figures in French public life are **énarques**, or former students of ENA.

2 *N'importe quoi !*

N'importe quoi is another of those useful phrases that can be used for a multitude of purposes. The root, **n'importe**, means *any*

One Hundred and Fifth Lesson

in compound forms. We have already seen **n'importe quoi** used to mean *anything*. **Donnez-moi quelque chose à boire, n'importe quoi**, *Give me something to drink, anything will do*. On the same pattern, we have **n'importe où**, *anywhere*, **n'importe qui**, *anyone* and **n'importe comment**, *anyhow*.

But, when uttered in tones of annoyance or dismissal, **n'importe quoi** takes on a whole different shade of meaning. For example, in lesson 99, Jean-Michel says something that he most certainly does not mean and his wife says : **Tu dis n'importe quoi**, *You don't really mean what you're saying* (lit. "you're saying any old thing that goes through your head"). Even more dismissive would be someone criticising, say, a politician who says anything to get elected. **Ne le croyez pas. Il dit n'importe quoi**, *Don't believe him, he talks rubbish*. If someone botches a job, you could say: **Regarde ! Tu fais n'importe quoi. C'est comme ça qu'il faut faire**, *Look at you, you're going about it all wrong*. Here's what you should do. Or if your child says that he or she intends to hitch to Mexico alone, you would probably say: **N'importe quoi !**, *You don't half talk nonsense!* (i.e. over my dead body). Get the idea?

3 Showing disinclination

Lesson 99 shows us how to express different degrees of disinclination. If you are not particularly keen on something, for example, to have dinner with an acquaintance, you would say **Je n'ai pas tellement envie de dîner avec Thierry**. If you actually don't want to, you would say **Je n'ai pas envie de dîner avec Thierry** and, if you're really against the idea, **Je n'ai vraiment pas envie de dîner avec Thierry**. Now, practise the different degrees yourself. Here are a few suggestions. You decide how little you want to do the actions suggested:

dîner avec ma belle-mère, *have dinner with my mother-in-law*
avoir mal aux dents, *have toothache*
aller chez le dentiste, *go to the dentist*

voir ce vieux film muet, *see that old silent film*
promener le chien, *take the dog for a walk*
payer plus d'impôts, *pay more tax*

Find some more things you don't want to do.

Two other ways of showing disinclination. First, mildly: **Je n'aime pas l'idée (de)** is equivalent to our *I don't like the thought of...* **Je n'aime pas l'idée de quitter la région**, *I don't like the thought of leaving the region*.
Now emphatically: **Pas question de quitter la région !**, *No way will I leave the region!*

Now re-read lesson 99 and see all these expressions in context.

4 The *faux-amis* (false friends)

Since English and French have common roots, many words are the same in both languages. However, there is a group of words known as **les faux-amis** (*false friends*), which look the same but have a different meaning. Very often, you don't realise the difference until something you say is met with a blank look or puzzled smile. We've already pointed out a few of the most common, but the best thing to do is make your own list.

Some **faux-amis** are easy to spot and remember: **une librairie**, *a bookshop* / *a library*; **une bibliothèque** or **une prune**, *a plum* / *a prune*, **un pruneau**.

French	English	English	French
un car	*a coach*	*a car*	**une voiture**
une cave	*a cellar*	*a cave*	**une grotte**
un coin	*corner*	*a coin*	**une pièce (de monnaie)**
un éditeur	*publisher*	*an editor*	**un rédacteur**
une librairie	*a bookshop*	*a library*	**une bibliothèque**
la monnaie *	*change*	*money **	**l'argent**

une prune	a plum	a prune	un pruneau
large (adj.)	*wide*	*large*	**grand**
sensible (adj.)	*sensitive*	*sensible*	**raisonnable**

* Both *money* and **la monnaie** are collective nouns, i.e. you cannot use the indefinite article *a*/**une** with either of them.

Others are more subtle. For example, **éventuellement** has nothing to do with *eventually*. It means *possibly* or *if the need arises* in phrases such as **Éventuellement, je pourrais donner des cours**, *If necessary, I could give lessons*. Or **On sera six, et éventuellement sept si François vient**, *They'll be six of us, and possibly seven if François comes*. The adjective **éventuel** has the same connotation: **Le successeur éventuel du patron est son fils**, *The possible successor to the boss will be his son*. So, **éventuel** always expresses possibility but uncertainty. (For the record, *eventually* in French is **enfin**: **On est arrivés enfin après cinq heures de marche**, *We eventually arrived after a 5-hour walk*.)

5 S'agir de...

Always used in the impersonal form, **s'agir de** basically means *it is a matter of* or *it is about*. **De quoi s'agit-il ?**, *What's this about?* **Quand il s'agit de travailler dur, il n'est jamais là**, *When it's a question of hard work, he's never there*. Or **Il faut qu'il m'appelle. Il s'agit de son avenir**, *He must call me. It's a question of his future* (i.e. his future is at stake). **Il veut me voir. Il s'agit de la lettre que je lui ai écrite**, *He wants to see me. It's about the letter I wrote him*. Now, try leaving it out when you come across it. Look at our example in lesson 103. **Il s'agit d'un poste de cadre**, *It is a management job*. Or **Il s'agit de ne pas oublier !** *Don't forget it!*, You see? Much simpler!

Bear in mind, then, that **s'agir de** basically means *concerning*, but that we can get along nicely without always finding an exact equivalent.

Second wave: 56th Lesson

106

Cent sixième leçon

On déménage

1 La prochaine étape : le déménagement.
Claude commence par acheter le *Journal des
Particuliers* ¹.

2 Mais, n'ayant ² rien trouvé d'intéressant, elle
décide de contacter une agence immobilière ³.

3 – Bonjour madame. Voilà, je suis_à la recherche
pour mon mari et moi d'un pavillon ⁴ près
des_Ulis,

4 de préférence avec un jardin et situé dans_un
village avec des commerces.

5 – Combien de pièces vous faut-il ?
– Il nous faut un grand séjour, deux chambres et
une cave. ⁵

6 En plus, il faut absolument un garage, une
cuisine aménagée et le chauffage central.

7 – Et quel loyer êtes-vous prêts ⁶ à mettre ?
– Pas plus de mille.

Notes

1 particulier (lit. "particular" or "special") is also used to mean a private
individual. **C'est pour un particulier ou une société ?**, *Is it for a private
individual or a company?* When buying or renting property, **une location** or **une vente de particulier à particulier** means *a private transac-
tion*, i.e. not handled by an agency. In this usage, there is no feminine
form.

2 As we saw in lesson 83, note 5, this use of the participle is very similar to
English. **N'ayant rien trouvé** works for both *Having found nothing* and
Not having found anything.

One Hundred and Sixth Lesson

Moving

1 The next stage: the move. Claude begins by buying the *Journal des Particuliers*.

2 But having found nothing interesting, she decides to contact an estate agent.

3 – Good morning madam. I'm looking for a house near Les Ulis for my husband and me,

4 preferably with a garden and located in a village with shops.

5 – How many rooms do you need?
  – We need a big living-room, two bedrooms and a cellar.

6 In addition, we absolutely must have a garage, a fitted kitchen and central heating.

7 – And how much rent are you prepared to pay?
  – No more than 1,000.

---

3 l'immobilier, *property*; un agent immobilier, *an estate agent.*

4 un pavillon, *a detached house.* The word is commonly used instead of une maison. (Be careful, it can also mean a ship's flag!)

5 Remember not to confuse une pièce, *a room*, with une chambre, *a bedroom.* Un séjour literally means *a stay* (un séjour de trois jours, *a three-day stay*). The room of a house in which one "stays" the longest is the living room, hence la salle de séjour. But in common usage, we drop la salle. Many French people also talk about le living. Please don't imitate them!

6 Not **prête** because the estate agent is talking about both Claude and Jean-Michel.

8 – Je pense qu'il faut que vous soyez [7] un peu moins_exigeants. À ce prix-là, il vaut mieux envisager un appartement.

9 Et pourquoi pas à Paris ? Vous pouvez prendre le RER pour aller aux_Ulis.

10 Justement, j'ai un trois-pièces [8] avec cuisine et salle de bains dans le quatorzième pour mille. Il y a un bail [9] de trois_ans, avec un mois de caution et deux mois de loyer.

11 Vous voulez le visiter ?
    – Il faut que je demande à mon mari. Je vous rappelle demain.

12 Jean-Michel, que penses-tu d'un appartement plutôt qu'une maison ? C'est plus facile à entretenir.

13 – Mais on_avait dit qu'on voulait un pavillon, non ? Pourquoi as-tu changé d'avis ?

14 – À cause du loyer. Un appartement coûte moins cher qu'une maison.
    – Bon_argument !

15 – D'accord, j'appelle l'agence à la première heure [10] demain matin.   □

⌐ Notes

7 Subjunctive of **être**: que je sois, que tu sois, qu'il soit, que nous soyons, que vous soyez, qu'ils soient. Pronunciation: apart from the first and second persons plural, *[swaï-ohn]* and *[swaï-yay]*, the other forms are pronounced *[swa]*. See lesson 98, note 2.

8 Two examples of commonly abridged forms: instead of referring to un appartement de trois (deux, etc.) pièces, most people say simply un trois-pièces, un deux-pièces, etc. And no Parisian worth their salt

8 – I think you'd better be a little less demanding. At that price, you'd better consider a flat.

9 And why not in Paris? The regional express goes to Les Ulis.

10 In fact, I have a three-roomed flat with a kitchen and bathroom in the 14th *(district)* for 1,000. It's a three-year lease with one month's deposit and two months rent.

11 Do you want to visit it?
– I'll have to ask my husband. I'll call you back tomorrow.

12 Jean-Michel, what do you think about a flat instead of a house? The upkeep is easier.

13 – But we said we wanted a house, didn't we? Why have you changed your mind?

14 – Because of the rent. A flat costs less than a house.
– That's a good argument!

15 – Right. I'll call the agency back first thing tomorrow morning.

would bother adding **arrondissement** to the number of the district in which they live.

9 The word for *a lease*, **un bail** *[buy]*, has an irregular plural, **les baux** *[boh]*.

10 There are many picturesque expressions in French to describe the early morning, but **à la première heure** is the most common. It corresponds to our *first thing in the morning*.

▶ Exercice 1 – Traduisez

❶ Il me faut un deux-pièces avec une cuisine aménagée dans le troisième. ❷ Combien es-tu prête à mettre ? – Pas plus de cinq cents. ❸ Il faut que nous soyons un peu moins exigeants. ❹ Je voudrais louer un pavillon, mais de particulier à particulier. ❺ Justement, j'ai l'appartement qu'il vous faut.

***

Exercice 2 – Complétez

❶ Having found nothing that interested him, he looked elsewhere.
. . . . d'intéressant, il a cherché ailleurs.

❷ You must be there first thing tomorrow morning.
Il . . . . vous . . . . . là demain à la . . . .

❸ A house costs more than a flat.
Une maison . . . . un . . . .

❹ Every morning, he takes the train to Les Ulis.
Tous les matins il . . . . . le train . . . . Ulis.

107

Cent septième leçon

▶ ### Montons à Paris

1 Jean-Michel décide d'aller à Paris en voiture. Il aime conduire sur l'autoroute,

2 et comme il n'y a pas trop de monde sur la route en semaine, il peut rouler tranquillement à 130 kilomètres à l'heure.

Answers to Exercice 1

❶ I need a two-roomed flat with a fitted kitchen in the 3rd district. ❷ How much are you prepared to pay? – Not more than 500. ❸ We have to be a little less demanding. ❹ I'd like to rent a house, but without going through an agency. ❺ I have the very flat you need.

***

❺ How much rent are you prepared to pay, madam?

Madame, quel ....- .... à mettre ?

Answers to Exercice 2

❶ N'ayant rien trouvé – ❷ – faut que – soyez – première heure ❸ – coûte plus cher qu' – appartement ❹ – prend – pour aller aux – ❺ – loyer êtes-vous prête –

Second wave: 57th Lesson

_____

107

One Hundred and Seventh Lesson

Let's go *(up)* to Paris

1 Jean-Michel decides to drive to Paris. He likes motorway driving,

2 and since the roads are not too crowded *(there are not too many people on the roads)* during the week, he can drive comfortably *(quietly)* at 130 km/h.

3 Le couple quitte Vannes à neuf_heures et arrive aux portes ¹ de la capitale à quinze heures ²,

4 pile ³ à l'heure pour le rendez-vous avec l'agent immobilier.

5 L'immeuble est situé dans_une petite rue calme dans le quatorzième arrondissement.

6 *(L'agent leur fait visiter l'appartement.)*

– Voici les deux chambres ; la cuisine est_au fond du couloir, les WC ⁴ sont_à gauche, avec la salle de bains juste à côté.

7 Comme vous voyez, le living est_assez grand, avec une belle vue. Qu'en pensez-vous ?

8 – Ça nous plaît ⁵ assez, mais il faut que nous_en discutions, mon mari et moi. Si vous le permettez, nous vous rappellerons vers dix-sept_heures trente.

: Notes

1 Although this is a figurative expression – to arrive at the gates of the capital – Paris does actually have its entry points called **portes** (see lesson 83, note 2). Many metro lines used to terminate at these points but are now tending to reach places beyond: **La ligne 4 du métro allait de la Porte d'Orléans à la Porte de Clignancourt ; elle se prolonge désormais jusqu'à la ville de Montrouge.**

2 The twenty-four hour clock is now very much in everyday use, not just for official purposes but also in everyday conversation. It's quite easy to get used to: just add (or substract twelve). **Dix-huit heures – six heures du soir.**

3 Used idiomatically, **pile** means *exactly*. **Mon rendez-vous chez le dentiste tombe pile le jour de mon anniversaire,** *My dental appointment is exactly the same day as my birthday*. But the word is most commonly used when telling the time: **À dix heures pile,** *Ten o'clock on the dot*.

3 The couple leave Vannes at 9 am and reach the outskirts *(gates)* of the capital at 3 pm,

4 exactly on time for the appointment with the estate agent.

5 The building is located in a small quiet street in the 14th *arrondissement*.

6 *(The estate agent shows them around the flat)*

  – Here are the two bedrooms; the kitchen is at the end of the corridor, the toilets are on the left and the bathroom is next door.

7 As you can see, the living [room] is fairly big, with a beautiful view. What do you think [of it]?

8 – We quite like it. But we'll have to discuss it, my husband and I. If you don't mind *(if you permit it)*, we'll call you back around 5.30 pm

---

4 Yes, that's right. The French sometimes use WC as a "polite" word for toilet. But they use it in the plural! **Les WCs.** This is sometimes written as it is pronounced, i.e. **les vécés.** Another variant is **les waters** *[wa-taire]*. It's better to be straightforward, though, and ask for **les toilettes.**

5 **Ça me/nous/lui/leur plaît** (lit. "It pleases me/us/him or her/ them") is another way of expressing one's liking for something. See line 12.

9 – Si vous voulez, mais ne perdez pas trop
de temps. J'ai d'autres personnes qui
sont_intéressées.

10 Jean-Michel et Claude trouvent un café et
s'installent à une table.

11 *(Le serveur arrive.)*
 – M'sieur-Dame ? [6]
 – Un thé au lait et un café, s'il vous plaît.
 – Bien monsieur.

12 *(Quelques minutes plus tard.)*
 – Alors, qu'est-ce que tu en penses ?
 – Moi, je l'aime bien.
 – Moi aussi, mais on devrait en voir plusieurs,
non ?

13 – On n'a tout simplement pas le temps. Regarde,
c'est pratique pour le boulot, l'endroit est
sympa [7] et le loyer est raisonnable.

14 – Je suppose que tu as raison. Allez, c'est décidé.
On le prend.

15 *(Le serveur revient.)*
 – Le thé, c'est pour ?
 – Pour madame. Tenez, je vous règle [8] tout de
suite.

☐

⌐ : Notes

6 We're no longer in a classy restaurant (lessons 72 and 104). These elided
forms are common in cafés, bars, etc. The waiter should have said
Bonjour monsieur, **Bonjour madame** (or, if he were addressing a group
of people, **Messieurs'Dames**). See also line 15. (Note that you have to
ask specially for milk when you order tea in France.)

9 – OK *(If you like)*, but don't be too long *(waste too much time)*. I have other people who are interested.

10 Jean-Michel and Claude find a café and sit down at a table.

11 *(The waiter arrives)*
  – What can I get you?
  – A tea with milk and a coffee, please.
  – **Sure** *(Very well, sir)*.

12 *(A few minutes later)*
  – Well, what do you think?
  – I like it.
  – Me too, but shouldn't we see several?

13 – We simply don't have the time. Look, it's practical for the office [job], the place is nice and the rent is affordable.

14 – I suppose you're right. So it's decided. We're taking it.

15 *(The waiter returns)*
  – Who's the tea for?
  – For the lady. Here, I'll settle up right away.

---

7 See lesson 31, note 4.

8 **régler** means *to pay*, but in the sense of paying a bill. For example, in a hotel, you might say: **Je voudrais régler ma note, s'il vous plaît**, *I would like to pay the bill, please*. The noun is a **règlement**. On the bottom of invoices (**une facture**, *commercial invoice*, **une note**, *bill for services*), you will often see an indication of payment times, e.g. **Règlement à 30 jours**, *Invoice settled in thirty days of receipt*.

▶ Exercice 1 – Traduisez

❶ J'aime conduire sur l'autoroute parce que je peux rouler à 130. ❷ Les toilettes sont au fond du couloir à gauche. ❸ Ne perds pas trop de temps. On a rendez-vous à neuf heures pile. ❹ M'sieur- Dame ? – Un café pour moi et un thé au lait pour ma femme. ❺ Qu'en penses-tu ? – L'endroit est sympa.

**

Exercice 2 – Complétez

❶ The flat has a nice view. That's what they like about *(pleases them)*.
L'. . . . . a une belle vue. C'est ça . . . .

❷ The appointment is exactly the same day as his/her birthday.
Le rendez-vous . . . . de son anniversaire.

❸ We'll settle your bill in thirty days' time.
Nous . . . . votre facture . . . .

108

Cent huitième leçon

▶ ## Le quartier

1 L'appartement de Jean-Michel et Claude se trouve dans le quatorzième arrondissement, près du parc Montsouris.

2 C'est_un quartier résidentiel, mais, comme certains quartiers de Paris, il ressemble à un petit village.

Answers to Exercice 1

❶ I like motorway driving because I can drive at 130. ❷ The toilets are at the end of the corridor on the left. ❸ Don't take too long. We have an appointment at 9 am on the dot. ❹ What will you have? – A coffee for me and a tea with milk for my wife. ❺ What do you think? – The place is nice.

***

❹ We simply don't have time.
   Nous .... le ..... .

❺ The rent is affordable.
   Le ..... est ....

Answers to Exercice 2

❶ – appartement – qui leur plaît ❷ – tombe pile le jour – ❸ – règlerons – à trente jours ❹ – n'avons tout simplement pas – temps ❺ – loyer – raisonnable

Second wave: 58th Lesson

108

One Hundred and Eighth Lesson

The neighbourhood

1   Jean-Michel and Claude's flat is in the 14th *arrondissement*, near Montsouris Park.
2   The neighbourhood is residential, but like some neighbourhoods in Paris, it resembles a little village.

3 Depuis une vingtaine d'années, les grandes surfaces ¹ se sont multipliées en France, et maintenant beaucoup de gens y ² font leurs courses ³.

4 Mais dans chaque ville, il y a un marché au moins une fois par semaine. Et à Paris il y en_a même une dizaine.

5 Nos_amis habitent une petite rue tranquille, loin des grands_axes qui mènent au boulevard périphérique ⁴.

6 Le déménagement s'est bien passé ⁵. Les meubles sont_arrivés en bon_état, et le couple s'est_installé rapidement.

7 Claude s'est_occupée de toutes les formalités, comme le changement d'adresse et l'immatriculation de la voiture ⁶,

---

Notes

1 **les grandes surfaces** (lit. "large surface areas") is a collective designation for mass distribution outlets. In practice, the term refers to *supermarkets*, **les supermarchés** (m.), and *hypermarkets*, **les hypermarchés** (m.). France has strict legislation governing the creation of **grandes surfaces**. Another category of store is **le grand magasin** (lit. "big shop"), *a department store*.

2 Note, both here and in line 15, how **y** allows us very neatly to say *here* or *there*. **Je suis né à Bordeaux et j'y ai vécu jusqu'à l'âge de huit ans**, *I was born in Bordeaux and I lived there until I was 8*.

3 Remember lesson 54? **Faire les courses**, *to do one's shopping* (generally for food). **Il faut faire les courses : je n'ai rien à manger à la maison**, *We have to go shopping: I've got nothing to eat at home*. If you shop in a market rather than a store, you could also say **faire mon marché** (see line 10). However, when the French go shopping for clothes, etc. they often refer to it as… **faire du shopping!**

3 For thirty years, the number of supermarkets in France has multiplied, and many people now do their shopping in one.

4 But each city has a market at least once a week. In fact, in Paris there are *(even)* around ten.

5 Our friends live in a small quiet street, away from the major roads that lead to the Boulevard Périphérique.

6 The move went off well. The furniture arrived in good condition, and the couple settled in quickly.

7 Claude took care of all the formalities, like the change of address and car registration,

---

4 Paris is quite small by comparison with, say, London or Los Angeles. Technically, one reason is that the city itself is bounded by an urban expressway, **le boulevard périphérique** (see lesson 83, note 2), so only what is within this boundary is Paris in the strict sense of the term. This is often called **Paris intra muros** (Latin for "within the walls"), to distinguish the city from its suburbs. In actual fact, as in most countries, the capital has the largest population, and the greater Paris area, called **l'Île de France**, has the highest population density in the country.

5 **se passer**, *to happen*. **Pourquoi tout ce bruit ? Qu'est-ce qui se passe ?**, *Why all the noise? What's happening?* But, in the reflexive form, the verb can also mean *to go smoothly*. **Tout s'est bien passé**, *Everything went smoothly*. When you are in the middle of a meal in a restaurant, the waiter may ask you **Tout se passe bien ?**, *Is everything OK?* Assuming that it is, you would say **Oui, très bien, merci.**

6 In France, when you move home and relocate to another **département**, you have to make a formal declaration to the authorities. You also had to re-register your car*. Each **département** – there are 96 in mainland France – has a number, and motor vehicle licence plates used to bear the number of the **département** in which they are registered. For Paris **intra muros**, the number is 75 (see line 9).

* Since 2009, people don't need to change their car's licence plate anymore when they move as each car is now attributed a number "for life".

8 et très vite, ils sont devenus de vrais Parisiens.

9 – "Nous_avons nos Cartes Oranges [7] et nous sommes_immatriculés dans le soixante-quinze –, mais la Bretagne me manque beaucoup !"

10 C'est dimanche, et Jean-Michel et Claude décident d'aller faire leur marché et de se balader dans leur quartier [8].

11 – Donnez-moi un kilo de pommes de terre, une livre de carottes et une demi-livre de champignons, s'il vous plaît.

12 – Et avec ça ?
– Une botte de radis, un filet d'oignons. Et une barquette de fraises. Ça sera tout.

13 Après_avoir fait les courses et mangé un croque-monsieur [9] dans_un bistrot près du marché, ils partent à la découverte du quatorzième.

14 Tout près du réservoir, ils découvrent une charmante impasse avec des maisons très_originales.

Notes

7 Specific to Paris, **la Carte Orange** (lit. "orange card") used to be the monthly travel pass for the public transport system. The name changed over the years, and it is now called the **passe Navigo**.

8 **se balader** is another way of saying **se promener**, i.e. *to go for a walk*. The emphasis is on recreation. Otherwise we say **marcher**: **Il faut marcher dix minutes pour arriver jusqu'au métro**, *You have to walk for ten minutes to get to the metro station*. The same remark applies to **faire une balade en voiture**, *to go for a drive*.

8   and in no time at all *(very quickly)*, they were *(became)* true Parisians.

9 – We have our travel passes and the car has Paris plates (registered in the 75) – but I miss Brittany a lot!

10   It's Sunday, and Jean-Michel and Claude decide to do their shopping at the market and stroll around their neighbourhood.

11 – Give me a kilo of potatoes, a half-kilo *(pound)* of carrots and 250 grams *(half-pound)* of mushrooms, please.

12 – Anything else? – A bunch of radishes, a bag of onions and a punnet of strawberries. That'll be all.

13   After finishing the shopping and eating a *croque-monsieur* in a bar near the market they set off to discover the 14th.

14   Just near the reservoir, they come across a charming cul-de-sac lined with very unusual houses.

9 un croque-monsieur (lit. "bite the gentleman!") is a toasted ham and cheese sandwich. When served with a fried egg on top, it becomes un croque-madame. You can also ask for un hot dog...

15 – D'après [10] le guide, c'est la villa Seurat*. Il y a
plein de gens célèbres [11] qui y ont vécu.

16 – Très jolie, mais il est temps de rentrer. Demain,
c'est mon premier jour de travail. ☐

Notes

10 Another way of saying **selon**. **D'après** means *according to*. **D'après
lui, cette église date du dix-huitième siècle** – *According to him, this
church dates back to the 18th century*. In France, **une villa** is not only *a
villa*; it also means a short street lined with detached houses.

* The charming Villa Seurat in the 14th **arrondissement** was home
to Salvador Dali, Henry Miller, Chaim Soutine and a number of other
writers and artists.

***

▶ Exercice 1 – Traduisez

❶ Y a-t-il un marché ? – Il y en a même une dizaine. ❷ J'y
fais mes courses au moins deux fois par semaine. ❸ Tout
s'est bien passé ? – Très bien, merci. Le repas était fameux.
❹ Paris me manque beaucoup. ❺ D'après eux, c'est une rue
où plein de gens célèbres ont vécu.

***

Exercice 2 – Complétez

❶ She was born in Paris and lived there until she was 10.
Elle . . . . . . à Paris et . . . . l'âge de dix ans.

❷ Let's go for a drive.
Allons . . . . . une . . . .

❸ I want a bunch of radishes, a punnet of strawberries and a half-
kilo of carrots.
Je veux . . . . de . . . . ., ... de fraises et . . .
. . . . . de carottes.

15 – According to the guide [book], this is the Villa Seurat. Loads of famous people have lived here.

16 – Very pretty, but it's time to go home. Tomorrow's my first day at work.

11 The adjective **fameux** does exist in French, but in everyday usage, it means *excellent* or *delicious*. **Fameux, ton gâteau au chocolat,** *Your chocolate cake was fabulous.* To describe famous people, events, etc., we use **célèbre**.

***

Answers to Exercise 1

❶ Is there a market? – In fact, there are around ten. ❷ I do my shopping there at least twice a week. ❸ Was everything to your satisfaction? – Fine, thank you. The meal was splendid. ❹ I miss Paris a lot. ❺ According to them, it's a street where loads of famous people have lived.

***

❹ Just next to the boulevard, but well away from the main roads, there is a charming little street.

. . . . boulevard, mais . . . . grands axes, ... une charmante villa.

❺ What happened here?

Qu'est- . . . . ici ?

Answers to Exercise 2

❶ – est née – y a vécu jusqu'à – ❷ – faire – balade en voiture ❸ – une botte – radis, une barquette – une livre – ❹ Tout près du – loin des – il y a – ❺ – ce qui s'est passé –

Second wave: 59th Lesson

Cent neuvième leçon

Le premier jour chez Toutvu

1 À neuf_heures pile le lundi matin, Jean- Michel se présente à l'accueil [1] de Toutvu.
– Bonjour, je suis le nouveau responsable de projet.

2 – Vous devez_être M. Bellon. Prenez l'ascenseur jusqu'au quatrième étage et présentez-vous au bureau 402.

3 – Bonjour, M. Fauconnier, comment_allez-vous ?
– Bonjour, Jean-Michel. Tu peux me dire "tu", tu sais. Tout le monde se tutoie ici. [2]

4 Jean-Michel est très_étonné, mais il joue le jeu.
– Bon, si vous voulez, euh, je veux dire, si tu veux...

Notes

1 **l'accueil** *(m.)* is used in many contexts. It basically means *a welcome*. In a public place, it means *the reception desk* (as here). Pronunciation: *[akeuy]*. The more abstract uses still have the meaning of *welcome* or *reception*. **Nous essayons d'améliorer l'accueil de nos clients**, *We are trying to improve the way we greet our customers*. In many cases, there is no one-for-one translation of **accueil**, but you will meet the word again in context. That's what we mean by assimilating the language: by using words, you quickly get the feel of them.

109

One Hundred and Ninth Lesson

The first day at Toutvu

1 At 9 a.m. on the dot on Monday morning, Jean-Michel arrives at the reception of Toutvu.
– Good morning, I'm the new project manager.

2 – You must be Mr Bellon. Take the lift to the fourth floor and go to office 402.

3 – Good morning, Mr Fauconnier, how are you?
– Good morning, Jean-Michel. You know, you can use the familiar form of address *(tu)* with me. We all use it, here.

4 Jean-Michel is very surprised, but he plays along *(plays the game)*.
– If you wish, I mean: sure, if you want...

---

2 We have seen already how the fact of having a familiar and a formal manner of address can complicate life for the English speaker. However, the old rules are being re-drawn and, although French is still a relatively formal language, the familiar form (**le tutoiement**) is becoming increasingly prevalent, notably in the workplace. But this "familiarity" can still take people by surprise. Basically, don't use the familiar form (**tutoyer**) with someone you do not know unless invited to do so. (**Tu peux me dire "tu"** or **On peut se tutoyer**.) If this happens, you have to shift gears quickly, and it doesn't always come naturally at first (see line 4).

5 – Bien, alors je vais te faire visiter les locaux [3]. Suis-moi [4], s'il te plaît.

6 Comme tu vois, chez Toutvu, nous_avons des bureaux paysagers. Ça facilite la communication.

7 Chaque poste de travail est_équipé d'un [5] ordinateur relié à un réseau local. Il y a une imprimante pour dix_ordinateurs.

8 Aux premier et deuxième étages, se trouvent les services administratifs, la direction [6] générale et les services généraux.

9 – Tiens, je te présente Dominique [7] Lestelle, qui est_ingénieur de projet. Dominique, voici Jean-Michel, notre nouveau chef d'équipe.

10 – Enchantée de te connaître. Tu vas vite apprendre tout ce qu'il faut savoir : comment faire le café, organiser des pots [8]...

Notes

3 un local, *a place, a space*. **Le groupe cherche un local pour répéter**, *The band is looking for a place to rehearse*. The plural is **les locaux**, meaning *premises*.

4 Don't confuse the verbs **suivre** and **être** in the present tense. The context makes all the difference. **Pourquoi tu me suis depuis une heure ? Mais je ne vous suis pas**, *Why have you been following me for an hour? – I'm not following you* (the **mais** adds emphasis). Compare this with **Je suis très étonné par cette accusation**, *I am very surprised by that accusation*.

5 Note the postposition: **équipé de**. Another, more formal way of saying this is **doté de** (lit. "endowed with"). **L'ordinateur est doté d'une carte modem**, *The computer is equipped with a modem card*.

5 – Right. I'll show you round. Follow me, please.

6 As you can see, at Toutvu we have open-plan offices. It makes it easier to communicate.

7 Each work station is equipped with a computer linked to a local-area network. There is one printer for ten computers.

8 The first and second floors house the administrative departments, the general management and the general services.

9 – Here, let me introduce you to Dominique Lestelle, who's a project engineer. Dominique, here's Jean-Michel, our new team manager.

10 – Pleased to meet you. You'll soon learn all you need to know: how to make the coffee, organise the drinks...

---

6 **la direction** of a company is its *management team* (**un directeur**, *a director*). **La gestion** is *the science of management* or (see line 13) *the task of administration*. But despite having two words to describe the concept, French has also felt the need to adopt the term **le management**, presumably because the Anglo-Saxon concept is more advanced... That said, see lesson 112, section 8.

7 Two common French Christian names, Dominique and Claude, can be used by either sex.

8 **un pot** *[poh]* is either *a drink*, **Tiens, je te paie un pot**, *Come on, I'll buy you a drink*, or *a drinks party* organised at work to celebrate a special event. **Avant de quitter la boîte, Patrice a organisé un pot d'adieu**, *Before leaving the company, Patrice organised a farewell drink*.

11 Une heure plus tard, Jean-Michel est_installé devant son ordinateur. Il est très_impressionné par le haut niveau de technicité de la société.

12 Le siège de Toutvu est_un bâtiment "intelligent", doté des derniers_outils de la bureautique.

13 La société développe et commercialise des logiciels et outils télématiques pour la gestion des télécommunications.

14 Submergé par sa matinée chargée, Jean-Michel murmure : "J'espère que je serai à la hauteur".

***

15 – M. Durand, on me signale [9] que vous_arrivez de plus_en plus tard au bureau. Avez-vous quelque chose à dire ?

16 – Je l'avoue, monsieur le Directeur. Mais n'oubliez pas que je pars de plus en plus tôt... □

Note

9 signaler, *to signal*, is often used formally with the meaning of *to inform* or *to point out*. **Nous nous permettons de vous signaler que votre compte est toujours débiteur**, *We would point out that your account has not been settled*. At this stage of your course, this is a word to be recognised rather than used.

***

▶ Exercice 1 – Traduisez

❶ Enchanté de te connaître. – Moi aussi. ❷ Merci pour votre accueil très chaleureux. ❸ On peut se tutoyer, tu sais. – Si tu veux. ❹ Vous allez vite apprendre tout ce qu'il faut savoir ici. ❺ Je suis sûr que tu seras à la hauteur.

11   One hour later, Jean-Michel is settled in front of his computer. He's very impressed by the company's high level of technical capability.

12   Toutvu headquarters is a "smart" building equipped with the latest office automation tools.

13   The company develops and sells software and data communications tools for telecoms management.

14   Overwelmed by his busy morning, Jean-Michel murmurs: "I hope I'll be up to the task".

***

15 – Mr Durand, I hear that you're arriving later and later at the office. Have you anything to say?

16 – I admit it, sir. But don't forget that I leave earlier and earlier...

Answers to Exercice 1

❶ Pleased to meet you. – Same here. ❷ Thank you for your warm welcome. ❸ Let's use the familiar form of address. – If you like. ❹ You'll soon learn everything you need to know here. ❺ I'm sure you'll be up to the task.

Exercice 2 – Complétez

❶ Why are you following me? – *(But)* I'm not following you.
Pourquoi vous ....? – Mais je .... pas.

❷ The general services are on the first floor of the premises.
Les .... sont .. premier étage ....

❸ The buildings are equipped with extremely hi-tech tools.
Les .... sont .... de très haute ....

110

Cent dixième leçon

La rentrée [1]

1   Deux mois plus tard, c'est_au tour [2] de Claude
    de commencer son nouveau travail.
2   Elle a été mutée dans_un collège de
    200_élèves dans le vingtième arrondissement
3   pour y assurer [3] les cours d'orthographe et de
    grammaire, comme elle le faisait [4] en Bretagne.

Notes

1   Despite recent trends, the year still revolves very much around the two-
    month holiday period in July and August. The month of September is
    known as **la rentrée** (lit. "the return"). And it does not only apply to **la
    rentrée scolaire** or **la rentrée des classes** (*back to school*). When the
    politicians return after the summer break, the press refers to **la rentrée
    politique**. Often, September is a time for organised labour to make its
    demands for the next parliamentary session. This is known as **la ren-
    trée sociale**. In short, just about everything has its **rentrée**!

❹ She is overwhelmed by her busy day.
Elle est .... sa journée ....

❺ I hope that I'll be up to the task.
J' ...... que je ....

❶ – me suivez – ne vous suis – ❷ – services généraux – au – des locaux ❸ – bâtiments – dotés d'outils – technicité ❹ – submergée par – chargée ❺ – espère – serai à la hauteur

Second wave: 60th Lesson

110

One Hundred and Tenth Lesson

Back to school

1 Two months later, it is Claude's turn to begin her new job.
2 She has been transferred to a college with *(of)* 200 pupils in the 20th *arrondissement*
3 to give writing and grammar classes, as she was doing in Britanny.

2 Remember not to confuse **une tour**, *a tower*, with **un tour**, which has several meanings. Here, it is used to mean *a turn*. **À chacun son tour**, *Everyone takes turns*. Note how the preposition **à** changes to **au**: **C'est au tour de Claude.**

3 An idiomatic usage: **assurer un cours**, *to give a lesson*. Note that, although **l'orthographe** *(f.)* is often translated as *spelling*, it has a broader meaning for the French. **Une faute d'orthographe** is not just *a mistake in spelling*, it also denotes an ignorance of the appropriate grammatical rule. We could say that **la grammaire** is the theory and **l'orthographe** the application.

4 The imperfect tense is used here because Claude <u>no longer</u> gives lessons in Brittany (she <u>used to</u> give them).

4 Mais_elle apprend très vite que les classes
à Paris sont bien différentes de celle de son
village breton [5].

5 Clément, un jeune professeur de vingt-
trois_ans, prend Claude sous son aile et lui
explique comment se passent les choses.

6 – D'abord, t'as [6] les classes très mixtes d'un point
de vue ethnique : il y a des beurs, des blacks [7],
des_asiatiques...

7 Plus mélangé que ça, tu meurs [8]. Mais ils sont
hyper-sympas [9].

8 Ensuite, les classes sont très grandes. Ça peut
être angoissant, mais il faut assumer [10].

Notes

[5] Remember that the adjective derived from a place name does not take
an initial capital: la Normandie but le beurre normand. However, as we
saw recently, the noun does: Paris, un Parisien.

[6] When speaking quickly, many people fail to enunciate the two vowels of
tu as, which becomes t'as *[ta]*. You can hear the same thing in line 10.

[7] As France becomes more multi-racial, different ethnic groups assert
themselves more forcefully. One such group consists of the French-
born children of immigrants from North Africa. They refer to themselves as les beurs, a back-slang formation from **arabe**. Young blacks
prefer to be called les blacks rather than les noirs, which many find
pejorative.

4 But she quickly learns that the classes in Paris are very different from the one in her Breton village.

5 Clément, a young 23-year-old teacher, takes Claude under his wing and tells her what's what (how things happen).

6 – First, your classes are very mixed ethnically: there are *beurs*, blacks, Asians…

7 You can't get more mixed than that! But they're really great kids.

8 Next, the classes are very big. That might be worrying, but you've just got to accept it.

8 This construction – **Plus … que ça, tu meurs**, *More …you could not get* (lit. "you die") – is often used to say that something could not be any more so than it actually is. It entered the language as a film title and is now heard at least once a day on the radio or television or in the press.

9 Inflation affects language as well as economies. What used to be **très sympa** is now **hyper sympa**. The new information technologies have also given us **mega-** and **giga-** as superlatives. What next, googol?

10 Psychiatry has added its buzzwords to the language, too. Used in this context, **assumer** means to accept personal responsibility for a situation. In "loose" usage, however, it simply means *to accept things*. **C'est dur, mais il faut assumer**, *It's hard, but there's no point complaining*.

9 Pour la plupart, les profs sont cool [11]. Le directeur [12] est vachement [13] strict, mais très réglo.

10 Donc, tu vois, on galère parfois, mais dans l'ensemble on s'éclate [14]. Mais attends, qu'est-ce que t'as ? Ça va pas ?

11 – Si, si [15]. Seulement, je n'ai compris que la moitié de ce que tu as dit.

***

12 En classe d'histoire : "Après quelle bataille le chef Vercingétorix [16] s'est-il rendu aux Romains ?"

13 Après un long silence, un élève dit timidement : "Sa dernière bataille, madame." □

Notes

11 No comment... (except that, being a loan word, the adjective **cool** does not agree with its subject).

12 The head teacher of a primary school is **le proviseur**. In a secondary school, he or she is **le directeur** or **la directrice**.

13 See lesson 81, note 3. Even though this all-purpose adjective has been around for many years, it is still considered a little informal.

***

▶ Exercice 1 – Traduisez

❶ C'est à qui le tour ? – C'est à moi. **❷** Je dois assurer des cours d'histoire à la rentrée, comme je faisais l'année dernière. **❸** Ça ne va pas ? – Si, si, je vais très bien, je t'assure. **❹** Est-ce que c'est vraiment difficile ? – Plus difficile que ça, tu meurs. **❺** Ils sont vachement sympas, nos profs.

9 Most of the teachers are cool. The headmaster is dead strict, but he's a regular kind of guy.

10 So you see, you really struggle sometimes, but in the main we have a good time. But what's the matter? Aren't you well?

11 – Yes, yes. But I only understood half of what you said!

***

12 In a history lesson: After what battle did Vercingetorix surrender to the Romans?

13 After a long silence, one pupil ventures shyly: "His last battle, miss".

14 **galérer** is an imaginative derivation from **une galère**, *a galley ship*, where conditions were far from comfortable. Already used figuratively as a noun – **Je me suis mis dans une vraie galère**, *I've got myself into a real mess* – it is now a verb. **Elle a trois gosses et pas de boulot. Elle galère pour les élever**, *She's got three kids and no job. She really struggles to bring them up.* The other verb, **s'éclater** (lit. "to burst"), means *to have a great time*.

15 **si** allows you to respond in the affirmative to a negative interrogative. **Ça ne va pas ? – Si, je vais très bien.**

16 Vercingétorix, a Gallic chieftan who led a revolt against Julius Caesar in 52 BC and was defeated at the battle of Alésia, is a symbol of French resistance against the invader.

***

Answers to Exercice 1

❶ Whose turn is it? – Mine. ❷ I have to give history classes when school resumes, like I was doing last year. ❸ Aren't you well? – Yes, yes I'm fine, honestly. ❹ Is it really difficult? – It doesn't get much more difficult than this! ❺ Our teachers are really great.

Exercice 2 – Complétez

❶ He took me under his wing on the very first day.
Il m'. . . . . dès le premier jour.

❷ He's a Breton, but he loves Normandy butter.
Il est . . . . . . mais il adore le . . . .

❸ Schools in Paris are very different to those in the provinces.
Les écoles à Paris . . . . de
province.

111

Cent onzième leçon

La routine

1 Que le temps passe vite ! Jean-Michel et Claude
sont à Paris depuis deux ans [1].

2 Et ils commencent à tomber dans la routine. Ils
n'ont pas pu prendre de vraies vacances, ni l'un
ni l'autre [2].

3 À présent, avec l'arrivée des beaux jours, ils
rêvent de partir loin de Paris.

Notes

[1] French has no real equivalent of the English "present perfect" tense (*She has lived* in France for five years; *I haven't seen* her since Christmas). To convey the same idea (i.e. a past action with a present aspect) we simply use **depuis** with the present tense, if the action is in the affirmative (**Elle vit en France depuis cinq ans**) or the past tense if the action is negative (**Je ne l'ai pas vue depuis Noël**) – see line 5.

❹ He only understood half of what I said.

Il n'a compris … … … … de … … … dit.

❺ After what battle did he surrender? – The last one.

… … … … bataille … … … … ? – La dernière.

Answers to Exercice 2

❶ – a pris sous son aile – ❷ – Breton – beurre normand ❸ – sont très différentes de celles – ❹ – que la moitié – ce que j'ai – ❺ Après quelle – s'est-il rendu –

Second wave: 61st Lesson

111

One Hundred and Eleventh Lesson

Routine

1 How time flies! Jean-Michel and Claude have been in Paris for two years.

2 And they are beginning to fall into a routine. Neither of them has been able to take a real holiday.

3 Now, with the fine weather (*arriving*), they dream of going far away from Paris.

---

2 Although the construction may seem a little cumbersome, the double negative is the rule in French: **Nous ne parlons pas le chinois, ni l'un ni l'autre**, *Neither of us speaks Chinese.*

4 – Métro-boulot-dodo [3]. Je commence à en_avoir
   marre. Ça te dirait [4] de quitter Paris pour
   quelques semaines ?

5 – Bien sûr que ça me dirait ! Nous n'avons pas
   pris de vacances depuis bientôt [5] trois_ans.

6 – Marché conclu [6] ! Il nous reste seulement à
   décider où et quand.

7   Nous sommes_obligés de partir pendant les
   vacances scolaires, donc est-ce qu'on va être
   juillettistes ou aoûtiens [7] ?

8 – Partons [8] plutôt en juillet. Il y a moins de
   monde, me semble-t_-il [9].

9 – Il me semble aussi. D'accord pour juillet.
   Maintenant, quel pays ?

10 – Et si nous restions [10] en France ? On pourrait
   faire du tourisme vert.

Notes

3 A famous catch phrase which could be loosely translated as "the rat
   race"! **Le dodo** is a children's word, equivalent to our *beddy-byes*. **Fais
   un gros dodo, mon petit**, *Time for beddy-byes, little one*. The phrase
   describes the typical day for most people: *commute* (**le métro**), *work*
   (**le boulot**) and *straight to bed* (**le dodo**). **Métro-boulot-dodo**, *the daily
   grind*.

4 In this lesson, we will see several different ways of making a suggestion
   to someone. **Ça te/vous dirait de**, *Would it please you to…* **Ça vous
   dirait d'aller au cinéma ce soir ?**, *Would you like to go to the cinema
   this evening?*

5 **bientôt**, *soon*. It can replace **presque** in expressions of time to give a
   greater sense of immediacy. Compare **Il est parti il y a presque deux
   ans**, *He left nearly two years ago* with **Cela fait bientôt deux ans qu'il
   est parti**, *It is nearly two years since he left*.

4 – Bloody routine! I'm starting to get fed up. Would it please you to leave Paris for a few weeks?

5 – Of course it would! We haven't had a holiday for nearly three years.

6 – It's a deal! All we have to do is decide where and when.

7 We have to leave during the school holidays, so will it be July or August?

8 – Better to leave *(Let's leave rather)* in July. It seems to me that there are fewer people.

9 – I think so, too. OK for July. Now, what country?

10 – Why don't we stay in France? We could do some eco-tourism.

---

6 un marché, *a market*. It also means *a contract* or *a deal*: **les marchés publics**, *public sector contracts*. The exclamation **Marché conclu !** is equivalent to *You've got a deal!*

7 Most of the country goes on holiday in *July*, **juillet** or *August*, **août**. This is so common that French has coined words – slightly tongue-in-cheek – for the people who leave in each month: **les juillettistes** and **les aoûtiens** *[a-oo-syehn]*.

8 Another, more assertive way of making a suggestion is to use the first person plural (the **nous** form) in the imperative. Returning to our example, in note 4, we could say **Allons au cinéma ce soir**, *Let's go to the cinema this evening*. And almost everyone knows the first line of **la Marseillaise**, the French national anthem: **Allons enfants de la patrie, le jour de gloire est arrivé** (see lesson 92).

9 A more elegant way of saying **Il me semble que...** Note that the **me semble-t-il** phrase comes at the end of the sentence. **Il me semble qu'il y a moins de monde**, BUT **Il y a moins de monde, me semble-t-il**. Line 9 shows you how to respond in the affirmative.

10 Another way of suggesting: **Et si** + conditional. This is similar to our *And what if we...?*: **Et si nous allions au cinéma ?**, *What if we went to the cinema?*

11 Pourquoi pas " louer un gîte dans_un_endroit isolé – la France profonde – et faire de la randonnée pédestre ¹² ?

12 Rien ne nous_empêche de faire des balades en voiture pour visiter les_environs. Et on serait tranquilles.

13 – Tiens, tu te souviens du petit village en Auvergne où on s'est_arrêtés pour déjeuner il y a cinq_ans ?

14 – Montézic ? Bien sûr. C'est un coin ravissant. Et que dirais-tu si j'écrivais au syndicat d'initiative ¹³ pour demander des renseignements ?

15 – Je dirais que tu as eu une idée de génie ! Je vais tout de suite chercher le numéro de téléphone sur le Minitel.

☐

Notes

11 A very simple way of making a suggestion: **Pourquoi pas** + infinitive. **Pourquoi pas aller au cinéma ce soir ?**, *Why don't we go to the cinema this evening?* A simple affirmative answer would be **Pourquoi pas ?** with a rising intonation (cf. Exercices), *Why not indeed*.

12 For the past decade, many people have been taking their holidays in the French countryside rather than travelling abroad. This has become known as **le tourisme vert**. One excellent way of discovering France is to use **les gîtes**, a well organised network that offers rural properties for rental for short periods. **La France profonde** (lit. "deep France") refers to the "real" France, remote and rural. However, city-dwellers often use the phrase to mean "backward, undeveloped France". Context is all!

11 Why not rent a *gîte* in some isolated spot – in the heart of France – and go hiking?

12 There's nothing to stop us going for drives and visiting the surroundings [countryside]. And we won't get disturbed *(We'll be peaceful)*.

13 – Do you remember that little village in Auvergne where we stopped for lunch five years ago?

14 – Montézic? Of course. It's a beautiful spot. What would you say if I wrote to the tourist office and asked for information?

15 – I'd say you had a brilliant idea! I'll look up the number right away on the Minitel.

13 le syndicat d'initiative (lit. "the initiative syndicate") is basically the tourist office of a small town: a group of local residents who "take the initiative" and attract tourists to the place. Most large towns and cities – and each **département** – has its own **office de tourisme** (m.). In everyday language, **un syndicat** is *a trade union*.

▶ Exercice 1 – Traduisez

❶ Que le temps passe vite ! ❷ Ça te dirait de venir dîner à la maison ce soir ? – Avec grand plaisir. ❸ J'en ai marre de cette routine ! ❹ Il me semble qu'il y a moins de monde aujourd'hui. – Il me semble aussi. ❺ Pourquoi ne pas partir en août cette année ? – Pourquoi pas ?

***

Exercice 2 – Complétez

❶ I've now been in Paris for 4 years.

. . . . quatre ans . . . . à Paris.

❷ Neither of them has been able to take a real holiday.
Elles . . . . prendre de vraies vacances, ...
. . . .

❸ We haven't been away on holiday for nearly three years.
Nous . . . . en vacances . . . . trois ans.

112

Cent douzième leçon

Révision – Revision

1 Going somewhere... À ? Aux ?

We know that we cannot say **à le** or **à les**: **Je vais** au **bureau** or **Nous allons** aux **courses**. This same rule applies if the **le** or **les** in question is part of the name of a city or town, e. g. Le Havre. **Ils habitent au Havre** or **Les Ulis**. **Je travaille aux Ulis** (note that neither **au** nor **aux** takes a capital).
The same rule applies if the preposition is **de** or **des**. *I come from*

Answers to Exercice 1

❶ How time flies! ❷ Would you like to come round for dinner this evening? – With great pleasure. ❸ I'm fed up with this routine! ❹ It seems to me that there are fewer people today. – Me too. ❺ Why don't we go away in August this year? – Why not?

***

❹ What if we went to the Auvergne this year?
. . . . **Auvergne cette année ?**

❺ Why not stay in France? We could go hiking.
Pourquoi pas rester en France ? Nous . . . . **de la** . . . . **pédestre.**

Answers to Exercice 2

❶ Cela fait maintenant – que je suis – ❷ – n'ont pas pu – ni l'une ni l'autre ❸ – ne sommes pas partis – depuis bientôt – ❹ Et si nous allions en – ❺ – pourrions faire – randonnée –

Second wave: 62nd Lesson

One Hundred and Twelfth Lesson

Le Havre: **Je viens du Havre**; *She comes from Les Ulis*, **Elle vient des Ulis.**
Now practise **Je viens de** and **Je travaille à** with the following place names:

Les Mureaux   **Le Mans**
Le Lavandou   **Les Essarts**

You see? The reflex comes fairly quickly after a short while.

2 *Il faut que* + subjunctive

Lesson 98 explained that **il faut que** is followed by the subjunctive. We see another example of the subjunctive mood in line 8 of lesson 106. But this rule only applies if **il faut que** is followed by another verb, allowing the two to be "sub-joined". Flip back to lesson 98 and take a look.

In some constructions, therefore, **falloir** can be followed by a noun or an infinitive (cf. lines 5 & 6). The secret is not to use a pronoun after **faut**:

Il (nous) faut un grand jardin, *We need a big garden.*
Il faut louer plutôt qu'acheter, *It's better to rent rather than buy.*

But once you use a pronoun, you are imposing your view on someone else. In that case, you need the subjunctive:

Il faut que nous **ayons un grand jardin**.
Il faut que vous **louiez plutôt que vous achetiez**.

3 Driving in French

In French, driving is a complicated business in more ways than one. There are three main verbs to express this simple idea. First, we have **aller en voiture**, literally *to go by car*, i.e. as opposed to taking another form of transport, etc. **Elle a décidé d'aller en voiture plutôt que de prendre le train**, *She decided to drive rather than take the train*. Variant: **prendre la voiture, Je n'ai pas envie de prendre la voiture. Je suis trop fatigué**, *I don't want to drive. I'm too tired* (i.e. let's take a bus, taxi, etc.)

Next comes **conduire**, which expresses the act of driving a car and serves as the root word for most of the nouns related to driving: **le permis de conduire**, *driving licence*, **la conduite**, *driving*, hence, **la conduite sur autoroute**, *motorway driving*, **la conduite de nuit**, *night driving*, etc., **un conducteur**, *a driver*. **Jean-Michel aime conduire sur l'autoroute**, *Jean-Michel likes driving on motorways*. (You've probably recognized the English verb *to conduct* by now.)

Lastly, we have **rouler** (lit. "to roll"). This describes the movement of the car and how the driver handles it: **Il roulait à 150 à l'heure**, *He was doing 150 km/h*. **Ils roulaient trop vite**, *They were driving too fast*. On the motorway, you will see signs warning you: **Ne roulez pas trop près**, *Don't drive too close together*.

So, to summarise: **Si vous prenez la voiture, conduisez prudemment – et ne roulez pas trop vite...**, *If you drive (i.e. take the car),* *drive carefully* (pay attention) *but don't drive* (i.e. make the car go) *too fast*. **Ça va ?**

4 Acute or grave accent in verbs... an explanation

We include the following rule simply to explain why certain verbs take acute or grave accents (**é** or **è**) in certain forms. As far as the pronunciation is concerned, the change is too slight to spot at this stage of your study.
Rule: verbs that have an **é** or **è** in the <u>next to last syllable</u> of the infinitive – **régler**, *to settle* or **répéter**, *to repeat*, take a grave accent – **è** instead of **é** or **e** – before a consonant followed by a mute **e**.
Read that again.
Now look:
je règle (the last **e** is mute), **tu règles**, **il règle**... changing to **nous répétons**, **vous répétez**... to go back to **ils/elles répètent**.

5 Past tense verbs conjugated with *être*

Another grammar rule, this time to explain why the past tense of verbs conjugated with **être** (rather than **avoir**) sometimes agree with the preceding subject.
First, we know that the <u>participle</u> agrees with the <u>direct object</u> if that object is placed before the verb, e.g. **J'ai** envoyé **la lettre** (object after the verb) BUT **La lettre que j'ai** envoyée (object before the verb).
Next, remember that, with a reflexive verb, the subject and object are often the same. And thus are bound to "agree". For example, **Il s'est rasé**, *He* (subject and object) *shaved*; **Elle s'est coupée**, *She* (subject and object) *cut herself*. Clear?
In some cases, however, the subject and object of a reflexive verb are NOT the same. So, following our original rule, if the direct object comes <u>after</u> the verb, there is no agreement. **Elle s'est coupé la main**. Look what happens.
Ils se sont disputés, *They argued* (S and O are the same = agreement).
Ils se sont disputé la première place, *They fought for first place* (S and O are not the same = no agreement).
You see, French really is a logical language. More importantly, this rule has little discernible effect on pronunciation.

6 To miss, *Manquer*

The verb **manquer**, *to miss*, is simple to use if we're talking about a train or a plane. **J'ai manqué mon avion**, *I've missed my plane*.

But if we're talking about missing someone or something, we adopt a totally different logic. Instead of saying *I miss Brittany*, a French person would say **La Bretagne me manque**, or *Brittany is missing to me*. So, *I miss you* would be **Tu me manques**. If you want to be sure that your loved one is experiencing the same feeling, you would ask whether you are missing to him/her: **Je te manque ?** Try it, you'll soon get used to it.

7 Buying food: the metric system

The French use the metric system. When buying food, the standard unit of measurement is usually **un kilogramme** (*2.2 lbs*), abbreviated to **un kilo**. The subdivision is **un gramme** (*15.4 grains*). When ordering loose items like potatoes, turnips, etc., you would ask for **un kilo de pommes de terre** or **deux kilos de navets**. If you want less, you generally order **un demi-kilo**, *a half-kilo*. However, for reasons that go back to France's old measurement system, **500 g** is also referred to as **une livre**, or *a pound*. You could also order *a half-pound* (**250 g**), or **une demi-livre**, of some commodity like mushrooms.

As in English, other items are ordered by the serving unit, so **une botte de radis, d'asperges** (*a bunch of radishes, asparagus*). Most soft fruits are sold in *a punnet*, **une barquette**. Butter generally comes in *a pat*, **une plaquette de beurre**. And as for cheese...

So if you are visiting France, avoid the temptation to do your grocery shopping in a supermarket. Head instead for the produce market, and soak up the sights and sounds of people going about the serious business of buying food.

8 Foreign words in the French language

France is extremely sensitive about the invasion of foreign words – as we have seen in recent lessons, many English words have already taken deep root in the French language. The problem has become so acute that various laws have been passed to prohibit "loan words".

In this context, it is noteworthy that French is one of the few European languages to have made a valiant – and largely successful – effort to coin its own words in the most sensitive field of all: advanced technologies. (In some cases, this is because the inventor of a particular application was French.)

This is not to say that people don't talk about **le soft** for "software" or **upgrader** for "to upgrade". But these are largely unnecessary. The words we list below are used every day without any feeling of linguistic chauvinism (a French word, incidentally). They have become common usage. In fact, a couple of them have even been borrowed by English!

l'ordinateur (m.)	*computer*
le logiciel	*software program*
le progiciel	*software package*
l'informatique (f.)	*computing, information technology*
la carte à puces	*smart card*
la télématique	*remote data services (telematics)*
la bureautique	*office automation systems*
le caméscope	*camcorder*
la télécopie	*facsimile* (although **le fax** is very common)

The French came up with the coinage based on **se balader** (see lesson 108, note 8) and the word **un baladeur** passed into the language. As technology evolved, so did the language. **Baladeur** was pressed into service to form the noun **baladodiffusion**, *a podcast*, and the verb **baladodiffuser** (or **baladiffuser**).

Similarly, when France began "importing" the British system of Bed & Breakfast, the language mavens were intent on not importing the term. So they came up with **le café-couette** (*coffee-quilt*), which has entered the language. Not all these efforts are so fortunate – **le mousse-lait** has failed to dethrone **le milk-shake**, for example – and some can seem over-zealous. But French will continue to coin its own words, and many of them will become second nature. OK?

Second wave: 63rd Lesson

113

Cent treizième leçon

Au revoir... et à bientôt !

1 Nous voici à la fin de notre livre, mais non pas à la fin du voyage.

2 Il ne faut pas que vous vous‿arrêtiez [1] maintenant.

3 Bien‿entendu, vous ne parlez pas‿encore le français comme un Parisien-né [2],

4 mais vous‿êtes capable de comprendre une conversation

5 et de vous faire comprendre [3] dans les circonstances usuelles de la vie quotidienne.

6 Reprenez le livre tous les jours et feuilletez-le. Choisissez une leçon,

7 ré-écoutez les‿enregistrements et continuez à faire la deuxième vague.

Notes

1 Subjunctive after **il faut que**. Remember lesson 112, § 2: we could avoid the subjunctive by not using *you* and making the sentence "imperso-nal". Il ne faut pas s'arrêter. Il faut que vous soyez‿à l'heure – or Il faut‿être à l'heure.

2 C'est‿un comédien-né, *He's a born actor.* C'est‿une Parisienne-née, *She is a native Parisian.* Il est né en mille neuf cent deux, *He was born in 1902.* (Some people would claim that it is not the Parisians that speak the best French, but the inhabitants of the Touraine region.)

113

One Hundred and Thirteenth Lesson

Goodbye... and see you soon!

1 Here we are at the end of our book, but not at the end of the journey.

2 You must not stop now.

3 Of course, you don't yet speak French like a born Parisian,

4 but you are capable of understanding a conversation

5 and of making yourself understood in the usual circumstances of daily life.

6 Take the book again every day and flip through it. Pick a lesson,

7 listen again to the recordings and continue to do the second wave.

AU REVOIR... ET À BIENTÔT !

3 Je me fais comprendre, *I make myself understood.* Vous me faites rire, *You make me laugh.* French also simplifies the English construction: *to have* + past participle. *I am having my watch repaired,* Je fais réparer ma montre. *Have him come in,* Faites-le entrer. If we use a pronoun for the direct object, we place it before faire: Je la fais réparer, *I am having it repaired.* If we use the noun itself, we place it after the infinitive: Il fait faire un costume, *He is having a suit made.*

8   Il y a des points de grammaire, des expressions
    et du vocabulaire que nous n'avons pas_encore
    vus.
9   Donc, n'arrêtez pas maintenant. Prenez un
    journal, lisez un roman,
10 écoutez la radio ou parlez avec un ami
    francophone,
11 mais surtout, continuez à apprendre et à
    pratiquer cette belle langue française
12 que vous avez_apprise ⁴ "sans peine".
13 "Ce qui n'est pas clair n'est pas français."
    – *Rivarol*   □

Note

4 Feminine form because the nearest preceding direct object is... **la
   langue française**.

Exercice 1 – Traduisez
❶ Écoutez-la ; c'est une vendeuse-née ! ❷ Non, je ne le lis
pas ; je le feuillette. ❸ Je voudrais prendre rendez-vous avec
le docteur, s'il vous plaît. ❹ Il se fait comprendre partout.
❺ C'est la fin de l'exercice, mais non pas de la leçon. ❻ Au
revoir et à bientôt.

***

Exercice 2 – Complétez
❶ You must stop at once.
   Il faut ... vous vous .... tout de suite.

❷ I flipped through the book and I chose a lesson.
   J'ai .... le livre et j'ai ...... une leçon.

❸ It must be understood that it is very hard.
   Il .... que c'est très dur.

❹ He is having a new suit made.
   Il .... un nouveau costume.

8 There are points of grammar, expressions and vocabulary that we have not seen yet.

9 So don't stop now. Pick up a newspaper, read a novel,

10 listen to the radio or talk with a French speaking friend,

11 but, above all, continue to learn and practise the *(this)* beautiful French language

12 which you have learned "with ease".

13 "What is not clear is not French."
   – *Rivarol*

Answers to Exercice 1

❶ Listen to her; she's born a saleswoman! ❷ No I'm not reading it, I'm flipping through it. ❸ I would like to make an appointment with the doctor, please. ❹ He makes himself understood everywhere. ❺ It's the end of the exercise but not of the lesson. ❻ Goodbye and see you soon.

***

❺ What is not clear is not French.

. . . .

Answers to Exercice 2

❶ – que – arrêtiez – ❷ – feuilleté – choisi – ❸ – faut comprendre – ❹ – fait faire – ❺ Ce qui n'est pas clair n'est pas français

Second wave: 64th Lesson

Grammatical appendix

This brief section is intended purely for reference. Use it to check a form, a tense or a rule.

1 Nouns

All French nouns are either masculine or feminine. The articles – the words for *a* or *the* change accordingly.

Masculine: **un livre** – **le livre**
Feminine: **une voiture** – **la voiture**
The plural for both genders is **les**.

Gender has to be learned parrot fashion. Always learn the gender when you learn the noun.

Here are a couple of hints to help you work out the gender:
• most nouns which end in a mute **e** are feminine
• all nouns ending in **-ée** are feminine (with a few exceptions)
• all nouns ending in **-ion** are feminine (with a few exceptions).

The plural of most nouns is formed by adding an **s** (unpronounced) to the end:
• nouns ending in **-eau** (masculine) add an **x**
• there is a series of seven nouns ending in **-ou** (masculine), the most common of which are **chou**, *cabbage*; **genou**, *knee;* **bijou**, *jewel*; they also form the plural by adding an **x**.

2 Adjectives

These words usually come **after** the word they describe and must "agree" i.e. they must be in the same gender and form. The usual form given in dictionaries is the masculine form. The feminine is formed in several different ways:

adjectives ending in:
-eux become **-euse** e.g. **dangereux-dangereuse**
adjectives ending in:
-en, **-on**, **-il**, double the final consonant and add **e** e.g. **bon-bonne**; **moyen-moyenne**, *average* ; **gentil-gentille**.
Most other adjectives simply add **e**.

Adjectives usually come after the noun they qualify (i.e. describe), but there are some common exceptions. Some examples:
bon, *good*; **mauvais**, *bad*; **beau**, *handsome*; **grand**, *big*; **petit**, *small*; **autre**, *other*; **long**, *long*.

This also applies to the feminine form. Adjectives which are placed before the noun have a second masculine form if they end in a vowel and the word they qualify begins with a vowel. For example: **un bel appartement**; this avoids any difficulty in pronunciation (called a "hiatus").

If two (or more) nouns of both genders are the subject of a sentence, we use the masculine plural form for a single adjective qualifying them:
Son fils et sa fille sont grands.
Adjectives of nationality do not take a capital letter:
une voiture française, un livre allemand.

3 Adverbs

Most of them are formed by simply adding **-ment** to the feminine form of the adjective.

lent – lente – lentement; heureux –heureuse – heureusement

Some adjectives are also adverbs:
dur; vite; haut.

Adverbs are placed directly after the verb.

4 Verbs

We have distinguished three main groups of verbs by their endings in the infinitive. They are: **-er** (the most common), **-re** and **-ir**.
Here is an example of each, using the tenses and the moods we have seen so far.

4.1 -er verbs: *acheter*, to buy

• **Present**

j'achète	nous achetons
tu achètes	vous achetez
il/elle achète	ils/elles achètent

This tense corresponds to the three English present forms:

I buy   *I am buying*   *I do buy*

Pronunciation: Remember the final **s** and **-ent** are both silent. Also there is a **liaison** between the final **s** of the pronoun and the initial vowel of the verb: **elles achètent** *[elzashet]*.

• **Future**

The endings that form this tense (which are, in fact, the present tense of **avoir**) are added to the infinitive:

j'achèterai	nous achèterons
tu achèteras	vous achèterez
il/elle achètera	ils/elles achèteront

This tense corresponds to the English form: *I shall / will buy*.

The future tense is also used in French after conjunctions of time (e.g. **dès que**; **aussitôt que**; **quand**) where English would use a present:

Quand elle me téléphonera, je te le dirai, *When she phones me, I will tell you*.

• **Imperfect**

The endings which form the imperfect tense are added to the stem of the first person plural present:

j'achetais	nous achetions
tu achetais	vous achetiez
il/elle achetait	ils/elles achetaient

This tense is used to describe any continuous action in the past e.g. *She was reading a book*, **Elle lisait un livre**, or a habitual action e.g. *He always drank wine*, **Il buvait toujours du vin**, or for the description of a state e.g.
The flat was small, **L'appartement était petit**.

The imperfect is also used in conditional sentences where English uses the past tense:
If he left now he would find a taxi, **S'il partait maintenant, il trouverait un taxi**.

• **Past tense**
This tense is called in French **le passé composé** because it is a compound tense formed with the auxiliary **avoir** and the past participle of the verb. The past participle of **-er** verbs is formed by removing the **r** from the infinitive and placing an acute accent on the **e**, e.g. **acheter-acheté**.
(Some verbs – mainly those expressing motion – and all reflexive verbs use **être** as the auxiliary).

j'ai acheté	**nous avons acheté**
tu as acheté	**vous avez acheté**
il/elle a acheté	**ils/elles ont acheté**

The tense translates both English forms: *I bought* and *I have bought*. Another past form does exist – **le passé simple** – but since this is never used in speech or correspondence, and is found less and less in modern literature, we have decided not to introduce it to you in this volume.

• **The agreement of the past participle**
Let it be said straight away that this rule rarely changes the pronunciation (except for some **-re** verbs) and also confuses a lot of native French speakers! Since the past participle is an adjective it must agree with any direct object which comes <u>before</u> the verb **avoir**.
For example, if we say: *I bought some books*, **J'ai acheté des livres**, there is no agreement since the direct object (**les livres**) comes <u>after</u> the verb **avoir**. But if we say: *The books which I have bought*,

Les livres que j'ai achetés, we must make the past participle agree. If the direct object is a feminine noun: **la voiture que j'ai achetée**.

Remember that this rule takes a lot of practice to master and for the time being is not our main priority.

• **Conditional**
The conditional tense is formed by adding the endings of the imperfect tense to the stem of the future:

j'achèterais	nous achèterions
tu achèterais	vous achèteriez
il/elle achèterait	ils/elles achèteraient

This tense corresponds fairly closely to the English use of *would* when that auxiliary denotes a condition. Remember that the polite use of *would* in English: *Would you like...* is usually expressed by: **Voulez-vous...**

• **Subjunctive**
We have touched briefly on the subjunctive, which is not a tense but a "mood". It presupposes some doubt or uncertainty that the action described will be completed. We can broadly distinguish two cases for its use, the first being where a subjunctive adds a shade of meaning to the sentence and the second an obligatory use after certain constructions. We shall deal only with the second case in this volume.

The subjunctive is generally formed from the stem of the third person plural present:

j'achète	nous achetions
tu achètes	vous achetiez
il/elle achète	ils/elles achètent

donner:

je donne	nous donnions
tu donnes	vous donniez
il/elle donne	ils/elles donnent

One of the most common uses of the subjunctive is after the impersonal form: **Il faut que...**, *It is necessary that... One must...*
Il faut que vous me donniez votre réponse demain, *You must give me your answer tomorrow*. It is also used after a construction with **vouloir** when a person imposes his will on someone else: *I want you to buy it*, **Je veux que vous l'achetiez**.
Other constructions after which the subjunctive must be used are:

avant que	*before*
pourvu que	*provided that*
jusqu'à ce que	*until*
à moins que	*unless*
bien que, **quoique**	*although*
afin que, **pour que**	*in order that*

You will notice that any verb which follows these constructions does not indicate a definite state or a certainty. The meaning of "subjunctive" is "sub-joined", which means that any verb in the subjunctive mood depends on (or is joined to) an initial state.

We have only given the present subjunctive in this volume because, in modern usage, both spoken and literary, it is the only form commonly found.

There are ways of avoiding the subjunctive; for example, replacing the impersonal **il faut que vous...** or **il faut que je...** by the appropriate form of **devoir** e.g. **Il faut que vous donniez votre réponse demain** → **Vous devez donner votre réponse demain**.
But there is no escaping the fact that the subjunctive is commonly used in modern French and that we must begin to learn it now.

4.2 *-re* verbs: *vendre*, to sell

• **Present**

je vends	**nous vendons**
tu vends	**vous vendez**
il/elle vend	**ils/elles vendent**

As always, the final **-s** and **-ent** are not pronounced.

• Future

Before adding the future endings, we drop the **-e** from the infinitive:

je vendrai	nous vendrons
tu vendras	vous vendrez
il/elle vendra	ils/elles vendront

• Imperfect

je vendais	nous vendions
tu vendais	vous vendiez
il/elle vendait	ils/elles vendaient

• Past tense

j'ai vendu	nous avons vendu
tu as vendu	vous avez vendu
il/elle a vendu	ils/elles ont vendu

Agreement of the past participle does not change the pronunciation, unless the past participle of the verb ends in **-is** (e.g. **prendre - pris**; **mettre - mis**. **Les pommes que j'ai prises**, *The apples I have taken*).

• Conditional

je vendrais	nous vendrions
tu vendrais	vous vendriez
il/elle vendrait	ils/elles vendraient

• Subjunctive

il faut que je vende	il faut que nous vendions
il faut que tu vendes	il faut que vous vendiez
il faut qu'il/elle vende	il faut qu'ils/elles vendent

4.3 *-ir* verbs: *finir*, to finish

• Present

je finis	nous finissons
tu finis	vous finissez
il/elle finit	ils/elles finissent

• **Future**

je finirai	nous finirons
tu finiras	vous finirez
il/elle finira	ils/elles finiront

• **Imperfect**

je finissais	nous finissions
tu finissais	vous finissiez
il/elle finissait	ils/elles finissaient

• **Past tense**

j'ai fini	nous avons fini
tu as fini	vous avez fini
il/elle a fini	ils/elles ont fini

• **Conditional**

je finirais	nous finirions
tu finirais	vous finiriez
il/elle finirait	ils/elles finiraient

• **Subjunctive**

il faut que je finisse	il faut que nous finissions
il faut que tu finisses	il faut que vous finissiez
il faut qu'il/elle finisse	il faut qu'ils/elles finissent

Notes on pronouns:

In modern French, the **nous** form of verbs (especially in tenses where pronunciation may be awkward e.g. **nous finirions**) tends to be replaced – to the dismay of purists – by the pronoun **on**. Even though this usage is somewhat "inelegant" it makes life so much easier that we can only recommend it.

tu – the familiar form of *you* also presents some problems as to when – or if – to use it. Here are a couple of guidelines:

• always use **vous** to people you do not know
• initially, only reply in the **tu** form if someone uses it with you first
• you use **tu** when talking to small children.

The tendency with younger people in French today is to use **tu** to most people of the same age and interests. We recommend that you do not initiate the **tutoiement** but that you should follow suit if someone addresses you as **tu**.

5 Pronoun order

Remember our "football team", which gives the order in which object pronouns must come:

me

te	**le**		
		lui	
se	**la**	**(y)**	**(en)**
		leur	
nous	**les**		

vous

Examples:
Il me le/la donne: *He gives it to me.*
On les demande au téléphone: *Someone wants them on the phone.*
J'y vais: *I am going (there).*
Je lui en parlerai: *I'll talk to him/her about it.*

Object pronouns are placed after the verb if it is the imperative form:
Donnez-le/la moi: *Give it to me.*
Dites-lui: *Tell him/her.*
(**moi** and **toi** are used instead of **me** and **te**)

This rule does not apply if the command is negative:
Ne lui dites pas: *Don't tell him/her.*
Ne le lui donnez pas: *Don't give it to him/her.*

5.1 *On*

We have already seen that this impersonal pronoun commonly replaces the **nous** form in modern speech. Here are two more uses:

• where English would use the passive form: **On dit qu'il est riche**, *He is said to be rich*.
• or a "false" subject: **En France, on boit beaucoup de vin**, *In France, people/we/they drink a lot of wine*.

6 The auxiliaries *avoir* and *être*

6.1 *Avoir*

Avoir, *to have*, is used as an auxiliary to form the past tense of most verbs and also in expressions where English uses *to be*, e.g. *I am hot*, **j'ai chaud**; *she is hungry*, **elle a faim**, etc.

• **Present**

j'ai	nous avons
tu as	vous avez
il/elle a	ils/elles ont

• **Future**

j'aurai	nous aurons
tu auras	vous aurez
il/elle aura	ils/elles auront

• **Imperfect**

j'avais	nous avions
tu avais	vous aviez
il/elle avait	ils/elles avaient

• **Past tense**
formed with the present form and the past participle **eu**

j'ai eu	nous avons eu
tu as eu	vous avez eu
il/elle a eu	ils/elles ont eu

• **Conditional**

j'aurais	nous aurions
tu aurais	vous auriez
il/elle aurait	ils/elles auraient

• Subjunctive

il faut que j'aie	il faut que nous ayons
il faut que tu aies	il faut que vous ayez
il faut qu'il/elle ait	il faut qu'ils/elles aient

6.2 *Être*

Être, *to be*, is used as an auxiliary to form the past tense of all reflexive verbs – those whose infinitive is preceded by **se** – and certain verbs of movement: **arriver**, *to arrive*; **partir**, *to leave*; **monter**, *to go up*; **descendre**, *to go/come down*; **aller**, *to go*; **venir**, *to come*; **entrer**, *to come/go in*; **sortir**, *to go/come out*; **retourner**, *to return*; **tomber**, *to fall* and also **naître**, *to be born*; **mourir**, *to die* and **rester**, *to remain*.

A note on agreement:
We have seen that verbs conjugated with **avoir** in the past tense must make the agreement between the past participle of the verb and the nearest preceding direct object. The rule for these verbs, conjugated with **être** in the past, is much simpler: the past participle must agree with the subject of the sentence.
Elle est partie, *She has left;* **Nous sommes descendus**, *We came down;* **Elles sont entrées**, *They came in;* **Ils sont nés en France**, *They were born in France.* (If you look at an official form in Britain, you will see that the space for a woman's maiden name is entitled: **Née**; notice that we retain the agreement of the past participle.)

• Present

je suis	nous sommes
tu es	vous êtes
il/elle est	ils/elles sont

• Future

je serai	nous serons
tu seras	vous serez
il/elle sera	ils/elles seront

• Imperfect

j'étais	nous étions
tu étais	vous étiez
il/elle était	ils/elles étaient

- **Past tense**

j'ai été	nous avons été
tu as été	vous avez été
il/elle a été	ils/elles ont été

- **Conditional**

je serais	nous serions
tu serais	vous seriez
il/elle serait	ils/elles seraient

- **Subjunctive**

il faut que je sois	il faut qu'il/elle soit
il faut que tu sois	il faut que vous soyez
il faut qu'il/elle soit	il faut qu'ils/elles soient

Just from this brief review we can see that French grammar is more rigorous than ours but, having realised this, it can often work in our favour since there is always a rule for a particular construction and – more often than not – the rules are as "logical" as any living language can make them.

7 Irregular verbs

The tenses not indicated are regular. Ex. imperfect, **j'allais, tu allais,** etc.

The past tense is formed by using **avoir** + past participle (except for these verbs mentioned in lesson 70).

7.1 Infinitive ending in -er

• **aller**, to go

Ind. prés.	je vais, tu vas, il va, nous allons, vous allez, ils vont
Futur	j'irai, tu iras, il ira, nous irons, vous irez, ils iront
Condit.	j'irais, tu irais, il irait, nous irions, vous iriez, ils iraient
Subj. prés.	que j'aille, que tu ailles, qu'il aille, que nous allions, que vous alliez, qu'ils aillent

• **envoyer**, *to send*

Futur	j'enverrai, tu enverras, il enverra, nous enverrons, vous enverrez, ils enverront

7.2 Infinitive ending in *-re*

• **apprendre**, *to learn* – voir **prendre**

• **atteindre**, *to reach* – voir **peindre**

• **battre**, *to beat*

Ind. prés.	je bats, tu bats, il bat, nous battons, vous battez, ils battent

• **boire**, *to drink*

Ind. prés.	je bois, tu bois, il boit, nous buvons, vous buvez, ils boivent
Imparf.	je buvais, tu buvais, il buvait, nous buvions, vous buviez, ils buvaient
Futur	je boirai, tu boiras, il boira, nous boirons, vous boirez, ils boiront
Condit.	je boirais, tu boirais, il boirait, nous boirions, vous boiriez, ils boiraient
Subj. prés.	que je boive, que tu boives, qu'il boive, que nous buvions, que vous buviez, qu'ils boivent
Impératif	bois, buvons, buvez
Part. passé	bu
Part. prés.	buvant

• **comprendre**, *to understand* – see **prendre**

• **conduire**, *to conduct, to drive, to lead*

Ind. prés.	je conduis, tu conduis, il conduit, nous conduisons, vous conduisez, ils conduisent
Imparf.	je conduisais, tu conduisais, il conduisait, nous conduisions, vous conduisiez, ils conduisaient

Futur	je conduirai, tu conduiras, il conduira, nous conduirons, vous conduirez, ils conduiront
Condit.	je conduirais, tu conduirais, etc.
Sub. prés.	que je conduise, que tu conduises, etc.
Part. passé	conduit
Part. prés.	conduisant

• **connaître**, *to know, be acquainted with*

Ind. prés.	je connais, tu connais, il connaît, nous connaissons, vous connaissez, ils connaissent
Imparf.	je connaissais, tu connaissais, il connaissait, nous connaissions, vous connaissiez, ils connaissaient
Subj. prés.	que je connaisse, que tu connaisses, qu'il connaisse, que nous connaissions, que vous connaissiez, qu'ils connaissent
Part. passé.	connu
Part. prés.	connaissant

• **construire**, *to construct, to build* – see **conduire**

• **coudre**, *to sew*

Ind. prés.	je couds, tu couds, il coud, nous cousons, vous cousez, ils cousent
Imparf.	je cousais, tu cousais, etc.
Subj. prés.	que je couse, que tu couses, etc.
Part. passé	cousu
Part. prés.	cousant

• **craindre**, *to fear*

Ind. prés.	je crains, tu crains, il craint, nous craignons, vous craignez, ils craignent
Imparf.	je craignais, tu craignais, etc.
Subj. prés.	que je craigne, que tu craignes, etc.
Part. passé	craint
Part. prés.	craignant

• **croire**, *to believe*

Ind. Prés.	je crois, tu crois, il croit, nous croyons, vous croyez, ils croient
Imparf.	je croyais, tu croyais, il croyait, nous croyions, vous croyiez, ils croyaient
Futur	je croirai, tu croiras, il croira, etc.
Condit.	je croirais, tu croirais, etc.
Subj. prés.	que je croie, que tu croies, qu'il croie, que nous croyions, que vous croyiez, qu'ils croient
Impératif	crois, croyons, croyez
Part. passé	cru
Part. prés.	croyant

• **croître**, *to grow* [intransitive]

Ind. prés.	je croîs, tu croîs, il croît, nous croissons, vous croissez, ils croissent
Imparf.	je croissais, tu croissais, etc.
Subj. prés.	que je croisse, etc.
Part. passé	crû
Part. prés.	croissant

• **détruire**, *to destroy* – see **conduire**

• **dire**, *to say, to tell*

Ind. prés.	je dis, tu dis, il dit, nous disons, vous dites, ils disent
Imparf.	je disais, tu disais, il disait, nous disions, vous disiez, ils disaient
Futur	je dirai, tu diras, il dira, nous dirons, vous direz, ils diront
Subj. prés.	que je dise, que tu dises, qu'il dise, que nous disions, que vous disiez, qu'ils disent
Impératif	dis, disons, dites
Part. passé	dit
Part. prés.	disant

• **écrire**, *to write*

Ind. prés.	j'écris, tu écris, il écrit, nous écrivons, vous écrivez, ils écrivent
Imparf.	j'écrivais, tu écrivais, il écrivait, nous écrivions, vous écriviez, ils écrivaient
Futur	j'écrirai, tu écriras, il écrira, nous écrirons, vous écrirez, ils écriront
Condit.	j'écrirais, tu écrirais, il écrirait, nous écririons, vous écririez, ils écriraient
Subj. prés.	que j'écrive, que tu écrives, qu'il écrive, que nous écrivions, que vous écriviez, qu'ils écrivent
Impératif	écris, écrivons, écrivez
Part. passé	écrit
Part. prés.	écrivant

• **éteindre**, *to extinguish* – see **peindre**

• **faire**, *to do, to make*

Ind. prés.	je fais, tu fais, il fait, nous faisons, vous faites, ils font
Imparf.	je faisais, tu faisais, il faisait, nous faisions, vous faisiez, ils faisaient
Futur	je ferai, tu feras, il fera, nous ferons, vous ferez, ils feront
Condit.	je ferais, tu ferais, il ferait, nous ferions, vous feriez, ils feraient
Subj. prés.	que je fasse, que tu fasses, qu'il fasse, que nous fassions, que vous fassiez, qu'ils fassent
Impératif	fais, faisons, faites
Part. passé	fait
Part. prés.	faisant

• **frire**, *to fry* (used only in these forms)

Ind. prés.	je fris, tu fris, il frit
Futur	je frirai, tu friras, il frira, nous frirons, vous frirez, ils friront
Part. passé	frit (in the other tenses, **faire frire** is used instead of **frire**)

• **instruire**, *to instruct* – see **conduire**

• **joindre**, *to join*

Ind. prés.	je joins, tu joins, il joint, nous joignons, vous joignez, ils joignent
Imparf.	je joignais, tu joignais, il joignait, nous joignions, vous joigniez, ils joignaient
Futur	je joindrai, tu joindras, etc.
Condit.	je joindrais, tu joindrais, etc.
Subj. prés.	que je joigne, etc.
Part. passé	joint
Part. prés.	joignant

• **lire**, *to read*

Ind. prés.	je lis, tu lis, il lit, nous lisons, vous lisez, ils lisent
Imparf.	je lisais, tu lisais, il lisait, nous lisions, vous lisiez, ils lisaient
Futur	je lirai, tu liras, il lira, nous lirons, vous lirez, ils liront
Condit.	je lirais, tu lirais, il lirait, nous lirions, vous liriez, ils liraient
Subj. prés.	que je lise, que tu lises, qu'il lise, que nous lisions, que vous lisiez, qu'ils lisent
Impératif	lis, lisons, lisez
Part. passé	lu
Part. prés.	lisant

• **mettre**, *to put*

Ind. prés.	je mets, tu mets, il met, nous mettons, vous mettez, ils mettent
Imparf.	je mettais, tu mettais, il mettait, nous mettions, vous mettiez, ils mettaient
Futur	je mettrai, tu mettras, etc.
Condit.	je mettrais, tu mettrais, etc.
Subj. prés.	que je mette, que tu mettes, qu'il mette, que nous mettions, que vous mettiez, qu'ils mettent

Impératif	mets, mettons, mettez
Part. passé	mis
Part. prés.	mettant

• **naître**, *to be born*

Ind. prés.	je nais, tu nais, il naît, nous naissons, vous naissez, ils naissent
Imparf.	je naissais, tu naissais, etc.
Subj. prés.	que je naisse, que tu naisses, etc.
Part. passé	né
Part. prés.	naissant

• **paraître**, *to appear, to seem* – see **connaître**

• **peindre**, *to paint*

Ind. prés.	je peins, tu peins, il peint, nous peignons, vous peignez, ils peignent
Imparf.	je peignais, tu peignais, il peignait, nous peignions, vous peigniez, ils peignaient
Subj. prés.	que je peigne, que tu peignes, etc.
Part. passé	peint
Part. prés.	peignant

• **permettre**, *to allow* – see **mettre**

• **plaindre**, *to pity* – **se plaindre** *(to complain)* – see **craindre**

• **plaire**, *to please*

Ind. prés.	je plais, tu plais, il plaît, nous plaisons, vous plaisez, ils plaisent
Imparf.	je plaisais, tu plaisais, il plaisait, nous plaisions, vous plaisiez, ils plaisaient
Subj. prés.	que je plaise, que tu plaises, qu'il plaise, que nous plaisions, que vous plaisiez, qu'ils plaisent
Part. passé	plu
Part. prés.	plaisant

• **prendre**, *to take*

Ind. prés.	je prends, tu prends, il prend, nous prenons, vous prenez, ils prennent
Imparf.	je prenais, tu prenais, il prenait, nous prenions, vous preniez, ils prenaient
Subj. prés.	que je prenne, que tu prennes, qu'il prenne, que nous prenions, que vous preniez, qu'ils prennent
Impératif	prends, prenons, prenez
Part. passé	pris
Part. prés.	prenant

• **produire**, *to produce* – see **conduire**

• **promettre**, *to promise* – see **mettre**

• **remettre**, *to put back* or *to hand over* – see **mettre**

• **rire**, *to laugh*

Ind. prés.	je ris, tu ris, il rit, nous rions, vous riez, ils rient
Imparf.	je riais, tu riais, il riait, nous riions, vous riiez, ils riaient
Futur	je rirai, tu riras, etc.
Conditionnel	je rirais, tu rirais, etc.
Subj. prés.	que je rie, que tu ries, qu'il rie, que nous riions, que vous riiez, qu'il rient
Impératif	ris, rions, riez
Part. passé	ri
Part. prés.	riant

• **suivre**, *to follow*

Ind. prés.	je suis, tu suis, il suit, nous suivons, vous suivez, ils suivent
Imparf.	je suivais, tu suivais, il suivait, nous suivions, vous suiviez, ils suivaient
Subj. prés.	que je suive, que tu suives, qu'il suive, que nous suivions, que vous suiviez, qu'ils suivent
Impératif	suis, suivons, suivez
Part. passé	suivi
Part. prés.	suivant

- **surprendre**, *to surprise* – see **prendre**

- **se taire**, *to keep silent, to shut up* – see **plaire**

- **vivre**, *to live*

Ind. prés.	je vis, tu vis, il vit, nous vivons, vous vivez, ils vivent
Imparf.	je vivais, tu vivais, il vivait, nous vivions, vous viviez, ils vivaient
Subj. prés.	que je vive, que tu vives, qu'il vive, que nous vivions, que vous viviez, qu'ils vivent
Impératif	vis, vivons, vivez
Part. passé	vécu
Part. prés.	vivant

7.3 Infinitive ending in *-ir*

- **acquérir**, *to acquire*

Ind. prés.	j'acquiers, tu acquiers, il acquiert, nous acqué-rons, vous acquérez, ils acquièrent
Imparf.	j'acquérais, tu acquérais, il acquérait, nous acqué-rions, vous acquériez, ils acquéraient
Futur	j'acquerrai, tu acquerras, il acquerra, nous acquerrons, vous acquerrez, ils acquerront
Condit.	j'acquerrais, tu acquerrais, il acquerrait, nous acquerrions, vous acquerriez, ils acquerraient
Subj. prés.	que j'acquière, que tu acquières, qu'il acquière, que nous acquérions, etc.
Part. passé	acquis
Part. prés.	acquérant

- **bouillir**, *to boil*

Ind. prés.	je bous, tu bous, il bout, nous bouillons, vous bouillez, ils bouillent
Imparf.	je bouillais, etc.
Subj. prés.	que je bouille, que tu bouilles, etc.
Part. passé	bouilli
Part. prés.	bouillant

- **conquérir**, *to conquer* – see **acquérir**

- **courir**, *to run*

Ind. prés.	je cours, tu cours, il court, nous courons, vous courez, ils courent
Imparf.	je courais, tu courais, il courait, etc.
Futur	je courrai, tu courras, il courra, nous courrons, vous courrez, ils courront
Condit.	je courrais, tu courrais, il courrait, nous courrions, vous courriez, ils courraient
Part. passé	couru
Part. prés.	courant

- **couvrir**, *to cover* – see **ouvrir**

- **cueillir**, *to gather*, *to pluck*

Ind. prés.	je cueille, etc.
Imparf.	je cueillais, etc.
Futur	je cueillerai, etc.
Condit.	je cueillerais, etc.
Subj. prés.	que je cueille, etc.
Part. passé	cueilli
Part. prés.	cueillant

- **découvrir**, *to discover* – see **couvrir**

- **dormir**, *to sleep*

Ind. prés.	je dors, tu dors, il dort, nous dormons, vous dormez, ils dorment
Imparf.	je dormais, etc.
Subj. prés.	que je dorme, etc.
Part. prés.	dormant

- **fuir**, *to flee*, *to leak*

| Ind. prés. | je fuis, tu fuis, il fuit, nous fuyons, vous fuyez, ils fuient |
| Imparf. | je fuyais, etc. |

Subj. présent	que je fuie, que tu fuies, qu'il fuie, que nous fuyions, que vous fuyiez, qu'ils fuient
Part. passé	fui
Part. prés.	fuyant

• **mentir**, *to lie – tell a lie*

Ind. prés.	je mens, tu mens, il ment, nous mentons, vous mentez, ils mentent
Imparf.	je mentais, etc.
Subj. présent	que je mente, que tu mentes, qu'il mente, que nous mentions, que vous mentiez, qu'ils mentent

• **mourir**, *to die*

Ind. prés.	je meurs, tu meurs, il meurt, nous mourons, vous mourez, ils meurent
Imparf.	je mourais, etc.
Futur	je mourrai, tu mourras, etc.
Subj. prés.	que je mente, que tu mentes, qu'il mente, que nous mentions, que vous mentiez, qu'ils mentent

• **offrir**, *to offer*

Ind. prés.	j'offre, etc.
Imparf.	j'offrais, etc.
Subj. prés.	que j'offre, etc.
Part. passé	offert
Part. prés.	offrant

• **ouvrir**, *to open* – see **offrir**

• **partir**, *to leave, to go away* – see **mentir**

• **repentir (se)**, *to repent* – see **mentir**

• **secourir**, *to succour* – see **courir**

• **sentir**, *to feel* or *to smell* – see **mentir**

• **servir**, *to serve*

Ind. prés.	je sers, tu sers, il sert, nous servons, vous servez, ils servent
Imparf.	je servais, tu servais, etc.
Impératif	sers, servons, servez
Part. passé	servi
Part. prés.	servant

• **souffrir**, *to suffer* – see **offrir**

• **tenir**, *to hold*

Ind. prés.	je tiens, tu tiens, il tient, nous tenons, vous tenez, ils tiennent
Imparf.	je tenais, etc.
Futur	je tiendrai, tu tiendras, il tiendra, etc.
Condit.	je tiendrais, tu tiendrais, il tiendrait, etc.
Subj. prés.	que je tienne, que tu tiennes, qu'il tienne, que nous tenions, que vous teniez, qu'ils tiennent
Impératif	tiens, tenons, tenez
Part. passé	tenu
Part. prés.	tenant

• **venir**, *to come* – see **tenir**

• **asseoir (s')**, *to sit down*

Ind. prés.	je m'assieds, tu t'assieds, il s'assied, nous nous asseyons, vous vous asseyez, ils s'asseyent
Imparf.	je m'asseyais, etc.
Futur	je m'assiérai, etc.
Condit.	je m'assiérais, etc.
Subj. prés.	que je m'asseye, etc.
Impératif	assieds-toi, asseyons-nous, asseyez-vous
Part. passé	assis
Part. prés.	s'asseyant

• **devoir**, *to owe*, or *must*

Ind. prés.	je dois, tu dois, il doit, nous devons, vous devez, ils doivent
Imparf.	je devais, tu devais, il devait, nous devions, vous deviez, ils devaient
Subj. prés.	que je doive, que tu doives, qu'il doive, que nous devions, que vous deviez, qu'ils doivent
Part. passé	dû (due)
Part. prés.	devant

• **falloir**, *to be necessary*, *must* (impersonal)

Ind. prés.	il faut
Imparf.	il fallait
Futur	il faudra
Condit.	il faudrait
Subj. prés.	qu'il faille
Part. passé	il a fallu

• **pleuvoir**, *to rain* (semi-impersonal)

Ind. prés.	il pleut, ils pleuvent
Imparf.	il pleuvait, ils pleuvaient
Futur	il pleuvra, ils pleuvront
Condit.	il pleuvrait, ils pleuvraient
Subj. prés.	qu'il pleuve, qu'ils pleuvent
Part. passé	plu

• **pouvoir**, *to be able to*, *can* or *may*

Ind. prés.	je peux, tu peux, il peut, nous pouvons, vous pouvez, ils peuvent
Futur	je pourrai, tu pourras, il pourra, nous pourrons, vous pourrez, ils pourront
Condit.	je pourrais, tu pourrais, il pourrait, nous pourrions, vous pourriez, ils pourraient
Subj. prés.	que je puisse, que tu puisses, qu'il puisse, que nous puissions, que vous puissiez, qu'ils puissent
Part. passé	pu
Part. prés.	pouvant

• **savoir**, *to know*

Ind. prés.	je sais, tu sais, il sait, nous savons, vous savez, ils savent
Futur	je saurai, tu sauras, il saura, nous saurons, vous saurez, ils sauront
Condit.	je saurais, tu saurais, il saurait, nous saurions, vous sauriez, ils sauraient
Subj. prés.	que je sache, que tu saches, qu'il sache, que nous sachions, que vous sachiez, qu'ils sachent
Impératif	sache, sachons, sachez
Part. passé	su
Part. prés.	sachant

• **valoir**, *to be worth*

Ind. prés.	je vaux, tu vaux, il vaut, nous valons, vous valez, ils valent
Imparf.	je valais, tu valais, il valait, nous valions, vous valiez, ils valaient
Futur	je vaudrai, tu vaudras, il vaudra, nous vaudrons, vous vaudrez, ils vaudront
Condit.	je vaudrais, tu vaudrais, il vaudrait, nous vaudrions, vous vaudriez, ils vaudraient
Subj. prés.	que je vaille, que tu vailles, qu'il vaille, que nous valions, que vous valiez, qu'ils vaillent
Part. passé	valu
Part. prés.	valant

• **voir**, *to see*

Ind. prés.	je vois, tu vois, il voit, nous voyons, vous voyez, ils voient
Imparf.	je voyais, tu voyais, il voyait, nous voyions, vous voyiez, ils voyaient
Futur	je verrai, tu verras, il verra, nous verrons, vous verrez, ils verront
Condit.	je verrais, tu verrais, il verrait, nous verrions, vous verriez, ils verraient

Subj. prés.	que je voie, que tu voies, qu'il voie, que nous voyions, que vous voyiez, qu'ils voient
Impératif	vois, voyons, voyez
Part. passé	vu
Part. prés.	voyant

• **vouloir**, *to want, to will*

Ind. prés.	je veux, tu veux, il veut, nous voulons, vous voulez, ils veulent
Imparf.	je voulais, tu voulais, il voulait, nous voulions, vous vouliez, ils voulaient
Futur	je voudrai, tu voudras, il voudra, nous voudrons, vous voudrez, ils voudront
Condit.	je voudrais, tu voudrais, il voudrait, nous voudrions, vous voudriez, ils voudraient
Subj. prés.	que je veuille, que tu veuilles, qu'il veuille, que nous voulions, que vous vouliez, qu'ils veuillent
Impératif	veuille, veuillons, veuillez
Part. passé	voulu
Part. prés.	voulant

Glossaries

We have organised the vocabulary used in the dialogues and notes of this book into an easy-to-use French/English glossary. Note that the corresponding translations are those given in the context of the lessons, and that other translations are therefore possible. The figure(s) after each word show(s) the lesson(s) in which it is used. The gender of nouns is shown by *(m.)* (masculine) or *(f.)* (feminine); *(sing.)* is for "singular" and *(pl.)* is for "plural"; *(adj.)* stands for "adjective" and *(adv.)* for "adverb"; *(v.)* is for "verb". To help you "back translate" when you reach the second wave, we have included a English/French glossary.

French - English glossary

A

à	in 1
à (jusqu'à)	until 18
à bientôt !	see you soon! 18, 95, 113
à propos de	about 64, 103
à tel point que	to such an extent that 76
à tout à l'heure	until later on 41; see you later 78
abandonner	to give up 99
absent/e	absent, out 5; not here 36
absolument	absolutely 52
accent *(m.)*	accent 44
accepter	to take 48; to accept 99, 104
accompagnement *(m.)*	accompaniment 72
accordéon *(m.)*	accordeon 40
accueil *(m.)*	reception (hotel, building) 44, 109
accueillir	to greet 44; to meet, to welcome 44, 74
accusation *(f.)*	accusation 109
achat *(m.)*	purchase 6, 16
acheter	to buy 10, 22, 27, 40, 50
acrylique *(f.)*	acrylic 2
acteur *(m.)*	actor 74
activement	energically 101
actrice *(f.)*	actress 62
actuel/le	current, present 52
actuellement	now, at the moment 52
addition *(f.)*	bill 19, 72

amené à (être ~)	to be required to 103
ami/e *(m.)*	friend 5, 9, 25, 39, 82
amour *(m.)*	love 37
amoureux *(m.)*	lover 37
an *(m.)*	year 67
Anglais/e	English 3, 94
Angleterre *(f.)*	England 94
angoissant/e	worrying 110
angoisse *(f.)*	anxiety 104
année *(f.)*	year 6, 43
annonce *(f.)*	advertisement, ad 15, 101
annoncer	to announce 104
annonces (petites ~) *(f. pl.)*	classified advertisement 15; small ads 81
annuaire (téléphonique) *(m.)*	directory 61
annuel/le	annual 38
antenne *(f.)*	aerial 65
août	August 19, 92
apéritif *(m.)*	drink 104
appareil *(m.)*	apparatus 17
appareil photo *(m.)*	camera 50
appart (= appartement) *(m.)*	apartment 10, 30, 81; flat 30, 31, 106
appartenir (à)	to belong to 31, 65
appeler	to call 15, 60
appeler (s'~)	to be called 9, 37
appétit *(m.)*	appetite 41
application *(f.)*	program 101
apporter	to take 50
apprécié/e	appreciated 38
apprécier	to appreciate 74
apprendre	to teach 68, 86; to learn 113
apprêter à (s'~)	to get ready to 66
après	after 25
après tout	after all 61
après-midi *(m.* or *f.)*	afternoon 5
araignée	spider 39
arbre *(m.)*	tree 58
argent *(m.)*	money 17, 22
argot *(m.)*	slang 47, 81
argument *(m.)*	argument 39, 89, 106
arme *(f.)*	weapon 92
armée *(f.)*	army 34, 74
armoire *(f.)*	wardrobe 31
arrêt de bus *(m.)*	bus stop 34
arrêter	to stop 16, 78
arrêter (s'~)	to stop 34, 40, 89

cependant	however 66
certainement	certainly 34
cerveau *(m.)*	brain 75
chaîne *(f.)*	channel 10, 88
chambre *(f.)*	room 26; bedroom 30, 31
champagne *(m.)*	champagne 55
champignon *(m.)*	mushroom 108
chance (avoir de la ~)	to be lucky 19
chance *(f.)*	luck 19
changement *(m.)*	change 60, 108
changer	to change 32, 89, 106
chanson *(f.)*	song 13, 25
chanteur/chanteuse	singer 13
chapeau *(m.)*	hat 2
chaque	each 6, 65; every 24
charbon *(m.)*	coal 102
charbons ardents *(m. pl.)*	tenterhooks 102
chargé/e	laden 83; busy 109
charger	to load 83
charmant/e	charming 108
chasseur (hotel) *(m.)*	page-boy 46
château *(m.)*	castle 22
chaud/e	hot 3, 26
chauffage *(m.)*	heating 106
chauffeur *(m.)*	driver 96
chauffeur de taxi *(m.)*	taxi driver 43
chaussette *(f.)*	sock 26
chaussure *(f.)*	shoe 26, 57
chauve	bald 68
chef d'équipe *(m.)*	project/team manager 104
chef d'orchestre	conductor 76
chemin *(m.)*	way 83
chemin de fer *(m.)*	railway 83
chemin des écoliers *(m.)*	long way round 83
chemise *(f.)*	shirt 26, 36, 52
chemisier *(m.)*	blouse 78
chèque *(m.)*	cheque 33, 57
cher/chère	dear 2, 39; expensive 18, 32, 40
chercher	to look for 8; to get 45
chercher (aller ~)	to fetch 66
chéri/e	darling 29, 99
cheval *(m.)*	horse 22
cheveu(x) *(m.)*	hair 68
cheville *(f.)*	ankle 69
chewing-gum *(m.)*	gum 11
chez	at 30

comme	like 17, 32; as 32
comme ça	like that 11
commémorer	to commemorate 92
commencer (à)	to begin (to) 12, 26, 37, 65
comment	how 6
comment ?	what? 2
comment ça va ?	how's things? 6
commerçant	shopkeeper 27
commerce (m.)	shop 106
commercialiser	to sell 109
commissariat (m.)	main police station 59
communication (f.)	communication 109
communication (f.)	public relations 102
compartiment (m.)	compartment 93
complémentaire	additional 64
complet/complète	full (up) 41, 46
complètement	completely 11
composé/e (de)	composed (of) 30, 68
composter	to stamp 102
comprendre	to understand 44, 59, 113
compte (m.)	account 5
compter	to count 81, 89
compteur (m.)	meter 96
concentration (f.)	concentration 24
concierge (m./f.)	concierge 30
condition (f.)	rate 61
conduire	to drive 52, 107
confier à	to confide to 88
confortable	comfortable 30
congélateur (m.)	freezer 36
connaissance (f.)	knowledge 22, 101
connaisseur (m.)	connaisseur 34
connaître	to know 11, 36, 64
conserve (f.)	tinned food 39
considérer	to reckon 103
construction (f.)	construction 65
construire	to build 52
consultation (f.)	consultation 75
consulter	to look at 101
contact (m.)	contact 64
contacter	to contact 106
continuer	to continue 59, 78, 83, 96, 113
contourner	to go around 59
contraire	opposite 79
contrat (m.)	agreement 64; contract 104
contre	against 89

couvert/e (de)	covered with 68
couvrir	to cover 83
cravate *(f.)*	tie 26
crayon *(m.)*	pencil 13, 78
création *(f.)*	creation 89
créer	to create 90
crème *(f.)*	cream 26, 27
crèmerie *(f.)*	creamery 27
crevé/e	whacked 101
crevé/e (fatigué/e)	worn out 89
crever	to have a puncture 89
crier	to shout 48
croire	to believe 54
croiser	to cross 43, 101
croissant *(m.)*	croissant 3, 27
croque-monsieur *(m.)*	toasted ham and cheese sandwich 108
cuillère *(f.)*	spoon 41
cuir *(m.)*	leather 15
cuisine *(f.)*	kitchen 30, 41, 106; cooking 88; cookery 90
cuisiner	to cook 24
cultivé/e	cultivated, grown 40; cultured 73, 94
cultiver	to grow 73
culturel/le	cultural 85
cycliste	cycle 89

D

d'abord	first of all 10; originally 12; first 45, 58
d'accord	OK 33, 57
d'ailleurs	moreover 33
dame *(f.)*	lady 9
dans	in 4, 8, 12
danser	to dance 26
dater de	to date from 58
daube de bœuf *(f.)*	beef stew 19
davantage	more 39, 80
débarrasser	to clear 53
débattre	to discuss 15
debout (se mettre ~)	to stand up 69
debout (se tenir ~)	to stand 69
débrancher	to unplug 20
débrouillard/e	resourceful 94
débrouiller (pas mal) (se ~)	to get by (quite well) 103
débrouiller (se ~)	to get by 94
début *(m.)*	beginning 47, 92, 99
débutant/e	beginner 13

emploi *(m.)*	job 43, 48, 100
emprunter	to take 32; to borrow 32, 50
ému/e	moved 38
enchaîner	to continue 88
enchanté/e	delighted 45; pleased 45, 109
encore	again 20, 53
encore (pas ~)	not yet 23
encre de Chine	Indian ink 26
endormir (s'~)	to fall asleep 73
endroit (à l'~)	the right way around 48
endroit *(m.)*	place 32
enfant *(m./f.)*	child 9, 62
enfants *(m./f.)*	children 15
enfin	finally 26; well 64
énorme	enormous 38, 47
énormément	enormously 74
enregistrement *(m.)*	recording 113
enregistrer	to record 48
ensemble (dans l'~)	in the main 110
ensuite	next 26, 78; afterwards 55, 74
entendre	to hear 37, 62
entendre parler	to hear of 80
entraînement *(m.)*	practice 95
entre	between 40
entrée *(f.)*	entrance hall 30; appetizer, entrance, lobby 46
entrer dans	to enter in 58
entrer en scène	to come on stage 37
entretenir	to upkeep 106
entretien *(m.)*	interview 52, 102
envers (à l'~)	back to front, backwards 48
envie de (avoir ~)	to want to 27
envie de (ne pas avoir ~)	to not want to 96
environs *(m. pl.)*	surroundings 85, 111
envisager	to consider 106
envoyer	to send 36
épée *(f.)*	sword 25
épeler	to spell 41
épicier/épicière	grocer 27
épisode *(m.)*	episode 85
époque *(f.)*	age 72; time 89
épuisé/e	exhausted 51
équipe *(f.)*	team 103

fenêtre *(f.)*	window 30, 55
fer *(m.)*	iron 65
férié	holiday 92
fermier *(m.)*	farmer 73
festival *(m.)*	festival 38
fête (faire la ~)	to celebrate 104
fête *(f.)*	party 71; holiday 92
fêter	to celebrate 62
feu (du ~) *(m.)*	a light 4
feu d'artifice *(m.)*	firework 92
feuille d'impôts *(f.)*	tax-form 53
feuilleter	to flip through 113
février	February 19
fier/fière	proud 25, 72
figurant *(m.)*	extra 74
filer à l'anglaise	to slip away, to take French leave 94
filet *(m.)*	bag 108
fille (ma ~)	my daughter 20
fille *(f.)*	girl 20, 62
film *(m.)*	film 11, 38, 53
film noir *(m.)*	gangster (film) 38
fils *(m.)*	son 9
fin *(f.)*	end 50, 61, 113
financer	to finance 88
finir	to end, to finish 25, 90
fisc *(m.)*	tax office 104
fleur *(f.)*	flower 32
fleurs (en ~)	in bloom 59
fois (une ~)	once 85, 89
fois *(f.)*	time 38
foncé/e	dark 26, 78
fonction (en ~)	according to 22
fond *(m.)*	end 107
fontaine *(f.)*	fountain 1
football *(m.)*	soccer 22
forêt *(f.)*	forest 58
forfait *(m.)*	all-in rate 64
formalité *(f.)*	formality 64, 108
former	to form 68
formulaire *(m.)*	form 9
fort	loudly 37; strong 44
forteresse *(f.)*	fortress 92
fortune *(f.)*	fortune 22
fortune du pot *(f.)*	pot-luck 39
fou *(f. folle)*	madman 37
foule *(f.)*	crowd 92

fournir	to provide 101
foyer (m.)	household 88
frais (m. pl.)	charges 81
frais bancaires (m. pl.)	bank charges 81
frais de déplacement (m. pl.)	travel expenses 81
frais/fraîche	fresh 73
fraise (f.)	strawberry 108
Français (m.)	Frenchman 32
français/e	French 3
France (f.)	France 94
franchement	downright 85
franc-jeu	fair-play 94
frapper	to hit 76
fric (m.)	bread, cash, money 81
frigo (m.)	fridge 36
froid (n.)	cold 43
froid/e	cold 26, 87, 94
fromage (m.)	cheese 6
fruit (m.)	fruit 27
fruits (m. pl.)	fruit 40
fruits de mer (m. pl.)	seafood 104
fumer	to smoke 4, 24
fumeur (m.)	smoking (smoker) 60
furieux/-se	furious 54
futé/e	bright, sharp, smart, cunning 76
futur (dans le ~)	in the future 43
futur (m.)	future 86

G

gaffe (f.)	blunder 87
gagnant	winner 22, 38
gagner	to win 23, 65, 87, 89; to earn 103
gagner de l'argent	to earn money 94
galère (f.)	difficult situation, galley ship 110
galérer	to struggle 110
gamme (f.)	range 61
gant (m.)	glove 2
garage (m.)	garage 106
garçon (m.)	waiter 3; boy 9, 62
garde-manger (m.)	larder 39
garder	to look after 15; to keep 62
gare (f.)	train station 32
gars (m.)	guy 74
gâteau (m.) (pl. gâteaux)	cake 27, 108
gauche (à ~)	on the left 107
gauche (f.)	left 1, 79

gêné/e	embarrassed 34
gêner	to bother 34
général/e	general 62
génie (de ~)	brilliant 111
genou (m.) (pl. genoux)	knee 37, 69, 86
genre (m.)	type 80; kind 102
gens (pl.)	people 24, 38
gentil/le	kind 3, 29
gestion (f.)	science of management 109
gîte (m.)	gîte 111
glace (f.)	ice-cream 52, 59
goût (m.)	taste 30, 88
goûter	to taste 30, 71
gouvernement (m.)	government 92
gouverneur (m.)	governor 92
grammaire (f.)	grammar 110
grand/e	big 16
grande surface (f.)	supermarket 108
grandir	to grow 73
grand-mère (f.)	grandmother 62
grand-parents	grandparents 62
grand-père (m.)	grandfather 62
gratter	to scratch 22
gratuit/e	free 17
grave	serious 17
Grèce	Greece 19
grippe (f.)	flu 18
gris foncé	dark grey 26
gris/e	grey 64
gros/se	big 22, 29; fat 69
grosse caisse (f.)	bass drum 76
groupe (music) (m.)	band 75
guerre (f.)	war 73
guichet (m.)	ticket office 33
guide (livre) (m.)	guide (book) 108
guide (m.)	guide 12, 34, 57
guitare (f.)	guitar 22, 40
guitariste	guitarist 75

H

habileté (f.)	skill 24
habillé/e	dressed 54
habiller (s'~)	to dress 26
habit (m.)	clothes 87
habitant/e	inhabitant 85
habité/e	inhabited 85

intérieur (à l'~)	inside 43
inutile	useless 11
inventaire *(m.)*	inventory 78
inviter	to invite 39, 102
ironique	ironic 45
isolé/e	isolated 111
Italie *(f.)*	Italy 94
ivre	drunk 55
ivrogne *(m.)*	drunkhard 37

J

jadis	in the past 43
jaloux/jalouse	jealous 19
jamais	never 31, 37
jambe *(f.)*	leg 68, 83
jambon *(m.)*	ham 27
janvier	January 19
Japonais/e	Japanese 78
jardin *(m.)*	garden 59, 106
jaune	yellow 89
je vous en prie	don't mention it 95
jeter	to throw 15
jeu *(m.) (pl.* jeux)	game 22, 88
jeu d'argent *(m.)*	gambling 22
jeune	young 10, 65
jeune fille *(f.)*	young girl 15
jeune homme *(m.)*	young man 47
jeûner	to fast 36
joindre	to get in touch 97
joindre à	to mix with 95
joli/e	pretty 1, 29, 59, 62
jouer	to play 22
jouer de (instrument)	to play 40, 52
jouer le jeu	to play along 109
joueur/joueuse	player 22
jour *(m.)*	day 6, 26, 32
jour férié *(m.)*	public holiday 92
journal (TV) *(m.)*	news 88
journal *(m.)*	paper 22
journaliste *(m.* or *f.)*	journalist 43, 62, 65
jours (de nos ~)	nowadays 43, 89
juillet	July 19
juin	June 19
jupe *(f.)*	skirt 78
jury *(m.)*	jury 38
jusqu'à présent	up to now 81
justement	exactly 38; in fact 106

K

L

loin	further 30; far 46
loin de	away from 108
Londres	London 3
long/longue	long 25, 50
longtemps	a long time 47
longueur *(f.)*	length 32, 65
lors de	during 89
lorsque	when 76
lot (gros ~)	jackpot 22
loto *(m.)*	Loto 22, 87
louer	to rent 15, 61, 81, 111
lourd/e	heavy 29
loyer *(m.)*	rent 81, 106
luxe *(m.)*	luxury 72
lycéen/ne	high school pupil 86

M

mâcher	to chew 11
machin *(m.)*	thing 48
maçon *(m.)*	builder 43
madame	madam 2
mademoiselle	miss 5, 36
magasin *(m.)*	shop 2, 13, 78
magazine *(m.)*	magazine 44
magnifique	magnificent 83
mai	May 19, 92
maigre	thin 69
maillot *(m.)*	jersey 89
maillot de bain *(m.)*	swimming costume 89
maillot de corps *(m.)*	man's vest 89
main *(f.)*	hand 25, 44
maintenant	now 26, 38, 47, 66, 108
mairie *(f.)*	town hall 9, 58
mais	but 1
maison (à la ~)	at home 8
maison *(f.)*	house 39, 52
majeur/e	major 88
majoration *(f.)*	increase 96
majorer	to increase 96
malade	ill 20; sick 48
malades *(m. pl.)*	sick people 85
malgré	despite 10, 47
malheureusement	unfortunately 43
maman	mum 50
manger	to eat 10, 16, 19, 24, 27, 41
manquer (à qqn)	to miss 108

mettre	to turn on 10; to put 23, 66
mettre à (se ~)	to start 101
meuble *(m.)*	piece of furniture 30, 31
meublé/e	furnished 30
meubles (les ~)	furniture 108
miche *(f.)*	loaf 27
Midi	south of France 24
midi	midday 50; noon 60
mien/ne (le/la ~)	mine 66
mieux	better 50, 73
migraine *(f.)*	migraine 86
milieu (au ~ de)	in the middle of 30, 40
million *(m.)*	million 22, 65
ministre *(m.)*	minister 102
Minitel *(m.)*	Minitel 111
minuit	midnight 10
minute *(f.)*	minute 1
miroir *(m.)*	mirror 34, 67
mise en scène *(f.)*	direction (film) 38
mixte	mixed 110
mode *(f.)*	fashion 13
modèle *(m.)*	model 16
moderne	modern 13, 72
modernisé/e	modernised 60
modestie *(f.)*	modesty 74
moi	me 3
moi-même	myself 12, 46
moine *(m.)*	monk 87
moins (au ~)	at least 50, 88, 97
moins (de ~)	less 67
moins de	under 60
mois *(m.)*	month 67
moitié (à ~)	half 67
moitié *(f.)*	half 110
moment (en ce ~)	at the moment 20, 50
moment *(m.)*	moment 24, 37, 38
monarchie *(f.)*	monarchy 92
monde (beaucoup de ~)	lots of people 40
monde *(m.)*	world 39; people 111
monnaie *(f.)*	change 62
monsieur *(m.)*	gentleman, sir 3
monter	to hop in 96; to go up 10, 107
monter à cheval	to ride a horse 50
montre *(f.)*	watch 89
monumental/e	monumental 87
mort *(f.)*	death 54

mort/e	dead 13
mortel/le	deadly 25
mot *(m.)*	word 62; note 76
multimédia	multimedia 101
multiplier (se ~)	to multiply 108
mur *(m.)*	wall 31
murmurer	to murmur 109
musée *(m.)*	art museum 34, 59; museum 59
musique *(f.)*	music 10, 13
muté/e	transferred 110

N

n'importe comment	in any way 82
n'importe où	aywhere 82
n'importe quand	at any time 82
n'importe qui	anybody 82; anyone 82, 105
n'importe quoi (dire ~)	to talk nonsense 99
naissance *(f.)*	birth 62
naturellement	naturally 38
né/e	born 113
né/e (être ~)	to be born 65
ne... que	only 60
néanmoins	nevertheless 31
nécessiter	to necessitate 43
nez *(m.)*	nose 68
niveau *(m.)*	level 71
niveau de (au ~) *(m.)*	in terms of 103
Noël *(m.)*	Christmas 76
noir/e	black 4, 26, 54, 110
nom *(m.)*	name 33, 46
nombre *(m.)*	number 88, 95
nombreux/nombreuse(s)	numerous 22
non plus	either 19
non-fumeur *(m.)*	non-smoking 60, 93
nord *(m.)*	north 24
normalement	normally 8
note *(f.)*	bill 53
nouveau riche *(m.)*	nouveau-riche 76
nouveau/nouvelle	new 9, 53, 76
nouveauté *(f.)*	novelty 38
Nouvel An *(m.)*	New Year 67
nouvelle *(f.)*	news 68, 101
novembre	November 19, 92
nuit (la ~)	at night 62
nuit *(f.)*	night 46

nulle part	nowhere 89
numéro *(m.)*	number 22, 23, 32, 61

O

obligatoire	vital 101
obtenir	to get 61; to obtain 79
occuper de (s'~)	to take care of 108
océan *(m.)*	ocean 72
octobre	October 19
œuf *(m.)*	egg 27, 68, 73
offre *(f.)*	offer 101
offre d'emploi *(f.)*	job advertisement, job offer 101
offrir	to give 76
oh ! là, là !	oh dear! 81
oignon *(m.)*	onion 108
on y va !	let's be off! 66
oncle *(m.)*	uncle 50, 62
optimiste	optmist 67
orchestre *(m.)*	orchestra 76
ordinaire	ordinary 6
ordinateur *(m.)*	computer 60, 101
ordre *(m.)*	order 22
organiser	to organise 109
original/e	unusual 108
origine (à l'~)	at the beginning 90
origine *(f.)*	beginning 89, 90
orthographe *(f.)*	writing 110
os *(m.)*	bone 68
oser	to dare 62
où	where 1, 12
oublier	to forget 9, 24, 50, 61, 62
ouest *(m.)*	west 24, 99
outil *(m.)*	tool 109
outil télématique *(m.)*	data communications tool 109
ouvrir	to open 16, 30, 55

P

Pages Jaunes *(f.)*	Yellow Pages 61
paiement à la séance *(m.)*	pay-per-view 88
pain *(m.)*	bread 27
pain complet *(m.)*	whole-grain bread 27
paisible	peaceful 10
panne (en ~)	not working 46
panne *(f.)*	breakdown 46
panneau *(m.)*	sign 46
papa	dad 50

pavillon *(m.)*	detached house, house 106
payer	to pay 29, 62, 81
pays *(m.)*	country 31, 90
paysage *(m.)*	landscape 31
paysager *(m.)*	open-plan 109
Pays-Bas *(pl.)*	the Netherlands 89
péage *(m.)*	toll booth 83
peindre	to paint 93
peine (pas la ~)	useless 48
pelouse *(f.)*	lawn 59
pendant	during 11, 62; for 11, 89
pendant que	while 66
penser	to think about 60
penser à	to think of 50
Pentecôte *(f.)*	Whitsun 92
perdre	to lose 22, 53, 87, 104
père *(m.)*	father 8
performance *(f.)*	performance 22
période *(f.)*	period 80
perle *(f.)*	pearl 76
permettre	to allow 44; to permit 107
permis de conduire *(m.)*	driver's licence 61, 64
perplexe	puzzled 45
personne	anybody 44
personne *(f.)*	person 41
pessimiste	pessimist 67
petit ami *(m.)*	boyfriend 29
petit/e	small 61
petit-déjeuner *(m.)*	breakfast 36
pétrole *(m.)*	mineral oil 83
pétrolier/pétrolière	oil 44
peu (un ~ de)	a little 11, 58
peur (faire ~)	to frighten 87
pharmacie *(f.)*	chemist 27
photo *(f.)*	photo 9, 25
photographie *(f.)*	photograph 31
phrase *(f.)*	sentence 47
piano *(m.)*	piano 52
pièce (de monnaie) *(f.)*	coin 37, 39
pièce (de théâtre) *(f.)*	play 37
pièce *(f.)*	room 30
pied (à ~)	on foot 32, 96
pied *(m.)*	feet 57
piège *(m.)*	trap 16
pile ("exactement")	exactly 107
pile *(adv.)*	on the dot 107

pile à l'heure	exactly on time 107
pilote de ligne *(m.)*	airline pilot 31
pipe *(f.)*	pipe 57
pizzeria *(f.)*	pizzeria 71
placard *(m.)*	cupboard 75
place *(f.)*	place 12, 24, 37, 58, 88
plaindre de (se ~)	to complain of/about 75
plaine *(f.)*	plain 25
plaisanterie *(f.)*	joke 54
plaisir *(m.)*	pleasure 17, 74
plaquette *(f.)*	pat 112
plat/e	flat 25
plateau *(m.)*	platter 104
plein (faire le ~) (d'essence)	to fill the tank 83
plein de	loads of 50
plein/e	full 16, 67
pleuvoir	to rain 2, 26
plier	to bend 69
plomb *(m.)*	lead 29
plombier *(m.)*	plumber 43
pluie *(f.)*	rain 47, 67
plume *(f.)*	feather 29
plupart (la ~)	most 58, 96, 110
plus	more 61
plus (en ~)	what's more 32; on top 81
plus en plus (de ~)	more and more 88
plus que	more than 80
plusieurs	several 43, 61
plutôt	instead 33; rather 33, 104
P.M.U.	totaliser (P.M.U.) 22
pneu *(m.)*	tire 89
pneumonie *(f.)*	pneumonia 75
poche *(f.)*	pocket 93
poids *(m.)*	weight 29
poignet *(m.)*	wrist 69
point *(m.)*	point 113
point de (sur le ~) (+ *v.*)	on the point of (+ *v.*) 93
pointe (de ~)	advanced 103
poisson *(m.)*	fish 104
poivre *(m.)*	pepper 41
policier *(m.)*	police officer 16; crime (films) 38
politesse (de ~)	polite 95
politique	political 40
politique *(f.)*	politics 79
pollution *(f.)*	pollution 100
Pologne	Poland 89

Polonais	Pole 94
polychrome	polychromatic 85
pomme (f.)	apple 29
pomme de terre (f.)	potato 108
pompier (m.)	fireman 78
pont (m.)	bridge 1
populaire	popular 92
porc (du ~) (m.)	pork 19
porte (d'une ville) (f.)	gate (for a town) 83; outskirt 107
porte (f.)	door 30, 57, 76; gate (airport) 44
porte à tambour (f.)	revolving door 76
portefeuille (m.)	wallet 9
porter	to carry 25, 46
porter (vêtements)	to wear 89; to put on 62
poser sa candidature	to apply for 101
poser une question	to ask a question 48, 71
posséder	to have 38, 88
possible	possible 41
poste (f.)	post office 101
poste (m.)	post 101; job 103
poste de police (m.)	police station 59
pot (m.)	post 48; drink 81, 109
pot d'adieu (m.)	farewell drink 109
pote (m.)	buddy 73
pot-pourri (m.)	pot-pourri 97
pouce (m.)	thumb 69
poulet (m.)	chicken 26
pour	for 5, 16, 38
pourboire (m.)	tip 96
pouvoir (m.)	power 92
pouvoir (v.)	to be able 27, 55; can 32, 57
pragmatique	pragmatic 94
pratiquant/e	practising 95
pratique	practical 61, 95, 107
pratiquer	to do 24; to practise 95
précipitation (f.)	rush 99
précipiter (se ~)	to rush 85
préférer	to prefer 5, 46, 60
premier de l'an (m.)	New Year's Day 92
premier/première	first 22, 65; former 43
première classe (f.)	first class 60
prendre	to catch 16; to take 19, 26, 29, 32, 36, 40, 60, 107
prendre place	to take a seat 79
préparer	to get together 82
près de	near 41

Q

qu'est-ce qu'il y a ?	what's the matter? 11
qualifié/e	qualified 99
qualité *(f.)*	quality 71, 74
qualité de vie *(f.)*	quality of life 100
quand	when 17, 26
quart (et ~)	fifteen (for time) 37
quart d'heure *(m.)*	quarter of an hour 37
quartier *(m.)*	quarter 32; neighbourhood 108
quatrième	fourth 99
quel/le, quels/quelles	what 8; which 17
quelqu'un	someone 55
quelque	some 10
quelque chose	something 10, 65
quelquefois	sometimes 10
quelques	some 20
quelques *(pl.)*	a few 47
question (pas ~)	there's no question 99
question *(f.)*	question 29, 33, 60
queue (faire la ~)	to queue up 47
queue *(f.)*	queue 47
qui est à l'appareil ?	who's speaking? 17
quinquennat *(m.)*	five-year term 79
quinzaine de jours *(f.)*	fortnight 79
quitter	to go away 17; to leave 74, 89
quoique	although 45
quotidien *(m.)*	daily newspaper 101

R

raccourci *(m.)*	short-cut 96
racine carrée *(f.)*	square root 71
radio *(f.)*	radio 11
radio-réveil *(m.)*	radio alarm clock 26, 31
radis *(m.)*	radish 108
raison (avoir ~)	to be right 19, 103, 107
raisonnable	reasonable 2; affordable 107
ranger	to put away 31
rapidement	quickly 32, 33, 108
rappeler	to call back 61, 106
rappeler (à qqn)	to remind sb. 79
rapporteur *(m.)*	tell-tale 76
rare	scarce 100
ras *(m.)*	lip, edge 97
ras bord (à ~)	to the brim 97
ras le bol (en avoir ~)	to be fed up (with) 97

revolver *(m.)*	revolver 39
riche	rich 48, 73, 76
rien	nothing 11, 37
rien (de ~)	you're welcome 5
rire	to laugh 17
riz *(m.)*	rice 39
robe *(f.)*	dress 20
Romain *(m.)*	Roman 110
roman *(m.)*	novel 11
roman policier *(m.)*	crime novel 90
romantique	romantic 5
rond *(n.)*	round shape 71
ronfler	to snore 37
rosier *(m.)*	rose bush 59
rouge	red 4
rouillé/e	rusty 86
route (bonne ~)	a good trip 64
route (en ~)	on the way 64
route *(f.)*	road 58, 64, 82
routine *(f.)*	routine 111
rue *(f.)*	street 4, 26, 40, 58

S

s'il vous plaît	please 1, 36
sac *(m.)*	bag 16
saisir	to seize 47
salaire *(m.)*	salary 103
salle à manger *(f.)*	dining room 30
salle d'eau *(f.)*	bathroom 15
salle de bains *(f.)*	bathroom 30
salle obscure *(f.)*	cinema 38
salon *(m.)*	linving-room 30
salut !	hi! 74
samedi *(m.)*	Saturday 17
sandwich *(m.)*	sandwich 55
sans	without 29
santé ! (à ta ~)	your health 104
santé (en bonne ~)	in good health 69
saoul/e	drunk 94
satellite *(m.)*	satellite 88
saucisson *(m.)*	sausage 27
sauf	except 96
savoir *(v.)*	to know 11, 50, 62
savoir-faire *(m.)*	know-how 93
scénario *(m.)*	screenplay 38
scie *(f.)*	saw 75

société à responsabilité limitée (f.)	private limited company 99
société anonyme (f.)	public limited company 99
sœur (f.)	sister 62
soie (f.)	silk 78
soif (avoir ~)	to be thirsty 19
soif (f.)	thirst 41
soigner (se ~)	to look after oneself 17
soins (m. pl.)	medical treatment 96
soir (m.)	evening 10, 11, 37, 54, 96
soirée (f.)	evening 10, 37, 88
soit	either 22
soit... soit	either... or 22
soldat (m.)	soldier 34
sole (f.)	sole 104
soleil (m.)	sun 67
solution (f.)	solution 100
sombre	dark 26
somme (f.)	sum 22, 96
somptueux/somptueuse	gorgeous 92
sondage (m.)	opinion poll 80
sondeur (m.)	pollster 80
sonner	to ring 26
sono (f.)	sound system 47
sorte (en quelque ~)	in a manner of speaking 52
sortie (f.)	exit 16, 44, 83
sortir	to come out 38
sortir de	to get off 58
sou (un ~)	a penny 53
sou (m.)	bean 53
souhaiter	to want 60; to wish 64
soupe (f.)	soup 23
sourcil (m.)	eyebrow 68
sourd/e	deaf 11, 31, 48
sourire (m.)	smile 45
sous huit jours	within a week 103
souvenir (de) (se ~)	to remember 64, 78
spécialité (f.)	speciality 71
spectateur/spectatrice	spectator 76
splendide	splendid 58
station (f.)	station 32
station de métro (f.)	metro station 32
station de taxis (f.)	taxi rank 96
station-service (f.)	service station 83
statue (f.)	statue 34
stéréotype (m.)	stereotype 94
stopper	to stop abruptly 78

strict/e	strict 110
strictement	strictly 22
studio *(m.)*	studio 15, 81
stylo *(m.)*	pen 25
submergé/e	overwelmed 109
sucre *(m.)*	sugar 24, 39
sud *(m.)*	south 24
suisse	Swiss 44
suite (de ~)	consecutive 89
suite *(f.)*	continued 31
suivant/e	following 101
suivre	to follow 45, 109
sujet (au ~ de)	about 15
superbe	superb 82
supérieur/e *(adj.)*	higher 43
supermarché *(m.)*	supermarket 10, 27
supplément *(m.)*	additional fee 102
supporter	to stand 43
supposer	to suppose 72, 90
sur	about 36
sûr/e	sure 1, 41
surpris/e	surprised 38
surtout	particularly 38
symboliser	to symbolise 92
sympa	nice 107
sympathique	nice 31, 85
symphonique	symphonic (symphony) 76
syndicat *(m.)*	trade union 111
syndicat d'initiative *(m.)*	tourist office 58, 111
systématiquement	systematically 94
système *(m.)*	system 32

T

tabac (place) *(m.)*	tobacco shop 4
tabac *(m.)*	tobacco 4
table *(f.)*	table 3, 30
table de nuit *(f.)*	night table 31
tableau *(m.)*	painting 87
taille *(f.)*	size 78
taire (se ~)	to shut up 62
tandis que	whereas 89
tant pis	shame, bad luck 18
tante *(f.)*	aunt 62
tard	late 18, 109
tarif *(m.)*	fare 96
tarte *(f.)*	tart 27

English - French glossary

able (to be ~) — pouvoir *(v.)* 27, 55
about — au sujet de 15; sur 36;
à propos de 64, 103
about 30 — trentaine *(f.)* 99
about twenty — vingtaine *(f.)* 79
above — au-dessus (de) 31
abroad — à l'étranger 103
absent — absent/e 5
absolutely — absolument 52
accent — accent *(m.)* 44
accept (to ~) — accepter 99, 104; assumer 110
accompaniment — accompagnement *(m.)* 72
accordeon — accordéon *(m.)* 40
according to — en fonction 22; selon 94
account — compte *(m.)* 5
accusation — accusation *(f.)* 109
acrylic — acrylique *(f.)* 2
actor — comédien/ne 37; acteur *(m.)* 74
actress — actrice *(f.)* 62
actually — en effet 52
add (to ~) — ajouter 13
additional — complémentaire 64
additional fee — supplément *(m.)* 102
address — adresse *(f.)* 8
administration — administration *(f.)* 43
administrative — administratif/administrative 109
admire (to ~) — admirer 59
admit (to ~) — avouer 109
adopt (to ~) — adopter 92
ads (small ~) — petites annonces *(f. pl.)* 81
advanced — de pointe 103
adventure — aventure *(f.)* 38
advertisement (classified ~) — petites annonces *(f. pl.)* 15
advertisement, ad — annonce *(f.)* 15, 101
advertiser — publicitaire 43
advertising — publicité *(f.)* 88
advice — tuyau *(m.)* 96
aerial — antenne *(f.)* 65
affordable — raisonnable 107
after — après 25
after all — après tout 61

afternoon	après-midi *(m. or f.)* 5
afterwards	ensuite 55, 74
again	encore 20, 53
against	contre 89
age	âge *(m.)* 9; époque *(f.)* 72
agency	agence *(f.)* 61
ago	il y a 53
agreement	contrat *(m.)* 64
air (in the open ~)	en plein air 58
airline pilot	pilote de ligne *(m.)* 31
airport	aéroport *(m.)* 44, 75
alike	pareil/le 72
alive	vif/vive 13; vivant/e 38
all	tous 3; tout 4
all over	partout 89, 92
all-in rate	forfait *(m.)* 64
allow (to ~)	permettre 44
almshouses	hospices *(m. pl.)* 82
already	déjà 19
also	aussi 22, 38
although	bien que, quoique 45
always	toujours 3, 65
among	parmi 92
and so on and so forth	et ainsi de suite 71
angry	fâché/e 93
ankle	cheville *(f.)* 69
annoucement	faire-part *(n.)* 103
announce (to ~)	annoncer 104
annual	annuel/le 38
answer	réponse *(f.)* 23, 57, 62, 102
answer (to ~)	répondre 12, 47, 54
answering machine	répondeur *(m.)* 10
anxiety	angoisse *(f.)* 104
anybody	personne 44; n'importe qui 82
anyone	n'importe qui 82, 105
anyway	de toute façon 13, 99
anywhere	n'importe où 82
apartment	appart (= appartement) *(m.)* 10, 30, 81
apparatus	appareil *(m.)* 17
appear (to ~)	paraître 76
appetite	appétit *(m.)* 41
appetizer	entrée *(f.)* 46
apple	pomme *(f.)* 29
application	candidature *(f.)* 101
apply for (to ~)	poser sa candidature 101
appointment	rendez-vous *(m.)* 102, 107

band	groupe (music) *(m.)* 75
bar	bistrot *(m.)* 108
barrel	tonneau *(m.)* 25
bass drum	grosse caisse *(f.)* 76
batallions	bataillons *(m. pl.)* 92
bathroom	salle d'eau *(f.)* 15; salle de bains *(f.)* 30
battle	bataille *(f.)* 110
be (to ~)	être *(v.)* 1, 7, 10, 45, 77
bean	haricot *(m.)* 40; sou *(m.)* 53
beautiful	beau/belle 13, 29, 68; ravissant/e 111
because	parce que 10
become (to ~)	devenir 65, 108
bed	lit *(m.)* 31, 36
beddy-byes	dodo *(m.)* 111
bedroom	chambre *(f.)* 30, 31
beef	du bœuf *(m.)* 19, 104
beef stew	daube de bœuf *(f.)* 19
beer	bière *(f.)* 4
beggar	mendiant *(m.)* 85
begin (to) (to ~)	commencer (à) 12, 26, 37, 65
beginner	débutant/e 13
beginning	début *(m.)* 47, 92, 99; origine *(f.)* 89, 90
beginning (at the ~)	à l'origine 90
behind	derrière 45
Belgian	Belge *(m. or f.)* 89
Belgium	Belgique 89
believe (to ~)	croire 54
belong (to ~ to)	appartenir (à) 31, 65
bend (to ~)	plier 69
best	meilleur/e 25, 32
bet	pari *(m.)* 22
better	mieux 50, 73
between	entre 40
beware (to ~)	se méfier 76
Bible	Bible *(f.)* 68
bicycle	bicyclette *(f.)* 65
big	grand/e 16; gros/se 22, 29
bill	addition *(f.)* 19, 72; note *(f.)* 53
bill (eletricity ~)	relevé d'électricité *(m.)* 53
birth	naissance *(f.)* 62
birth certificate	extrait de naissance *(m.)* 9
biscuit	biscuit *(m.)* 39
black	noir/e 4, 26, 54, 110
block of flats	immeuble *(m.)* 30
blocked	bloqué/e 25, 82
bloody	vachement 75, 81

brush (to ~)	brosser 26
buddy	pote *(m.)* 73
build (to ~)	construire 52
builder	maçon *(m.)* 43
building	immeuble *(m.)* 30; bâtiment *(m.)* 85
bunch	botte (flowers, radishes) *(f.)* 108
bus	bus *(m.)* 11
bus stop	arrêt de bus *(m.)* 34
business card	carte de visite *(f.)* 64
busy	chargé/e 109
but	mais 1
butcher	boucher *(m.)* 27
butt in (to ~)	couper la parole 93
butter	beurre *(m.)* 27
buy (to ~)	acheter 10, 22, 27, 40, 50
buzz	coup de fil *(m.)* 48

C

cabaret	cabaret *(m.)* 52
cabbage	chou *(pl.* choux*)* 37
cable	câble *(m.)* 10, 88
café (place)	café *(m.)* 3, 107; bistrot *(m.)* 62
cake	gâteau *(m.) (pl.* gâteaux*)* 27, 108
calculator	calculatrice *(f.)* 99
calf	un veau *(m.)* 19
call (to ~)	appeler 15, 60
call back (to ~)	rappeler 61, 106
called (to be ~)	s'appeler 9, 37
called for (to be ~)	s'imposer 58
calm	calme 10
calmly	calmement 57
camera	appareil photo *(m.)* 50
can	pouvoir *(v.)* 32, 57
canapé	canapé *(m.)* 55
candidate	candidat *(m.)* 79, 80
capable	capable 113
capable of (to be fully ~)	être à même de 103
capitalism	capitalisme *(m.)* 79
car	voiture *(f.)* 25, 55, 64
car (by ~)	en voiture 32
car park	parking *(m.)* 55
card	carte *(f.)* 9; ticket *(m.)* 22
career	carrière *(f.)* 74
careful (be ~)	attention ! 96
careful with (to be ~)	faire attention à 87
carrot	carotte *(f.)* 40, 108

carry (to ~)	porter 25, 46
cartoon	dessin animé *(m.)* 38
case	cas *(m.)* 22, 94
case (in any ~)	en tout cas 69
case (in that ~)	alors 4, 60
cash	fric *(m.)* 81
cash desk	caisse *(f.)* 9, 76
casino	casino *(m.)* 22
castle	château *(m.)* 22
catastrophe	en catastrophe 90
catch (to ~)	prendre 16
category	catégorie *(f.)* 61
catholic	catholique 58
celebrate (to ~)	fêter 62; faire la fête 104
celebration	kermesse *(f.)* 92
cellar	cave *(f.)* 85, 106
century	siècle *(m.)* 58
certainly	certainement 34
champagne	champagne *(m.)* 55
chance	hasard *(m.)* 22
chance (by ~)	par hasard 36
change	changement *(m.)* 60, 108; monnaie *(f.)* 62
change (to ~)	changer 32, 89, 106
channel	chaîne *(f.)* 10, 88
charges	frais *(m. pl.)* 81
charges (bank ~)	frais bancaires *(m. pl.)* 81
charming	charmant/e 108
chat up (to ~)	baratiner 62; draguer 76
cheap	bon marché 33
cheaper	meilleur marché 33
cheese	fromage *(m.)* 6
chemist	pharmacie *(f.)* 27
cheque	chèque *(m.)* 33, 57
chess	échecs *(m. pl.)* 76
chew (to ~)	mâcher 11
chicken	poulet *(m.)* 26
child	enfant *(m./f.)* 9, 62
children	enfants *(m./f.)* 15
chin	menton *(m.)* 68
Chinese	chinois *(m.)* 111
choice	choix *(m.)* 38, 101
choose (to ~)	choisir 22, 23, 82, 113
Christmas	Noël *(m.)* 76
church	église *(f.)* 12, 58
cigar	cigare *(m.)* 4, 93

composed (of)	composé/e (de) 30, 68
computer	ordinateur (m.) 60, 101
computer engineer	ingénieur informaticien (m.) 99
computer specialist	informaticien/ne 43
concentration	concentration (f.) 24
concierge	concierge (m./f.) 30
condition (in good ~)	en bon état 108
conductor	chef d'orchestre 76
conference	colloque (m.) 60
confide to (to ~)	confier à 88
confuse (to ~)	se tromper 34
congratulations	félicitations (f. pl.) 104
connaisseur	connaisseur (m.) 34
consecutive	de suite 89
consider (to ~)	envisager 106
construction	construction (f.) 65
consultation	consultation (f.) 75
contact	contact (m.) 64
contact (to ~)	contacter 106
continue (to ~)	continuer 59, 78, 83, 96, 113;
	enchaîner 88
continued	suite (f.) 31
contract	contrat (m.) 104
contrast (in ~)	en revanche 22
conversation	conversation (f.) 5, 19
convinced	convaincu/e 103
convincing	convaincant/e 39
cook (to ~)	cuisiner 24
cookery	cuisine (f.) 90
cooking	cuisine (f.) 88
cool	frais/fraîche 73; cool 110
correspond (to ~)	correspondre 61
corridor	couloir (m.) 107
cost (to ~)	coûter 18, 19, 32, 65
couch	canapé (m.) 30
count (to ~)	compter 81, 89
country	pays (m.) 31, 90
country(side)	campagne (f.) 31
couple	couple (m.) 107
courtyard	cour (f.) 30
cousin	cousin/e 62
cover (to ~)	couvrir 83
covered with	couvert/e (de) 68

eat (to ~)	manger 10, 16, 19, 24, 27, 41; déjeuner *(v.)* 66
eco-tourism	tourisme vert *(m.)* 111
edge	ras *(m.)* 97
efficient	efficace 32, 60
egg	œuf *(m.)* 27, 68, 73
either	non plus 19; soit 22
either... or	soit... soit 22
elbow	coude *(m.)* 69
elect (to ~)	élire 79
election	élection *(f.)* 79
electric	électrique 65
elsewhere	ailleurs 33, 82
embarrassed	gêné/e 34
employ (to ~)	embaucher 102
empty	vide 67
empty (to ~)	vider 55
encounter	rencontre *(f.)* 54
end	fin *(f.)* 50, 61, 113; bout *(m.)* 58; fond *(m.)* 107
end (at the ~ of)	au bout de 58
end (to ~)	finir 25, 90
endowed with	doté/e (de) 109
energically	activement 101
engineer	ingénieur *(m./f.)* 43, 65
engineering	ingénierie *(f.)* 101
England	Angleterre *(f.)* 94
English	Anglais/e 3, 94
engrave (to ~)	inscrire 57
enjoy (to ~)	bénéficier (de) 92
enormous	énorme 38, 47
enormously	énormément 74
enough	assez 13, 17
enter in (to ~)	entrer dans 58
entertainment	divertissement *(m.)* 88
entrance	entrée *(f.)* 46
entrance hall	entrée *(f.)* 30
environment	écologie *(f.)* 86
episode	épisode *(m.)* 85
equipped with	doté/e (de) 109
especially	exprès 95
estate agent	agence immobilière *(f.)* 106
etc	et tout et tout 71
ethnic	ethnique 110
euro	euro *(m.)* 70
even	même 9

evening	soir *(m.)* 10, 11, 37, 54, 96; soirée *(f.)* 10, 37, 88
every	tout/e(s), tous 10; chaque 24
every ten minutes	toutes les dix minutes 79
everybody	tout le monde 10, 17, 47
everywhere	partout 24, 88
exactly	parfaitement 16, 101; justement 38; pile ("exactement") 107
exactly on time	pile à l'heure 107
exam	examen *(m.)* 97
examine (to ~)	examiner 75; scruter 101
example	exemple *(m.)* 87
example (for ~)	par exemple 13
excellent	excellent/e 96; fameux/fameuse 108
except	sauf 96
exciting	passionnant/e 89
exclaim (to ~)	s'exclamer 16, 93
excuse me	pardon 1; excusez-moi 3
executive	cadre *(m.)* 44, 103
exhausted	épuisé/e 51
exhibition	exposition *(f.)* 65
exit	sortie *(f.)* 16, 44, 83
expensive	cher/chère 18, 32, 40
experience	expérience *(f.)* 103
experienced	expérimenté/e 13, 101
explanation	explication *(f.)* 61
exploitation	exploitation *(f.)* 79
express train	express (train) 95
expression	expression *(f.)* 20, 48, 95, 97
expresso	express (coffee) 95
extra	figurant *(m.)* 74
extraordinary	extraordinaire 65
extremity	bout *(m.)* 58
eyebrow	sourcil *(m.)* 68
eyes	yeux *(sing.* œil) 68

F

fabulous	fabuleux/-se 74
face	visage *(m.)* 26, 68
fact (in ~)	en effet 62
factory	usine *(f.)* 43
failing	défaut *(m.)* 29
fair-play	franc-jeu 94
fall asleep (to ~)	s'endormir 73
fall into (to ~)	tomber dans 111
false	faux/fausse 76

familiar form of address (tu) (to use the ~)	se tutoyer 109
family	famille *(f.)* 60, 66
famous	célèbre 43, 89, 108
far	loin 46
fare	tarif *(m.)* 96
farmer	fermier *(m.)* 73
fascinated	passionné/e 22; fasciné/e 103
fascinating	passionnant/e 90
fashion	mode *(f.)* 13; haute couture *(f.)* 52
fast	vite 47
fast (to ~)	jeûner 36
fat	gros/se 69
father	père *(m.)* 8
father-in-law	beau-père *(m.)* 62
fault	défaut *(m.)* 71
favour	service *(m.)* 102
feather	plume *(f.)* 29
February	février 19
fed up (to be ~)	en avoir marre (de) 111
fed up (with) (to be ~)	en avoir marre (de) 81, 82; en avoir ras le bol 97
feel (to ~)	se sentir 75
feet	pied *(m.)* 57
festival	festival *(m.)* 38
fetch (to ~)	aller chercher 66
few (a ~)	quelques *(pl.)* 47
fifteen (for time)	et quart 37
fill (to ~)	remplir 41
fill the tank (to ~)	faire le plein (d'essence) 83
film	film *(m.)* 11, 38, 53
film buff	cinéphile 38
filmic	cinématographique 38
finally	enfin 26
finance (to ~)	financer 88
find (to ~)	trouver 10, 13, 37, 43, 45, 53, 83, 85
find oneself (to ~)	se retrouver 99
fine	bien *(adv.)* 9; amende *(f.)* 93
finger	doigt *(m.)* 69, 101
finish (to ~)	terminer 12, 47; finir 25, 90
fireman	pompier *(m.)* 78
firework	feu d'artifice *(m.)* 92
firm	société *(f.)* 44
first	premier/première 22, 65; d'abord 45, 58
first class	première classe 60
first of all	d'abord 10

fish	poisson *(m.)* 104
fitted	aménagé/e 106
flagfall	prise en charge (taxi) *(f.)* 96
flat	plat/e 25; appart (= appartement) *(m.)* 30, 31, 106
flight	vol *(m.)* 44
flip through (to ~)	feuilleter 113
floor	étage *(m.)* 30, 46, 65, 109
floor (on the ~)	à terre 15
flower	fleur *(f.)* 32
flu	grippe *(f.)* 18
fly (time) (to ~)	passer 111
fog	brouillard *(m.)* 94
follow (to ~)	suivre 45, 109
following	suivant/e 101
foot (on ~)	à pied 32, 96
for	pour 5, 16, 38; pendant 11, 89; depuis 38
foreign	étranger/étrangère *(adj.)* 38
foreigner	étranger/étrangère 89
forest	forêt *(f.)* 58
forget (to ~)	oublier 9, 24, 50, 61, 62
form	formulaire *(m.)* 9
form (printed ~)	imprimé *(m.)* 9
form (to ~)	former 68
formality	formalité *(f.)* 64, 108
former	premier/première 43
fortnight	quinzaine de jours *(f.)* 79
fortress	forteresse *(f.)* 92
fortunately	heureusement 17, 65
fortune	fortune *(f.)* 22
fountain	fontaine *(f.)* 1
fourth	quatrième 99
frame (painting)	cadre (tableau) *(m.)* 44
France	France *(f.)* 94
free	gratuit/e 17; libre 17, 101
free (to ~)	libérer 92
freezer	congélateur *(m.)* 36
French	français/e 3
Frenchman	Français *(m.)* 32
fresh	frais/fraîche 73
Friday	vendredi 60
fridge	frigo *(m.)* 36
friend	ami/e *(m.)* 5, 9, 25, 39, 82; copain/copine 102

frighten (to ~)	effrayer 54; faire peur 87
from	en provenance de 44
fruit	fruit *(m.)* 27; fruits *(m. pl.)* 40
full	plein/e 16, 67
full (up)	complet/complète 41, 46
full time	plein temps *(m.)* 13, 103
funny	drôle 5, 25
furious	furieux/-se 54
furnished	meublé/e 30
furniture	les meubles 108
further	loin 30
future	futur *(m.)* 86
future (in the ~)	dans le futur 43

G

galley ship	galère *(f.)* 110
gambling	jeu d'argent *(m.)* 22
game	jeu *(m.)* *(pl.* jeux*)* 22, 88
game of cards	partie de cartes *(f.)* 71
gangster (film)	film noir *(m.)* 38
garage	garage *(m.)* 106
garden	jardin *(m.)* 59, 106
garden city	cité-jardin *(f.)* 65
gate (airport)	porte *(f.)* 44
gate (for a town)	porte (d'une ville) *(f.)* 83
general	général/e 62
gentleman	monsieur *(m.)* 3
German	allemand/e 4, 44; Allemand/e 94
Germany	Allemagne *(f.)* 94
get (to ~)	chercher 45; obtenir 61; décrocher 104
get at (to ~)	en venir à 72
get by (quite well) (to ~)	se débrouiller (pas mal) 103
get by (to ~)	se débrouiller 94
get hey up (to ~)	se tracasser 99
get home safely!	bon retour ! 64, 95
get in touch (to ~)	joindre 97
get off (to ~)	descendre 32; sortir de 58
get through (to ~)	passer 47
get to the point (to ~)	en venir à 72
get together (to ~)	préparer 82
get up (to ~)	se lever 26, 75
get used to (to ~)	s'habituer à 68
get-together	rendez-vous *(m.)* 38
gift	don *(m.)* 74
girl	fille *(f.)* 20, 62
give (to ~)	donner 6, 37, 38, 76; offrir 76; passer 78

guess (to ~)	deviner 101
guide	guide *(m.)* 12, 34, 57
guide (book)	guide (livre) *(m.)* 108
guitar	guitare *(f.)* 22, 40
guitarist	guitariste 75
gum	chewing-gum *(m.)* 11
gunshot	coup de fusil *(m.)* 69
guy	gars *(m.)*, type *(m.)* 74

H

habit	habitude *(f.)* 10
hail (to ~)	héler 96
hair	cheveu(x) *(m.)* 68
half	à moitié 67; moitié *(f.)* 110
half (and a ~)	et demie 11
half hour	demi-heure *(f.)* 60
ham	jambon *(m.)* 27
hand	main *(f.)* 25, 44
hand (a ~)	un coup de main *(m.)* 69
handsome	beau/belle 29
hang on in there!	bon courage ! 64
happen (to ~)	se passer 79, 108
happily	heureusement 32
happy	heureux/heureuse 32, 36, 38
happy new year!	bonne année ! 67
hard	dur/e 67
hard rock	hard-rock *(m.)* 75
harpsichord	clavecin *(m.)* 76
hat	chapeau *(m.)* 2
hate (to ~)	détester 99
have (to ~)	avoir 7, 22; posséder 38, 88
have a safe journey back!	bon retour ! 64
have to (to ~)	devoir *(v.)* 60
head	tête *(f.)* 22, 68
head of personnel	directeur/directrice des ressources humaines (DRH) 101
headaches	maux *(sing.*: mal) de tête 75
headmaster	directeur *(m.)* 110
headquarters	siège *(m.)* 102
health (in good ~)	en bonne santé 69
health (your ~)	à ta santé ! 104
hear (to ~)	entendre 37, 62
hear of (to ~)	entendre parler 80
hear the news (to ~)	être au courant 97
heating	chauffage *(m.)* 106
heavy	lourd/e 29

hefty (man)	costaud *(m.)* 47
height	hauteur *(f.)* 65
height (in ~)	de haut 65
hello!	allô ? 17
help (to ~)	aider 37, 64, 95
here	ici 12; voilà 46
here (not ~)	absent/e 36
here are	voici *(pl.)* 3
here is	voici *(sing.)* 1, 64
hi!	salut ! 74
high	haut/e 29; élevé/e 71, 100; aigu/aiguë (voice, sound) 79
higher	supérieur/e *(adj.)* 43
highly	hautement 85
hill	colline *(f.)* 83
hire (to ~)	embaucher 104
hiring	embauche *(f.)* 52
history	histoire *(f.)* 59, 110
hit (to ~)	frapper 76
hitch-hike (to ~)	faire de l'auto-stop 78
hitch-hiker	auto-stoppeur/auto-stoppeuse 78
hold (to ~)	tenir 44
hold out (to ~)	tendre *(v.)* 44
holiday	férié, fête *(f.)* 92
holidays	vacances *(f. pl.)* 17, 18, 50, 67
home (at ~)	à la maison 8
honesty	honnêteté *(f.)* 74
hop in (to ~)	monter 96
hope	espoir *(m.)* 36, 104
hope (to ~)	espérer 17, 45, 69
horse	cheval *(m.)* 22
hot	chaud/e 3, 26
hotel	hôtel *(m.)* 45
hour	heure *(f.)* 2
hour (at what ~)	à quelle heure *(f.)* 8
house	maison *(f.)* 39, 52; pavillon *(m.)* 106
household	foyer *(m.)* 88
how	comment 6
how's things?	comment ça va ? 6
however	cependant 66
human	humain/e 68
humour	humour *(m.)* 74
hundred	cent 88
hungry (to be ~)	avoir faim 19, 69

jump the gun (to ~)	brûler les étapes 100
June	juin 19
jury	jury *(m.)* 38

K

keep (to ~)	garder 62
key	clef *(f.)* 55; clé *(f.)* 64
kill (to ~)	tuer 92
kilo	kilo *(m.)* 29, 40, 108
kind	gentil/le 3, 29; aimable 95; genre *(m.)* 102
kiss	bise *(f.)*, bisou *(m.)* 18
kiss (to ~)	embrasser 18
kitchen	cuisine *(f.)* 30, 41, 106
km (kilometre)	kilomètre *(m.)* 58
knee	genou *(m.) (pl.* genoux) 37, 69, 86
knife	couteau *(m.)* 25, 41
know (to ~)	connaître 11, 36, 64; savoir *(v.)* 11, 50, 62
know-how	savoir-faire *(m.)* 93
knowledge	connaissance *(f.)* 22, 101

L

ladder	échelle *(f.)* 78
laden	chargé/e 83
lady	dame *(f.)* 9
laid-back	relax 103
lamb	agneau *(m.)* 19
landlord	patron *(m.)* 62
landscape	paysage *(m.)* 31
language	langue *(f.)* 87, 113
larder	garde-manger *(m.)* 39
last	dernier/dernière 43
late	tard 18, 109; en retard 43
later	tout à l'heure 12
latter	dernier/dernière 43
laugh (to ~)	rire 17
lawn	pelouse *(f.)* 59
lawyer	avocat/e 43
lead	plomb *(m.)* 29
lead to (to ~)	mener à 108
learn (to ~)	apprendre 113
lease	bail *(m.) (pl.* baux) 106
least (at ~)	au moins 50, 88, 97
leather	cuir *(m.)* 15
leave (to ~)	partir 36, 60, 109; laisser 55;

	quitter 74, 89
leave again (to ~)	repartir 85
leave for (to ~)	partir pour 54, 83
left	gauche (f.) 1, 79
left (on the ~)	à gauche 107
leg	jambe (f.) 68, 83
legal (to be ~)	être en règle 93
lend (to ~)	prêter 90
length	longueur (f.) 32, 65
less	de moins 67
lesson	leçon (f.), 67; leçon (f.) 86; cours (m.) 99
let (to ~)	laisser 12, 61
let know (to ~)	faire part de 103
let's be off!	on y va ! 66
let's go	allons ! 66
let's see	voyons 86
letter	lettre (f.) 50
level	niveau (m.) 71
library	bibliothèque (f.) 57
licence	redevance (f.) 88
lie	mensonge (m.) 22
life	vie (f.) 10, 43, 88, 100, 113
lift	ascenseur (m.) 45, 65, 109
lift (to ~)	lever 37
light	clair/e 15, 78; léger/légère 26
light (a ~)	du feu (m.) 4
light (to ~)	allumer 93
lighter	briquet (m.) 4
like	comme 17, 32
like (to ~)	aimer 10, 45
like that	comme ça 11
likeable	aimable 73
limb	membre (m.) 68
line	ligne (f.) 32
lined with	bordé/e (de) 58
link (to ~)	relier 109
linving-room	salon (m.) 30
lip	ras (m.) 97
listen (to ~)	écouter 10
little (a ~)	un peu de 11, 58
live (to ~)	habiter 9, 27, 75; vivre 24, 31, 73, 108
live in (to ~)	habiter 85
lively	vivant/e 40
living	vie (f.) 100
living-room	séjour (m.) 106
load (to ~)	charger 83

loads of	plein de 50
loaf	miche *(f.)* 27
lobby	entrée *(f.)* 46
lobster	homard *(m.)* 72
located	situé/e 106
located (to be ~)	se trouver 30
London	Londres 3
long	long/longue 25, 50
long way round	chemin des écoliers *(m.)* 83
look (to ~)	regarder 23, 39
look after (to ~)	garder 15
look after oneself (to ~)	se soigner 17
look at (to ~)	regarder 11, 25, 63; consulter 101
look for (to ~)	chercher 8; rechercher 13, 81
lorry	camion *(m.)* 52
lose (to ~)	perdre 22, 53, 87, 104
lot (a ~)	beaucoup 31
lot of (a ~)	beaucoup 17
loto	loto *(m.)* 22, 87
loudly	fort 37
love	amour *(m.)* 37
love (to ~)	aimer 37
love at first sight	coup de foudre *(m.)* 69
lovely	chouette *(adj.)* 81
lover	amoureux *(m.)* 37
low	bas/se 30
luck	chance *(f.)* 19; veine *(f.)* 81
luck (bad ~)	tant pis 18
luck devil	veinard *(m.)* 81
lucky (to be ~)	avoir de la chance 19
lukewarm	tiède 73
lunch	déjeuner *(m.)* 36
lunch (to have ~)	déjeuner *(v.)* 36
luxury	luxe *(m.)* 72
lying	couché/e 69

M

madam	madame 2
madman	fou *(f.* folle*)* 37
magazine	magazine *(m.)* 44
magnificent	magnifique 83
main	principal/e 22, 30
main (in the ~)	dans l'ensemble 110
major	majeur/e 88
make (to ~)	faire 5, 17; fabriquer 76
make a film (to ~)	tourner un film 38

make a fuss (to ~)	faire des histoires 87
make a mistake (to ~)	se tromper 34
make it easier (to ~)	faciliter 109
man	homme *(m.)* 22
management	direction *(f.)* 109
manager (project/team ~)	chef d'équipe *(m.)* 104; responsable de projet *(m.)* 109
manner of speaking (in a ~)	en quelque sorte 52
many	beaucoup 11, 18
many (as ~)	autant de 73
many (how ~)	combien 33
many (so ~)	tellement 36
many (too ~)	trop de 96
map	carte (geog.) *(f.)* 58
March	mars 19
marked	marqué/e 46
market	marché *(m.)* 24, 40, 54
martial	martial 94
marvel	merveille *(f.)* 50, 72
match	allumette *(f.)* 27
match (to ~)	correspondre 101
mate	copain/copine 73
maths	maths *(f. pl.)* 99
May	mai 19, 92
me	moi 3
meal	repas *(m.)* 36, 53
meaning	sens *(m.)* 97
measure (to ~)	mesurer 65
meat	viande *(f.)* 27, 73
medical treatment	soins *(m. pl.)* 96
medicine	médicament *(m.)* 20
medieval	médiéval/e 65
meet (to ~)	rencontrer 36; accueillir 44, 74
meeting	meeting *(m.)* 44, 80; rendez-vous *(m.)* 54; réunion *(f.)* 79
members of a government	membre (d'un gouvernement) 68
menu	carte *(f.)* 72
message	message *(m.)* 36, 97
messenger	coursier *(m.)* 102
meteorology	météorologie *(f.)* 88
meter	mètre *(m.)* 65; compteur *(m.)* 96
metro	métro *(m.)* 1
metro station	station de métro *(f.)* 32
midday	midi 50
middle (in the ~ of)	au milieu de 30, 40
midnight	minuit 10

migraine	migraine *(f.)* 86
milk	lait *(m.)* 24, 27, 73, 107
million	million *(m.)* 22, 65
mind	tête *(f.)* 22; avis *(m.)* 106
mine	le/la mien/ne 66
mineral oil	pétrole *(m.)* 83
minister	ministre *(m.)* 102
Minitel	Minitel *(m.)* 111
minute	minute *(f.)* 1
mirror	miroir *(m.)* 34, 67
miss	mademoiselle 5, 36
miss (to ~)	manquer (à qqn) 108
mix with (to ~)	joindre à 95
mixed	mélangé/e, mixte 110
model	modèle *(m.)* 16
modem card	carte modem *(f.)* 109
modern	moderne 13, 72
modernised	modernisé/e 60
modesty	modestie *(f.)* 74
moment	moment *(m.)* 24, 37, 38
moment (at the ~)	en ce moment 20, 50; actuellement 52
monarchy	monarchie *(f.)* 92
money	argent *(m.)* 17, 22; fric *(m.)* 81
monk	moine *(m.)* 87
month	mois *(m.)* 67
monumental	monumental/e 87
more	davantage 39, 80; plus 61
more and more	de plus en plus 88
more than	plus que 80
moreover	d'ailleurs 33
morning	matin *(m.)* 15, 26, 32, 37, 53, 109
most	la plupart 58, 96, 110
mother	mère *(f.)* 8, 36
mother-in-law	belle-mère *(f.)* 62
motorway	autoroute *(f.)* 58
mouth	bouche *(f.)* 57, 68
move	déménagement *(m.)* 108
move (to ~)	déménager 106
moved	ému/e 38
movie camera	caméra *(f.)* 50
much	beaucoup 15
much (as ~)	autant de 73
much (how ~)	combien 33
much (not too ~)	pas tellement 51
much (so ~)	tellement 51, 88
multimedia	multimédia 101

multiply (to ~)	se multiplier 108
mum	maman 50
murmur (to ~)	murmurer 109
museum	musée *(m.)* 59
museum (art ~)	musée *(m.)* 34, 59
mushroom	champignon *(m.)* 108
music	musique *(f.)* 10, 13
music-loving	mélomane 94
must (to be a ~)	s'imposer 38
mutter (to ~)	marmonner 80
myself	moi-même 12, 46

N

name	nom *(m.)* 33, 46
nap	sieste *(f.)* 66
napkin	serviette *(f.)* 41
narrow	étroit/e 40
naturally	naturellement 38
navy-blue	bleu marine 78
near	près de 41
nearly	bientôt 111
necessitate (to ~)	nécessiter 43
neck	cou *(m.)* 25, 68
necklace	collier *(m.)* 76
need (to ~)	avoir besoin de 27, 47, 64
neighbour	voisin *(m.)* 31, 55
neighbourhood	quartier *(m.)* 108
Netherlands (the ~)	Pays-Bas *(pl.)* 89
network	réseau *(m.)* 109
network (local-area ~)	réseau local *(m.)* 109
never	jamais 31, 37
nevertheless	néanmoins 31
new	nouveau/nouvelle 9, 53, 76
New Year	Nouvel An *(m.)* 67
New Year's Day	premier de l'an *(m.)* 92
news	informations *(f. pl.)* 10, 31; nouvelle *(f.)* 68, 101; journal (TV) *(m.)* 88
newspaper (daily ~)	quotidien *(m.)* 101
next	prochain/e 17, 106; ensuite 26, 78
next (to)	à côté (de) 30
next door	à côté 107
nice	sympathique 31, 85; sympa 107
night	nuit *(f.)* 46
night (at ~)	la nuit 62
night club	boîte de nuit *(f.)* 47
night table	table de nuit *(f.)* 31

noise	bruit *(m.)* 31, 48, 100
none	aucun/e 80
non-smoking	non-fumeur *(m.)* 60, 93
noon	midi 60
normally	normalement 8
north	nord *(m.)* 24
nose	nez *(m.)* 68
not at all	pas du tout 13, 90
not to mention	sans parler de 67
note	mot *(m.)* 76
nothing	rien 11, 37
nouveau-riche	nouveau riche *(m.)* 76
novel	roman *(m.)* 11
novel (crime ~)	roman policier *(m.)* 90
novelty	nouveauté *(f.)* 38
November	novembre 19, 92
now	maintenant 26, 38, 47, 66, 108; actuellement 52; à présent 111
nowadays	de nos jours 43, 89
nowhere	nulle part 89
number	numéro *(m.)* 22, 23, 32, 61; nombre *(m.)* 88, 95
numerous	nombreux/nombreuse(s) 22

O

obtain (to ~)	obtenir 79
obviously	évidemment 9
ocean	océan *(m.)* 72
October	octobre 19
of course	bien sûr 1, 29, 34, 52; évidemment 96; bien entendu 113
offer	offre *(f.)* 101
office	bureau *(m.)* 8, 43, 55, 109; cabinet *(m.)* 102
office automation	bureautique *(f.)* 109
oil	pétrolier/pétrolière 44; huile *(f.)* 83
OK	d'accord 33, 57
old	vieux/vieil (vieille) 11, 30, 37, 86
once	une fois 85, 89
one in two	un sur deux 79
one-way	sens unique *(m.)* 86
onion	oignon *(m.)* 108
only	seulement 13, 27, 29; ne... que 60
only (not ~)	non seulement 75
open (to ~)	ouvrir 16, 30, 55
open-plan	paysager *(m.)* 109

opposite	en face 11, 64; contraire 79
optimist	optimiste 67
orchestra	orchestre (m.) 76
order	ordre (m.) 22; commande (f.) 104
order (to ~)	commander 4, 78, 85
ordinary	ordinaire 6
organise (to ~)	organiser 109
original version	version originale (f.) 38
originally	d'abord 12
other	autre 22
out	absent/e 5
outside	dehors 2, 59
outskirt	porte (d'une ville) (f.) 107
overwelmed	submergé/e 109
ox	un bœuf (m.) 19
oxen	des bœufs (m. pl.) 68

P

pack one's case (to ~)	faire sa valise 54
packet	paquet (m.) 4
packing-case	caisse (f.) 76
page-boy	chasseur (hotel) (m.) 46
paint (to ~)	peindre 93
painting	tableau (m.) 87
paper	journal (m.) 22
parade	défilé (m.) 92
pardon	pardon 1, 3, 46
pardon?	pardon ? 95
parents	parents (m. pl.) 32
Paris (of ~)	parisien/ne 30
Parisian	Parisien/ne 32, 108
park	parc (m.) 24, 108
part	partie (f.) 68; part (f.) 72
part of (to be ~)	faire partie de 71
part time	temps partiel 13
participant	participant (m.) 89
particularly	surtout 38
party	fête (f.) 71
pass (an exam) (to ~)	réussir (un examen) 76, 97
pass (to ~)	passer 58
pass by (to ~)	passer 45
passenger	passager (m.) 93
passion	passion (f.) 24
past	passé (m.) 53, 86
past (in the ~)	jadis, dans le passé 43
pasta	pâtes (f. pl.) 6

pastime	passe-temps *(m.)* 22
pat	plaquette *(f.)* 112
pâté	pâté *(m.)* 27
path	parcours *(m.)* 101
patiently	patiemment 47
pay (to ~)	régler 9; payer 29, 62, 81
pay back (to ~)	renvoyer l'ascenseur 102
payment	règlement *(m.)* 93
pay-per-view	paiement à la séance *(m.)* 88
pay-per-view (on a ~ basis)	à la séance *(f.)* 88
peace (in ~)	tranquillement 72
peaceful	paisible 10
pearl	perle *(f.)* 76
pen	stylo *(m.)* 25
pencil	crayon *(m.)* 13, 78
penny (a ~)	un sou 53
people	gens *(pl.)* 24, 38; monde *(m.)* 111
people (lots of ~)	beaucoup de monde 40
pepper	poivre *(m.)* 41
perfect	parfait/e 17, 101
perfectly	parfaitement 61
performance	performance *(f.)* 22
period	période *(f.)* 80
perks	avantages en nature *(m. pl.)* 103
permit (to ~)	permettre 107
person	personne *(f.)* 41
pessimist	pessimiste 67
phone	téléphone *(m.)* 17
phone call	coup de fil *(m.)* 69
photo	photo *(f.)* 9, 25
photograph	photographie *(f.)* 31
piano	piano *(m.)* 52
piece of furniture	meuble *(m.)* 30, 31
piece of information	information *(f.)* 31; renseignement *(m.)* 61
pig	cochon *(m.)* 19
pipe	pipe *(f.)* 57; tuyau *(m.)* 96
pity	dommage 6
pizzeria	pizzeria *(f.)* 71
place	place *(f.)* 12, 24, 37, 58, 88; endroit *(m.)* 32; local *(m.) (pl.* locaux) 109
plain	plaine *(f.)* 25
plan	projet *(m.)* 65
plane	avion *(m.)* 16, 32, 45
plate	assiette *(f.)* 10, 66
platter	plateau *(m.)* 104

play	pièce (de théâtre) *(f.)* 37
play (to ~)	jouer 22; jouer de (instrument) 40, 52
play along (to ~)	jouer le jeu 109
player	joueur/joueuse 22
please	s'il vous plaît 1, 36
pleased	enchanté/e 45, 109
pleasure	plaisir *(m.)* 17, 74; agréable *(adj.)* 95
plug in (to ~)	brancher 20
plumber	plombier *(m.)* 43
pneumonia	pneumonie *(f.)* 75
pocket	poche *(f.)* 93
point	point *(m.)* 113
point of (on the ~) (+ v.)	sur le point de (+ v.) 93
point out (to ~)	signaler 76
Poland	Pologne 89
Pole	Polonais 94
police officer	policier *(m.)* 16
police station	poste de police *(m.)* 59
police station (main ~)	commissariat *(m.)* 59
polite	de politesse 95
political	politique 40
political rally	meeting *(m.)* 55
politician	homme politique *(m.)* 67
politics	politique *(f.)* 79
poll (opinion ~)	sondage *(m.)* 80
pollster	sondeur *(m.)* 80
pollution	pollution *(f.)* 100
polychromatic	polychrome 85
pond	étang *(m.)* 58
poor	pauvre 48
popular	populaire 92
popular (to be ~)	avoir la cote 74
pork	du porc *(m.)* 19
possible	possible 41
possibly	éventuellement 100
possibly so	admettons 100
post	pot *(m.)* 48; poste *(m.)* 101
post office	poste *(f.)* 101
postcard	carte postale *(f.)* 50
potato	pomme de terre *(f.)* 108
pot-luck	fortune du pot *(f.)* 39
pot-pourri	pot-pourri *(m.)* 97
poultry	volaille *(f.)* 27
pound	livre *(f.)* 108
power	pouvoir *(m.)* 92
practical	pratique 61, 95, 107

practice	entraînement *(m.)* 95
practise (to ~)	pratiquer 95
practising	pratiquant/e 95
pragmatic	pragmatique 94
precisely	exactement 92
prefer (to ~)	préférer 5, 46, 60
premises	locaux *(m. pl.)* 109
prepared to (to be ~)	être prêt à 106
present	cadeau *(m.)* 50; actuel/le 52; présent *(m.)* 86
present oneself (to ~)	se présenter 79
presentation	remise *(f.)* 38
president	président *(m.)* 79
pretend (to ~)	faire semblant 97
pretty	joli/e 1, 29, 59, 62
price	prix *(m.)* 15, 32, 67
primary school	école primaire *(f.)* 86
printer	imprimante *(f.)* 109
prison	prison *(f.)* 52, 92
prisoner	prisonnier *(m.)* 92
private	privé/e 96
private individual	particulier *(m.)* 106
prize (award)	prix *(m.)* 38, 65
prized	coté/e 74
problem	problème *(m.)* 31
processing/processor (word ~)	traitement de texte *(m.)* 101
proclaim (to ~)	proclamer 92
produce (fresh ~)	produit frais *(m.)* 71
producer	producteur *(m.)* 25
profession	profession *(f.)* 43
profile	profil *(m.)* 101
profitable	rentable 71
program	application *(f.)* 101
programme	émission *(f.)* 10, 88
property	l'immobilier 106
propose (to ~)	proposer 72
proud	fier/fière 25, 72
prove (to ~)	prouver 50
proverb	proverbe *(m.)* 37
provide (to ~)	fournir 101
province	province *(f.)* 64
psychiatrist	psychiatre *(m.)* 75
psychologist	psychologue *(m./f.)* 75
public	public *(m.)* 38; public/publique 59
public holiday	jour férié *(m.)* 92
public relations	communication *(f.)* 102

publisher	éditeur *(m.)* 88
pull a face (to ~)	faire la tête 68
punch	coup de poing *(m.)* 69
puncture (to have a ~)	crever 89
punnet	barquette *(f.)* 108
pupil	élève *(m./f.)* 86, 110
pupil (high school ~)	lycéen/ne 86
purchase	achat *(m.)* 6, 16
put (to ~)	mettre 23, 66
put away (to ~)	ranger 31
put on (to ~)	porter (vêtements) 62
put out (to ~)	éteindre 93
puzzled	perplexe 45

Q

qualified	qualifié/e 99
quality	qualité *(f.)* 71, 74
quality of life	qualité de vie *(f.)* 100
quarter	quartier *(m.)* 32
quarter of an hour	quart d'heure *(m.)* 37
question	question *(f.)* 29, 33, 60
question (there's no ~)	pas question 99
queue	queue *(f.)* 47
queue jumper	resquilleur *(m.)* 47
queue up (to ~)	faire la queue 47
quickly	rapidement 32, 33, 108
quiet	tranquille 10; calme 107

R

rabbit	lapin *(m.)* 16
race	course *(f.)* 22, 54, 89
radio	radio *(f.)* 11
radio alarm clock	radio-réveil *(m.)* 26, 31
radish	radis *(m.)* 108
railway	chemin de fer *(m.)* 83
rain	pluie *(f.)* 47, 67
rain (to ~)	pleuvoir 2, 26
raincoat	imperméable *(m.)* 26, 66
range	gamme *(f.)* 61
rat	rat/e 16
rate	condition *(f.)* 61
rather	plutôt 33, 104
read (to ~)	lire 11
ready	prêt/e 66, 99
ready to (to get ~)	s'apprêter à 66
real	vrai/e 59, 71, 111

realise (to ~)	réaliser 55
really (oh ~?)	ah bon ? 37
reasonable	raisonnable 2
receive (to ~)	recevoir 88
reception (hotel, building)	accueil *(m.)* 44, 109
reckon (to ~)	considérer 103
recognize (to ~)	reconnaître 34, 44, 83
record (to ~)	enregistrer 48
recording	enregistrement *(m.)* 113
red	rouge 4
reduction	réduction *(f.)* 60
reflect (to ~)	réfléchir 67
refusal	refus *(m.)* 99
refuse (to ~)	refuser 69
region	région *(f.)* 99
registration	immatriculation *(f.)* 108
regular kind of guy	réglo 110
regulated	réglementé/e 22
relatives	parents *(m. pl.)* 62
relax (to ~)	se détendre 76
relaxed	décontracté/e 38
remain (to ~)	rester 38, 79
remember (to ~)	se souvenir (de) 64, 78
remind sb. (to ~)	rappeler (à qqn) 79
remote control	télécommande *(f.)* 88
rent	loyer *(m.)* 81, 106
rent (to ~)	louer 15, 61, 81, 111
rental	location *(f.)* 61
rental agency	agence de location *(f.)* 64
repair (to ~)	réparer 113
repair man	dépanneur *(m.)* 46
reply (to ~)	répondre 12, 62
representative	représentant/e 43
reputation	réputation *(f.)* 69
required to (to be ~)	être amené à 103
research	recherche *(f.)* 103
resemble (to ~)	ressembler à 108
reservation	réservation *(f.)* 60
reservoir	réservoir *(m.)* 108
residential	résidentiel/le 108
resolutely	résolument 47
resourceful	débrouillard/e 94
respect (to ~)	respecter 74
restaurant	restaurant *(m.)* 19, 41
result	résultat *(m.)* 23, 50, 80
return	rentrée *(f.)* 67; retour *(m.)* 101

return (ticket)	billet aller-retour *(m.)* 33, 60
return (to ~)	revenir 107
revision	révision *(f.)* 20
revolution	révolution *(f.)* 92
revolutionary	révolutionnaire *(m.)* 92
revolutionise (to ~)	révolutionner 103
revolver	revolver *(m.)* 39
revolving door	porte à tambour *(f.)* 76
reward (to ~)	récompenser 38
rib	côte *(f.)* 104
rice	riz *(m.)* 39
rich	riche 48, 73, 76
ride a horse (to ~)	monter à cheval 50
right	droite *(f.)* 1, 79; droit *(m.)* 79
right (on the ~)	du côté droit 88
right (to be ~)	avoir raison 19, 103, 107
right away	tout de suite 111
ring	coup de fil *(m.)* 48
ring (to ~)	sonner 26
ripe	fait/e 87
rise (to ~)	lever 37; augmenter 96
road	route *(f.)* 58, 64, 82; axe *(m.)* 108
road map	carte routière *(f.)* 58, 64
Roman	Romain *(m.)* 110
romantic	romantique 5
roof	toit *(m.)* 85
room	chambre *(f.)* 26; pièce *(f.)* 30
rope	corde *(f.)* 67
rose bush	rosier *(m.)* 59
round	tournée *(f.)* 62
round (election)	tour (élection) *(m.)* 79
round shape	rond *(n.)* 71
routine	routine *(f.)* 111
rule	règle *(f.)* 93
run (to ~)	circuler 32
rush	précipitation *(f.)* 99
rush (to ~)	se précipiter 85
rush hour	heure de pointe *(f.)* 82
rusty	rouillé/e 86

S

sad	triste 13, 67
salary	salaire *(m.)* 103
salesman/saleswoman	vendeur/vendeuse 13
salt	sel *(m.)* 41
same	même 12, 29

same (the ~)	pareil/le 72
sandwich	sandwich *(m.)* 55
satellite	satellite *(m.)* 88
Saturday	samedi *(m.)* 17
sausage	saucisson *(m.)* 27
saw	scie *(f.)* 75
say (to ~)	dire 11, 16, 34
saying	dicton *(m.)* 5, 79
scan (to ~)	scruter 101
scarce	rare 100
scarf	écharpe *(f.)* 25, 78
school	école *(f.)* 18, 74; scolaire *(adj.)* 111
school (back to ~)	la rentrée *(f.)* 110
science of management	gestion *(f.)* 109
scratch (to ~)	gratter 22
screen	écran *(m.)* 74
screen (small ~)	petit écran *(m.)* 88
screenplay	scénario *(m.)* 38
seafood	fruits de mer *(m. pl.)* 104
second	deuxième 79
secretary	secrétaire *(m./f.)* 36
see (to ~)	voir 2, 24
see again (to ~)	revoir 20
see you later	à tout à l'heure 78
see you soon!	à bientôt ! 18, 95, 113
seem (to ~)	sembler 101
seize (to ~)	saisir 47
select (to ~)	sélectionner 22
self-service	libre-service 17
self-service restaurant	self *(m.)* 69
sell (to ~)	vendre 15, 52, 97; commercialiser 109
send (to ~)	envoyer 36
senior citizen	troisième âge *(m.)* 85
sentence	phrase *(f.)* 47
September	septembre 19
series	série *(f.)* 23; série (TV) *(f.)* 88
serious	grave 17; sérieux/sérieuse 62
service	service *(m.)* 60, 61
service station	station-service *(f.)* 83
settle down (to ~)	s'installer 37
settle in (to ~)	s'installer 108
settle up (to ~)	régler 107
several	plusieurs 43, 61
shame	tant pis 18
sharp	futé/e 76
shave (to ~)	se raser 26

so	alors 1; donc 65
soccer	football (m.) 22
social climber	arriviste (m.) 76
socialism	socialisme (m.) 79
sock	chaussette (f.) 26
sofa	canapé (m.) 15
software	logiciel (m.) 109
soldier	soldat (m.) 34
sole	sole (f.) 104
solution	solution (f.) 100
some	quelque 10; quelques 20
someone	quelqu'un 55
something	quelque chose 10, 65
something else	autre chose 73
sometimes	quelquefois 10; parfois 31, 110
son	fils (m.) 9
song	chanson (f.) 13, 25
soon	bientôt 18, 99, 111; tout à l'heure 78
sorry	désolé/e 4, 15
sound system	sono (f.) 47
soup	soupe (f.) 23
south	sud (m.) 24
space	espace (m.) 24; local (m.) (pl. locaux) 109
Spain	Espagne 89
Spanish	espagnol/e 11, 94
speak (to) (to ~)	parler (à) 3, 36, 67
speciality	spécialité (f.) 71
spectator	spectateur/spectatrice 76
spell (to ~)	épeler 41
spend (to ~)	passer 10
spider	araignée 39
spleen	rate (f.) 16
splendid	splendide 58
spoon	cuillère (f.) 41
spot	coin (m.) 111
spring	printemps (m.) 5, 67
square meter	mètre carré (m.) 71
square root	racine carrée (f.) 71
square shape	carré (m.) 71
stage	étape (f.) 89
stammer (to ~)	bégayer 29, 85
stamp (to ~)	composter 102
stand	éventaire (m.) 40
stand (to ~)	supporter 43; se tenir debout 69
stand up (to ~)	se mettre debout 69

star	étoile *(f.)* 46
start (to ~)	démarrer 93; se mettre à 101
state (to ~)	prétendre 97
statement (bank ~)	relevé de banque *(m.)* 53
station	station *(f.)* 32
statue	statue *(f.)* 34
stay	séjour *(m.)* 106
stay (to ~)	rester 74, 111
stay at a hotel (to ~)	descendre à l'hôtel 64
stay in (to ~)	séjourner 94
step-ladder	escabeau *(m.)* 78
stereotype	stéréotype *(m.)* 94
stick out (to ~)	dépasser 93
still	toujours 56, 59, 82
stop (to ~)	arrêter 16, 78; s'arrêter 34, 40, 89; empêcher 111
stop abruptly (to ~)	stopper 78
story	histoire *(f.)* 5, 25
straight away	tout de suite 58, 82
strange	étrange 54
stranger	étranger/étrangère 54
strawberry	fraise *(f.)* 108
street	rue *(f.)* 4, 26, 40, 58
stretch (to ~)	se dégourdir 83
strict	strict/e 110
strictly	strictement 22
stroll around (to ~)	se balader 108
strong	fort 44
struggle (to ~)	galérer 110
student	étudiant/e 67
studio	studio *(m.)* 15, 81
study	étude *(f.)* 43
study (to ~)	étudier 97
stunt man	cascadeur *(m.)* 74
stupid	bête *(adj.)* 13, 80
suburb(s)	banlieue *(f.)* 30, 32
suburbs (outer ~)	grande banlieue *(f.)* 32, 100
succeed in (to ~)	réussir à 76
success	réussite *(f.)* 76
such	tel/le, tels/telles 43
suddenly	tout à coup 47, 55, 66
sugar	sucre *(m.)* 24, 39
suit	costume *(m.)* 26, 44, 113
suit (dinner ~)	smoking *(m.)* 55
suit (to ~)	aller 20; convenir 61
suitcase	valise *(f.)* 46, 83

thingamy	truc *(m.)* 81
think about (to ~)	penser 60; réfléchir 61
think of (to ~)	penser à 50
third	troisième 46, 65
thirst	soif *(f.)* 41
thirsty (to be ~)	avoir soif 19
three-roomed flat	trois-pièces *(m.)* 106
throw (to ~)	jeter 15
thumb	pouce *(m.)* 69
ticket	ticket *(m.)* 22, 87; billet *(m.)* 33, 60
ticket office	guichet *(m.)* 33
tie	cravate *(f.)* 26
tights	collant *(m.)* 78
time	temps *(m.)* 24; fois *(f.)* 38; horaire *(m.)* 60; époque *(f.)* 89
time (a long ~)	longtemps 47
time (at any ~)	n'importe quand 82
time (at the same ~)	en même temps 40
time (in no ~)	vite 108
time (to have ~)	avoir le temps 48
time (to have a good ~)	s'éclater 110
timidly	timidement 34
tinned food	conserve *(f.)* 39
tip	bout *(m.)* 58; pourboire *(m.)*, tuyau *(m.)* 96
tire	pneu *(m.)* 89
tired	fatigué/e 78
to such an extent that	à tel point que 76
tobacco	tabac *(m.)* 4
tobacco shop	tabac (place) *(m.)* 4
tobacconist	bureau de tabac *(m.)* 22
today	aujourd'hui 6, 38, 44, 90, 95
toilets	toilettes *(f. pl.)* 12; WC *(m. pl.)* 107
toll booth	péage *(m.)* 83
tomorrow	demain 67, 71
too	aussi 1; trop 15
tool	outil *(m.)* 109
toothbrush	brosse à dents *(f.)* 16
top (on ~)	en plus 81
top of (at the ~)	en haut de 40
top-of-the-range	haut de gamme 61
totaliser (P.M.U.)	P.M.U. 22
tour	tour *(m.)* 12
tourist	touriste *(m. or f.)* 1, 12
tourist office	syndicat d'initiative *(m.)* 58, 111
towards (direction)	vers 41, 44

tower	tour *(f.)* 65
town	cité *(f.)*, ville *(f.)* 65
town centre	centre-ville *(m.)* 83
town hall	mairie *(f.)* 9, 58
tract	tract *(m.)* 40
trade union	syndicat *(m.)* 111
tradition	coutume *(f.)* 16; tradition *(f.)* 38
traffic	circulation *(f.)* 100
traffic jam	embouteillage *(m.)* 82, 96
train	train *(m.)* 24, 32, 57
train station	gare *(f.)* 32
transferred	muté/e 110
trap	piège *(m.)* 16
travel (to ~)	voyager 31, 48; se déplacer 103
travel agent	agent de voyages *(m.)* 36
travel expenses	frais de déplacement *(m. pl.)* 81
traveller	voyageur/voyageuse 16
tree	arbre *(m.)* 58
trip	voyage *(m.)* 36
trip (a good ~)	bonne route 64
trip (have a good ~)	bonne route 64
trip (on a ~)	en voyage 36
triumphal	triomphal/e 89
truffle	truffe *(f.)* 72
trunk	tronc *(m.)* 68
try (to) (to ~)	essayer (de) 38, 50
turn	tour *(m.)* 47, 110
turn on (to ~)	allumer, mettre 10
twentieth	vingtième 8
two-roomed appartment	deux-pièces *(m.)* 30
type	genre *(m.)* 80
typical	typique 71, 88

U

ugly	laid/e 68
uncle	oncle *(m.)* 50, 62
under	moins de 60
underground	métro *(m.)* 32
underneath	en dessous 13, 31
understand (to ~)	comprendre 44, 59, 113
undisciplined	indiscipliné/e 94
unemployed	chômeur *(m.)* 43; au chômage 99
unfortunate	mauvais/e 54
unfortunately	malheureusement 43
United States (the ~)	les États-Unis 19
university	université *(f.)* 43

unplug (to ~)	débrancher 20
unpublished	inédit/e 88
until	à (jusqu'à) 18
until later on	à tout à l'heure 41
unusual	étrange 54; original/e 108
up to now	jusqu'à présent 81
up to the task (to be ~)	être à la hauteur 109
upkeep (to ~)	entretenir 106
use	usage *(m.)* 68
used to (to be ~)	avoir l'habitude 48, 68
useful	utile 20, 76
useless	inutile 11; pas la peine 48
usual	usuel/le 113
usually	d'habitude 10, 68

V

varied	varié/e 74
variety	variété *(f.)* 43
veal	du veau *(m.)* 19
vegetable	légume *(m.)* 27, 40, 73
very	très 2
vest (man's ~)	maillot de corps *(m.)* 89
vice	étau *(m.)* 22
view	vue *(f.)* 107
villa	villa *(f.)* 108
village	village *(m.)* 58, 106
vineyard	vignoble *(m.)* 83
visit	visite *(f.)* 8, 58
visit (to ~)	visiter 32, 34, 50, 57
visitor	visiteur/visiteuse 65
vital	obligatoire 101
vocabulary	vocabulaire *(m.)* 113
voice	voix *(f.)* 13, 79
voluptuous	pulpeux/pulpeuse 62
vote (to ~)	voter 79
voter	électeur/électrice 79

W

wait (for) (to ~)	attendre 2, 8, 44, 47, 67
waiter	garçon *(m.)* 3; serveur *(m.)* 107
waitress	serveuse *(f.)* 62
wake up (to ~)	réveiller 26
walk	promenade *(f.)* 59, 66
walk (to ~)	marcher (on foot) 57, 66
wall	mur *(m.)* 31
wallet	portefeuille *(m.)* 9

want (to ~)	désirer 3; vouloir 8, 12, 16, 53; souhaiter 60
want to (to ~)	avoir envie de 27
want to (to not ~)	ne pas avoir envie de 96
war	guerre *(f.)* 73
wardrobe	armoire *(f.)* 31
warm	tiède 73
wash (to ~)	se laver 26, 86
watch	montre *(f.)* 89
watch (to ~)	regarder 10
water	eau *(f.)* 26
wave	vague *(f.)* 113
way	façon *(f.)* 32, 94; chemin *(m.)* 83
way (in another ~)	autrement 95
way (in any ~)	n'importe comment 82
way (on the ~)	en route 64
way around (the right ~)	à l'endroit 48
way of doing (sth.)	façon *(f.)* 13
weapon	arme *(f.)* 92
wear (to ~)	porter (vêtement) 89
weather	temps *(m.)* 67
weather (forecast)	météo *(f.)* 88
web (spider)	toile *(f.)* 39
week	semaine *(f.)* 19, 22, 78
week (a ~)	par semaine 38
weekend	week-end *(m.)* 64
weight	poids *(m.)* 29
welcome	bienvenue *(f.)* 74
welcome (to ~)	accueillir 44, 74
welcome (you're ~)	de rien 5
well	bien *(adv.)* 3; alors 4; eh bien 6; enfin 64
well and truly	bel et bien 38
west	ouest *(m.)* 24, 99
whacked	crevé/e 101
what	quel/le, quels/quelles 8
what?	comment ? 2
what's more	en plus 32
what's the matter?	qu'est-ce qu'il y a ? 11
when	quand 17, 26; lorsque 76
where	où 1, 12
whereas	alors que 67; tandis que 89
which	quel/le, quels/quelles 17; lequel/laquelle 48
while	pendant que 66
while ago (a little ~)	tout à l'heure 78

whipping boy	tête de Turc *(f.)* 94
whisky	whisky *(m.)* 55
white	blanc/blanche 4, 26
Whitsun	Pentecôte *(f.)* 92
who's speaking?	qui est à l'appareil ? 17
width	largeur *(f.)* 65
wife	femme *(f.)* 9, 20
willingly	volontiers 104
win (to ~)	gagner 23, 65, 87, 89
window	vitrine *(f.)* 13; fenêtre *(f.)* 30, 55
window-pane	carreau *(m.)* 55
wine	vin *(m.)* 4, 71, 85
wing	aile *(f.)* 110
winner	gagnant 22, 38
wish (to ~)	souhaiter 64
within a week	sous huit jours 103
without	sans 29
woman	femme *(f.)* 9, 36
wonderful	excellent/e 37; chouette *(adj.)* 81; fameux/fameuse 85
wood	bois *(m.)* 66
wool	laine *(f.)* 2
word	parole *(f.)* 13; mot *(m.)* 62
work (to ~)	travailler 43, 73, 97; marcher (device) 50
working (not ~)	en panne 46
workshop	atelier *(m.)* 43
world	monde *(m.)* 39
worn out	crevé/e (fatigué/e) 89
worry (to ~)	s'inquiéter 46; s'en faire 71, 100; se tracasser 99
worrying	angoissant/e 110
would it please you?	ça te dirait ? 111
wrist	poignet *(m.)* 69
write (to ~)	écrire 15, 48
writing	orthographe *(f.)* 110
wrong	faux/fausse 23
wrong (to be ~)	avoir tort 99

Y

year	année *(f.)* 6, 43; an *(m.)* 67
yellow	jaune 89
Yellow Pages	Pages Jaunes *(f.)* 61
yet (not ~)	pas encore 23
you	toi 37
young	jeune 10, 65

young girl	jeune fille *(f.)* 15
young man	jeune homme *(m.)* 47
yours	le/la tien/ne 66
yourself	vous-même 12
yuk!	beurk ! 85

▶▶▶ French

Also available from Assimil

Using French
French Phrasebook*
French Workbook (false beginners)
Sing Your Way To French

*also available with audio

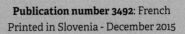

Publication number 3492: French
Printed in Slovenia - December 2015